THE TRANSCENDENT FUNCTION:

INDIVIDUAL AND COLLECTIVE ASPECTS

The Transcendent Function:
Individual and Collective Aspects

Proceedings of
The Twelfth International Congress
For Analytical Psychology
Chicago, 1992

Mary Ann Mattoon
Editor

DAIMON
VERLAG

Copyright © 1993 by Daimon Verlag,
Am Klosterplatz, CH-8840 Einsiedeln, Switzerland.

The Transcendent Function: Individual and Collective Aspects
edited by Mary Ann Mattoon.
The translators of individual papers are given on the final page of each
translation.

Cover design: Jeanne Fountain, Meta4.
Cover photo: "Chicago: Home Insurance Building."
               Undated photograph, courtesy of The Bettmann Archive,
               Underwood Collection.

ISBN 3-85630-537-8 (hard-cover)
ISBN 3-85630-538-6 (paper)

Contents

Editor's Preface
Mary Ann Mattoon   11

The Transcendent Function: A Critical Re-Evaluation
Jef Dehing   15
Response
Donald F. Sandner   31

*The Transcendent Function in Therapy after Incestuous
Violence*
Petra Affeld-Niemeyer   38
Response
Betty De Shong Meador   53

Political Leadership and the Transcendent Function
Louis H. Stewart   59
Response
Beverley Zabriskie   75

Esthetic Experience and the Transcendent Function
Basilio Reale   79
Response
Maria Pia Rosati   94

Another Degree of Complexity
Aimé Agnel   101
Response
John Beebe   116

Hegel's Dialectical Vision and the Transcendent Function
Hester McFarland Solomon   123
Response
Sherry Salman   143

Locating the Transcendent: Inference, Rupture, Irony
Polly Young-Eisendrath   151
Response
Andreas Wöhrle   166

The Transcendent Function and Psychodrama
Helmut Barz   173

Response
Elizabeth Strahan   189

Living, Ignoring, and Regressing
Lee Roloff   195

The Perverse and the Transcendent
Ann Belford Ulanov   212

Aspects of the Person

Decoding the Diamond Body
Robert L. Moore   233

The Body as Container for the Transcendent Function
Gustav Bovensiepen   242

Disguise as a Transition to Homecoming
Henry Hanoch Abramovitch   250

A Midsummer Night's Dream
William Willeford   257

Narcissistic Disorder and the Transcendent Function
Rushi Ledermann   265

The Chaotic Dynamics of the Transcendent Function
John R. Van Eenwyk   273

*Illness as Oracle: Psychosomatic Symptoms as
Synchronistic Occurrences*
Kaspar Kiepenheuer   281

Religious and Cultural Perspectives

Reflections on Self as Internalized Value
Marilyn Nagy   293

Confucian Contributions to Individuation
Bou-Young Rhi   302

Culture and the Transcendent Function
Makoto Takeuchi   310

*Eshu-Elegba, Master of Paradox: An African Experience of
the Transcendent Function*
Pedro Kujawski   315

Beyond the Dreamtime
  Leon Petchkovsky   326

Viewing Typology from the Star Maiden Circle
  Mary Loomis   334

African Healers: Called to Be Isangoma or Prophet
  Margaret P. Johnson   343

The Political World

*Analytical Psychology and Politics; the Political
  Development of the Person*
  Andrew Samuels   353

Armageddon Next Time: The Los Angeles Riots
  William O. Walcott   361

Eastern Europe and Analytical Psychology
  Renos Papadopoulos   368

Clinical Issues

Mirabile Dictu
  Sidney Handel   387

Therapist Mediation of the Transcendent Function
  Lionel Corbett   395

The Marionettes of the Self
  Carlos Amadeu B. Byington   402

Developmental and Archetypal Images in Sandplay:
  Joel Ryce-Menuhin   409

The Transcendent Function in Couples and Groups
  Peter Schellenbaum   414

Out of the Mouths of Babes
  Elizabeth Urban   421

Psychotherapy Research
  Seth Isaiah Rubin   428

Play and the Transcendent Function in Child-Analysis
  Verena Rossetti-Gsell   436

From the Three Suns to the Three Bridges
  Jean-Pierre Falaise   443

Forum: Psychology and Art

Leonardo's Mother Revisited
  Christian Gaillard   451

Anselm Kiefer: The Psychology of after the Catastrophe
  Rafael López-Pedraza   467

Minotauromaquia
  James Wyly   475

Forum: Ethics in Analysis

  Murray Stein   487
  Peter Rutter   489
  Denyse Zémor   493
  Aldo Carotenuto   498
  Paul Brutsche   505
  Beverley Zabriskie   508

Forum: Supervision in Training

Supervision and the Interactive Field
  Mario Jacoby   517

Styles of Supervision
  Judith Hubback   524

From Training Candidate to Supervising Analyst
  Paul Kugler   528

Selection and Training of Supervisors
  Marga Speicher   536

Index of Authors   540
Subject Index   543

Alphabetical List of Authors

Abramovitch, Henry Hanoch 250

Affeld-Niemeyer, Petra 38

Agnel, Aimé 101

Barz, Helmut 173

Beebe, John 116

Bovensiepen, Gustav 242

Brutsche, Paul 505

Byington, Carlos Amadeu B. 402

Carotenuto, Aldo 498

Corbett, Lionel 395

Dehing, Jef 15

Eenwyk, John R. Van 273

Falaise, Jean-Pierre 443

Gaillard, Christian 451

Handel, Sidney 387

Hubback, Judith 524

Jacoby, Mario 517

Johnson, Margaret P. 343

Kiepenheuer, Kaspar 281

Kugler, Paul 528

Kujawski, Pedro 315

Ledermann, Rushi 265

Loomis, Mary 334

López-Pedraza, Rafael 467

Meador, Betty De Shong 53

Moore, Robert L. 233

Nagy, Marilyn 293

Papadopoulos, Renos 368

Petchkovsky, Leon 326

Reale, Basilio 79

Rhi, Bou-Young 302

Roloff, Lee 195

Rosati, Maria Pia 94

Rossetti-Gsell, Verena 436

Rubin, Seth Isaiah 428

Rutter, Peter 489

Ryce-Menuhin, Joel 409

Salman, Sherry 143

Samuels, Andrew 353

Sandner, Donald F. 31

Schellenbaum, Peter 414

Solomon, Hester McFarland 123

Speicher, Marga 536

Stein, Murray 487

Stewart, Louis H. 59

Strahan, Elizabeth 189

Takeuchi, Makoto 310

Ulanov, Ann Belford 212

Urban, Elizabeth 421

Walcott, William O. 361

Willeford, William 257

Wöhrle, Andreas 166

Wyly, James 475

Young-Eisendrath, Polly 151

Zabriskie, Beverley 75, 508

Zémor, Denyse 493

Editor's Preface

The XIIth International Congress for Analytical Psychology was held August 23-28, 1992 in Chicago, Illinois. It was the second such meeting to be held in the United States. Of the 554 participants numbered, 360 were analysts, 118 were candidates and 76 were "auditors." Twenty-eight countries were represented.

Since the 1962 Congress (the first was in 1958), such meetings have been triennal gatherings of the International Association for Analytical Psychology (IAAP), the professional organization of Jungian analysts. (A person must be a member of the IAAP to use the title "Jungian Analyst.")

The IAAP was founded in 1955, with 40 members. At the time of the first Congress, in 1958, the membership had increased to 150, in eight member groups. By 1972, the 11 groups then extant were composed of about 360 members. New groups have been admitted at nearly every Congress until, by the end of the Chicago Congress, the member groups numbered 32 (including a roster of "individual members" – those who had been designated as analysts by the IAAP rather than through member groups) and the membership had increased to about 2000. Currently, the members are about half women. This percentage is far greater than those in such non-Jungian organizations as associations of psychologists and psychiatrists.

$$*\overset{*}{}*$$

Nearly everyone who is familiar with Jungian psychology is aware that Jung had a deep interest in symbols and a symbolic understanding of events and images. When students of Jungian psychology first hear of the "transcendent function," however, many are surprised to learn that Jung equated it with "symbol." It is well that he did so; a true symbol is indeed transcendent and "function" suggests its active nature. The symbol transforms by bringing opposites together and transcending them. As Jung put it, the transcendent function is "the transition from one condition to another" (Let-I, p. 268). When this Congress theme was adopted, it elicited a remarkable variety of papers devoted to broadening and deepening our understanding of the transcendent function.

* * *

Presentations at the Congress took the form of longer morning papers and shorter afternoon papers, including some grouped in forums. "Responses" to the morning papers, by designated presenters, were given in the afternoon, parallel (in time) to the other afternoon papers. The morning papers (the first ten chapters of this book) adhered to the theme. Afternoon papers (other than responses) dealt with a wider variety of topics.

Each presenter is a Jungian analyst (except where indicated), identified by place of practice and by group membership. If a presenter belongs to more than one IAAP group, the member organization named is the one through which that person holds a vote in the IAAP. (In a few instances, an IAAP member practices in one place and retains voting membership in another city or even another country.)

Many presenters delivered longer papers than appear here. They have graciously abbreviated their remarks to facilitate the publication of a book of reasonable size.

Although all presenters were invited to provide manuscripts for publication, some chose not to do so. Their reasons for this decision included: (1) the interactive nature of the sessions in which the material was presented; (2) the centrality of visual materials, such as videos, which cannot be reproduced in a book, and (3) the need for more than the space available for adequate representation of the presenter's material. The presenters who made this choice are, with their topics: Peter Amman and Robert Hinshaw (both of Zurich, Switzerland) on "Wilderness Within –

Wilderness Without"; Ruth Amman (Zurich, Switzerland) on "The Transcendent Function in Sandplay"; Francesco Bisagni (Milan, Italy) on "Infantile States and the Transcendent Function"; Mara Sidoli (Santa Fe, New Mexico, USA) on "When Meaning Gets Lost in the Body"; Richard Stein (San Francisco, California, USA) on "The Transcendent Function as Revealed in Unconscious Drawings" and Harry Wilmer (Salado, Texas, USA) on "Dream: A Jungian Interview with Vera von der Heydt."

***

A book comprising papers by many individuals inevitably includes disparate writing styles and points of view. The goal of the editing has been to retain individuality of style, while clarifying and enhancing each author's contribution.

Jung's works are indicated in the text, wherever possible, by CW (*Collected Works*), volume number and paragraph number. Other Jung references include DA1 (*Dream Analysis, Vol. 1*), MDR (*Memories, Dreams, Reflections*), Let-1 and Let-2 (Jung's *Letters*, Vols. 1 & 2), FJ (Freud-Jung Letters), VS (*The Visions Seminars*), Z (*Nietzsche's Zarathustra*). Several papers mentioned *VII Sermones ad Mortuos* (Seven Sermons to the Dead). It was published privately in 1925, republished in German (Rascher, 1962) and in English (Stuart & Watkins, 1967). It appears in some versions of *Memories, Dreams, Reflections*. Freud's works are indicated as SE (*Standard Edition*) and their volume number.

Other textual citations follow the format of the *Publication Manual* of the American Psychological Association: They indicate author and date, keyed to the reference at the end of the paper. Each reference is in the language cited by the presenter.

American-style punctuation and spelling have been used, according to the University of Chicago *Manual of Style*. Non-English words in the texts have been translated into English, unless they are terms – such as those from alchemy – that are well-known to readers of Jungian works, or are available in a standard English dictionary. Names of archetypes are capitalized when it is necessary to distinguish them from often-used words, such as Great Mother. Except for its appearance in direct quotations, "Self" (capitalized) refers to Jung's concept of the center, totality and integrating factor of the psyche; "self" (not capitalized) carries a variety of other meanings.

The official languages of the Congress were English, French, German and Italian. If a paper was delivered in a language other than English, the language from which it was translated is indicated. The translator's name follows, if it is available. Jennette Cook Jones assisted the editor with refining some translations from Italian. Manuscripts were typed on computer disks by Beverly Cicchese. Final proof-reading of the papers was done by Bonnie L. Marsh, as well as by the Editor.

Mary Ann Mattoon
Minneapolis, Minnesota, USA
June 1993

The Transcendent Function:
A Critical Re-Evaluation

Jef Dehing
Brussels, Belgium
Belgium Society of Analytical
Psychology

Jung's use of the expression "transcendent function" is surprisingly infrequent. He coined the term in a 1916 manuscript which was to await official publication (CW8) for more than 40 years. Curiously enough, in spite of its obvious relevance to the analytic process, no explicit mention of the concept is to be found in Jung's main writings on psychotherapeutic practice (CW16), although we find it in seven articles or books, three of the published seminars and four letters.[1] These publication peculiarities raise two questions:

1) What restrained Jung from publishing his main paper on the subject in 1916?

2) Why did he neglect the concept in his later writings on psychotherapy?

Other problems arise when we inquire into the content of his formulations. Jung sometimes defined the transcendent function as a *function*: a specific action or, by analogy with the mathematical term, an expression of a relationship, a dependence between elements of different sets. But more often than not he referred to it as a *method*, a *process* or the *effect* brought about by these dynamics. This leads us to a third question:

3) What are the reasons for this seeming inconsistency?

Before formulating possible answers we begin with an analysis of Jung's statements about the transcendent function. This

---

1. One or more of these works were published in each of the years 1920, 1930, 1934, 1935, 1936, 1939, 1942, 1950, 1954, 1955 and 1958 (CW5; CW6; CW7, parts 1 & 2; CW10, par. 855; CW11, ch. 7; CW14; DA1; VS; Z2; Let-1, pp. 267-69; Let-2, pp. 166 & 283; CW18, par. 1554.)

investigation adds a few items to our query. For instance, Jung opened his main text with a denial: "There is nothing mysterious or metaphysical about the term 'transcendent function'" (CW8, par. 131). Yet Jung's prefatory note announces a tentative answer to the question: "How does one come to terms in practice with the unconscious?" He defined "the unconscious" as "the Unknown as it immediately affects us" (CW8, pp. 67-68). Wouldn't this be a preeminently metaphysical matter?

Definitions

Now let us have a closer look at Jung's definitions of the transcendent function.

1. A Function

"It means a psychological function" (CW8, par. 131), "combined... of conscious and unconscious elements" (CW6, par. 184), "a... discursive co-operation of conscious and unconscious factors" (CW10, par. 855). It is called transcendent "because it makes the transition from one attitude to another organically possible, without loss of the unconscious" (CW8, par. 145) and "because it facilitates the transition from one psychic condition to another by means of the mutual confrontation of opposites" (CW11, par. 780). The transcendent function "unites the pairs of opposites" (DA1, p. 648; CW14, par. 261; CW18, par. 1554). It is linked closely to symbol formation: "The Self, as being the reconciling symbol" is considered its most desired fruit (VS, p. 472). This set of definitions is summarized in the following diagram:

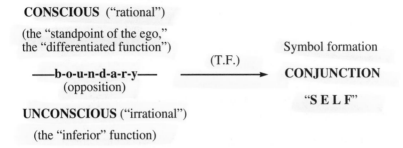

CONSCIOUS ("rational")

(the "standpoint of the ego,"
the "differentiated function")

——b-o-u-n-d-a-r-y——
(opposition)

(T.F.)

Symbol formation

CONJUNCTION

"S E L F"

UNCONSCIOUS ("irrational")

(the "inferior" function)

This "complex experience… comes from within, i.e., from the unconscious" (CW11, par. 822). "The initiative is with the unconscious, but all criticism, choice, and decision lie with the conscious mind" (CW7, par. 189). "In normal people, the transcendent function works only in the unconscious, which is continually tending to maintain the psychic balance… The transcendent function is not something one does oneself; it comes rather from experiencing the conflict of the struggle between opposites" (Let-1, p. 269). It "reveals itself as a mode of apprehension mediated by the archetypes and capable of uniting the opposites" (CW7, par. 184). Jung thus clearly postulated the archetypal nature of the function.

2. A Process

Thus far the transcendent function has been referred to as a function. Other passages define it as a "transition to a new attitude" (CW6, par. 427), "an involuntary personal experience" (Let-1, p. 268), "a purely natural process" (CW7, par. 186). It "is not a partial process running a conditioned course; it is a total and integral event in which all aspects are, or should be, included" (CW8, par. 183)

In later texts the reference to the individuation process becomes more explicit; the transcendent function is considered to be "a part" (CW18, par. 1554) of that process. Sometimes the transcendent function is identified with "the conjunction of conscious and unconscious" (CW5, par. 672), "the *transitus* to the self" (Let-2, p. 392). "Constructive treatment of the unconscious, that is, the question of meaning and purpose, paves the way for the patient's insight into that process which I call the transcendent function" (CW8, par. 147).

3. A Method

We are left with the transcendent function as a psychological function, a natural process.

> But it can be used as a method too; that is, when the contrary will of the unconscious is sought for and recognized in dreams and other unconscious products. In this way the conscious personality is brought face to face with the counterposition of the unconscious. The resulting conflict – thanks precisely to the transcendent function – leads to a symbol uniting the opposed positions. The symbol cannot be consciously chosen nor constructed; it is a sort of intuition or revelation. (Let-1, p. 268)

The transcendent function is linked closely to the constructive or synthetic method (Jung, 1916; CW6, par. 427; CW7, par. 121; CW8, par. 147). But here again Jung is a bit equivocal: "I entreat my reader to understand that I write about things which actually happen, and am not propounding methods of treatment" (CW7, par. 369). "This natural process of individuation served me both as a model and guiding principle for my method of treatment." (CW7, par. 187).

4. The Final Result

To complicate matters, a fourth definition appears every now and then: The transcendent function is the result of "the union of conscious and unconscious contents" (CW8, par. 131), "the reconciliation of the pairs of opposites. From this reconciliation a new thing is always created, a new thing is realized. That is the transcendent function" (DA1, p. 648). It is "born of the union of opposites" (CW7, par. 368).

I conclude this inquiry into Jung's pronouncements about our topic with a quotation which gives a lively description of the function, the method, the process and the final result:

The shuttling to and fro of arguments and affects represents the transcendent function of opposites. The confrontation of the two opposites generates a tension charged with energy and creates a living, third thing,... a living birth that leads to a new level of being, a new situation. The transcendent function manifests itself as a quality of conjoined opposites. (CW8, par. 189)

I consider the transcendent function as a "function of mediation between the opposites" (CW6, par. 184) which is archetypally founded. This function may start and sustain a process; certain therapeutic methods may foster it. Its activity may lead to a process of symbol formation and to the union of opposites; the latter term must not be considered as a mere merging of antithetical poles. Rather the conflict must be borne, sacrifices are demanded (CW8, pars. 166, 178, 186), pain and suffering cannot be bypassed, the tension has to be endured. Even then the patient – the suffering human being – "has to rely upon the possibility that they *may* be produced" (CW11, par. 784). This "something" is by no means a fusional amalgamate of the conflicting tendencies; it is a "living, third thing," a symbol, which truly transcends the existing predicament.

I have tried to render Jung's ideas about the transcendent function faithfully, to show that his formulations, as a whole, still conserve their original richness. But the concept is 76 years old now; perhaps the time has come for some critical re-evaluation. My questioning follows three parallel courses:

1) Inspired by Jung's repeated statement that any psychological theory is the expression of its author's subjectivity, I inquire into the personal elements that prompted Jung to lay down his concept;

2) On the theoretical level I focus chiefly on the nature and direction of the splitting line which keeps the opposites apart;

3) I examine the genetic origins of the transcendent function in infancy, and its relevance to the analytic process.

1916

The year 1916 was very special in Jung's life. It was marked by the resolution of the severe crisis that followed his break from Freud and the psychoanalytic movement. Several texts came into being in that year, but only two of them saw daylight in a direct way: the precursors of the *Two Essays on Analytical Psychology* (CW7). One booklet was published anonymously: *The Seven Sermons to the Dead* (MDR). It showed the amazing results of Jung's own active imagination. Finally there is a paper which was to remain in Jung's drawer for a very long time: "Adaptation, Individuation and Collectivity" (CW18). In it Jung developed a rather peculiar theory according to which individuation and collectivity are "absolute" opposites; individuation is possible only when the individual is able to tender an equivalent work for the benefit of society. "Anyone who cannot do this must submit directly to the collective demands" (CW18, par. 1099) by imitation. Thus Jung was far from taking the right to individuation for granted.

"Conscious" and "Unconscious"

During the years of his friendship with Freud, Jung had made honest efforts to assimilate psychoanalytic theory; in 1916 he was still entangled in confusion between Freud's ideas and his own. This situation makes his use of the terms "conscious" and "unconscious" confusing. The conscious and unconscious of classical psychoanalysis have a very restricted meaning and presuppose a rather mature development. It is one of Bion's (1962) merits to have established that the distinction between the two systems, and the mechanisms of repression, can only bear on rather sophisticated psychic components which he called "alpha-elements." Thinking, dreaming and the very possibility of repressing by displacement or condensation depend on the presence of alpha-elements, "digested" perceptions of the emotional experience. Of this personal unconscious we can say, with Jacques Lacan, that it is "structured like a language."

Jung never fully understood Freudian metapsychology; his conception of the unconscious was radically different, and "repression" meant little to him. He was far more at ease in the domain of dissociation and split-off sub-personalities. This divergent viewpoint was partly accounted for by his psychiatric experience, partly by his own psychological structure.

The World of Psychosis

Ironically, Freud insisted that Jung adopt psychoanalysis in the treatment of psychotic patients. Quite a few of these attempts failed miserably, and Jung would inform his Viennese friend: "Fragmentary complexes came pouring out, *with no resistance*" (FJ, p. 31) but no personality change occurred. Jung could not know that he was dealing with undigested facts – Bion's "beta-elements" and that classical psycho-analysis was bound to fall short for such elements.

The Freudian approach turned out to be useless for Jung himself when, a few years later, he suffered a severe breakdown. This predicament confronted him, once again, with another unconscious, which appeared to be all but personal. At this moment Jung developed new psychotherapeutic techniques, in a successful attempt at self-healing. His paper on the transcendent function describes this novel approach and the ensuing process. Its analogy with "the initial stages of certain forms of schizophrenia" (CW7, par. 121) did not escape Jung's notice. Many years later he still stressed that this method "is not a plaything for children;" it may give rise to a schizophrenia-like condition and "even lead to a genuine 'psychotic interval'" (CW8, p. 68). I do not want to venture a psychiatric diagnosis of Jung's crisis; anyway, it slips out of any nosological compartment. But, this "creative disease" most certainly had a psychotic structure, analytically speaking. Winnicott (1964), in his review of Jung's memoirs is quite plain in this respect:

> If I want to say that Jung was mad, and that he recovered, I am doing nothing worse than I would do in saying of myself that I was sane and that through analysis and self-analysis I achieved some measure

of insanity. Freud's flight to sanity could be something we psycho-analysts are trying to recover from, just as Jungians are trying to recover from Jung's 'divided self,' and from the way he himself dealt with it." (p. 483)

Winnicott argued that "Jung knew truths that are unavailable to most men and women," but that he lacked "a place to keep his inner psychic reality" (p. 488). It seems that Jung was unremittingly in search of such a container; mythology, Gnosis, alchemy and Christianity provided him with that space. He gave us a lively description of the dissociation between his well-adapted Number 1 personality, a "False Self" in Winnicott's language, and the Number 2 personality, which carried for him the sense of the real, a "Real Self" in search of a place to hide. Winnicott, assuming that Jung's dissociation was based on a splitting-off of primitive destructiveness, insisted that spontaneity and creativity have destruction as their "next-door-neighbor" (p. 491).

We return to the origins of the concept of the transcendent function. Clearly Jung found no solace in classical psychoanalysis; his problem was not one of repressed personal material, but overcoming a dissociation – a divided self. We are not faced with a horizontal division here, such as Freud presented between conscious and personal unconscious; the split is vertical and leaves no room for Freud's unconscious.

Jung found himself forced to devise a new approach which was remarkable in more than one respect. It took intuition and an uncommon courage to bring this attempt to a favorable conclusion. His self-healing was by no means the only result of his search; from it he brought along the essential germs of his life-work: the *Seven Sermons* contained the crux of Analytical Psychology in the form of emotions and images, while *The Transcendent Function* introduced the main renewal of analytic technique.

Jung seemed to be in serious doubt about the acceptability of these brand-new findings; he may have been afraid that his ideas would be rejected as invalid concoctions, as patent utterances of insanity, psychotic delusions. One can imagine that he mistrusted his newly created approach; hence his publishing the *Seven Ser-*

mons anonymously and allowing *The Transcendent Function* to sink into oblivion.

Methodological Problems

This explanation does not elucidate Jung's apparent incoherence in his definitions of the transcendent function, nor does it explain his later neglect of the concept. A methodological difficulty may account for these peculiarities.

First there is the epistemological problem of the unconscious, personal or collective. Again and again we tend to forget that we are talking about the Unknown; in fact we can say nothing about it – as Jung vigorously reminded us in the *Seven Sermons*. We can speak only of its manifestations, insofar as they can be registered by our restricted consciousness. Therefore an expression such as "cooperation of conscious and unconscious factors" is in fact pointless; the latter are bound to be hypothetical and should never be hypostatized. To avoid this error it would be more accurate to speak about "a conscious attitude which endeavors to be as unbiased as possible toward possible manifestations of a hypothetical unconscious." This formulation would do justice to the transcendent character of the unconscious; its phenomenological outlook avoids both the naive illusion that we know something by naming it and the oversimplification of scientistic reification. The shortened expression is more elegant and easier to handle but we should take care that it not become reified.

Psychoanalysis, certainly in its early years, claimed to be an objective science that described psychic facts as observed from the outside. This model was scientistic and organistic; Freud expected that it would comprehend the unconscious almost totally. This hope was in vain, even though the unconscious was by definition restricted to the personal portion: Its contents are rather familiar to the conscious mind, since they are made up of "repressed" representations which have once been conscious.

Jung, even before his first encounter with Freud, adopted a radically opposite view. His attention was focused on the *subjec-*

tive experience. One cannot consider the psychological phenomena he described as objective concepts; they appear rather as a lively account of the clash with unknown psychic phenomena. The unconscious which is supposed to lie behind these manifestations has little to do with the orderly structure of the personal unconscious.

The Collective Unconscious

Very soon, however, Jung assumed that this non-personal, or collective, unconscious has an order, a structure of its own. In the original paper on the transcendent function he mentioned the idea once again. The unconscious, he argued, reacts to an exaggerated one-sidedness of the conscious by adopting a dynamic counter-position. The latter's energy is "really dangerous" (CW8, par. 183), possibly overwhelming for the conscious ego. From the first version on, Jung propounded his new definition of the symbol: "the best possible expression for a complex fact not yet clearly apprehended by consciousness" (CW8, par. 148).

 Perhaps we are able now to understand Jung's definitional profusion. In the subjective experience the transcendent function must be sensed as a spontaneous *process* leading to a *result*. As a psychotherapist Jung was interested in *methods* that would foster this process. As a scientist he postulated a *function* accountable for the facts described. This last definition, the most logical one, also runs the biggest risks of reification.

Thus, Jung's rational inconsistency once more saves him from organistic hypostasizing and could be the reason why he neglected the concept in his later writings on psychotherapy. He certainly preferred mercurial liveliness to rigid systematization!

The Transference

As we have seen, Jung identified the transcendent function in the process of his own self-healing, his sole interlocutor being the Unconscious. This explains his life-long search for external corroborations of his experience. It also accounts for his not assessing the enormous importance, in relation to the transcendent function, of transference/countertransference dynamics. In his major work, "The Psychology of the Transference" (CW16), the transcendent function is never mentioned explicitly, although we can recognize its mechanisms, both clinically and metaphorically.

Jung enounced one important technical rule, however: The analyst "mediates the transcendent function for the patient, i.e. helps him to bring conscious and unconscious together" (CW8, par. 146), making sure that the conflict be borne, that the tension be not evacuated. In 1958 he acknowledged one transferential aspect: the conflict, and the ensuing rapprochement, may "just as well take place between patient and analyst" (CW8, par. 186). That is, one of the poles is projected onto the analyst.

Genetic Aspects

Another lacuna in Jung's study of the transcendent function concerns its genetic aspects. He even stated: "The understanding of the transference is to be sought not in its historical antecedents but in its purpose" (CW8, par. 146). I prefer to maintain the tension between the two possibilities. One of the purposes of the transference could very well be an attempt at resolving infantile problems. At the same time, if there exists such a thing as the transcendent function it should be possible, and worthwhile, to trace it back to its origins and to describe its avatars during psychic development.

It is hard to imagine the newborn's mind as a tabula rasa. Just as physical characteristics and development are engraved in the genetic material, so are psychic features and potentialities.

From Inborn Potential to Psychic Reality

The difficult question is: How do these inborn structures, registered in the biochemical patterns of DNA, genes, chromosomes and brain cells, acquire psychic quality? This mysterious interface between the material, physical substrate and the psyche is far from elucidated. On the contrary, the rise of modern physics has robbed us even of the naive illusion that at least we know what matter is. We don't know either what psyche is and I do not agree with Jung that we have "immediate knowledge" of psychic existence. He argued that "nothing can be known unless it first appears as a psychic image" (CW11, par. 769). I agree with that, but in my view this knowledge has to be *mediated*: "The original feeling of unity... is lost." Here I am quoting Jung again; no gnosis can restore that unity, unless "we fall into the pleroma and cease to be creatures" (*Seven Sermons*). Psychologically speaking this would mean that ego-consciousness is swallowed by the unconscious – tantamount to a psychotic breakdown.

A baby too, notwithstanding a rich supply of innate possibilities, has no immediate knowledge of psychic existence; in order to construct it the infant needs another human being. Several models account for this delicate interaction. Winnicott (1963) argued that a "good enough" mother succeeds in meeting the spontaneous gesture of her baby and in doing so strengthens the baby's "Real Self" – the inborn potential – and humanizes it. Bion (1962) stressed the containing functions of the mother; by the process of projective identification she receives the undigested psychic elements ("beta-elements") of the infant, works on them with her "alpha-function" (maternal reverie), and returns them to the baby in the form of alpha-elements. According to Bion the child starts its psychic existence "contained" within the maternal psyche.

Would this maternal attitude be the precursor or the catalyzer of the transcendent function? We find these dynamics back in the analytic situation in which the analyst continuously functions as a container for the analysand's psychic reality. The analyst will try to understand the analysand's utterances, including on the level of projective identification, and give them back in digested form. This analytic attitude clearly aims at transcending some essential difficulty. The archetype – the inborn structure as it is engraved in physical reality – sustains and directs raw sensorial and emotional experiences. These beta-elements are not met by maternal alpha-function; the encounter with the mother's response confers alpha-quality to the early mental representations of the newborn, humanizes and enriches them. If the maternal response fails, the child is left with agony: unspeakable, unrepresentable anxiety. More often than not these non-accepted archetypal expressions are split off, not repressed. This "second personality," inaccessible to conscious life, may remain active and even obtrusive.

According to Moore (1975) and Powell (1985) the transcendent function is an essential component of successful maternal reverie. In the analytic situation, too, the transcendent function – first embodied by the therapist – will gradually transform the analysand's beta-elements into alpha-elements. This process depends on the analyst's capacity to endure the tensions engendered by the analysand's projections; a therapist who succeeds in "transcending" the patient's dissociation may offer an interpretation that enables the latter to overcome splitting mechanisms.

Intermediate Area

Any human being probably presents some degree of splitting. For the luckiest, who enjoyed a reasonably good adaptation of the environment to their needs, this splitting may remain minimal. Nevertheless, the very development of ego-consciousness necessarily leads us to divide our subjective experience into poles: for example, good and bad, love and hate, life and death. These conscious discriminations, vital for the beginning organization of psychic life, may become hampering and impoverishing. Thus, even the healthy neurotic may profit by the dynamics of the transcendent function. For the more severely split persons its importance will be the more vital. This conception of the transcendent function bears strong resemblance to Winnicott's idea of "transitional phenomena." In this intermediary area, too, oppositions are tolerated; from the paradox thus created and respected symbolic activity may come into being. Spare (1986) provides us with a poetic illustration of this "flux of in-between states" (p. 28).

Our approach to the transcendent function remains quite close
to the scheme proposed by Jung: When a conflict appears between two opposite positions it is important to make the poles as
conscious as possible. If the conflict is borne, the pain endured, a
third element may emerge: a living symbol that transcends the
opposition. Thus, in the analytic situation, the therapist should
avoid any intervention that would mitigate the conflict or evacu-
ate the suffering. I consider the transcendent function itself as a
given; this possible transcending of antithetic stands is the very
foundation of our psychotherapeutic endeavor. The results are
given *Deo concedente*; all we can do is to bear the conflict.

The Question of Meaning

Interestingly, Jung himself sometimes withdrew from the tension that some opposites provoke. For instance, he would examine "the fact that there are two distinct and mutually contradictory views eagerly advocated on either side concerning the meaning or meaninglessness of things" (CW6, par. 822), a question as
frightening as it is vital. Sometimes he bore the suspense of the
agnostic position: "Any honest thinker has to admit the insecurity of all metaphysical speculations, and in particular of all
creeds" (CW11, par. 764). But at other times he fled to the
security of a position of knowledge. In the painful doubt about
meaning or meaninglessness he concluded that the very existence of the two opposite views "shows that processes obviously
exist which express no particular meaning...; and that there are
other processes which bear within them a hidden meaning, processes which... seek to become something." He called the latter
"symbols," the former "symptoms," and admitted that "it is left
to our discretion and critical judgment to decide whether the
thing we are dealing with is a symptom or a symbol" (CW6, par.
822.)

Surreptitiously, however, he introduced the gnostic assumption that somewhere meaning *must* exist. The conflict collapses,
the pole of meaninglessness is evacuated. The fact that Jung
needed to resort to dogmatic affirmations every now and then

probably had to do with his serious doubt regarding the possibility of constructing and fostering meaning without investing it with absolute certainty. Was he frightened by the split-off primitive destructiveness which he could not integrate in childhood?

A Dream

I conclude with a clinical example. My analysand is D.W. Winnicott. While reviewing Jung's memoirs (MDR) he had a significant dream of which he said: "I was dreaming... for Jung and for some of my patients, as well as for myself." Obviously he felt strongly affected by Jung's book. The dream had three parts:

"1. There was absolute destruction, and I was part of the world and of all the people, and therefore I was being destroyed.

"2. There was absolute destruction, and I was the destructive agent. Here then was a problem for the ego, how to integrate these two aspects of destruction?

"3. In the dream I awakened.... I knew I had dreamed both (1) and (2). I had therefore solved the problem.... Here I was awake, in the dream, and I knew I had dreamed of being destroyed and of being the destructive agent. There was no dissociation."

He woke with a "splitting headache" and realized that, without the third position, he would have remained split, "solving the problem alternately in sadism and masochism" (Winnicott, 1963, pp. 228-29).

Winnicott was on the edge of inflation when he stated: "I had... solved the problem." His ego maintained the tension between the opposites and endured the pain, but the solution was no conscious construction. It came about as a gift, a new creation beyond ego control: the transcendent function at work.

References

Bion, W. (1962/1988). *Learning by Experience*. London: Maresfield
        Library.

Jung, C. G. (1916). *Die Transzendente Function*, manuscript. Jung-
        Archiv der ETH - Bibliothek, Zurich.

Jung, C. G. (1957). *The Transcendent Function* (1916). Translated by
        A. R. Pope. Privately printed for the Students' Association,
        C.G. Jung Institute, Zurich, 1957.

Moore, N. (1975). The transcendent function and the forming ego.
        Journal of Analytical Psychology, 20, 164-182.

Powell, S. (1985). A bridge to understanding: the transcendent function
        in the analyst. *Journal of Analytical Psychology, 30,* 29-45.

Spare, G. (1986). The Celtic tradition: Reflections on winter and the
        Celtic spiritual attitude. *San Francisco Jung Institute Library
        Journal, 6*-2, 26-33.

Winnicott, D.W. (1963). D.W.W.'s dream related to reviewing Jung.
        An account enclosed in a letter to a colleague. Dec. 29, 1963.

Winnicott, D.W. (1964). Review of C.G.Jung's Memories, Dreams,
        Reflections (pp. 482-492). In Winnicott, C; Shephard, R;
        Davies, M. (Eds.), *Psycho-Analytic Explorations.* London:
        Karnac, 1989.

Response

Donald F. Sandner
San Francisco, California, USA
Society of Jungian Analysts of
Northern California

Jef Dehing has provided an excellent overview of the use and meaning of the transcendent function in Jung's thought. It is characteristic of Jung to define his important terms ambiguously; the transcendent function is no exception. As Dehing demonstrates, it is defined at different times as a function (relationship), process, method, or final effect. Jung was never much concerned with strict definition. In spite of this – or perhaps because of this – his accumulated definitions denote an intuitive concept embracing and containing process and effect, function and method, showing now one facet of the concept, now another. What a concept lacks in intellectual clarity it sometimes – not always – gains in intuitive breadth and power. Since confusion often results, it is worth the effort to pin Jung down as Dehing has done. Then we can see Jung's intellectual process working in both its intuitive power and its logical inconsistencies.

Regarding Winnicott's criticism and diagnosis of Jung I find myself wanting to add something. I do not for a moment agree with Winnicott's (1964) diagnosis of Jung as a case of recovered childhood schizophrenia. My therapist's sensitivity picks up a measure of petulant denial when Winnicott assures us (twice) that he does not mind his self-identification with Jung's description of ordinary people who are like "optimistic tadpoles who bask in a puddle in the sun, in the shallowest waters crowding together and amiably wriggling their tails, totally unaware that the next morning the puddle will have dried up and left them stranded" (pp. 482-483).

Winnicott says further, "I am not running down Jung by labeling him a recovered case of infantile psychosis." I might be able to swallow that, but not the next line of Winnicott's review: "I may be a 'tadpole amiably unknowing of my fate' but I am not besmirching Jung's personality or character. If I want to say that Jung was mad [note the progression here from schizophrenia to psychosis to madness] and that he recovered, I am doing nothing worse than I would do in saying of myself that I was sane and that through analysis and self-analysis I achieved some measure of insanity." I find this to be a piece of sophistry that thinly veils the negativity underneath. Then, only a little later, Winnicott says: "At the end of a long life Jung reached to the centre of his self, which turned out to be a blind alley" (p. 483). I am cross-eyed with indignation.

I think that Jung, like many other people – some of them Jungians – was not schizophrenic, psychotic or mad, but suffered a childhood wound which resulted in an initiatory illness. Through such studies as Dr. Henderson's (1967) and others, we are now familiar with this occurrence in the lives of shamans, healers, visionaries and mystics as well as certain Jungian analysts and some analysands. Walsh (1990) has shown, in an excellent phenomenological study, that schizophrenic and initiatory illnesses differ markedly in such phenomena as ability to be in control, level of mental concentration, type of emotional accompaniment, and stability of one's sense of identity. The content of the psyche in initiatory illness is much better organized, with coherent imagery and overall conscious purpose, than in any sort of psychotic state.

Winnicott's opinion that Jung repressed destructive impulses in himself and others is more convincing to me. Jung, who was so enormously original and creative, seemed not to appreciate fully the psyche's destructive capability. He mentioned and described the shadow but did not do justice to the full scope of lust, greed and malice in human affairs. Because he was so close to the spiritual side of the psyche, everything in Jung's psychology is a bit idealized and needs the test of hard reality to complete it. For example, he barely mentioned the Holocaust, one of the most cruel and destructive events of our time.

But do not Winnicott and his followers also deny something important? Coming to mind at once are meaning and purpose, without which health and sanity have no true foundation. True meaning cannot be found only in sexuality, childhood injury or personal relationship, though all of these are important. It must come through connection with higher power, a principle upon which Jung has based his psychology. A most important part of this connection is the transcendent function.

Dehing reminds us that one partner in this function, the unconscious, is largely unknown. But it is not entirely unknown. It contains in each individual a symbolic, structural layer which is collective and mythic. This collective aspect is seen clearly in tribal cultures in which there are coherent bodies of myth and ritual. In the cultures of modern Western civilization this coherent structure has been fragmented and dispersed. It remains for the modern individual to take what is given by the unconscious in dreams, visions and active imagination, and to combine and shape the material according to his or her unique psyche. If this work is done in any thorough-going way it begins with a lowering of conscious intensity, a flooding of consciousness with previously unconscious symbolic material – often fragmented – and a final structuring of a new consciousness with the ego's active participation.

I think this is what happened to Jung during his period of initiatory – creative – illness in 1914-16. A torrent of unconscious material came flooding in, temporarily overwhelming him but resulting finally in a strikingly original vision. This vision was first expressed in *VII Sermons Ad Mortuos* (Seven Sermons to the Dead; Jung, 1967); the method of dealing with it is described in the article on the transcendent function (CW8). Neither of these works, as Dehing mentions, was immediately made available to the world. There were many reasons why they were not. They were both lacking in polish. The article on the transcendent function was very short and sketchy for such original material, and the seven sermons were written in an inflated mythic style. But even more to the point, they both were concerned with intensely personal encounters with the collective unconscious. Part of that encounter, as recorded in the "Red Book," still has not been published.

What is of greatest interest to us here is that the first three sermons in particular represent mythic prefigurations of Jung's concept of pairs of opposites and their reconciliation by means of the transcendent function. It is Jung's vision of a creation myth which emerged from his interaction between conscious and unconscious, and which forms a mythic background – along with the other sermons – to much of Jung's later work.

The sermons begin with the *Pleroma*, which is characterized as at the same time everything and nothing. It has no being and no differentiation. Yet out of it come all the opposites: for example, good and evil, force and matter, male and female. Our Being is distinct from the *Pleroma*; from this individual being we must deal with the pairs of opposites that issue from the *Pleroma*. Jung said:

At bottom, therefore, there is only one striving, namely the striving after your own being. If ye had this striving ye would not need to know anything about the pleroma and its qualities, and yet would ye come to your right goal by virtue of your own being. Since, however, thought estranges from being, that knowledge must I teach you where-with you may be able to hold your thought in leash. (Jung, 1967, p. 14).

In the second sermon Jung recognizes a higher power which is God but which contains both poles of the opposites, including both good and evil. That god he calls Abraxas. Without the transcendent function we can never free ourselves from entanglement with pairs of opposites, especially good and evil.

In the third sermon Jung not only continues to use mythic language, but transforms it into a long spiritual poem. First he once again sets the opposites in place: "What the god-sun speaketh is life; what the devil speaketh is death. But Abraxas speaketh that hallowed and accursed work which is life and death at the same time" (Jung, 1967, pp. 19-20).

In the middle of this amazing poem, from the very depths of his being, Jung finds the ground for reconciliation. For me, this is one of the most exciting and revealing passages in all of Jung's work.

> It is abundance that seeketh union with emptiness.
> It is holy begetting.
> It is love and love's murder.
> It is the saint and his betrayer.
> It is the brightest light of day and the darkest night of madness.
> To look upon it, is blindness.
> To know it, is sickness.
> To worship it, is death.
> To fear it, is wisdom.
> To resist it not, is redemption. (Jung, 1967, pp. 20-21)

It is remarkable that at the same time that Jung conceptualized the transcendent function, he immediately applied it to the deepest and most poignant human dilemma, the inseparability of good and evil: "We labour to attain to the good and the beautiful, yet at the same time we also lay hold of the evil and the ugly" (Jung, 1967, p. 12). What is even more remarkable is that he brought forth an answer – his answer at least. He urged us to differentiate from Abraxas, to turn our eyes from "the flaming spectacle of Abraxas" and to resist it not; to go on the long journey of the soul to the far away star of our own being, "the god and the goal of man" (Jung, 1967, p. 33).

Abraxas is a Gnostic word; undoubtedly, the quotation is from a text inspired by Gnosticism. But Jung did not just sit down to write a Gnostic poem. *Seven Sermons* is a passionate work that came from the depth of his being. He said: "Then it began to flow out of me and in the course of three evenings the thing was written. As soon as I took up the pen, the whole ghostly assemblage evaporated. The room quietened and the atmosphere cleared. The haunting was over" (MDR, p. 191). This was a shamanic vision but more importantly this was a vision that gave meaning to Jung's life and work, and to our lives and to the world. That is what Winnicott did not understand.

We are very lucky that later Jung was confident and secure enough to allow these two important works to be published, even though what is to me one of his greatest masterpieces – *Seven Sermons* – did not at first bear his name.

I am greatly indebted to Dehing for his section on the transference. I had never before realized that the transference is a striking example of the transcendent function in which the analyst takes one pole of the oppositorum and the analysand takes the other. There are many times when there is no other solution but to wait on the slow development of a third possibility, a new life, in the unconscious. If the analyst is genuinely involved, the new life is also born in him or her as well as in the analysand.

Finally, Dehing challenges us with a most difficult pair of opposites: meaning vs. meaninglessness. We as well as the Gnostics are partial to meaning. In putting this pair of opposites side by side, and opening my mind to whatever comes, I first felt a great repugnance for meaninglessness; then the figure of Coyote and one of his stories came to mind and I felt great relief. Here is my adaptation of the story: Coyote loves to style himself as a Jungian analyst. It would be improper here to say why. But one day he was sitting with one of his candidates, who had just read reverently one of the *Collected Works*. "Oh sir," the candidate said, "I have just been reading about the authentic, true, inner self. Tell me, sir, can the authentic true inner self ever be diminished or destroyed?" Coyote immediately said, "Of course it can." The candidate looked at Coyote doubtfully, as if he were thinking he might have picked the wrong control analyst. "But how, sir, can the authentic true inner self ever be destroyed?" "It's easy," said Coyote who took the book from the candidate, looked at the pages he had been reading, ripped them out, tore them into shreds, and scattered them to the winds. "Like that," he said to the aghast candidate, and danced away. Then I knew that only life, for which Coyote stands, can transcend meaning and meaninglessness.

References

Henderson, J. (1967). *Thresholds of Initiation*. Middletown, CT: Wesleyan University Press.

Jung, C. G. (1967). *VII Sermones Ad Mortuos*. London: Stuart and Watkins.

Walsh, R. (1990). *The Spirit of Shamanism*. Los Angeles: Tarcher.

Winnicott, D.W. (1964/1989). "C. G. Jung: Review of *Memories, Dreams, Reflections*." In Winnicott, C.; Shepherd, R.; Davies, M. (Eds.), *Psycho-Analytic Explorations*. London: Karnac.

The Transcendent Function in Therapy after Incestuous Violence

Petra Affeld-Niemeyer
Berlin, Germany
German Society for Analytical
Psychology

Literature on the consequences of sexual trauma in childhood largely accepts the idea that such violence results in severe impairment to the development of personality. This impairment is especially severe if the perpetrator is the father, step-father or mother's partner, whom the children through their dependency cannot avoid. Further, it is accepted that children are victims of strategies for secrecy, with which they – the only witnesses of the violence – are silenced.

It is part of the coping and survival strategies of violated children to ignore their instinctive perceptions that would lead to an escape from the violence. A result may be a long-term repression of instinct and an on-going threat of being violated again in later life.

The child victims seem to concentrate on enduring the terrible experience; their coping strategies are molded by denial and threats of punishment from the perpetrator. Reality is perceived in a distorted manner. Negative affects are split off; seemingly harmless partial experiences remain in their consciousness. The victims relinquish their perception of reality under the pressure of the perpetrator's system of interpretation. They must become "deaf" and "blind."

Reality functions are impaired in the adults they become, even apparently "well-functioning" survivors. Just as in children, differentiation in the development of adult personality can be paralyzed. Or a regression can occur, handicapping them severely in their relationship with the Self and the Other.

In keeping with research on the consequences of other extreme forms of social violence – political terror and concentration camps – I assign the extent of the regression and the blocking of parts of personality development in incest victims to a particular developmental phase: the undifferentiated state of *primary ambiguity* (Bleger, 1981) or *primordial unconscious identity* (CW6).

In my view, archetypal images form early instinctual reactions in the victims of incest. Thus, changes in theory and therapeutic technique can be understood in a historical context: Jung, who had been sexually molested, formulated his "declaration of independence" following his separation from Freud. Jung's experience is reflected in the essay "The Transcendent Function" (CW8). Taking examples from analytic work with a woman who was sexually abused as a child and whose daughter also was traumatized by incest, I will show how the activation of the symbolic experience – the transcendent function – rather than the reductive reconstruction of the traumatic reality, provides the therapeutic orientation.

A dialectic tension is placed between imagination reflecting a present emotional state and reality constructed out of present and past experiences; a dialogue is opened in therapy and in outside relationships. Remembering is not the goal; as Ferenczi (1933) warned, an attending retraumatization can occur. The reanimation of immediate instinctive reactions and emotional perceptions of actual experiences, with the help of the transcendent function, forms the basis for remembrance and reconstruction of the individual history. However, this reconstruction in its violence – unbearable possibly for both the analysand and the analyst – may remain incomplete.

Developmental-Psychological Concepts and Historical Background

It is not by accident that psychoanalytic thinking on the consequences of sexual violence is oriented more and more by experiences with adult victims of other extreme forms of social violence (Wirtz, 1989). This research often describes the loss of soul and identity as "Soul-Murder" (Freud, SE12).

I find helpful the model proposed by Bleger (1981) which I encountered through the work of Amati (1990) on the victims of abduction, concentration camps and torture. Bleger proceeded from a personality nucleus, stemming from the primordial time of the soul, full of existential uncertainty. This he called "cementing nucleus" or "ambiguity nucleus." For the experience of identity it is necessary to put this nucleus into a container in the outside world.

I agree with his explanations to the extent that these processes – postulated to take place before a rudimentary psychic differentiation of inside and outside, subject and object – are not to be equated with projective identification. Both concepts, "identification" and "projection," suggest activity. Instead, I emphasize the passivity of this primary undifferentiated state. As a presupposition for every development, every differentiation of an inside and every relation to an outside, a passive readiness to let this nucleus be taken over needs to exist as well. In a state of ambiguity, not only the cementing of the nucleus matter in itself would be possible but also its fusion, its "being identical" and "being in identity with the other." This use of the concept, which distinguishes between "identification" and "being in identity," can be traced back to Jung: "Psychological identity... is... the real foundation of the *participation mystique*..., which is nothing but a relic of the original non-differentiation of subject and object" (CW6, par. 741).

In this primordial unconscious state, a center of consciousness has not yet formed nor has the ego separated from the Self. It is important that this phase of undifferentiation offers the possibility that an Other, not yet conceived as being outside, can usurp this identity: *the fusion of the Other inside the Self*. Jung impressively described the resulting state of identity confusion in a childhood experience with his stone.

In front of this wall was a slope in which was embedded a stone that jutted out – my stone. Often, when I was alone, I sat down on this stone, and then began an imaginary game that went something like this: "I am sitting on top of this stone and it is underneath." But this stone could also say "I" and think: "I am lying here on this slope and he is sitting on top of me." The question then arose: Am I the one who is sitting on the stone, or am I the stone on which he is sitting?" This question always perplexed me, and I would stand up, wondering who was what now. (MDR, p. 20)

According to Bleger (1981), to the ambiguity nucleus belong "feelings that despite their contrariness do not mutually exclude each other" (p. 208). When the more mature Self and ego are driven by extreme outside situations into severe regression and are flooded by ambiguity so that the defense mechanisms of splitting and denial no longer function, various symptoms may result. Their mutuality consists of a dulling of thought and a numbing of perceptions and emotions. The experience of extreme destruction (e.g., by the atomic bomb) and violence (e.g., in a concentration camp) may block secondary processes such as grief and suspend the "formative-symbolizing process." We can assume – for the victims of incest as well – that a permanent traumatic state of threat may lead to a *"standstill or a mimicry of thinking"* (Lifton, 1980, p. 251).

In the flooding by ambiguity which allows the preservation of life at any cost, the victims can respond only as drilled to familiar signals. An empty adaptation mechanism is functioning. In extreme fear this mechanism makes a threat seem to provide assistance through familiarity, even if it is not so. "Torture and other extreme forms of social violence are intended to mobilize in massive and perfidious ways those aspects of the human being that are connected the most strongly with adaptation, opportunism, and conformism" (Amati, 1990, p. 727).

In this adaptation, *identity on the level of instincts* is often conceived as that of a prey. Eibl-Eibesfeld (1990), has pointed to the atavistic male traits of capturing prey in the behavior of perpetrators: their hierarchic sexuality toward children and adolescents. These traits are mirrored in the soul-images of their victims. On the level of instincts, death and thanatosis (a shock-like state with reduced metabolic processes) apparently stand unsevered next to each other, although in thanatosis a spark of hope still survives: that a rescuer, and not a killer, may carry one off. In the archetypal images that Jung took to be the soul's shaping of the instincts, the image of a star or shining lapis often appears for this spark of life and hope. For example, in the mythical transformation into a star of the youth Ganymede; he had been sexually desired and taken as a prey by Zeus in the form of an eagle.

As another counter-movement against death I see the finding of *identity as a sacrifice*, where a meaning can be discerned which otherwise cannot be comprehended. The divine sacrifice of life often becomes a model and consolation. The active sacrifice of the incest victim in the family – to protect the mother, younger siblings or the suicide-threatening perpetrator – is often a reality which gives meaning to life. It transforms the compelled adaptation, the petrifying conformity to the violator, into a meaningful spiritual act of resistance and deliverance.

I understand also Jung's theoretical revolt against Freud's theory of the drives and the Oedipus complex. In Freud's presentation, the rape of the boy Chrysippus by Laius – Oedipus' father – and the murderous child abandonment, remains a largely split-off part of the myth. The "sexual assault" on the boy Jung by a man he had "once worshipped" gave Jung's transference onto Freud "the character of a 'religious' crush" that was "disgusting and ridiculous because of its undeniably erotic undertone" and that had made him "fear [Freud's] confidence" (FJ, p. 95). The separation from Freud enabled Jung to reformulate incest as symbolic and spiritual, negating the reality of his own experience.

Following the separation from Freud was a time of Jung's increasing withdrawal into an inner life. During this time he developed the concept of the transcendent function. In it he opposed Freud's postulate of the dominance of a consciousness for the incest victim identical with that of the violator. Jung posited instead, a creative dialectical process between conscious and unconscious. The symbol-creating power of the personal history is contrasted here with the dynamics of inherited archetypal symbols. Thus violence that is experienced as life-threatening can be compensated by a positive archetypal image.

From My Analytic Work

A 39-year-old nurse, "H.," reported that she experienced sexual violence between ages eight and ten. The perpetrator was then living with the family of seven children whose father was in prison. The analysand suffered from severe anxiety states and painful somatizations. Before beginning therapy H. informed me in a letter that she remembered "indecent touching" which caused her insomnia and night terrors. When the man wanted to penetrate her one night, she fled to the bed of her mother who angrily turned her away. "Further memories are missing. I only remember that I wanted to kill myself afterward."

H. had been referred to me by the therapist of her 10-year-old daughter, "T." The therapist had confronted H. and her husband with suspected ongoing father-daughter incest. The analysand had separated from her husband and recently found a new boyfriend. The daughter still had contact with her father, probably with continuing sexual violence.

The Path out of Petrification

From the beginning, in the transference, the submissive obedience is felt; H. can hardly conceal her distrust and her fears of being violated and manipulated in therapy. We also have to cope with her dread of the violent images of her dreams and hallucinations. Like other victims of incest, she fears being overwhelmed from the inside and losing the ability to differentiate between fantasy and reality. This process of differentiation between dream and conscious experience, between inside and outside, and the disentanglement of identities is illustrated in the following excerpts from my notes.

H. says in the fourth session: "Every time I have the feeling of security with my boyfriend, I have wild nightmares afterwards; for example, our hands, his hand and mine, were intertwined, that was nice. After such beautiful things – as with the hands – I don't know if it is a dream or reality. I provoke my own punishment."

The intertwining of dream and reality returns in the seemingly beautiful image of the intertwined hands; only much later do I learn the contents of her *recurring hallucinations and nightmares of terrible hands on a stone* "that drive one crazy." Then H. reports how "the fear creeps up on her" when T. tells her: "I want to go to Daddy, I can sleep in one bed with him and cuddle." Soon after that H. "had a terrible bad dream," her initial dream:

> In front of an orthogenic children's home, educators are in the process of "hot-wiring" her car [to steal it]. She says: "I went there and asked, what are you doing there?" They wanted to drive into town. I did not do anything. In the dream I got angry: Why can't I say that I find it a damn beastly mess that one does that in this manner? The other thing I remember is: "My God, the sky is clear and starry."

As an observer of the unwanted manipulation of her car, H. cannot act. The symbolic relation to the sexual manipulation of her past becomes clear, and to the present in which she is incapable of acting and tolerates incest. But she gets angry at her speechlessness: "Why can't I say that I find it a damn beastly mess?" With this emotional clarity the stars appear as positive counter-images to the negative petrification symbols. In the sequence of the dream H. clearly recognizes T.'s current reality:

> She returns to the children's home and meets a newly-admitted, sad little girl who says: "No matter what happens, no matter if the parents drink and beat me up badly, I want to go home." H. continues: "I caress her. With that a very peculiar thing happens. She pulls down her pants. "This is the reality of T." shot through my head. I give some sort of signals – she has to react to them according to what she has learned. Afterward I could not remember what I had dreamt. I felt bad and helpless." (Session 7)

The dream's clarity as to the reality of the daughter who reacts as if trained to signals nevertheless cannot remain conscious, because the mother still experiences herself as a giver of signals

– identical with the perpetrator. She fights her inner knowledge instead of the perpetrator. She is incapable of realizing what it means to "cuddle;" she cannot ask the daughter, cannot clarify the confusion of speech, as the identities of the perpetrator, observer, and victim are still too much cemented together.

A reductive interpretation of the car image and insistence on the "clarity of the dream" would have paralyzed H. further and stifled in guilt the anger about her silence. Yet the outside has been reflected emotionally on the inside and is understood as a reaction to reality; no longer is it interpreted as a self-punishing reaction to a beautiful feeling. The bad, helpless feeling "afterward" is real for both mother and daughter. I must accept that – as I often feel just as bad and helpless in the face of continued incest-violence.

Only the archetypal symbolism of a fairy-tale experience opens the dialogue between mother and daughter, differentiation of subject and object. H. suspects the threat to T. in another dream:

> She is quarreling with the "foolish" daughter and lets her get out of the car on a drive through a dark forest. Suddenly she is grabbed by panic and wants to find it, but her car has disappeared. Another faster car stalls. "It was like Hansel and Gretel."

In therapy H. is in panic. She reports dark premonitions of a fatal "accident" of her younger sister who also was violated. She has the feeling that an angel of death steps icily into the room. I am warned not to offer her an "analytic car" that is too fast and that would only stall. In order to emphasize fantasy, I ask to tell her the Hansel and Gretel fairy tale. As in the fairy tale H. idealizes the "kind-hearted father," splitting the violence from the male and projecting it onto the step-mother. Her own feminine identity is occupied by the archaic negative pole of the mother-archetype, the child-devouring witch, who is also an image of the violator.

As if, by the fairy tale comparison, H. is slipping back into the emotions of childhood, she describes the desperate children coming upon the witch; Gretel is locked up. Hansel and Gretel have

also switched roles: The victim incapable of action is female.
The memory of the fairy tale blocks when the witch is pushed
into the fire. H. experiences strong emotions against the death
penalty, as if she had to protect the witch. I ask her to write the
end of the fairy tale at home. Instead, as she tells me in the next
session, she asked T. "She insisted that the witch is the good one;
the children are the wicked ones." In the dialogue with her
daughter, H. sees as in a mirror her own reversal of good and
evil. Full of shame she asks why she keeps blaming her innocent
child. She now tackles her own witch side; shamefully she reports how she aggressively loses self-control against her daughter. Her tantrums remind her of her foster mother, a social worker, who had taken in an elder brother and H. in her tenth year of
life – like Hansel and Gretel.

In another dream a witch-like therapist, a lesbian, confronts
H. and her daughter:

> The therapist wanted to give T. some candy. T. likes to eat sweets
> but she refused the candy from this woman, who returned enraged
> and said: "My God, whose child is this?" This went straight to my
> belly; it was clear that the child was mine. There was this feeling:
> Something is wrong with the child. And then it shot through my
> head: Only because she refused the candy. A little bit of pride – a lot
> of pride: My daughter reacted, and I cannot stand her [the therapist]
> either. The old woman said: "She is too distrustful." She added
> something else that was much more to the point. This knowledge
> was uncomfortable for me. She is right; everybody around knows it.
> I felt that I had to do something. It was an honest matter. It was a
> feeling like a stone struck inside oneself; one cannot throw it off, but
> it presses. She called forth something, she hit the sore spot." (Ses-
> sion 17)

The unconscious identification of the violator and the therapist seemingly can be experienced and dissolved only in the
symbolic representation of her emotion. It is not that a stone is
taken off her heart; for the first time she feels the pressing stone
inside her as a foreign body with which she is no longer identical.
A difference is set, although she cannot yet throw off the stone.
The sore spot is hit; this is a sign of reanimation, at first through
pain and distrust. Proud of her daughter's distrust, H. accepts

herself as the mother and T. as her child. At the same time she can realize that her daughter's symptoms are danger signals that remind her of her own primordial symptoms.

Thereafter H. can communicate to me "scraps from recurring dreams and hallucinations" that have long put her into a state of paralyzing fear:

> There is a tombstone; a cold, charred hand looks over it. Soldiers march very often, stamping over the fields, trampling with their feet. It is a premonition: Oh my God, what is being announced there? (Session 25)

In the image of the tombstone under the charred hand the emotional petrification is experienced. The symbolic memory of the violation is there, not the real scene, and I have not interpreted it – as I did the previous scenes – in a reductive way. A deadly fury is released from the petrification. It is first projected onto the friend and auto-aggressively hits the maternal imago:

> Then I had a dream that my boyfriend slaughters his mother. I had a quarrel with T., could have killed her. (Session 26)

Integrating her fury, H. increasingly recognizes that she is directing old affects against her daughter. She also recognizes her own childhood fear in her daughter's panic:

> My daughter had a nightmare, cried, screamed, a monster wanted to devour her. I always had nightmares in my childhood. For example, with my foster mother who always wanted to give a deadly injection to my youngest brother on the changing table. I screamed, kept saying that she should not do it. I feel a lot of rage.

With the lifting of the petrification, the symbolic representation of the violation changes. What follows is the splitting into the screaming victim and the observing, screamingly protesting child-ego. The violence is still ascribed to a female figure. In the liberation of this rage H. complains desperately: "I am destructive." She gives more and more examples and speaks of her loss of control against her daughter and her disgust with her own body. It is as if, in this complaint, she finds her speech again, like the screaming children in the dream.

Now she remembers scenes from her childhood in which –
complementary to the helplessness at the baby-killing – the siblings thwarted the suicide attempts of the mother by hiding her
deadly "red candies." It seems that precisely the remembered
ability to act, for the rescue of the mother, and the conscious
analysis of her own current destructiveness make the archetypal
positive pole appear in the form of the "laughing child." For the
first time she reports a positive dream, "that rumbles deep down
inside":

> Somehow it concerns a child, a three-year-old boy. It was a beautiful
> dream, also scary. He was a cheerful child who had ended up in
> geriatrics. He was playing in bed. This picture: the cheerful child
> among the old people. He winked at me and could walk; he just
> wanted to get out of his crib. Somehow he did that and he laughed
> awfully much. (Session 36)

After the inner birth of the child, H. finds the strength to face
the reality of the incestuous violence against her daughter. With
the help of the transcendent function a differentiation between
her daughter's experience and her own evolves in a conscious act
of fantasizing over her daughter's drawings, which she brings to
therapy. On these drawings a small animal lifts its human mouth
toward the phallic arm of a headless man. The drawing is torn in
two. The analysand is full of rage: "I could go and tell him that
he should keep his dirty paws off her." She re-orientates her
verbal aggressiveness – against the aggressor – on the outside!
She forbids the father any contact with the daughter.

The Sacrifice and the Appropriation of the Will

Subsequently, H. and I must deal with the secret sexual violence against the daughter. She explains to me what being a man
means to her: To force his will on the woman – "that which she
does not want – she does want after all." Through a nightmare-
like hallucination in which the identities merge again, she realizes that T. does not sleep at her friend's home:

It is nonsense she is telling me. She secretly goes to her father. It happened to me twice in a half-awake state: Someone wanted to kill me. It is like in the childhood dream of my little brother where I dreamt he was killed by my foster mother. (Session 57)

The patient feels overstressed by this renewed secret abuse, as if she herself were to be killed. Again she feels the rage rising against her daughter and asks herself: "Why am I so angry when T. is in pain?" She ponders the question of a friend: "Are you angry at T. because she surrenders?" She does not dare ask her daughter directly and acts against the child's analyst because "all the analyst wants to do is sound out my daughter." It is as if she again merges with the perpetrator to protect him from betrayal.

In this phase of tension she becomes ill. She has a painful cyst in her ear. After the cyst has opened and the pus drained off, H. remembers how the violator came to her bed at night and whispered in her ear: After all, you also want this." H. experiences the symbolic reference between the pus and the foreign will that has to drain off so that her perceptive organs become purified.

Now she increasingly develops a "counterwill;" she checks at what time her daughter comes home and where she has been. The daughter at first reacts with furious resistance. In a quarrel she suddenly bursts out screaming: "If you take my cuddle [stuffed] animal I will kill myself!" (Session 60). The mother has seen the "cuddle animal" in the drawing and she knows that her husband attempted suicide at the beginning of her therapy. She now realizes that her daughter, who can be blackmailed, sacrifices herself and, like the perpetrator, threatens suicide in order to protect him. The fusion of the predatory animal, the prey and the animal of sacrifice in the "cuddle animal" becomes apparent.

H. somatizes with unclear abdominal pains; she has her intra-uterine device removed and feels insecure "without protection."

In memory she sees her six-day-old daughter whom she hands naked to the father to bathe her: "Suddenly she stopped breathing; she turned all blue. Is she still breathing? I was sure she was dead. I turned her upside down and shook her. Before I could run to the doctor downstairs she started breathing again." Such aggressions surfaced. (Session 69)

Through the depiction of this early "participation mystique" I understood the real death-threatening paralysis of the child as a passive process of identity with the panic-stricken and aggressive mother. I could empathize better with the fear of the mother who plants her will against her furious panic and thus against her intuitive perception of reality in order to keep herself and her daughter from "becoming crazy" to the point of death.

In the following stressful phase her furious "counterwill" against her daughter escalates again:

> She dreams that she spends the night with her daughter in a witch-house in a dark forest and has to put up a fight against the killer-witch who moans in a bed. The daughter is asleep in another bed. The dreamer happens on her daughter's bed in the dark. Already she has her hands around her daughter's neck to strangle her, when the dreamer finds herself mistaken and stops. Relieved she determines that the daughter is alive. "The witch in the other bed wants something sexual and I provide it to her – in the role of the male." (Session 89)

With the help of the changing dream fairy-tale, H. can dissolve her own cementing of identity and release the daughter from the identification with the witch-violator. Before, she had feared suffocation when her daughter, in her sleeplessness, called her to her bed and clung to her. Now she can comfort her during night terrors: "She did not grab me by the neck and did not threaten me otherwise."

H. no longer has to sacrifice her daughter as the representative of the violator; she sheds another piece of identity with him, so that she can now seek help and better enforce her "counterwill" against him: In agreement with the youth welfare office and through a lawyer she forbids the father any contact with the daughter. He does not file an objection. The daughter accepts protection. When she sees her father's car she hides in school and finally calls home to be picked up; she no longer needs to sacrifice herself either.

Although the analysand again and again has to work herself out of the floods of ambiguity, she can perceive increasingly the inner signals of violence – in her symptoms and dreams and in those of her daughter. She can also check their relationship to outside reality. The escape into petrification, victimization or sacrifice has become rarer; her own will has become more available.

On the basis of the inner images of analysands I do not believe any more that children who were victims of incestuous violence and helplessly experienced the deadly reversal of their adaptability "also wanted" this violence because of their infantile sexuality or any positive feelings. In the end they wanted what they did not want because the will of the perpetrator flowed into them like poison and usurped and petrified the Self. In the state of ambiguity they were paralyzed in the final protective reflex before the retreat into death. It is as if the soul stops breathing. I consider the attempted explanation of the betrayal of the body by pleasure a language confusion emanating from the perpetrator and, by way of the analysands, intruding into the therapists and the theory. It does not do justice to the damage done nor the regression forced upon the victims. Neither does it do justice to their desperate attempt to give meaning to the terror through their self-sacrifice. The symbolic experience with the help of the transcendent function offers images of the emotional experiences of the child victims. These images show that the body does not feel good; it feels pain and death – like the soul.

Translated from German by
Yvonne Cherne

References

Amati, S. (1990) Die Rückgewinnung des Schamgefühls. *Psyche 44*-8, 724-740.

Bleger, J. (1981). *Symbiose et ambiguité*. Paris: PUF Le fil rouge.

Eibl-Eibesfeldt, I. (1990). Dominance, submission, and love: Sexual pathology from the perspectives of ethology. In Feierman, J.R. (Ed.), *Pedophilia: Biosocial Dimensions*. New York/Berlin: Springer.

Lifton, R. (1980). *Der Verlust des Todes*. Munchen/Wien: Hanser.

Wirtz, U. (1989). *Seelenmord, Inzest und Therapie*. Zurich: Kreuz.

Response

Betty De Shong Meador
Berkeley, California, USA
Society of Jungian Analysts of
Northern California

Petra Affeld-Niemeyer's paper is informative, inspiring and boldly creative. She has refuted Freud's presumptuous opinion that the child "after all also wanted" the incestuous sexual involvement. Freud's observations were based on a child's nascent, crude, undifferentiated, instinctual desire for the parent. Freud's statement, that the child "after all also wanted," places the level of want or desire of the child in the same developmental category as the will and desire of the adult. In refuting this obvious fallacy Affeld-Niemeyer has offered a description of the child's experience of forced identification with the perpetrator who, in the child's desperate wish for survival, becomes the object of the child's protection.

Affeld-Niemeyer has presented a thoughtful theoretical construction to support her thesis. She has brought new thinking to our understanding of the core primitive, ambiguous states. Her case material skillfully exemplifies her argument that it is the activation of the transcendent function not the reconstruction of the trauma, that provides the healing in these cases.

The psychological phenomenon in whose grip the traumatized individual lives is that of unconscious fantasy. The original trauma has seared into the child's unconscious psyche a set of unchallengable beliefs, whether the trauma was sexual violation, as in this case, or emotional abuse in any of its many forms. As a result of the abuse, the child exists in a web of unconscious meanings based on the world-defining experience of the trauma. Ever after, no matter how adapted the individual becomes, the dramatic story of original abuse remains the foundation of an unconscious matrix of meaning whose emotions, images, and events forever color the person's self-perception and perception of others. In her case presentation Affeld-Niemeyer clearly demonstrates the tenacious grip childhood trauma has on the unconscious psyche of its victim.

Understanding this unconscious fantasy is the work of the analyst, who has the task of articulating the fantasy clearly to herself or himself. This is a primary task, necessary to the comprehension of the analysand's dreams, transference, and relationship to life events. The analyst must remain always objectively aware of the analysand's primitive, unconscious fantasy. A danger arises when the analyst's own unconscious fantasy happens to fit synchronistically into that of the analysand. In that case the analyst may collapse out of the position of objectivity and enter the potent, compelling, archetypal drama of the analysand as a real-life participant, not an "as-if" participant. The analyst, then, re-enacts the abuse. This action aborts the nascent transcendent function and reinforces the concrete identification of the analysand with the violator. Such action on the part of the analyst may be sexual or, more subtly, emotional. In either case Affeld-Niemeyer has described the coercive power of archetypal unconscious fantasy to pull all significant relationships under its spell. The task of the analyst is to walk the thin paradoxical line of relatedness to the analysand, yet outside the seductive whirlwind of unconscious fantasy.

In my own practice I have experienced numerous analysands with histories of severe childhood sexual and emotional abuse. Most of them are well-functioning adults in spite of the residue of unconscious fantasy shaped by the original trauma. I have been helped to understand the wide range and the paradoxical nature of their functioning by the work of the psychoanalyst, Thomas Ogden (1986, 1989). Ogden's work is influenced by Melanie Klein, although he is not a Kleinian. To Klein's two modes of generating experience, the depressive position and the paranoid-schizoid position, Ogden has added a third which he calls the autistic-contiguous position. This mode of generating experience is more primitive than the other two and has many of the characteristics of the locus of regression which Affeld-Niemeyer describes. This third mode, and its relationship to Klein's other two modes, adds to our understanding of the regression experienced by Affeld-Niemeyer's analysand.

Ogden asserts that all three modes remain active and functioning in adults, and that one does not replace the others developmentally. The three modes interact and support, as well as negate, each other. This situation requires the analyst to discern which mode dominates the functioning of the analysand, and to which mode the analyst is speaking in the interpretations the analyst offers.

In the depressive mode, the individual has available an interpreting subject who is able to observe and to weigh experience and to symbolize. In this mode the person is able to hold the opposites in consciousness and to experience self-generated ambiguity. Because the individual in this mode is able to tolerate pain, she or he may well be able to reconstruct and relive the intensity of the original trauma.

In the paranoid-schizoid mode the individual is much less able to contain pain and tends to get rid of it by the defenses of splitting and denial. Emotions, thoughts, and sensations appear to happen *to* this individual, because she or he is only minimally able to experience being the author of them. An individual who functions primarily in this mode can approach the original trauma only as its effects on the unconscious psyche reverberate in everyday life. Healing, as in Affeld-Niemeyer's case, can come about through the symbols of the transcendent function.

The autistic-contiguous mode which concerns us here is generated by the infant's very first sensate experiences of its body pressing against a surface, the experience of touch, of being rubbed, patted, handled, as well as the experience of the rhythm of being rocked, walked, jiggled, or the rhythm of sucking. The newborn forms a rudimentary sense of self as it becomes familiar with repeated sensory experiences; it becomes aware of externality through the sensation of the mothering-person's body against its skin. As Affeld-Niemeyer describes, the infant bestows itself into the mother's body.

It develops a sensory contiguity, a bounded sensory surface on which its experience occurs. This sensation, Ogden (1989) says, is the beginning of a feeling of a place where one lives, feels thinks and has experiences of "shape, hardness, coldness, warmth, and texture" (p. 54). A child's experience of the autistic-contiguous mode is presymbolic. A holding matrix is being formed which later will enable the child to create symbols and to expand into the unknown.

In a situation of trauma the growing child may regress to this primitive, non-symbolizing state. The child's experience is one of a deteriorating sense of the cohesiveness of its skin surface. There is an acute threat that the primary sense of boundedness will be lost, and the child will dissolve into a vast ocean or fog, or that its insides will leak out through the holes in its skin surface, that it will not be able to contain feces or urine, and ultimately that it will cease to exist – an overwhelming archetypal terror of disappearance and total annihilation.

The threat of such an occurrence is so great that the child reverts to the most primitive forms of maintaining cohesiveness. Primary among these, in the case of trauma, is to make use of the cohesive will of the perpetrator. The child attempts to patch its disintegrating sense of boundedness with the skin of the aggressor. The child loses the ability to think and adopts through mimicry and imitation the "skin" of the violator. This occurrence in Ogden's description matches Affeld-Niemeyer's observance of a flooding of ambiguity, cloudiness of thought, and the numbing of perceptions and emotions. The individual in this mode clearly cannot tolerate the reconstruction of the events of the trauma. Even when this mode is not primary, the analyst, when speaking to this part of an individual's unconscious fantasy, must be sensitive to the drastic limitation of functioning in the autistic-contiguous state.

In my own experience I find clues of the autistic-contiguous mode operating not only in regressed individuals, but also in well-functioning adults. In the latter the operation of unconscious fantasy easily could go unnoticed. One analysand wore shoes like mine. One day I changed to another model, and the next session she appeared with a similar change. This woman experienced severe infant deprivation and possible physical abuse. Through imitation of me she is rebuilding the safety of boundedness and cohesiveness.

Another analysand, who was sexually molested by her grandfather, frequently believes she is bleeding into the couch with her menstrual blood. The holes in her sense of self occur at this primary level of a failure of containment of her bodily fluids.

The repair of such a trauma is heartening and sometimes dramatic. One analysand, who was sexually abused by her brother, after many years of analytic work decided the time had come to disconnect from me. She communicated this to me in a long letter sent just before her vacation. I was dubious about the outcome; she had just recovered from a period of psychosis. In addition to cutting down our sessions drastically, she decided to stop her medication.

She managed the vacation, although she was somewhat shaky. We began to see each other on a curtailed basis. I felt I had to trust her sense of independence. A few months after the vacation, she was being examined by a doctor when she realized he was pressing his erect penis against her leg. Instead of dissociating, which was her usual defense, she immediately asked that her husband come in for the remainder of the exam. Following this very upsetting experience, she angrily dismissed a psychiatrist who questioned whether the erection was real or imaginary on her part. For this woman the perpetrator was now clearly outside, not inside.

Affeld-Niemeyer's sensitive and intelligent handling of the case she presented has given me a renewed trust in the wisdom of the psyche. I have an esthetic feeling for the beauty of her work. She is truly practicing the art of analysis.

References

Ogden, T. (1986). *The Matrix of the Mind*. Northvale, NJ: Jason
    Aronson.
Ogden, T. (1989). *The Primitive Edge of Experience*. Northvale, NJ:
    Jason Aronson.

The World Cycle of Change: Political Leadership and the Transcendent Function

Louis H. Stewart
San Francisco, California
Society of Jungian Analysts of
Northern California

This is an extraordinary time in the history of the world. The Cold War is over and democracy is breaking out all over Eastern Europe. But almost immediately new threats appear on the horizon: yet other kinds of dictatorships that hark back to the old religious wars. Democracy and dictatorship appear to be locked in a fateful struggle.

What may Analytical Psychology have to say about the world situation? Basic questions are: What is democracy? What are its origins? The psychic origins of democracy are to be found in the transcendent function, the innate dialectical relationship between the opposites. As Jung put it when he described his method of active imagination: "It is technically very simple to note down the 'other' voice in writing and to answer its statements from the standpoint of the ego. It is exactly as if a dialogue were taking place between two human beings with equal rights" (CW8, par. 186). Projected onto the plane of society, is this not the core of democracy: a dialogue between two people with equal rights?

This paper begins with a review of my studies of the family situation of political leaders, studies which have provided insights into the ways in which particular leaders appear at critical moments in history. The studies approach the family from two perspectives: sibling position – which determines certain fundamental elements of leadership style – and family atmosphere, which has to do with the ruthless demands of the "spirit." I shall then explore the psychological roots of democracy and dictatorship, illustrating my statements with mythical and historical material, as well as biographical data on individual leaders. What is most significant is the understanding we gain of an individual's being "seized by the spirit," and the impact this event may have in the world for good or for evil, democracy or dictatorship.

Studies of Political Leadership

Little did I know when I undertook my first study over 30 years ago that I would be swept into the maelstrom of United States and British history. This was an early attempt to understand the fateful intertwining of individual, family and society. I examined the sibling position of 31 elected USA presidents, George Washington to John F. Kennedy, as well as 44 defeated candidates and 123 presidential hopefuls. I found convincing evidence that sibling position is a critical factor in the selection of presidents. In a majority of elections, by the time the party primaries are over and the two, or sometimes three, principal candidates are known, they prove to be of the same or very closely related ordinal positions. My study also showed that the distribution of birth order positions is not random. Presidents of the same or similar birth ranks follow each other in close succession. Further examination showed that the sibling position of leaders mirrors meaningful developments and shifts in the political zeitgeist.

For example, the first decades of the American presidency (1789-1828) comprised a period of expansion and confrontation. The newly-established government was engaged primarily in expanding and consolidating its boundaries and asserting its sovereignty. During those years, eight of ten elected presidents were first-born sons. In sharp contrast, the period following the election of Andrew Jackson (1828-1860) was a time primarily devoted to mediation of internal factions. The issues of the day were in large part monetary and political, with the dispute over slavery gaining in ascendance. During this period there were eight presidential elections. Six of the eight elected presidents were younger sons.

Then, in that decisive election year of 1860, when the nation anxiously faced the threat of the South seceding, the choice of presidential candidates made certain that, no matter what party won the election, the presidency would be held by an only son. Like Lincoln, both Douglas and Breckenridge were only sons. Douglas was of exactly the same sibling position as Lincoln, each having a single older sister. The ability of the only child or only son/daughter to hold the opposites and work toward a synthesis was sorely needed. Would the country hold together as "one union," or would it split into two separate nations? Lincoln's strong, compassionate leadership and his unshaken conviction that the Union must survive were major factors in the outcome of that struggle.

[In presenting data regarding sibling positions, F is for a female, M for a male. A number giving the ordinal position, follows the F or M under consideration. Sometimes a particular sequence of siblings is underlined when that configuration is under discussion.]

In the Confederacy, a different type of leadership was needed. The president chosen by the rebellious southern states was Jefferson Davis, a last-born son, the youngest of ten children (MMMFMFFFFM10). Is this a characteristic sibling position for revolutionary leaders? In many cases they are last-born children, for example, Sun Yat-Sen (MMM3), Gandhi (MFMM4), Bolivar (FFMM4). Others – such as Lenin (FMM3FFM), Castro (FMM3MF), Garibaldi (MM2MMF), Ho Chi Minh (FMM3M), Aquino (MFFF4MF) and Joan of Arc (MMFF4M) – although not last-borns, are younger sons or younger daughters.

For cross-validation, I studied the British political system and examined the sibling position of 31 Prime Ministers, William Pitt to Harold Macmillan, 1783-1963. Here, too, I found an impressive degree of correspondence between the sibling position of British leaders and the political zeitgeist.

From these early studies, I have come to understand sibling position to be the major influence that shapes four basic styles of leadership, not only in politics but in every field of endeavor, including depth psychology. The basic styles correspond to the four sibling situations: only, first-born, intermediate, and last-born child. The last born is the rebel, finely tuned to the winds of change. The intermediate born is also frequently a rebel but, because of the vantage point between older and younger, an expert at accommodation and mediation. The first-born is the preserver, the extender and developer, the carrier of tradition. The only child is the synthesizer, the carrier of the opposites, being both first and last.

There are many factors of family size, gender and age-spacing between siblings. There is also the complexity of step-brothers, step-sisters, siblings who grow up in different homes, and siblings who die in childhood. But as a whole, the child's experiences with or without siblings during the formative years determine the essential sibling position. For example, Mikhail Gorbachev was the only child in his family until he was 17; psychologically he is an only child.

Through the years sibling position has been widely studied, but with mixed results. The main problem is that by attempting to relate sibling position to either high achievement or pathology, an amazing number of studies persist in asking the wrong questions. Also, many investigators focus on the interaction of children with their parents and assume that differences among siblings are due to different socialization by the parents (Ernst & Angst, 1983). These studies seem to ignore the fact that siblings also interact with and have effect upon each other.

Certain universal features of family life face children everywhere, time after time after time, with the often painful awareness of just where it is they stand with the siblings in the hierarchies: of size and strength, of mobility, of privilege and of knowledge and experience which must exist simply because of age differences and, in turn, by virtue of the order of their births. The deep, flowing currents of emotion implicit in sibling relationships are surely what make birth-order related experiences so binding and so freighted with far-reaching consequences.

Ten-year-olds tell us of the tactics they employ to get a sibling to do what they want: "I beat him up, hit him, boss him, spook him, belt him, exclude him." Or: "I get mad, shout and yell, cry, pout, sulk, ask other kids for help, threaten to tell Mom and Dad" (Sutton-Smith & Rosenberg, 1970). So elemental and universal are these responses that no one need be told that the participants are older and younger brothers and sisters, nor need anyone be in doubt that the power tactics are those of the older siblings. This is the litany of sibling rivalry. But is this not the raw material of power politics? It requires no great leap of imagination to perceive in adult political leaders the same kind of behavior: Lyndon Johnson, a first-born son, in the Capitol cloakroom "twisting arms." Richard Nixon, a second-born son, angry, pouting, crying on television. John Foster Dulles, a first-born son, exploiting atomic brinkmanship. Or Dwight Eisenhower, a third-born son, holding Nixon at arm's length.

Sibling complexes may be projected also between nations. Early in 1992, a news report described increasing tension between Russia and Ukraine. The two republics clashed over nuclear weapons, the Black Sea fleet, even time zones. Les Taniuk, a leader of the opposition in the Ukraine parliament identified the problem of such projection as a kind of sickness: "Russia needs to recover from this disease to be the big brother, and Ukraine should recover from the disease to be the little brother" (Freedberg 1992, pp. A1, A19, A21).

The Family Atmosphere

My studies of sibling position led me, inevitably, to explore the other major dimension of the family, the family atmosphere. Whereas sibling position determines a particular view of the world and the self that shapes the style of leadership, it is the family atmosphere that is responsible for the psychological dynamics that lead a particular individual to be "chosen" by the spirit, so to speak, to become the leader at a specific moment in history. Moses was called by Yahweh from the burning bush, Joan of Arc was guided by her angels and Gandhi listened to the voice of the people.

Seizure by the spirit does not tell us whether the resultant development will manifest as good or evil, as history well illustrates. Gandhi, for example, was seized by the spirit with the aim of taking back his native land from the rule of the British, and giving to his people their rights as citizens of a sovereign state. He created a non-violent revolution which in the end achieved his aim. Hitler, too, was presumably seized by the spirit with the aim of taking back his divided homeland from the allied countries that had defeated the Germans in World War I, and giving his people their rights and privileges. In *Mein Kampf*, he described his virulent hatred of the Jewish people as a "spiritual upheaval":

> Wherever I went, I began to see Jews, and the more I saw, the more sharply they became distinguished in my eyes from the rest of humanity.... Gradually I began to hate them.... For me this was the greatest spiritual upheaval I have ever had to go through. I had ceased to be a weak-kneed cosmopolitan and become an anti-Semite.... Hence today I believe that I am acting in accordance with the will of the Almighty Creator: *By defending myself against the Jew, I am fighting for the work of the Lord.* (1927, pp. 56-65)

Hitler created a violent revolution with a commitment to his notion of a Utopian society: a society that would breed a perfect race of blond, blue-eyed heroes; rid itself of all those who were Jewish, or weak, disabled and unfit and then impose its rule on the rest of the world.

What makes the difference between a Hitler and a Gandhi, both of whom were younger sons engaged in revolution? Here we must look to the family atmosphere, that indescribable amalgam created by the behavior, values, cultural development and (perhaps most significantly) the unconscious parental complexes which carry the unanswered questions of the ancestors and represent the unlived lives of the parents. It is to these family influences that we should look for the difference between a Hitler and a Gandhi.

I believe that it will be accepted eventually, as Alice Miller (1983) and others have advocated for some time, that the emergence of evil in the world has its roots in deep-seated disturbances in the family. In the Western world, these disturbances may be traced back to attitudes and doctrines based on views of human nature that were spiritually conceived and intellectually defended, but which have no basis in reality. That children should be beaten for the good of their souls can only be understood as a desperate measure by parents to ward off awareness of their own spiritual wasteland. That Hitler could achieve such a hold on the German people is due in part to his own baptism in these brutal methods aimed at inspiriting the child's soul, but which achieve such a perverse outcome. Of course it took more than a brutal family atmosphere to produce Hitler's hatred and vengeance toward the Jews. Anti-Semitism was a widespread aspect of European society and elsewhere. The specter that haunted his father, and that found its way into Hitler's psyche, was the uncertainty as to whether an ancestral ghost was Jewish.

Hitler's obsession can be likened, on a massive scale, to the obsession of the serial murderer. Other comparisons can be made of Hitler and the serial murders: their home lives were nightmares of drunkenness, brutality and degradation of one kind or another.

If we ask the same questions of Gandhi's family we find that it was essentially humane and moral. There is, to be sure, evidence of qualities of the family atmosphere which account for Gandhi's particular woundedness and suggest the reasons for his having been "called." But there is nothing of the brutal horror of Hitler's upbringing.

Democracy

The psychological origins of democracy are to be found, surely, in the inner dialogue of individuation – becoming oneself – the dialectic between conscious and unconscious. It is as if Jung's image of the dialogue were taking place between two human beings with equal rights. This statement conveys the essence of Jung's method of active imagination, which is a re-activation in psychotherapy of the innate process of individuation. If we look to the socio-political world for a projection of this process, it would appear to be democracy. A dialogue between two human beings with equal rights is the essence of democracy. It is also the essence of true friendship and of true marriage. We need only look to ourselves, to our friends, our spouses, our families, to realize how imperfect is our commitment to "true" democracy. Nevertheless, the ideal exists; it is the intrinsic goal as well as the process of psychological development.

Speaking of the nature of political democracy, Jung characterized the Swiss experience of some 400 years of struggle toward the democratic ideal. In 1946 he wrote:

> We came to the conclusion that it is better to avoid external wars, so we went home and took the strife with us. In Switzerland we have built up the "perfect democracy," where our warlike instincts expend themselves in the form of domestic quarrels called "political life." We fight each other within the limits of the law and the constitution, and we are inclined to think of democracy as a chronic state of mitigated civil war. Thus far we have succeeded, but we are still a long way from the ultimate goal. (CW10, par. 455)

Jung concluded that a further step, an introversion of the dialectic of conscious and unconscious, is yet to be taken.

> We still have enemies in the flesh, and we have not yet managed to introvert our political disharmonies. We still labour under the unwholesome delusion that we should be at peace within ourselves. Yet even our national, mitigated state of war would soon come to an end if everybody could see his own shadow and begin the only struggle that is really worth while: the fight against the overwhelming power drive of the shadow. We have a tolerable social order in Switzerland because we fight among ourselves. Our order would be perfect if only everybody could direct his aggressiveness inwards, into his own psyche. (CW10, par. 455)

Then, in the face of the tragic world situation following World War II, Jung commented on his hopes and fears for the future. The individual is the sole carrier of mind and life, yet there are those who seek to destroy the individual. This reminds us of the urgent need to understand better what it is in human nature, or human circumstances, that thwarts the normal individuation process and leads to authoritarianism and evil. The major factor appears to be a failure of the family atmosphere to "inspirit" the dialogue of outer and inner, conscious and unconscious, personified as ego and shadow in Jung's terminology.

Dictatorship

The archetypal roots of both democracy and dictatorship are intrinsic to the psyche. The psychological origins of dictatorship, then, are found in repression. As we know well from the practice of analysis, repression is an unconscious function that excludes or forces out thoughts and feelings that are incompatible with the ego. Projected onto the socio-political plane, is this not dictatorship? A state under dictatorial rule cannot tolerate freedom of the individual. A dictatorship seeks to establish absolute control over the thoughts and actions of its citizens. Is this not a mirror of the intrapsychic landscape wherein severe repression and dissociation bring the normal dialectical process of individuation to a halt?

Another facet of this question is that of the process by which an individual becomes a leader. For Jung, it is not just the will to power of the individual leader, but rather a combination of the individual's will to lead and the desire of the community to be led.

> Since society as a whole needs the magically effective figure, it uses this need of the will to power in the individual, and the will to submit in the mass, as a vehicle, and thus brings about the creation of personal prestige. The latter is a phenomenon which, as the history of political institutions shows, is of the utmost importance for the comity of nations. (CW7, par. 237)

Jung's perspective essentially grounds our understanding of dictatorship by postulating that there must be a common need shared by a potential leader and the society. But we have not yet a satisfactory understanding of dictatorship from a psychological perspective. For that we must try to understand good and evil.

Good and Evil

To approach the nature of good and evil, I begin with an effort to identify the psychological dynamics that account for our experience of good and evil. If we consider the emotional core of this dynamic, we are led directly to the innate archetypal affects –

contempt and shame – and their development through the imagination toward the highest ideals of human community.

Contempt and shame are not the only affects that are involved with good and evil. Joy and interest, as well as fear, grief, anger and startle are the other inherited affects. Then, in addition to the inherited affects there are those mixtures and modulations that Darwin (1872) described as the "complex" emotions. Complex emotions include such opposites as jealousy and love, envy and admiration, guilt and compassion, greed and generosity. In my view, these universal experiences develop simply and solely because there is a family; consequently, I have come to call them "complex family emotions." It seems obvious that all the inherited emotions and all the complex family emotions are interwoven with the human experience of good and evil.

Nevertheless, there is an essential difference between contempt/shame and all the other emotions. What makes contempt and shame different is the extent to which self-evaluation is involved. Nothing in the world has such a potential for inducing us to take stock of ourselves and our relations with others. It seems evident that contempt and shame have evolved directly as a function of the social needs of the mammalian species.

Both contempt and shame are fundamental emotions that seem to have evolved out of the inherited affective reflex, disgust, which is present in infants from birth. The survival function of disgust is to identify noxious, potentially poisonous substances. For example, using the senses of smell and taste, we turn away from rotten food, or reject it by spitting it out. In the extremity of disgust we may experience the primal reaction of vomiting.

In accord with the classic study by Lynd (1958), contempt and shame may be understood as two faces of a single bi-polar affect; the stimulus is rejection. Whether one experiences contempt or shame is determined by the direction of rejection, either toward the other (contempt), or toward the self (shame). Contempt is expressed along a continuum of intensity that ranges from mild antipathy and distaste to the extreme of disgust. Shame ranges from shyness and mild embarrassment to the extreme of humiliation. To describe both poles of the affect, I have put the two words together: contempt/shame.

When contempt/shame is constellated, the experience is terrible, toxic, withering. It is as if one is banished, driven into the wilderness, far from human community. When such profound alienation is in consciousness, the opposite is constellated in the unconscious. A state of alienation evokes the deepest longing for "fairness" and "justice," a "good" community. The imagination of human relationship has evolved out of humanity's experience of alienation. Here we find the incipient forms of utopian fantasies. Depending on the development of the individual, these fantasies may be about dictatorial power (as with Hitler) or they may be shaped by the democratic ideal.

The Spirit Chooses

The innate emotions are the energic source of choice by the spirit. The "choice" of an individual to carry forward an idea or a task, such as that of leadership in politics (or, of course, in any field of endeavor), depends in part on a concatenation of the individual's sibling position in the family and the specifics of the social-political situation. But more is required for the choice of a particular leader in a specific political situation than just the match of sibling position and political zeitgeist. The question is then: What is that "more?"

From time immemorial the answer to that question has been referred to as "spirit." The heroic man or woman who takes on a task is said to have been "called." As we know, Moses (FMM3) was called by Yahweh, who was in the burning bush. In that confrontation Yahweh distinguished between Moses and his elder brother Aaron. For when Moses sought to decline the invitation because he was not eloquent of speech, Yahweh proposed that Aaron could speak for him. Why did Yahweh not simply call Aaron rather than Moses? The reason is to be found, presumably, in Yahweh's discernment of "spirit." Yahweh recognized in Moses a "natural" revolutionary leader, and the "soon to become" spiritual leader of the Israelites, Yahweh's "chosen" people. In our terms that would mean recognition that Moses' sibling position was that of a last-born and that he would make himself accessible to the ruthless demands of the "spirit."

Now we are left with the question: how does a particular leader of the appropriate sibling position come to dedicate himself or herself to preparation for the role for which a call will come? Not every last-born would aspire to the task that Moses took on, and not every last-born would be adequate for it. At first Moses did not feel that he was equal to the task, but he rallied and assumed the role assigned to him. Why was this? Obviously he had little choice. He could not deny Yahweh. But what does that mean psychologically? Moses must have come to recognize his own fitness for the task, just as do contemporary leaders in similar situations. Moses knew that he had a strong commitment to freedom: he had been banned from Egypt because he killed a slave owner who was abusing a slave. Moreover, at birth Moses had been saved by his mother and elder sister from the Pharaoh's command to kill all male babies born to the Jews. He had been adopted by the Pharaoh's daughter and raised in the palace. He had, then, a dual identity, and knew from the inside the ways in which the Pharaoh dealt with power. He was prepared to contend with the Pharaoh with the help, of course, of Yahweh.

Perhaps the most extraordinary example of being chosen by the spirit is the history of Joan of Arc (MMFF4M). A young peasant girl from the provinces of France, Joan knew at the age of 13 that France could be saved from her enemies only through the crowning of the dauphin as King. By 17 or 18 years of age she had accomplished that. At 19, she was burned at the stake for heresy. It is no wonder that the historian Dunham speaks in hyperbole when he approaches this subject:

> The new world which, five centuries later, we still live in and have not yet built arrived with more flame and mystery than would attend a collision of comets or sudden perturbations among the stars. For the whole new world, the modern world, existed in concept, in the mind of an illiterate, teen-age peasant girl, who, in the year 1429, knew, though no one else knew, what was necessary to be known. (1963, p. 240)

And we too may marvel. Imagine, how thunderstruck Joan's brothers and sisters must have been when she revealed to them the commands of her voices: Saints Michael, Catherine and Margaret. For the Western world Joan is unquestionably an historical paradigm of the coalescence of the heroine of myth and the heroic leader. Joan's inspiration came to her through the voices of her saints, who called her the Maid of Orleans, daughter of God. Any lurking doubts we may have that a sense of destiny erupting in the right person at the right time can move mountains and sweep masses of people along in its wake are quickly dispelled as we contemplate the towering figure of Joan of Arc.

Joan's role as a revolutionary is not unexpected in view of her sibling position. The fourth of five children; she had two older brothers, a next older sister and a younger brother (MMFF4M). As a second-born daughter with an older brother who was the first-born child she is in precisely the same sibling position as that held by other revolutionaries of the likes of Lenin (FMM3-FFM), Castro (FMM3MF) and others. (For males, the family configuration is an eldest sister, then a brother and then the revolutionary hero). From Moses (FMM3) to Joan of Arc (MM-FF4M) to Gandhi (MFMM4) to Polish leader Walesa (FMM3) one voice speaks, one word is heard: freedom – freedom from the tyranny of authority, be it the authority of unjust government or of dogmatic opinion. With this the archetypal image of the rebel takes form: Zeus overthrowing Chronos, the exemplary model of the younger son or daughter with an intimate knowledge of the human spirit in defiance.

Democracy or Dictatorship

Dickens' well-worn phrase is strangely apropos again: These are the best of times; these are the worst of times. It is as if the spirit of the French revolution were once more in the air. The similarity of what has been happening in the countries of Eastern Europe, the Philippines, South Africa and the beginning attempt in China, to the period of the French revolution is striking:

masses of people in the streets bringing down the Bastille again and again. Central to all these revolutionary movements is the sense of a new era of freedom and support for the rights of the individual citizen. But will this euphoria be followed by the atmosphere of the tribunal, as in the French revolution: the desperate attempt to preserve the "purity" of the revolution by purging those who dissent, thus creating the very instrument of God-given vision and authority which the revolution had sought to transform?

In the revolution of the American colonies this self-destructive enantiodromia was avoided, through what mysterious mix of good will and luck we shall never know. Was it the background of British history and its struggle toward democracy, or the aid and inspiration of the French? Perhaps it was the separateness on a new continent, or the high quality of the founders of the new Republic. Or was it the creation of a constitution and bill of rights which allowed for a democratic transfer of power at regular intervals, as well as the establishment of inalienable rights of the individual citizen?

To be sure, the new republic was soon put to the test of its high ideals in the secession of the southern states over the issue of slavery. The Civil War was won by the northern states and slavery was abolished, yet the issue of full rights for all citizens had not been settled. In the South, economic slavery replaced the old form of slavery. In the USA women did not win the right to vote until 1920. The non-violent civil rights movement of the 1960s led to considerable improvement in the rights of African-Americans and other minorities, but full equality for all citizens has not yet been achieved.

On the plane of society as well as in the psyche, the struggle for democracy still goes on.

Postscript: Reflections on the 1992 campaign

President Bill Clinton was an only child throughout his early formative years; his younger half-brother was born when he was 10. In the 1992 presidential campaign, it was remarkable to see that all the democratic hopefuls who continued through the primaries were only children or only sons. Jerry Brown and Paul Tsongas are both only sons with sisters. Brown has two older sisters and a younger sister; Tsongas has an older sister and a twin sister. (Ross Perot and Al Gore are only sons, each with one sister).

The question arises: What is the situation in the body politic that cries out for a leader who is an only child or only son (or only daughter)? The continuing recession, rising unemployment, and threat of another depression seem to call for a leader who is a natural expert in balancing the opposites and seeking a synthesis. It is remarkable that the Democratic ticket of 1992 offered both an only child – Clinton – and an only son, Al Gore. (The Republican ticket offered the incumbents: a younger son – Bush – and a first-born, Quayle.) The election of 1992 ended a period of 40 years of presidents who were predominantly younger sons. Since the election of Dwight Eisenhower in 1952, eight of ten elected presidents were younger sons.

References

Darwin, C. (1872/1965). *The Expression of the Emotions in Man and Animals*. Chicago/London: University of Chicago Press.

Dunham, B. (1963). *Heroes and Heretics: A Social History of Dissent*. New York: Dell.

Ernst, C. and Angst, J. (1983). *Birth Order: Its Influence on Personality*. Berlin/Heidelberg/New York: Springer.

Freedberg, L. (1992). Tension between Russia and the Ukraine. *San Francisco Chronicle*, February 7.

Hitler, A. (1927/1971). *Mein Kampf* (R. Mannheim, Trans.). Boston: Houghton Mifflin.

Lynd, H. (1958). *On Shame and the Search for Identity*. New York: Harcourt, Brace.

Miller, A. (1983). *For your Own Good: Hidden Cruelty in Child-Rearing and the Roots of violence*. New York: Farrar, Straus, Giroux.

Sutton-Smith, B. & Rosenberg, B. (1970). *The Sibling*. New York: Holt, Rinehart & Winston.

Note: Portions of this paper are drawn from:

Stewart, L. (1992). *Changemakers: A Jungian Perspective on Sibling Position and the Family Atmosphere*. London/New York: Routledge.

Response

Beverley Zabriskie
New York, NY, USA
New York Association for Analytical
Psychology

Jung's view of the psyche and its workings may be seen as through the prism of a systems approach. In this approach to complexes, the psyche may be perceived as inter-related nucleus energies sharing kinship but each responding with its own gestalt. In this respect, Jungian analysis is not unlike an intrapsychic family therapy, which assumes that the roles of family members are not singular but are affected by an intricate web of inter-related influences.

We speak of the mother and father complexes, the positive and negative shadow, animus and anima as if they are relatives of the ego, and sometimes speak of the ego itself as if it were son, daughter or perhaps grandchild of the Self. We speak of one's consciousness as being the effect of various specific archetypal figures as if these are the great aunts and uncles of an extended family, who stimulate an individual to behave in typical ways and repeat inherited patterns even when unaware of their existence. And when we describe anima and animus relating with each other and with the ego, we might well be describing in-laws meeting and engaging – sometimes benignly, sometimes explosively.

We are accustomed to apprehending the psychic life as an elaborate weaving, in which significant outer persons in each individual's life give shape to the contours of inner figures, which in turn influence choices of outer persons as viewed in relation to oneself.

We may also speak of Jung's typological functions as a sibling-systems inner structure. With the primary function as the eldest, the intermediate functions in the middle, and the inferior function youngest, their "birth order" determines the way we engage and interpret the world. The same functions in the opposite orientation are "half" relations, so to speak. For example, the introverted feeling function is akin to and yet apart from the extraverted feeling approach. These multiple figures, modes, functions and complexes establish a nuclear and extended family within each psyche. Even within an individual session, sometimes one member of this inner family is in dialogue, sometimes another, depending on which complex is most actively constellated.

We can tell much, as Stewart suggests, about the outer family by the way the inner figures relate to each other and to the ego. Sometimes their interaction is determined by overt behaviors within the family, and sometimes, as the author remarks, by "unconscious parental complexes which carry the unanswered questions of the ancestors and carry the unlived lives of the parents." To the old adage that children are more affected by what their parents do than by what they say must be added: and by what they do not do or say, will not look at or live through.

Stewart's focus on the sibling bond is most valuable in exploring an individual's *modus vivendi*, relationships and, for our purposes, transference. Bank and Kahn (1982) have written that, except for Alfred Adler,

> When psychotherapists have written about siblings, they have tended to focus on rivalry for the love of parents during early childhood. This point of view appears to be a legacy from psychoanalysis, where a heavy emphasis on rivalry has dominated the literature about siblings. The psychoanalysts have had little to say about the larger family context which affects the way brothers and sisters conduct their relationship. (p. 5)

On the other hand, they note: "Family-systems experts do not acknowledge narcissism as an important aspect of sibling relationships, and the birth order researchers appear uninterested in the riptide of circular influences that make siblings a special social system" (p. 7). They also quote the belief of Robert W. White (author of *Family as a Social System*) that "in actual life, pairs of siblings cannot be isolated from their surroundings...

The way in which they affect one another's development is always subordinate to the total pattern of influences prevailing in the family" (pp. 87-88). They examine many variables, including the difference in the effect of birth order, depending on whether there exists close, partial, or distant identification among siblings, on "low or high" access among siblings, and on parental influence.

In his expanded work, I hope that Stewart pursues these issues and explores what must be significant consequences which follow from sibling gender difference. In analytic work, we meet with sibling transferences as well as parent-child, although Bank and Kahn believe that the "vertical parent-to-child vector is so deeply embedded in dynamic theory that master therapists ignore the parallel, peer-related, horizontal vectors of sibling-to-sibling relationships." They also posit that therapists tend to avoid sibling issues because "most therapists are first-borns" (pp. 299-301).

As Jungians, we work with an awareness of the existence and implications of archetypal families – the House of Atreus, for instance – and sibling pairs: Cain and Abel, Jacob and Esau, Orisis and Set, Isis and Nepthys, Apollo and Artemis. We are also alert to the adept and *soror mystica* bond of alchemy. Stewart's paper stimulates us to attend more fully to the implications of the sibling relationships in the personal, political and archetypal realm.

I see Jung's understanding of the transcendent function as far more an introverted activity than is suggested by Stewart. Jung wrote of it as identical with the alchemical "incubation by self-heating, a state of introversion in which the unconscious content is brooded over and digested" (CW14, par. 262), a dialogue between the conscious and that which is emerging from the unconscious. In contrast, the dialogue in democracy is among egos. Here, we diverge – let us hope in a friendly, professional sibling spirit.

Reference

Bank, S. & Kahn, M. (1982). *The Sibling Bond.* New York: Basic
    Books.

Esthetic Experience and
the Transcendent Function

Basilio Reale
Milan, Italy
Centro Italiano di Psicologia
Analitsea (CIPA)

During the past 15 years, analysts have been returning to the genesis of the projected symbol, which bases the theory and the practice of Analytical Psychology on the opening of the senses. Thus, we go back to the crucial moments of the analytic process where we face a nebula of potentialities that wait to receive a direction and a form. This itinerary is complex and multidirectional. It does not leave tracks in the literary text, as Paul Valery (1957) indicated when he wrote:

> It might be interesting, once, to create a work that would show in each of its crucial points, the diversity which the soul faces and from which it chooses the only result that will be given in the text. In this case it would mean substituting the illusion of a single choice which imitates the reality with that 'possible in every instant' which seems more real to me. (p. 1470)

Poets, novelists and painters never lack real models, so that references to reality are detectable in their works even when the alteration of the form becomes a privileged element of new and autonomous dimensions of expression. Still, Leonardo da Vinci suggested to the artists of his time that they look at the stains on the walls, the veins in the marbles, the clouds and the ashes, in order to discern landscapes, animals, and monstrous unusual things as he himself did, taking his inspirational power from "confusing things" because "among confusing things genius awakens to new inventions" (*Trattato della Pittura, I*).

Order emerges from chaos; clues and invisible tracks lead to a form and a project. As in the preliminary phase of active imagination, Leonardo's attention focused on evoking the interior imagination, which is an expression of the vitality and creativity of the psyche, says Silvia di Lorenzo (1970, p. 377).

But let us hear how the imagination insinuates itself into the methods of a great contemporary Italian novelist, Alberto Moravia:

> The first thing I notice is the existence of some outward behavior that is somehow magical: ... You must sit at your desk, have a blank piece of paper in front of you, and hold a pen or a pencil or sit in front of a typewriter. However, this entire objective ritual may elicit only dead words if a strange osmosis is not produced, so that the utensils of the writer become the transparent *medium* of what I would define as the entry of the voice.

The writer asks himself: "How should I put the voice in order for the ups and downs of the story to meander happily between recording devices and interior resonance? Who is it that speaks after all? What ego directs the accumulation and bend of the signals? Also by using the third person... the enigma of the voice of the narrator's ego, who is neither the writer nor a conventional ego but is a *quid*[1] between them; it is very mysterious and imposes itself conclusively" (1981, pp. 108-109).

The Enigma of the Voice

If we focus on the mystery that the author shows us, the minuscule subject pronoun behind which "an identity which is the one which regulates writing" hides, so that once the voice is attuned, it could be possible in theory "to write the novel all at once" whereas usually it is necessary to take "heaps of notes" (Moravia, 1981, p. 109). Moravia intended to get out of the conventional way of representing reality in order to grab and express the fiction which is considered an action that parallels reality.

Apart from the elements that remind us of the *rite d'entrée*, an attentive reader would understand the gap, however minimal,

---

1. Editor's Note: "something" or "whatever."

between the just-described experience and the tradition of great Western poetry, according to which it is "another being" – be it a Muse, a devil, a god – who whispers what to write and imposes the words of inspiration.

I will stay out of the realm of historical figures and refer to the unique example of a contemporary Italian poet, Franco Loi. Thinking back to the time when he wrote his poems, Loi says: "I was writing verses 14 hours a day.... In my poetry experience my ego was not very relevant. I would walk in my room laughing, crying, reciting. I would look outside the window, see a truck go by and make it into a poem. I would write and then type. I would recite, but there was a being that would dictate... inside me" (*Corriere della Sera*, 1989, p. 18).

Loi has always considered himself "someone's clerk." However, even taking note of the auxiliary role that he attributes to the ego – he has been repeating for years: "I haven't written poetry, someone else has" – we know that he has not passively submitted to the images that populated his silence.

I would receive small impulses. I would measure the sounds, and the quality and weight of words. I would type the rhythms and then correct them. All this was quick, sometimes instantaneous. The sinuous movement of emotions was investigated by my mind for its expressive possibilities. And there was no "before" and no "after." You could almost say that the emotions and even the impulses would dictate the words that the mind would put down at the same instant. Sometimes the impetus to write was so great that I would let myself be carried along by this torrential flow. And my mind would scarcely intervene at all. At the most I would leave a brief pause in the verse. However, there was still someone else or something else indifferent to everything, but at the same time contemplating. (1987, p. 25)

Thus the artist would abandon himself to his internal images and set his ego apart. He would cut his ties from everything else to enter completely each emotion and transcribe it. But he would also converse and intervene actively in the constant exchange between the ego and the Self. In the meanwhile, a contemplative conscience, as the god of the creation of the universe, would be present and, indifferently would help the formation of life. It was like an "interior eye," a "warm spot right on top of my head" (1987, p. 18), which observed the visible reason of being between the world of the senses and the world of the intellect.

Moments of fervent creative activity and enthusiasm, of force that transforms every emotion into energy are the emotions of the archetype that appear as a magnet attracting consciousness. Loi talks of poetry as a fusion of music and word, emotions, intelligence, geometric and rhythmic order made possible by the work of "technical" revision done afterwards. He says that his work is doing and redoing, correcting, adjusting and organizing to a "minimal degree in comparison to the volume of expression" (1987, p. 25). But the modifications sometimes involve rewriting a work from the first to the last word. From the connection of Eros and Logos, understood as reflective intellect, is born poetry which carries Loi's personal stamp but which nevertheless rises above what is personal.

Complex, Symbol, Work of Art

It is very possible that Moravia never had to test himself with a real invasion of his unconscious. "The imagination," he wrote (1981), "comes about as an unconscious situation of the writer. It is a projection of the collective unconscious and the writer becomes more or less its interpreter, its vehicle or its spokesman. But the word spokesman is very limiting," he added. "We may say that on one hand there is an expressive capacity mediated through language acting within the writer, and on the other hand there is the interpretive capacity of the writer's experiences, his heritage, and the atavism – the archetypal – that exists in him, to use Jung's expression" (p. 109).

In Moravia's reference to Jung we recall the distinction between the visionary artistic creation and the psychological one, their genetic diversity and the belief that the creative impulse characterized by discontinuity, irregularity, and despotism is an autonomous complex and a demonstration of the separation of the psyche. As a consequence, certain contents are capable of opposing or imposing themselves upon the conscious intent.

There is no difference between invasion and inspiration in this sense. The difference lies rather in the state of consciousness of the ego. Neumann (1975) noticed that in those cases where the complex situation leads "to an activity instead of a neurosis" (p. 61) the temperament is able to overcome the personal nature of the complex and reaches a meaning valid for everyone. The complex therefore becomes creative.

Inspiration is a normal event that appears every once in a while and allows the artist to live an adequate social life. Within certain limits it is even possible to favor inspiration, preparing for the appearance of new models and symbols by suspending everyday life and thereby dissolving or weakening the normative social structures.

The structural process of the rite of passage presents obvious analogies with the transcendent function: in our case the transformation of psychic energy from the undifferentiated biological form to the cultural-spiritual form of esthetic activity.

The symbolic function in artistic activity only rarely involves individual psychological development, since the artist exists as an extension of the daemon within. The artist's ethical nature is achieved by the absorbing tension of the work, its impersonal quality, the innovative strokes and the transformative potential of the work itself.

Of course in the case of an analysis it is possible that the esthetic creativity may reveal individualized factors. Or in any case it may favor the harmonious development of the personality.

I had an analysand who demonstrated a striking bent for poetry from the time of her adolescence. But for years she was influenced by current literary trends. She would pay more attention to which way the wind was blowing than to listening to herself; she wrote verses distinguished by an abundance of parentheses in an attempt to classify her work as experimental and avant-garde. All this went on until she had the following dream:

It was night and she was in a classroom with walls made of glass in a country school. A limping teacher was writing sentences at the blackboard using many parentheses (perhaps they were equations). Suddenly the attention of the people in the class (all adults, as was the dreamer) was taken by the arrival of a girl riding a bicycle and ringing the bell. Soon after, from behind the blackboard, a black man appeared. He had a book to give to the dreamer. She had the same book and at the same time she wanted to give the book to him. "Keep it," insisted the young man. "Now you can publish it. In this book there are the stories of the ghosts of all the houses in the world."

This dream emphasizes natural instincts and physical dimensions. The black man holding the book in his hand seems to represent the link between opposites; he symbolically expresses the transcendent function within a context in which up to that moment the spirit was shown as a limping man.

In the artistic experience it is difficult to detect the phases which prepare and produce the link between opposites, as is sometimes possible in the clinical experience. If you have first-hand elements some moments of the dream can be clarified.

Moravia, in his work that – according to Jung's theory – could be classified as a psychological creation, emphasized the perception of a synthesis. It is time to return to that strange osmosis, already pointed out, that prepares the entry of the voice: the voice of a partial personality, no longer an enigmatic voice. (This is a *quid* between the writer's ego and a conventional ego as Moravia, 1981, indicated when he suggested that the psyche use "what" and not "who" as a pronoun.)

This voice brings to consciousness the imaginative component of the creative complex which is acting at that time. This is the complex which becomes work X or Y, within that intermediate area of experience to which Winnicott (1974) gave the name "transitional space," where it is not known whether the work was invented or found within or outside oneself.

Concerning the genesis of arts, Trevi (1975) wrote that "in a dialectic process several pairs of opposites are involved: individual conscious and personal unconscious, cultural canons and archetypal structures, form and event, ego and Self" (p. 10). The dialectical interpretation places genetic differences between symbolic works and works originating in the author's personal unconscious. According to Trevi, artistic creativity is the product of various factors and also the unpredictable synthesis of various elements.

However, this synthesis should be considered as a single indivisible symbol from the moment when the artwork, belonging to any gender, develops organically according to an "internal purpose which is the future form" (Pareyson, 1988, p. 77) and it cannot go back, even if it is a literary work, to a series of elements arranged according to linguistic laws such as that of informative communications.

The text of a literary work, as well as almost any work of art, has a literal and metaphoric sense. However, the receiver may attribute to it a symbolic function because the symbolic way is "a procedure which does not necessarily belong to the production but is nevertheless always 'in use' within the text," as Eco (1984, p. 253) has said. "Every physical product can be conceived as a symbol," Jung said repeatedly.

With respect to the "forest of symbols" coming from Romanticism and Symbolism, there is no doubt that the language of art is less inclined, nowadays, to welcome the darkness of the primitive symbol and instead prefers the immediacy of the word, sign and gesture which intervene with their communicative function "on the... fleeting reality of the things" (Conte, 1990, p. 16). Finally, a work of art is an autonomous microcosm of primitive emotional relations and a privileged place for the synthesis of opposites. A work of art is an event as well as a decisive presence that has its own meaning and, as the symbol, reveals and hides its own sense and significance.

There may be a parallelism among complex, symbol, and work of art; even if different they are established firmly in an archetypal nucleus of meaning. In them the link between a universal psychic element and a personal psychic element is always realized.

Philosopher Luigi Pareyson, wrote (1988): "Before existing as a finished work, the form acts as a law of organization" (pp.

78-79). He pointed out the paradox of the harmonic dual presence between the direction of the artist and the spontaneous development of his work.

> When I am inside one of my paintings I am not sure of what I am doing. It is only after I have been working on becoming acquainted with the painting, that I am able to see the direction that it has taken. At that point I am not afraid to make changes and to destroy the image, because I know that the painting has its own life and I am only trying to make it come out. It is only when I lose contact with the canvas that the result is disastrous. Otherwise a status of pure harmony and of spontaneous reciprocity are established and the work comes out well. (pp. 67-68)

Jackson Pollock (1960) told about his "absolute" experience, where the space of the canvas, the color, the technique – dripping – and the author himself appear as a single organic entity. Picasso used to say that this happened between the player and the violin when they are together. We are not impressed by the unawareness to which Pollock abandons himself and by the status of "pure harmony" and of "spontaneous reciprocity" that he talked about. Also, in this case, we must refer to the potential space between the individual and the environment, where the work of art is born with its own life and where the artist alternates moments of fusion with the object with moments where he is linked to it as if it were something external and separated. The canvas is still partially open to the experimentation of the omnipotence of the artist, such that the artist's "not me" would be compatible with a series of manipulations that aim to collect perceptions and experiences suitable to represent the ego's consciousness of an archetypal condition. It is true that all roads lead to Rome, to use an outdated saying, but it is certainly also true that all roads depart from Rome.

Trevi (1988) says "the logic of Ego alternates, in man's life, with the logic of the 'Self' so that 'the thought of Self' prepares the thought of the Ego and the thought of the latter prepares the thought of the former" (pp. 117-118), in a circular relationship. The circularity and the complementary ego-Self model are helpful in approaching phenomena which are as difficult to interpret psychologically as those of the arts, starting with poetry.

Words Speak Both From Within and Outside

Valery (1988) says, "Myth is the name of everything existing and subsisting, having only words as a cause." While in the early words there is no dark or bizarre "speech" which would not be able to "give sense to the language," to transform "the word into gesture and into a constructive action," (p. 49) the word of *logos* has no power and is silent.

Such considerations do not surprise us. The quote of the most cartesian of the poets only attempts to attract our attention to the expressive language; proceeding to the imagination that departs from the word to reach the image, or that gives image to the word. Valery would say that it is a poetic word instead of a *poietica* in the etymological sense recalled by Hillman (1984): a *verbum* that becomes incarnate.

I do not refer to the use of the metaphoric and analogic language in psychotherapeutic practice, but to the usefulness of extending toward the direction of the analyzed, the invitation from Hillman (1984) to become "more literate" and less "literal" (p. 36).

Poetry-writing is an "imaginative activity" different from automatic writing and every other method of active imagination; it is a technique that can survive as long as it is continually betrayed. It takes form by listening to the unconscious pushed by a special affectivity and perception. This fact fills the poetry writing with a marked polyvalence and a deep inner resonance, empowered by rhythm and sound, an expression of that elementary embodiment from which the conventional language has been expropriated. Loi (1987) writes:

> The language of poetry is not a medium of expression but a body. If it were only a medium it would not give any emotion. The work of a poet is get the thing and add flavor to it. Therefore the language of poetry is the language behind languages; it is universal, because

it includes sensations, emotions, thoughts, as well as what is not felt and thought (p. 20).

In the evocative world of poetry the word "assumes in itself everything that escapes to the *logos*." Quoting Vico (1963): "The spirit expresses itself freely through metaphors and similarities tied to the root metaphors of the human body and of the natural world in order to give sense and reason to seeming absurdities" (p. 203). But it also works by violating the order of communicative language and reassembling it according to its own combinatory power, which produces a new synthesis of image and meaning. Think for a moment of the onomatopoetic and phonetic linguistic formations.

This way the word of poetry brings us back to the time when we were babies and used to organize reactions in words and when play and fantasy were "factors" of poietic elements of growing up (from the Greek *poiein*, "to make").

Poetry writing shares with figurative and plastic expression the capacity to stimulate the imagination. In addition to being free from psychic tensions, poetic imagination accomplishes the ancient function of catharsis and illuminates the nuclear complex and its related emotions. Thus it promotes a real extension of consciousness and lays the groundwork for the operation of the transcendent function.

Poetry is perhaps preferable to visual artistic expression in cases where analysands have emotions – together with the inferior function – that are so unconscious as to be locked inside their bodies. It may be that these persons are inhibited by color. It could also happen that the analysand, asked to draw his or her interior images, would pass from one sheet to the other, as if passing from one complex to another without becoming self aware but convinced of being involved in psychotherapy.

As with every other imaginative activity, poetry writing is considered in relation to typology and to the natural inclination of the subject to use written language. Hillman (1984) recalls that "there is a part of us which functions by poetry and that belongs to the poetic realm" (p. iv). It is equally important to remember that the specificity of oral language, and therefore of written, lies in its capacity for concrete reference. Consequently, even when it is most free and most intensely connotative it maintains an objective capacity to communicate.

Before they were separated the Greek words Mythos and Logos both meant "word." Therefore Cassirer (1961) said: "The mythic language does not belong exclusively to the language of the myth. There is another force, the force of the Logos" (p. 143).

The following examples demonstrate the way a perceptive and passive attitude is overcome by poetry writing. This is the short poem through which a patient was able to look inside her cockroach phobia:

> They assault me while I am sleeping / when I am in the dark and alone / During the day I do not abandon myself / I am alert, I am very attentive / that they do not show up / because no one would like me / no one knows the evil eye / the grin in the night / at night instead every one is free / and from the outside they assault me / as many as they are / they run throughout my body / big white without a shield / and get in everywhere.

She is the first one who is astonished that "no one would like me" escaped from her. Immediately she adds: "For me writing is like speaking of a part of myself. The cockroaches could represent the fact that I feel guilty because I do nothing to change my situation. Where there is no life there are insects untouchable by atomic radiation."

Those troubling cockroaches were also a sign of her becoming depressed frequently; their proliferation, which from dreams tended to trespass into daily life, transformed the dissolving aspect of a complex into something to fear.

> At night they go out / their mother nurtures them
> with love / in her stinking bed

she would write. Taking care of them without avoiding the nausea given by their stink of the sewer freed the patient from the bad mood that she often had and let her hope to find inside herself good things to say to her analyst.

Sometimes a dream can be noticed while one is still sleeping. In such a case it is useful to let the images of memory settle and then get back to the dream, entering into every detail without exiting from the language, in a sort of rhythmic and expressive reexamination, which is both elaboration and deep examination.

An example is a case (1984) that I published some years ago. Going deeper and deeper into a forest the dreamer meets a pheasant of extraordinary beauty. Looking closer, he sees the pheasant expelling something from its anus. This something turns out to be a mixing of interiors: intestine, earth and other organs. Then the bird disappears. The dreamer follows it and finally finds it or thinks he has found the bird, but it is only a chicken among other chickens, in the forest. This is the "record" from which the dream becomes a psychic manifestation: *poiesis*.

In the forest where he entered / path trees bushes grass / the bird that I saw / was going ahead flapping / in the
path / plumes bent tail bridge of colors / splendid regal /

Here the bird / its legs stoop on its knees /
the toes stretch / then again expands / rhythmic /

Astonished I look at the colored bird / noble pheasant / whose bottom / in the path of the forest /

Here it expels a soft bunch of twisted things / pure grey pink / descend while the body contracted helped the
movement / the grey pink clot / expelled on the path /

I look / on the ground and then behind / I look inside / there is an opening /

I see a huge cavity / a golden cave / I look inside with great anguish / a layer of straw covers the bottom / and everything is empty / golden cavity / I stare at it / nothing else

And the opening close again / the pure tuft of the rump covers the bottom / the loosened plumes stretch out again / the wings flap / quickly the bird with mobility / dives
into the forest that protects and hides it / trees bushes leaves / I run

To see and to find it again / I run / among the bushes searching / here / the green screen once again closes

a yellow clearing made of low grass and in the middle /
bird that trots and pecks / its neck bent toward the

ground / short feathers of the same color / low sitting chicken?/

Astonished and incredulous / I look and feel pain /

Its round grey eye looks sidelong at me / he looks at me
and then turns around and pecks away /

Confusion overcomes me / in the yellow clearing of the forest / and
shame and pain.

Life Which Takes Form, Form Which Comes Alive

The person who comes to analysis is escaping from the fear
and pain of an empty life, seeking to find in the confusion and
fragmentation of personal history some order and meaning – a
form.

"What we call art is the process of formation: it is at once a
'doing' and the invention of a way of doing; a production and
also an invention," Pareyson (1988) writes.… It is only by taking
form that the work becomes a unique and unrepeatable reality, by
now detached from its author and having its own life (p. 18).
Therefore if it is possible to see an artistic aspect in every activity
of the spirit, we can no longer consider the esthetic dimension to
be an end in itself, since it is both the expression of the vital
impulse at the highest level and the tangible thought by which
every formal invention is born.

Therefore art is to make, to produce. Pareyson here resumes
the *poiein* of Valéry, who had recognized Leonardo as the genius
of accomplishing and construing, before the temporary and mod-
ifiable attempts of research and formal experimentation to the
perfection of the defined and definite work. "The goal is important only as idea," Jung wrote. "What is important is the opus that
brings you to the end. This is the one which gives meaning to the
length of life, and to get it… you need the cooperation of the
conscious and the unconscious" (CW16, par. 400). According to
Valéry, the first, most human and primordial idea is the idea of
making, "which impersonates the thickness of the myth, sensation that becomes sound, gesture, action, and modification of the
prime matter in new forms" (cited in Franzini, 1988, p. 11). The

esthetic of forms, where genesis and formal characters permeate each other, where to understand is to produce, according to the original meaning of *hermeneuein*, brings us back to the narrative construction of analysis. On this threshold Hermes comes forward; as "Mercury's spirit" Hermes represents the *principium individuationis*. Next to him, and as to complete him, there is Ephes, god of constructive concentration, incomparable producer and finisher. Throughout their mediation, our analytic practice proceeds from the true-false dialectic, in the attempt to answer the requests of forms and sensation, by disposing projected events and hints according to their intrinsic necessity.

There is an internal plausibility sustained by the structural balance, by the order and the harmony of composition, by the esthetic feeling which is also a feeling of proof. Both correspond to a need of truth, according to a "very strong known obsession that wants to compare Truth, Order and Harmony" (Morin, 1989, pp. 148-149).

But more important than the end is the opus that brings us to the end, Jung has recalled. The opus of the analysis goes ahead slowly and tortuously through the word that acts.

Translated from Italian

References

Cassirer, E. (1961). *Linguaggio e Mito*. Milano: Il Saggiatore.

Conte, G. (1990). *La Lirica d'Occidente*. Parma: Guanda.

Corriere della Sera, Milano, 15.1.1989.

Di Lorenzo, S. (1970). Il metodo dell'immaginazione attiva nella psicologia di C.G. Jung. *Rivista di Psicologia Analitica, I-2*.

Eco, U. (1984). *Semiotica e Filosofia del Linguaggio*. Torino: Einaudi.

Franzini, E. (1988). Introduzione ã P. Valery, *All'Inizio Era la Favola*. Milano: Guerinie Associati.

Hillman, J. (1984). *Le Storie Che Curano*. Milano: Cortina.

Loi, F. (1987). *Diverse Lingue*. Udine: Campanotto.

Moravia, A. (1981). *Il Viandante e la Sua Orma*, Bologna: Cappelli.

Morin, E. (1987). *La Conoscenza della Conoscenza*. Milano: Feltrinelli.

Neumann, E. (1975). *L'Uomo Creativo e la Trasformazione*. Venezia: Marsilio.

Pareyson, L. (1988). *Estetica*. Milano: Bompiani.

Pollock, J. (1960). In *La Nuova Pittura Americana*. Milano: Silvana Editrice d'Arte.

Reale, B. (1984). *Quando in un'Analisi Prende Corpo la Poesia* in *la Pratica Analitica*. Roma: Alpha Print.

Trevi, M. (1975). Introduzione a E. Neumann. *L'Uomo Creativo e la Trasformazione*. Venezia: Marsilio.

Trevi, M. (1988). *L'Altra Lettura di Jung*. Milano: Cortina.

Valéry, P. (1957). *Oeuvres* (Vol. I). Paris: Gaillimard.

Valéry, P. (1988). *All'Inizio era la Favola*. Milano: Guerini e Associati.

Vico, G.B. (1963). *La Scienza Nuova*. Milano: Rizzoli.

Winnicott, D.W. (1974). *Gioco a Realità*. Roma: Armando.

Response

Maria Pia Rosati
Rome, Italy
Italian Association For the Study of
Analytical Psychology (AIPA)

As Reale says, psychoanalysis made a significant change during the last decades by moving away from a reductive, scientific positivist model. This change agrees with the spirit that characterized Jung's research. Jung perceived the inadequacy and danger of interpretation, such as Freud's, which aimed to reduce the complexity and depth of the psyche to an absolute model, with biological impulses viewed as the ultimate requirement.

Therefore, with Jung, psychoanalysis upholds its calling as the discipline that seeks meaning and yet never pretends to exhaust it, always remaining open to the dynamic and transcendent possibility of the symbol.

The relationship between psychoanalysis and art, which has been underlined by Reale, is strictly connected with the dynamic function of the symbol. For that reason, it is interesting to look at the model given by a work of art, which offers a possible ontological opening for its own "finality without a goal," (as Kant says) for its irreducibility as a tool and for its sending us toward the undetermined.

A psychoanalyst, nowadays, deals mainly with psychic pain due to a feeling of loss in a daily life where particular dominates universal, where the interests of the singular interferes with inquiry into the sense of everything, and where tools and techniques are more significant than the goals that must be achieved. Our hypothesis is that the analytic process should not be just technical but should have the same ontological dignity of the process of artistic creation.

Since the first historic definition, the artist, whose duty is called "holy duty," is regarded as an interpreter of human destiny. This concept dominates all philosophic thought from Plato – who considered the artist as a person of God – to Heidegger, according to whom only art can break the silence of being and communicate the meaning of living in the world. Homer thought that holiness in art, particularly in the song of a Greek poet, is indicated by the fact that human disasters are defused in art.

Plato in *Phaedrus*, one of the most beautiful and important dialogues, saw in the divine foolishness that invades or inspires poets a purifying force able to heal and set free from evil. This concept is even better explained in *The Symposium* where it is pointed out that the peculiarly human function, is to generate and introduce immortality into mortal life. Generation comes through the body but also through the soul. But Plato said:

> It is impossible that it happens in disharmony, and disharmony is ugly compared with all things divine; beauty is instead harmony,... and when the pregnant creature approaches beauty, she becomes joyous, spreads her joy, gives birth and generates. On the contrary, when she approaches the ugly, she becomes gloomy and contracts herself in sadness and does not generate; but when she cannot generate she suffers. Therefore in the creature, pregnant and burning with desire, there is a great yearning for what is beautiful, because beauty liberates whoever possesses it in the pangs of labor. Because... love is not love of beauty... but it is love to generate and give birth in beauty.... It is desire to generate immortality in good and... love is love for immortality. (Symposium 206)

We all know the Aristotelian theory about art as catharsis, as a moment of humanity's education in knowledge and virtue when we see human reality in the light of those ideal structures, a reality that otherwise could become confused and get lost in daily life. Even more obvious is the relationship between poetry and holiness in the world of the Bible where, next to the prophets, all the people of Israel – the Chosen People – through their singing gave expression to their hope to be saved and set free. Singing is an expression of wisdom which is the word of God, the real Author, the real Creator and therefore the real Poet.

In the universe of Cabala we notice that:

> Din (rigor) and Hesed (mercy) come together in Tipheret (Beauty), the Sephirah mediator par excellence, place of synthesis of the following antinomies: Life and Joy, Measure and Freedom, Harmony and Fullness. It is the union of those principles gathered together in Tipheret that determines the over-formal form of cosmic creation and, by analogy, the ideal form of art. This is definitely accomplished and finished when the following are united in it: the harmonic measure of proportions, the nature of the subject matter that pushes toward the outside, and the dissolution of the obscure elements and the spiritual fullness that make the substance alive. Art is this whole body providing a foundation for happiness, without which there are only structures in their spareness and nudity, and truth, without which there is nothing but subjective pleasure. (Bies, 1992, pp. 242-43)

We have here an esthetic concept that gives art dignity and metaphysical importance and recognizes that beauty has the ontological function of filling the abyss between ideal and real, thus forming one of the basic elements of being. This concept is present in Plotinus, for whom the merit of art is not limited to producing tangible things, but includes the achievement of ideal patterns that are models for natural entities.

My intention, here, is not to give a history lesson about esthetics and concepts of art. However, it is important to point out the great distance between an archaic concept such as the one from Homer and the Bible – where the artist has a high civil, religious, and therapeutic calling (because he is a spokesman of the permanent and eternal being) – and the concept of art in the contemporary world.

Coomaraswamy (1939) recalled that, according to the Platonic lesson, art must harmonize and attune our distorted way of thinking to the harmony of the universe; through the assimilation of the knower with the known, we can get the best from life given to humans from gods in this world or in the other. Or, according to the Hindu Upanishad, we can become a harmonic whole with the universe through the imitation of divine forms in order to "become what we think". Coomaraswamy concluded that "the real consists of a symbolic and insignificant representation of aspects of reality that otherwise are not seen except by the intellect" (p. 10).

His teaching is precious for our work as analysts, as he points out the substantial difference between modern art and the abstract algebraic forms of archaic art – various unique forms in which there is a balance between physical and metaphysical). Modern art is defined as sentimental, esthetic, materialistic – because the instinctive expression is preferred to the formal beauty of rational art. It is a kind of mannerism whose aim is decoration, not that beauty which has the attractive power of perfection and is achievable only if one can understand life on its own terms.

Therefore, only apparently contradicting his previous thought, Plato, in the *Republic*, banishes poetic arts from his program for a state because he considers them bad for education when they limit themselves to pure imitation and do not aim to help minds to pass from becoming to being, and from accidental emotions to the contemplation of pure and constant ideas. From the Stone Age to the present, it is possible to see a decline of the intellectual creativity inversely proportional to the progress of technique.

Contemporary art is connected mainly to the world of contingency and of personal and individualistic living. Therefore, it brings elements of endlessness and instability. It is no longer a release of existence from the alienation, dispersion and fragmentation of daily life. It seeks to achieve a beauty that, though it may be identical with spirit, reduces it to an emphasis on appearances.

Invention, the importance of creative capabilities and imagination are taught today in our schools and in other arenas where pedagogy is studied. But once again we should remember that *imago* comes from *imitor*; imagination is not arbitrary invention, but imitation. It is bringing up-to-date, a never-ending repetition of models. Imagination means to be able to see the world in its complexity, to sense the essence of things on reference levels that are higher than empirical ones. Thus, according to St. Augustine, intuition means an intellectual activity beyond dialectic reason, in the realm of eternal reason.

In the same way, artistic contemplation must raise the reference from the empiric to the ideal level, from observation to vision, from acoustic sensation to pure hearing. The misfortune of a person who lacks imagination consists in becoming sterile, cutting oneself off from the deep reality of life and soul. And as analysts we should avoid (paraphrasing Coomaraswamy) evoking a devil rather than a daimon and avoid classifying as libido what may be divine Eros.

The psychotherapist should keep in mind the distinction between the sense of art in the contemporary world and that in the traditional world. Artistic creation can be a therapeutic and redeeming factor only if it is able to effect a transformation, a metanoia; that is, if it is able to activate the transcendent function, and if the subject is able to avoid the petrifying, tearing, depressing daily hell in order to contact what is beyond the contingent and urgent situation which causes trouble, anxiety and pain. Only an art that is not inspired by an instinctive and unconscious will, but instead is authentic art, an expression of ontological reality, can cast light upon a tragic historic period and give sense to absurd and incomprehensible human events. Such an art redeems and gives dignity to suffering, and offers the hermeneutic assumption, the key to understanding and thus to redeeming. This art can help us, even in the ephemeral and fleeting ray of beauty, to light up the epiphany of being. In this way, I think we can repeat after Dostoevsky that "Beauty can save the world."

In order to be able to be therapeutic, art must help us to read the deepest meaning of reality – also, according to Heidegger, "putting the facts to work" in order and to create and invent. Human will should aim to create as it tries to change history, humanity, society and the world. It should invent because it reaches the essential point of things, revealing and disclosing them. Thus, the example of Goethe is valid; he gave to his biography the title *Poetry and Truth*. Thanks to poetry, giving to isolated events a symbolic form, he reached the deepest knowledge of himself and of life.

In this sense the *Confessions* of St. Augustine is a great example of artistic creation. He was able to see in his personal tragedy the reflection of the religious tragedy of humanity, which through guilt and the Fall reaches redemption.

Indeed, the symbolic function is the fundamental function of art. But symbolon, according to Greek tradition, is the pottery broken in two parts, one for the host who stays, the other for the guest who leaves, so that there will always be a link between them and a hope to meet again. According to the story told by Plato in *The Symposium*, there was a similar link between a man and a woman, because they were the two halves of the original androgen who, with his arrogance and self-sufficiency, provoked the anger of Zeus, who cut the androgen into two parts that thereafter always wished to meet and merge again. A human is in essence a symbolon, a fragment waiting for another part to become complete and provide a complete happiness.

"The language of art," Gadamer (1964) writes, "is unique in that a single work of art is able to... give expression to that symbolic character which from the hermeneutic point of view belongs to every being. Unlike any other linguistic or non-linguistic tradition, it is an absolute presence. At the same time, in a mysterious way, it conserves the confusion and ruin of whatever is considered usual. Not only does it tell us, in a horror mixed with happiness and fear: This is you. It also tells us: You must change your life (pp. 1-7).

Psychoanalysis is in danger of facing hell. Indeed, if psychoanalysis does not consider its task to transform present reality – thanks to the symbolizing capabilities of the transcendent function – by connecting it to situations that are archetypal and thus fundamental, it risks finding itself imprisoned and overwhelmed by the same problems and dynamics that it tries to solve.

The hell of the present (and hell is a situation without light, hope, future and safety) can be overcome only if the soul can have confidence in the future, that symbolic future which is not a simple prospect of what will happen, but transcends the empirical reality. Thanks to the ability to deny the limits imposed by empirical reality, that is, thanks to the symbolic capability, the soul sets an ideal goal and has confidence in the hope of a new possibility. Consequently, as a paradox, it is from denying the empirical reality that a safe integration at a higher level can have birth, bringing a decisive change in a person's life.

To the objection that the psyche which analysts must cure is not the soul of theologians, we can answer that analysis must contemplate in its horizon of research the sense of human life which is strictly connected to our ontological function. Today this ontological function is denied and humans have become tools, a "resource to direct"; the deepest psychic pains are dangerously spread out not only among the fringes of population, but among people who reach the most important positions of social life.

And perhaps it will be up to psychologists to help to bring about that deep transformation, that metanoia, by means of living symbols, full of meaning and able to represent the ineffable and the unknown. These vivifying, regenerative and restoring symbols will then replace symptoms of discomfort and discord.

Translated from Italian

References

Bias, J. (1992). *Connaissance des Religions*, (Vol. 7). Chaumont, France: Cedex.

Coomaraswamy, A. (1939). *Christian and Oriental Philosophy of Art.* New York: John Day.

Gadamer, H.G. (1964). Aesthetik und Hermeneutik. *Algemeen Nederlands Tijdschriftfur Wigsbegerte, 56,* 1-7.

Another Degree of Complexity

Aimé Agnel
Paris, France
French Society of Analytical
Psychology

As a child at the end of the war, while turning on the family radio set at random, I came across a piece of music that immediately captivated me. It was a modern, unprecedented piece of music, made of heterogeneous elements that nevertheless seemed to form a whole. It turned out to be "Petites Liturgies" by Olivier Messiaen. I knew right away that this was my music. It supported my intuition about "modernity" and made me understand what I found too simple in the pieces from light opera and operetta that my father used to strum on his mandolin. Female voices in unison sang a strange repetitive melody with unusual gaps in an indescribable blend of bird songs and chaotic noises.

I liked this complexity that brought together contrary forms which traditionally were in separate categories: a singing voice that for everyone signifies the essence of music, and noise. I was still unaware that in Europe and the United States toward the end of the war and immediately after it several composers, independently, were experimenting with mixing music and noise in surprisingly fresh works: Pierre Schaeffer and his "concrete" music, John Cage and his prepared piano, Stockhausen, Berio and many others.

Pondering Jung's concept of the transcendent function, I understood why these works appeared simultaneously. They were an unconscious response to the disaster of the war and to the terrible dissociation that it had engendered. The bringing closer together of the opposites, the heterogeneous mix of music and noise – of "noble elements" and of "crude components," as the alchemists would have said – fulfilled a compensatory function. The postwar composers were in a conscious position that was critical enough to be able to accommodate intuitively the new contents that came from the unconscious. Thus, their different works all expressed a new attitude of listening, a new conception of musical forms and esthetics including, in a more complex whole, the music that until then had been rejected as noise, a shadow entity.

The context in which these works were created – a time of war marked by the collapse of ancient values – is an explicit illustration of the contradictory work of the unconscious, the work of the Self in spirit and form. Likewise, in order to grasp better the clinical importance of the transcendent function, it is appropriate to link it to the historic circumstances that surrounded its appearance in Jung's thinking; to his preoccupations and inner experiences, which he dated (MDR) from 1913 – the year of his break with Freud – to 1917.

These five years of inner uncertainty coincide (within a year) to the five years of World War I, which affected Jung deeply. The tragic context of the war and the circumstances surrounding his "confrontation with the unconscious" give full meaning and power to the 1916 essay, "The Transcendent Function" (CW8). This text is an initial formulation and theorization of the chaos of affects and images which Jung had to confront in himself. At the same time, it testifies to a profound transformation of his conception of the unconscious.

In freeing himself from the partial identity that linked him to Freud, Jung discovered his own method: phenomenology (in the same sense as Husserl's) that inclined him to describe rather than construct and to be surprised by the "world of life." The object can be perceived and reflected upon only by a consciousness that has broken from the pseudo-familiarity which has bound it to the world. The unconscious is a complex phenomenon which is experienced in the conflictual relations the ego maintains with it. Indeed, Freudian theory does not account sufficiently for the heterogeneous and contradictory values of conscious and unconscious. The questions Jung asked himself are eminently practical: "What should be done with the unconscious?" How can one confront this "stranger who immediately influences us"? The transcendent function is an initial, paradoxical response to this question.

The theory of complexes elaborated by Jung between 1904 and 1907 was generally compatible with Freudian theory. The resulting conscious/unconscious system is a linear system that never really questions the continuity of the ego except, of course, in psychosis. The conscious ego of the neurotic is disturbed by repressed complexes. Yet the source of these complexes is the ego itself. The unity of the psyche (conceived of as a closed system), which Freud defended until the end of his life, is preserved. In the coherent and relatively simple scheme of drive repression, the ego remains in control, even if it must be diminished as a result.

However, by accentuating the autonomy of complexes, which is most severe in dementia praecox, Jung opened the first breach in the linear conception. Repression alone cannot account for this autonomy and the discontinuities that it implies.

About ten years later, especially with "The Transcendent Function" and its poetic twin "The Seven Sermons to the Dead" (both dated 1916), the unconscious described by Jung is no longer the troublemaker or even a complex that in more serious cases can take possession of the ego, but a chaos within which, oddly, a certain order appears to emerge.

In 1923, Freud approached this chaos (which for him was dominated by drives) but only to say that it has no organization; the best one can do is to differentiate the ego from the chaos so that it can fill the vacuum left by the id: Where ego was, id shall be. This is a major clinical task, but there is a risk of maintaining the ego's illusion of unity and failing to liberate it from paranoia.

For Jung, the matter is entirely different. The 1913 breakdown forced him to confront a chaos that is not the id, does not come only from the drives. His break from Freud was the break from the ideal father, initiator and interpreter of the world. Such a break is more painful and loaded with consequences than the separation between the son and his actual father, because it sends the son back to his earliest weakness, an "un-knowingness," and condemns him to rely on his own strength alone, like the orphaned child of mythology.

When Jung separated himself from Freud he was deeply disoriented. Certain patients attest to the same feeling when they lose the landmarks that have enabled them to find their way in the world. The entire container-world collapses; a world in which order seemed self-evident is revealed as a world in which order was taught, given, or imposed by the Other.

The loss of this learned knowledge is a prerequisite to the transcendent function. The painful early symptoms of the function are the unsettling of certainties and the loss of reference points. If Jung made little or no mention of this prerequisite it is because he preferred to omit subjective observations from his description of the phenomenon. It seems appropriate here to restore the subjective context, without which, vital clues to comprehending the concept are missing. With it, the concept becomes more operational, more directly applicable.

The time when the analysand's doubt may attack the very foundation of the transference, undermining even the trust that made the transference possible, is an exceedingly delicate one in analysis. Indeed, transference loses its magic when the analysand is confronted with the void and solitude. If the analyst holds back from filling this void and succeeds in containing the "unknowingness" of analysand – who for a time resembles a lost child – the solitude and void can take on therapeutic value. However painful, this experience seems to be the necessary condition for the emergence of the transcendent function; the analysand must look inward, gradually discovering a more personal, more complex image of reality.

An example from literature that is quite close to the therapeutic experience is a passage from a novel (de Troyes, 1974). Parsifal is contemplating three drops of blood on the snow – the blood shed by a goose wounded by a falcon. He has just learned that due to his negligence, the Fisher King cannot heal his injury. For the first time, he doubts himself. He discovers with astonishment the presence of an inner enemy, a shadow; he had always been certain that the enemy was the Other who could be engaged in combat and vanquished. He can no longer rely on his naive unconscious, an innocence that provided all his strength. His state of mind could be likened to the one Jung described in himself: "floating, in suspense." He is halted. Motionless, he contemplates "the way the snow and the blood look together" (p. 111). He is leaning on his spear; his surroundings no longer exist. The image that he quietly contemplates in which he believes he sees the face of his beloved, seems to lead him slowly to a new meaning, that had hitherto been inaccessible to his consciousness. Nothing is really understood but something is intuited that is the property of the reverie alone. It is a hybrid state, half conscious, half unconscious, that must not be diverted by anyone or anything.

Thus Gauvin, a knight of the Round Table, like an analyst who would know not to intervene and to respect the duration of the process, wants to wait until Parsifal is "out of his reverie" before seeking him and bringing him to King Arthur. The spell will break when the sun dries the three drops of blood. Indeed, when consciousness re-awakens the *abaissement du niveau mental* (lowering of mental level) ends. Nevertheless, the imprint of the image remains with Parsifal; it continues to act, preparing a change in attitude.

Such is the role of the symbol that formulates the unconscious and brings compensation into play. In this case, it combines opposites in a single image: the hot, red blood with its finite nature and the cold, white infinite expanse of snow. Rational understanding is sorely tried. According to Jung, one of the roles of the transcendent function is to assemble within a more complex whole elements that are rational and irrational, imaginary and real. The image is one of a bridge between two worlds; the symbol serves as the conveyor. By combining things that the conscious distinguishes and sets apart, the symbol causes us to question our linear mode of understanding and saps the ego's authoritative orientation.

Parsifal's values are those of the knight errant who travels over mountain and plain to earn honor and praise from humanity. These solely masculine values are contradicted with all the force of an unconscious compensation which appears at just the right moment, by the face of the anima, fortuitous and unexpected, portrayed in the snow. Blanchefleur, the faraway and abandoned lady-love, becomes present in this way. The vision on the snow of her pale cheek exorcises oblivion and reconstructs the continuity of the love bond.

The contradictory image thus makes room for another logic: that of feeling. The image's subtly shifting borders are congruent with the complex judgments of feeling, capable of integrating and synthesizing a large number of heterogeneous elements. What other function could process such a high degree of complexity?

The lengthy contemplation of the image also fashions a new type of attitude where reflection and introversion are mingled. Parsifal's pathological extraversion, which binds him to reality without giving him any perspective, gradually makes room for a type of introversion that fosters the reflective attitude. The world no longer dominates the conscious; the *participation mystique* with things becomes evident. According to Jung, it is the epitome of the therapeutic effect. Via this phenomenological reduction, this loss of "worldly illusion," the conscious "discovers that it is… giving of meaning" (Ricoeur, 1987, p. 25).

The moment in analysis when the analysand acquires this capacity to reflect is very moving. It is as if the ego ceased to be flat and expanded into a new dimension; as if the analysand had finally become the psychologist by gaining access to his or her own psychology. It is a major transition that often affects the transference, by freeing the analysand of burdensome projections and by developing a new ability for self-analysis.

Jung described two moments characteristic of the transcendent function. Initially, when the unconscious takes over because the conscious is in a critical situation; a second, marked by the association of opposites, where it is no longer the unconscious that takes the lead, but the ego. The advent of reflection can serve as a criterion for determining the second phase. In order for the ego's authority to be effective it must indeed be capable of thinking for itself.

Jung gave two different explanations for the use of the adjective "transcendent" in the expression "transcendent function." It combines conscious and unconscious, rational and irrational elements in a way analogous to the mathematical functions in which real and imaginary magnitudes meet. But "this function is called 'transcendent' because it facilitates the transition from one psychic condition to another by means of the mutual confrontation of opposites" (CW11, par. 780).

Thus, the function can be understood as a key moment of the individuation process, for which theory came later. In 1916, it was from the ego that Jung derived his eventual identification of another center of the personality, located between the conscious and the unconscious. The transcendent function is an initial intuitive approach, an initial experience of the Self.

Consequently, I chose the singular scene in the de Troyes novel where Parsifal, confronted with the irrational symbol, can finally have an intuition of what his life has been and what it could be. It is a moment of transcendence, of transition: the passage from one attitude to another through the integration of new contents.

The second part of the novel is the tale of Parsifal's individuation process. It is a story full of hazards of an individual destiny. By becoming conscious, Parsifal chooses to become a unique, detached creature, cut off from knowledge. The tree of a thousand candles no longer blinds him with fantasies. The Fisher King, to whom he can finally pose his question, explains it to him. The tree is the tree of sorcery; we would call it the "participation mystique." With each step Parsifal takes toward the tree the deceptive lights are extinguished. "You are the one who destroyed them" concludes the Fisher King (de-Troyes, 1974, p. 269). Following the upheaval caused by the transcendent function, individuation really begins with this withdrawal of projections, enabling the ego to detach itself from the world in which it wandered, lost, as a naive consciousness.

The distinction between transcendent function and individuation process is therefore not merely historically-based. It is also useful from a clinical point of view. It makes it possible to place the accent on the ego's work in moments of "transcendence," that is, when the ego is confronted with a reality that is overwhelming by its apparent irrationality and its degree of complexity. The ego is thus required to open itself to another, more paradoxical concept of the world which includes the problematic opposites.

Two fairly typical clinical cases illustrate the transformation of the personality, which Jung defined as a characteristic of the transcendent function. They proceed in opposite ways; the unconscious compensation, or factor of change, operates in an inverse way in the two cases.

The first case, "Mathilde," is one of neurosis. The psychic space in which the ego felt protected from anxiety and death, was the mother. Fear, inhibition and taboo were wherever the mother was not present. The archetype the ego had to confront and through which the unconscious counterposition was expressed was that of the Stranger, who represented the strongest opposition to the mother but who was also the object of the greatest fear. Its separating character and the conflict it introduced made it a forerunner or a representative of the Self.

In the second case, "Pierre," the secure psychic space was not at all maternal. As in other borderline cases this man, rejected by his family when he was still a small child, was forced – in order to survive – to project his personality into an imaginary self which was experienced as a real self. It carried him efficiently and provided his best defenses. In this Divine Infant position, he found in God and Nature an archetypal Father and Mother who were substituted for the defective real parents. In contrast to the preceding case, the missing opposite was not the Self or its representatives, but the ego belonging to a world and a human family. The fear was not so much of the Stranger, as more generally a fear of the Other, any Other. Indeed, lacking a body, how could one enter into a relationship with one's fellow creatures?

In discussing these cases I emphasize two different types of transition from one attitude to another, through analysis of the transference. In the case of Mathilde, it is the compensation of the ego by the Self (via the symbol of the Stranger) which triggers the change in attitude. In the case of Pierre, it is the compensation of the Self by the ego. There are, indeed, two opposite forms of unconscious compensation: two opposing orientations of the transcendent function. The first, compensation by the unconscious, is decisive when the pathology is of the neurotic type while the second, compensation of the unconscious by the conscious, is usually encountered in borderline cases. Compensation is always unconscious. But this counter-position forces consciousness either to open itself to the unconscious and its compensatory values (as for Mathilde) or to reduce the domination of the unconscious in a readjustment that benefits the conscious ego and gives it its true place (as for Pierre).

Transference opens a relational field that is attached to two opposing poles, a "familiar" pole and a "foreign" pole: one an experience of closeness and warmth, but banning incest; the other separated, providing a non-incestuous psychic field where one can experience a sexual encounter with the Other, an experience of distance and separation. The analyst's role is paradoxical, maintaining the constant presence of both poles. That is, the analyst must not be only the good mother who understands and forgives, nor only a distant and indifferent stranger. Some Jungian analysts have a tendency to favor the familiar pole; Freudian analysts have a tendency to favor the distant one. It is difficult to contain the complexity, and tempting to reduce it to a single element.

In the case of Mathilde, her conscious desire caused her to seek in me all possible signs of emotionality and warmth, all the reassuring similarities to the familiar world of the mother; on several occasions, she reproached me for being too Freudian. A contrary desire, which was unconscious, oriented her toward what seemed "unknown" in me, that is, the parts of myself and my way of relating to her that enabled her to experience, or to imagine, a bold and brazen relationship with a stranger.

It is this characteristic of the transference that made possible the conflict, hitherto avoided, between her infantile tendencies and her vital need to break free of the maternal bosom. Indeed, many strange faces would appear in her dreams, the faces of unknown men, characterized at first by negative associations: rapists and AIDS-carriers. Then, as a certain trust was built in the transference, as the two opposing poles "familiar" and "unknown" gradually drew closer to one another, these strangers ceased to be so threatening.

The bridge of transference by which Mathilde now ventured as far as possible from the zone of maternal security, now allowed her to confront a symbol that was to shatter all her certainties: In a dream, she had to cross a wall of shit. This image clashed with the childish reveries fed by fairy tales and idealizations that masked her fear, reveries that magically recreated the Mother and served as a conception of the world.

The wall of shit disturbed this false knowledge, acting as a counter-thought. It was a brutal return to the rawest sensation. It was appropriate, in Mathilde's case, to analyze the dream in terms of drives, but more effective was considering it as a symbolic test. Reflection on the dream was filled with disgust and fears, decisions and hesitations, developing in Mathilde a capacity for introversion to which she had never before had access. Her speech, usually so smooth and continuous, broke off, crumbled, allowed glimpses of lively and meaningful expression, of impulsive movements and desires that she was no longer able to control. After her long passage through the wall Mathilde found herself in the depths of herself, in that cultureless and empty place in whose utter solitude the humiliated being renews contact with her fundamental unconscious origin, the seat of her own creativity.

In Pierre's case, the transference took an entirely different direction. The analyst's "familiar" role was solicited because the unconscious desire, or the intuition of the goal, was for the Self, which Pierre had experienced in its cosmic aspect, to be limited at last and contained by a body, an ego, an actual person, the offspring of real parents. It was this quest, this transition from a foreign Self to a familiar ego, that dominated the transference.

The borderline experience of the Self – the Divine Infant position – is tragic and often poorly understood. It is an intuitive, instinctive reaction to serious parental failings. The child is pro-jected out of the protective shell of the family and cut off from roots. In psychiatric circles this reaction is often interpreted as a flight from reality. This interpretation takes little account of the Self's very real intuition that is the basis of the reaction. It is real, but alienating, because it is inexpressible. The question appropri-ate to a therapeutic perspective would be rather: How can the ego-body and its speech be retrieved without a loss of the Self? What the borderline patient, who is at odds with the family circle, has conveyed – into the imaginary psychic space where the child is the protege of the gods – is the secret of radical originality, intuited as simultaneously intimate and impersonal, the Self's paradoxical secret: the "anonymous singularity" of which the poet Charles Juliet speaks.

Pierre very accurately compared it to gold – which has no value unless it is traded. Jung indicated the appropriate method to use in such a case. "The conscious," he wrote "must lend its means of expression to the unconscious material" (CW8, par. 178). Nevertheless, this method was applicable to Pierre only when the physical and psychic body of the analyst was invested and recognized as a sufficiently proper and viable container able to acquire, conserve, respect and share the secret. This process was a very slow one, with long periods of doubt and back-tracking, stagnation, silences and withdrawals.

No intimate word can be uttered if the hollow of a body is not available to receive it and give it resonance. The body grows and becomes aware of itself not only in the mirror where the other is reflected, but also by this dangerous attempt at an intimate speech that returns to us as an echo. It is less a matter of commu-nication as it is usually understood than of a structural experi-mentation involving the internal and the external. This experi-mentation cannot be carried out in solitude. Even if the word is thrown out into depths, the Other is vital for a conscious separa-tion between the inside and the outside. The Other must be receptive and present: not obligated to reply, but merely to bear witness to a possible meaning. This speech that seemed crazy contains a grain of truth. Through the word the body is awakened to the pleasure of sensations. The word takes on substance and, armed with its power to resound from within and from without the body, makes the ego capable of extraverting and giving the secret a form "by lending it a means of expression."

In Pierre's case, the secret took on a poetic form. He brought me several texts written in a complicated language, expressive of opposites, through which he finally succeeded in trading the gold of the Self without betraying it. The formulating was difficult, because, according to Pierre, it always resulted in a frustrating reduction of the unutterable experience of what he called "the other side," this psychic space where he was in contact with the world of archetypes. These reduced texts needed to attain an extreme authenticity, in order to retain some of their value and not simply be thrown away. They were re-worked at length, until an expression that appeared as truthful and adequate as possible was attained. There is such a great demand for wholeness, truth and meaning emanating from the Self! Often, there remained only very few words, as in a Japanese haiku poem. The All of the Self became an "almost nothing," but in this almost-nothing the ego/Self opposition was finally reconciled.

This pathetic, yet necessary reduction often reminded me of the tiny statuettes that Giacometti sculpted in the 1940s. They dwindled all by themselves, becoming so small that they could no longer carry any details. He couldn't understand it, but it was what made them good likenesses.

Certain atonal compositions of Schoenberg, Webern and Berg, written between 1910 and 1913, participate in the same esthetic of extreme brevity. They are pieces of great intensity, written at a time when the abandonment of the tonal system forced these composers to resort to their own unconscious roots in order to continue to compose. It is during these moments of alienation, of radical disorientation, that the "transcendent" process is activated and that compensation can play its regulating role.

These examples illustrate that compensation can induce a re-adjustment of the Self's tendencies through the ego's opposing values. The Self is indeed an alienating value that remains foreign to the subject if it is not connected to the familiar ego, if it is not reduced to its human dimension.

Jung mentioned this modality several times in his lifework but, to my knowledge, did not develop it. He called it assimilation of the ego by the Self and considered it a psychic catastrophe that makes way for accidents. Jung's constant references to psychosis explain this analysis in part. Today we encounter borderline states – that are at the outer limit but not psychotic – in which the ego, no matter what identification game it is engaged in, remains a relatively stable entity. When the body can contain it, it reveals itself as skillful at channeling the archetypal contents.

Moreover, as Pierre's case showed, a development of extraversion goes hand-in-hand with this type of compensation of the Self by the ego. However, this extraversion interests Jung less than the opposing movement of introversion whose full value he discovered through his personal experience. This introversion was considered pathological by Freud. By setting up the transcendent function, Jung was able to go against the current of received wisdom and show that this attitude could be natural and even essential to personal development.

One of Jung's greatest contributions following his separation from Freud was indeed the integration into normality, via the problematics of opposites – of attitudes, tendencies, functions – simple psychic facts hitherto classified as either symptoms of pathology or obstacles to relationship with the real world. This is the case not only with introversion, but also with affect, which for Jung not only expressed drive energy – as Freud understood it – but which is also the vehicle by which the subject is implicated, the object that makes him aware of the full weight of reality. It is also the case for intuition, raised to the rank of ego function on an equal footing with sensation, and for feeling, judge of values and indispensable complement to the intellect for the description and comprehension of phenomena. In his description of the transcendent function, Jung again emphasized the importance of the constructive method – opposing finality to the principle of causality then reigning unchallenged in the sciences and in psychoanalysis – and of active imagination, which is not a mere neurotic fantasy, but is the trigger of a state that makes possible an objective grasp of unconscious material.

Finally, he brings up the existence, still argued today, of a factor of order in the unconscious, of a psychic self-regulation system. It was only in the distant past, with the Paracelsus' "lumen naturae" (of the alchemists' Mercury), that Jung was able to find an intuition and a hypothesis similar to his own. "Order may appear at the heart of disorder," we are currently being told, as if the physicians and mathematicians working on chaos theory echoed Jung. Jung's very modernity is contradictory insofar as it participates in a dual movement: toward past history which must be reinterpreted and reintegrated with the present, and toward the unknown that is yet to be discovered.

The problem of opposites, as revealed to us by the transcendent function, requires a fundamental reevaluation which arouses many resistances from the norm and from what we could call mental health. Jung's paradoxical position, which postulates the existence of an unconscious that is as much nature as it is nurture, opens a broader field to psychology and psychotherapy. It also has the merit of removing guilt from the subject by the diminishing of the Freudian categories of suspicion and shame. Conversely it makes the subject more responsible, by confronting it with the shadow and the evil without which the good would not exist.

The integration of such a concept is slowed only by the fact that the problem of opposites is less a theory that can be taught in a university classroom than an experience that is lived in solitude when, as one patient said, "there's no shelter where you can rest."

This independent and contradictory meaning that can reach us from the unconscious commits us to a journey from which there is no turning back. Once the process is begun, the choice is no longer available. In several essays Jung emphasized that the transcendent function can develop without the knowledge or cooperation of the subject, it can even impose itself despite resistances.

Jung's recognition of a counter-thought that wells up in the very chaos of the unconscious has nothing euphoric about it. Its complexity forces us to proceed with a formidable and dangerous revision of our homogeneous conception of the world. In a 1951 letter written to a Protestant theologian regarding *Answer to Job*, Jung confided that he would have "preferred to remain a child in the Father's protection and shun the problem of opposites" (Let-2, p. 29).

> *Translated from French*
> *by Anita Conrade and Yvonne Cherne*

References

de Troyes, C. (1974). *Perceval ou le Roman du Graal*. Paris: Gallimard.

Ricoeur, P. (1987). *A l'École de la Phenomenologie*. Paris: Vrin.

Salzmann, M. (1989). Le complexe-mère chez un homme: Essais de théorisation à partir de la vie et de l'oeuvre d'Alberto Giacometti. *Cahiers Jungiens de Psychanalyse*, *60*, 47-48.

Response

John Beebe
San Francisco, California, USA
Society of Jungian Analysts of
Northern California

I hate to add my noise to the music of this paper. Yet this is a paper that invites noise in, welcoming disruption as part of the background that completes thought. The paper raises the noise of psychological thinking to the level of creative sounding, precisely by introducing what its author well calls "another degree of complexity."

My disruption will take the form of a thinking – and therefore, categorically, more seemingly knowing – response to what he has given us, superbly, with feeling. Aimé Agnel allows his thinking to play below the surface of his argument, illuminating his ideas from within. I come from without, like the Stranger to whom his patient Mathilde must somehow relate. If I am in the role of forcing this subtle author's thought to the surface I start intrusively, by posing a question to his text which it has already answered, as a beginning point for an inquiry that may deintegrate the paper and stimulate discussion. Only then will we see if we can provoke the transcendent function to emerge. Here is my question. The title of Agnel's paper is "another" – an added – "degree of complexity." What, then, is the first degree of complexity that this paper invites us to complicate?

Agnel himself gives us an historical answer. The first degree of complexity that Jung uncovered in the evolution of his psychological thought was the complex theory. It enabled the academic, white-coated, laboratory Jung of 1904-1909 to map out the structure of the unconscious without sacrificing what Agnel calls the "continuity of consciousness" that had allowed the philosophic and scientific thought of his "fathers" in academic psychology to get as far as they had. And clearly, the developing evidence for the shadow that Jung was able to adduce in his experimental researches with the Word Association Test was a complication; it had led Jung to introduce what truly was a complex – complicated – theory of mind.

Nevertheless, complex theory was a conservative theory, given what Nietzsche (1880/1986) and even Fechner (1846/1991) had already thought to do with the idea of mind's shadow. Complex theory did not announce that mind is dead, still less that the shadow is alive. It merely allowed that mind is challenged by "other" mentation, and offered a way for mind to investigate this otherness in its midst.

Let us add to this history the observation from my own experience that to admit even a little bit of the unconscious into consciousness is like accepting a touch of pregnancy into the body. Once admitted to the threshold of consciousness, the complexes Jung had befriended were sure to assert themselves as unruly guests, as indeed they did in the stormy and disruptive relationships of his personal and professional life in the years between 1909 and 1913. According to Jung's own account, "Aside from Theodore Flournoy [William James] was the only outstanding mind with whom I could conduct an uncomplicated conversation." According to a 1958 letter from Jung to Kurt Wolff, the editor of Pantheon Books, that conversation lasted "little over an hour" (Taylor, 1980, pp. 160-161).

It must not have been hard for Jung, on the basis of the other experiences he was having at that time – with Freud, Sabina Spielrein, Toni Wolff, Johann Honegger and Emma Jung – to feel confirmed in his earlier intuition, dating at least from his doctoral dissertation of 1902, that the psyche is autonomous and that its complexity lives a life of its own. Nor was it hard for him to see how that complexity was lived out in interpersonal relationships. By 1909, Jung had become the first object relations theorist, mapping the "games people play" in terms of the complexes they manifested. (It is amusing nowadays to read the Word Association Test protocols in which Jung details the complex-indicators in the associations of himself, Spielrein, and Emma Jung [McGuire, 1984].)

What is startling is Jung's next step after he had accepted the consequences of his discovery of this "first degree of complexity" – that is, after the sacrifice of his relationship with Freud and his acceptance of the relationship with Toni Wolff, those chronologically paired events that shattered his persona and shaped his fate as the eternally controversial psychologist. For it was just after these professional and social catastrophes, from which his reputation has still to recover, that he decided to invert the game of delineating the complexity that is lived in relationship – a game that even today is often imagined to be the ultimate business of psychotherapy – and to seek not the complexes in relationship, but relationship with the complexes themselves. This was the "other degree of complexity" for which Jung reached; with this psychological move he sacrificed forever the scientist's goal of mastery through understanding. Instead he fashioned a new goal of understanding through relationship, a form of psychological knowing that accepts its dependency upon what is known, and for which the relationship that is built up with the unconscious object is indispensable.

Jung's identification of the transcendent function must be seen not merely as an event in his own history, however, but as a moment in the history of the evolution of the psychological attitude, a moment that is recapitulated whenever anyone manages to become psychological. The transcendent function is realized synchronistically when there is a shift away from a desire to know and control toward a desire to relate and understand. That is, I agree with Agnel that this formulation by Jung was a consequence of the extremity to which he, in 1913, had been brought. Nothing other than the humiliating events of 1911-1913 could have led him to the appreciation that not the ego, but the psyche itself, provides the bridge across the "yawning ravine" between the ego and its otherwise unknowable shadow. This bridge is only available to those who know that they do not know, and whose connection to those who would know for them is interrupted. Jung's break with Freud was a traumatic interruption of contact with an analyst who knew, and would tell him, in what his shadow consisted.

Agnel makes it clear that this separation from analytic know-ing can be achieved also, with tact, within an uninterrupted analytic situation. But, as he rightly points out, it is the cessation of knowing that is itself the essential precursor for the emergence of the transcendent function, not the tact with which the cessation is achieved. Nowhere in his paper is Agnel's empathy for Jung's state of mind at the time of his recognition of the transcendent function more satisfying than in Agnel's rendering of that time- and space- transcending moment when, in a state of profoundest self-doubt, *Parsifal* ("leaning on his lance; his surroundings no longer exist") contemplates the three drops of blood on the snow.

This, as Agnel knows, is the psychological moment, when the lost battle with the shadow enables the anima to emerge as the symbol of the bridge between two worlds, when the psychologi-cal attitude of reflection replaces all Faustian search for knowl-edge – knowledge which inevitably sunders worlds with its sep-arating distinctions. Unfortunately, Jungian psychology does not usually do right by such moments. It has often tried to rob this moment in Jung's own development of its reflective humility by trying to know too much about it, reintroducing a note of triumph as if the anima and the reality stumbled upon through contempla-tion were but trophies of a new psychological age of heroic discovery in which, if Jung was not exactly the Columbus of the unconscious, he was at the very least its Cortez. We reintroduce this confusion in our patients whenever we permit ourselves to speak of their "courage" in confronting the unconscious, or tell them about Jung's. Nothing could more falsify the real spirit of our psychology – for which Jung's own rather Christian words – "sacrifice" and "transcendence" – seem far more appropriate than this Freudian language of conquest.

The Christianity, also present in the story of *Parsifal*, need not embarrass us. I am in some agreement with Giegerich (1991) that "we can scarcely speak of the rise of the psychological attitude outside a context of Christian thought" (p. 89). It is that thought, particularly in St. Paul, who said, "For the good that I would I do not: but the evil which I would not, that I do" (Romans 7:19), which introduced the idea of the shadow as an autonomous being to which we must find it in us to relate with a forgiving attitude, as if it were part of ourselves.

To the list of Christian words that seek to explicate the mystery of the transcendent function, I add one other: "grace." Jung said at least once that in his confrontation with the unconscious he was saved from petrification by the grace of God. Grace, in Christian tradition, also involves the humility and penitence that enables us to receive it. But in common usage grace also refers to the gift of beauty, the delight of art and the esthetic attitude. Here Jung's Christian background sometimes made him too severe, as if creative elaboration of the image were irrevocably separate from its conscious understanding.

Agnel has shown us that we can hardly approach the uncanny power of the transcendent function without evoking the magic of art. Just his mention of Messiaen and Giacometti evokes that magic; the grace that these great psychological artists bring to the uniting of extreme opposites: whether birdsong and chaotic sounds, as in Messiaen's work, or scooped out remains of matter and the empty spaces around them, as in Giacometti's.

The artist of transcendent rank is granted the way to bridge incommensurables at times of historical caesura, such as the period from 1942 to 1945, when the possibilities, even the morality, of old forms seem exhausted. Just as the scientific understanding of psychology seemed exhausted for Jung in the midst of the First World War, the possibilities of representation appeared to stop with the Holocaust and Hiroshima. Yet the Second World War was the germinative moment for Messiaen and Giacometti, as the First World War had been for Jung. At such a time, only grace could have given their exhausted consciousness access to the continued unfolding of unconscious meaning.

But, to ask a final question, what is it in the person that enables him or her to receive the grace that is the gift of the transcendent function? At these difficult moments of near-cessation of psychological movement, Agnel attests that this gift was the bridge that led to nothing less than incarnation in Pierre, whose personhood had been lost in an unborn Self and to a first authentic discovery of the Self in Mathilde, whose personhood, though secure, had been too contained by a mother-bound ego to encompass her affective depths. But what was the psychological capacity that enabled these one-sided people to access this bridge that led in one case toward ego, in the other case toward Self, but in both cases to a deepening of humanness? Jung I think gives us a key in his *Seven Sermons to the Dead* (1967), that shadow text to which the essay "The Transcendent Function" must be related. In these psychological sermons, written, like "The Transcendent Function," in the midst of the First World War, Jung described the part of us that receives impressions from the pleromatic unconscious and acts psychologically on what we receive, as *creatura*. In English, as Agnel reminds us, this word is creature. For much too long, Analytical Psychology has tried to equate creatura with ego. But ego, like Parsifal, like Jung, needs a *caesura* to become *creatura*.

By understanding Parsifal's caesura, and Jung's, and that of Western art and culture in the mid-1940s, Agnel has helped us to feel what creatura means. It is a capacity to reflect upon distinctions from within a standpoint of vulnerability. Creatura permits grace, where ego would heroically defend against it or push for transcendent consciousness as a hero's reward for psychological tasks completed. Creatura constellates the transcendent function with the chastened receptivity of a consciousness dissociated from the containing world of both Mother and Father psychology. With his consciousness securely rooted in creatura, Agnel understands that containment, no less than interpretation, is not enough for the analysand, who is after all alone with the real problems. I think it is Agnel's feeling for the analysand's authentic dilemma, and his grasp of the necessity of the vulnerability that it produces, that has enabled him to assist so skillfully and to formulate so well his analysands' creative discovery and use of a new psychological structure of unexpected benefit to them, the transcendent function.

References

Fechner, G. (1846/1991). The shadow is alive (S. Simmer, Trans.). *Spring*, 80-85.

Giegerich, W. (1991). The advent of the guest: Shadow integration and the rise of psychology. *Spring*, 86-106.

Jung, C. G. (1967). *VII Sermones ad Mortuos* (H. G. Baynes, Trans.). London: Stuart & Watkins.

McGuire, W. (1984). Jung's complex reactions (1907). *Spring*, 2-43.

Nietzsche, F. (1880/1986). The wanderer and his shadow. In *Human, All Too Human: A Book for Free Spirits* (R. J. Hollingdale, Trans.). New York: Cambridge University Press.

Taylor, E. (1990). William James and C. G. Jung. *Spring*, 157-168.

Hegel's Dialectical Vision and the Transcendent Function

Hester McFarland Solomon
London, England
British Association of
Psychotherapists – Jungian Section

Jung's concept of the transcendent function derives its philosophical basis from the notion of dialectical change, first expounded by the German Romantic philosopher, Friedrich Hegel (1770-1831). The dialectical model was developed in Germany, at the time of the Romantic revolution and the Napoleonic Wars; Marx and his followers applied it to theories of social, political, and economic change. It formed an essential core of twentieth century European philosophical traditions, such as phenomenology and its derivatives, as well as the version of psychoanalysis developed by Lacan and his followers in France.

In Hegel's dialectical model the development of self-consciousness unfolds internally in what he calls the World Spirit (Geist). It can be likened to Jung's theory that the individual develops a sense of identity over time through the interplay between inner and outer, and between collective and personal psychological contents, both at conscious and unconscious levels. Although he had philosophical antecedents – Plato, Spinoza, Kant – and parallels in other philosophical traditions, Hegel expounded (in his *Phenomenology of the Spirit Science of Logic*, Encyclopedia of the Philosophical Sciences and *Philosophy of Right*) a philosophy that reflects a deep structural view of the world which has had a profound effect on the thinking of people schooled in European culture since the nineteenth century. Hegel's dialectic reflects an understanding of fundamental truths, including psychological truths, concerning reality, its perception and how the Self comes into being. The dialectic attains its full actualization through the interaction between self-consciousness and consciousness of an Other.

Both Hegel and Jung expounded models of those deeply embedded, inherited structures and dynamic processes that underlie our perceptions of ourselves, our reality and the ways in which we become the individuals we are. Both employ an archetypal model of the Self expressed in terms of an image of wholeness, achieved through successive conflict-ridden steps toward individuation and integration.

Hegel's model is fundamentally about spirit as the product of the dialectical interaction between subjective thought and the objective world and between logic and nature. As such, spirit finds its fullest manifestation in human consciousness. Moreover, "the only true and complete reality is spiritual, which is the dialectical result of the interaction of subjective thought and objective world" (Stepelevich, 1990, p. 19).

For Hegel, the history of reality is equivalent to human history as it engages in the struggle to reconcile itself to itself. In so doing it achieves a synthesis, arriving at successive and increasingly comprehensive states of consciousness. *The Phenomenology of Mind*, Hegel's (1807) great work, relates the story of this dynamic between conflict and integration, the goal of which is wholeness.

Although I am concentrating on the relationship between Jung's model of the transcendent function and Hegel's dialectical model, there is a deeper implication. An understanding of the dialectical model contributes to a broader recognition of the philosophical bedrock which underpins the ways of thinking about human nature and development that we call analytic and psychoanalytic theory. It is able to contribute to an understanding of the differential roles of inner and outer influences in the development of personality. Thus it contributes conceptually to a central debate in current depth psychology: whether a primary self or a primary instinct for relatedness forms the basis of personality structure. It can lead us to think about a possible resolution of the debate through a view of the Self as the result of successive interactions between the contents of the inner world and those objects in the outer world with which it relates. It is a model of Self's combining and interacting with its objects from birth to maturity: in Jungian terms, the primary self becoming the individuated Self.

The Hegelian notion of dialectical change permeates the psychological theories of Freud, Jung and their followers, steeped as they were in the German-speaking culture of their times. Neither Jung nor Freud acknowledged a debt to Hegel. In fact, nearly all the few references to Hegel in Jung's Collected Works are quite scathing. In another context, Jung called Hegel "that great psychologist in philosopher's garb" (CW18, par. 1734).

We know, however, from the libraries of each, that both Freud and Jung read and carefully annotated Hegel's work. Freud's debt to Hegel would be the basis of another study; it may suffice to mention Freud's tripartite model of the mind and the three levels of consciousness, each in dynamic relationship within and between the various structures with ego synthesizing the opposing demands of id and superego. My contention is that the dialectical vision can be seen as the essence of Jung's concept of the transcendent function.

The Transcendent Function

Jung considered the transcendent function to be a process central to the psyche. He thought of the conscious and unconscious as being in dynamic opposition to each other, resulting in an intense interaction, full of conflict and of potential for growth. For him the transcendent function was the way through this conflict: "a natural process, a manifestation of the energy that springs from the tension of opposites;... it consists in a sequence of fantasy-occurrences which appears spontaneously in dreams and visions" (CW7, par. 121). Thus, "it forms the raw material for a process... in which thesis and antithesis both play their part,... forcing the energy of the opposites into a common channel" (CW6, par. 827).

The following diagram (Fig. 1) illustrates Jung's model.

The Transcendent Function
Jung

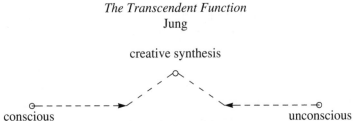

Figure 1

The resulting image contains the possibility of a creative synthesis and a way out of what had appeared to be a locked state of polar opposition. This achievement, in turn, creates a position against which further elements will stand in opposition, leading to new conflictual polarities which will require further integration, mediation and synthesis. So the process continues, inexorably and relentlessly, each time reaching a higher level of synthesis.

Far from claiming it as a philosophical idea, Jung compared the transcendent function to a mathematical function: "a function of real and imaginary numbers. The psychological 'transcendent function' arises from the union of conscious and unconscious contents" (CW8, par. 131).

Jung wrote in the same year, 1916, both the "Seven Sermons to the Dead" (MDR) and "The Transcendent Function" (CW8), although the latter would not be published until 1957. It was a time of crisis for him. He had broken with Freud and allowed himself to descend into the depths of his own unconscious – a self-exploration with dramatic consequences. At that time he began his studies in alchemy and the writings of the Gnostics, using images therein as metaphors for the dialectic within and between internal and external relationship. Hubback (1966) speculated that the abstract thinking which formulated "The Transcendent Function" was based on the personal experiences contained in the "Seven Sermons," and that Jung hesitated to publish it for that reason. She pointed out that Jung was looking for "a pattern of order and interpretation in face of the confused and frightening contents of the unconscious" (p. 107).

Building on Hubback's understanding, I suggest that Jung may have found containment for the highly personal and disruptive experiences found in the "Seven Sermons" through the philosophical and intellectual rigor of the dialectical model as expressed in "The Transcendent Function." I think Jung was deeply indebted, however unconsciously, to the systematic philosophical vision of Hegel's dialectic.

In the immediacy of Jung's disintegrating psychological experiences in the years around 1916, he swung from one pole of experience to the other, from the chaos and destabilization of unconscious eruptions witnessed in the "Seven Sermons," to the structuring and orderliness of thinking as expressed in "The Transcendent Function." Through this dynamic interplay he was able to achieve a personal synthesis, a position of relative integration between the conscious and unconscious attitudes. Thus, Jung himself was living the dialectic. He may have had this experience in mind when he wrote: "The confrontation of the two positions generates a tension charged with energy and creates a living, third thing... a living birth that leads to a new level of being, a new situation" (CW 8, par. 189).

Jung called the synthesis of what is oppositional at a particular moment in the unconscious and in the conscious "transcendent" because, as he says, "it makes the transition from one attitude to another organically possible.... The constructive or synthetic method of treatment presupposes insights which are at least potentially present in the patient" (CW8, par. 145). It is especially through the transference and the catalytic contribution of the analyst that "the suitably trained analyst mediates the transcendent function for the patient, i.e., helps him to bring conscious and unconscious together and so arrive at a new attitude" (CW8, par. 146).

Jung's vision of a bound-together dynamic between related and relating opposite functions which lead to change forms the basis of my comparison of the transcendent function and the dialectical vision. These opposites may be situated intrapsychically, or between the self and an Other (for example, between infant and mother, or analysand and analyst). Through the tension and conflict created by the dynamic relationship a creative, forward-moving resolution, a synthesis is achieved. Death or stagnation resides in holding these factors separate and apart.

The Dialectical Vision

Hegel's grand design is an attempt to understand reality as constructed historically in pairs of opposites which are not dichotomous but are rather intimate and dynamic, albeit oppositional in relation to one another. The dialectical model allows for a two-fold view of reality: bipolar opposites in dynamic relation to each other, a unity of opposites toward which each strives.

When any thought, notion, or understanding becomes fixed or defined, the mind's tendency to achieve a more comprehensive view is stunted momentarily. A potentially creative conflict may then occur which enables the rigidly-held position to be mediated, superseded or overcome. The task of dialectical philosophy is to strive for greater and greater comprehension until a totality of understanding is achieved. This understanding is what Hegel called "Absolute Reason." I will discuss later how it relates to Jung's archetypal notion of the Self as an image of wholeness.

The dialectical process begins with a "thesis": any definable reality that is considered to be an unconditioned beginning, a starting point from which future developments proceed. In the course of time, the thesis is seen to entail an opposite – "antithesis" – or "the Other." A third stage is achieved, called the "synthesis," the result of the dynamic, conflictual, and reciprocal relationship between thesis and antithesis. A resolution is achieved that has the capacity to hold the two apparent opposites together. Thus, Hegel's creative synthesis, like Jung's, arises out of a dynamic opposition.

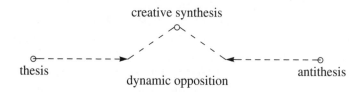

Figure 2

> "Dialectic is the process of thought that leads the mind from one idea into its complementary opposite, and reveals the unexpected conclusion that their fundamental truth is found only in their unity. Dialectical philosophy proceeds from the premise that true reality is a 'unity of opposites'" (Stepelevich, 1990, p. 16).

Dialectical thinking is illustrated by the idea of "pure being" as the fundamental starting point of philosophical inquiry. The next step is immediately, almost simultaneously, to require pure being's opposite, "nothingness." Thus "being" as thesis implies "nothingness" as antithesis. As long as these fundamental opposites remain in stagnant and mutually annihilating conflict without authentic interaction, no resolution, no creative change is possible. Hegel demonstrated that the only possible dynamic and creative outcome between these opposite positions is "becoming." This brilliant and immediately accessible understanding of the fundaments of existence is matched by a similar understanding of the fundaments of the human psyche and its relationship to others.

Hegel's major illustration of the dialectic between self and others appears in his analysis (1907) of "Lordship and Bondage." It is supremely psychological, in that it is concerned with the development of self-consciousness. The process begins at the moment when one person first becomes aware of another as being similar but also different, an Other. Each is filled by the desire for recognition by the other. A living relationship is thus established between them, so authentic that the basic core identity of each is touched, threatened with takeover by the other, and then, in some way, reconciled. As Hegel said, "Self-consciousness... exists only in being acknowledged" (1907, p. 111).

The tripartite structure of the dialectical model reflects an archetypal pattern that we meet in the world and in the human mind as it mirrors the structures of the world. The Christian idea of the threefold nature of God as Father, Son, and Holy Spirit; Spinoza and Descartes' threefold vision of reality as thought, nature and God; the Socratic dialect whereby rigid positions are changed by adroit questioning leading to deeper understanding – all attest to the ubiquitous, deep structural nature of the tripartite dialectical vision.

As an explanation of how change occurs psychologically, the dialectical model also gives us a way of thinking about another deep human structure: how a two-person becomes a three- or more- person psychology. The primary mother-infant dyad, if maintained for too long, becomes a stultifying, anti-life set-up, which does not allow for change, as is described in the Kleinian model of the oppositional paranoid-schizoid position. The presence of the father, or the mediatory inner element, acts as a catalyst for forward movement where change may be possible. The central psychoanalytic concept of the Oepidus complex is about this, whether at the classical psychosexual phase, creating emotional space for the individuation process to occur, or at the level of very early unconscious fantasy, creating mental space in which thoughts may occur.

From Symbol to Self

Hegel's *Phenomenology* concerns the steps by which the World Spirit or Psyche (Geist) achieves wholeness. Each moment in the dialectical process corresponds to a center or point of consciousness, and "they stimulate each other into activity... [so that] each has its 'other' within it and they are only one unity" (1807, p. 99).

Hegel's choice of language in the inquiry concerning the processes of self-consciousness begins as if it were a statement concerning the primary self: "the simple essence of life, the soul of the world, the universal blood... [that] pulsates within itself but does not move, inwardly vibrates, yet is at rest" (1807, p. 100).

This primary state of undifferentiated unity, this "restless infinity" (1807, p. 107) holds the potential for all the differences to come. It is from out of "this self-identical essence" that an "I" and an "Other" appear. For this to happen, consciousness must become self-consciousness, and this in turn can only occur when the self is conscious of itself in relation to another. To describe this achievement, Hegel used the violent image of self-sundering: "These *sundered moments* are thus *in and for themselves* each an opposite – *of an other*, thus in each moment the 'other' is at the same time expressed... and so each is therefore in its own self the opposite of itself (1807, p. 100).

Hegel carried the argument further. For the "I" to differentiate itself from the "first distinct moment," something other than purely passive self-contemplation must occur. This other thing is the "second distinct moment," a moment of antithesis, which Hegel called desire (1807, p. 105). The living, immediate quality achieved at this level of philosophical analysis, the introduction of psychological states of desire as the catalytic factor in the dialectic of the self, is remarkable. Hegel, "that great psychologist in philosopher's garb," as Jung called him (CW18, par. 1734), related inner states of desire to the foundation of the self in its relation to others: I know myself through my desire in relation to an Other.

The immediacy of Hegel's (1809) language – "restless infinity," for example – is similar to the living quality in Jung's writing.

Working as a deep structural system, the dialectical model offers the means of liberation from the either/or way of thinking that characterizes so much of philosophy, just as it characterizes the primitive mental polarization of the infant caught in the paranoid-schizoid position. By positing a dynamic threefold structural model, Hegel provided a model of reality, philosophy, and the evolution of the human spirit or mind; a model which describes the development to more mature, individuated, as opposed to more infantile, splitting states of mind.

The Self: Bridging the Transcendent Function and the Dialectic

The archetype of the Self can be thought of as the analytic equivalent of Hegel's model of spirit. Both involve a vision that includes opposites, the conflict between them, and the resolution of the conflict through synthesis. In discussing this progression, three steps in Jung's theoretical development relate to the dialectic: (a) from libido to symbol; (b) from symbol to Self; (c) From Self to coniunctio. My intent is to relate Fordham's notion of a primary self with its integrates and deintegrates to Jung's idea of the Self in relation to the transcendent function, and to explore how these may be expressions in psychological language with origins in dialectical philosophy.

Let us consider the I and the Other or – in Hegel's language – the subject and object. The two interact and conflict; each makes its own internal synthesis of the experience.

If the I and the Other can be thought of as elements, each of which internalizes its own experience of a joint interaction; a similar bipolar configuration is considered to occur in the rhythmic back and forth movement between deintegration and reintegration. This movement occurs externally between persons and internally between parts of persons. Through the play between deintegration and reintegration, the infant achieves a synthesis of particular elements in the inner and outer world. All these processes, internal and external, result in steps in the establishment of the self. For the Kleinians, states of gratitude, concern, and forgiveness toward objects and toward oneself is achieved within "the repeated rhythmic experience of destruction and restoration, of despair and hope, of mental pain and joy" (Meltzer, 1967, pp. 40-41). Perhaps these states and Jung's use of mandala figures as Self representations, are parallel attempts at representing a synthesis arising from the conflict between opposites.

From Libido to Symbol

Jung's theory of libido differed from Freud's original drive model of libido as a release of instinctual energy according to erotogenic zones. Jung's view of libido was consistent with an overall teleological position, in that instinctual energy was available to be transformed at the psychological level, especially via the production of symbols. The publication of Jung's view (CW5) marked the end of his professional and personal collaboration with Freud. The steps that took Jung from the concept of libido to that of symbol and then to Self reach a final point when Self and the coniunctio are bridge.

Instead of the psychoanalytic view of symbol formation as the "prevention of the primary incest tendency" Jung's view was that the symbol designated "phenomena requiring a teleological explanation [rather than] simple causalities [with] the purpose of canalizing the libido into new forms." Through this new definition Jung offered an alternative view of the purely psychosexual nature of libido; he claimed that the effect of the canalization of libido is to "stimulate the creative imagination which gradually opens up possible avenues for the self-realization of libido. In this way the libido becomes imperceptibly spiritualized" (CW5, par. 332).

In juxtaposing the instinctual and the spiritual, while uniting them through the concept of symbol, Jung offered a demonstration of both the form and the content of the dialectical process. Only a few years later he wrote "The Transcendent Function," in which he expounded the dialectical view of psychological change. A few years after that (1921), in *Psychological Types* (CW6), he gave us a definition of symbol in relation to the transcendent function: "*living* thing,… not to be characterised in any other or better way… pregnant in meaning" (CW6, par. 816). He then gave a description of the symbol in dialectical terms:

> But precisely because the new symbol is born out of man's highest spiritual aspirations and must at the same time spring from the deepest roots of his being, it cannot be a onesided product of the most highly differentiated mental functions but must derive equally

from the lowest and most primitive levels of the psyche. For this collaboration of opposing states to be possible at all, they must first face one another in the fullest conscious opposition. This necessarily entails a violent disunion with oneself, to the point where thesis and antithesis negate one another, while the ego is forced to acknowledge its absolute participation in both. (CW6, par. 824)

Having posited thesis and antithesis, he went on to state:

Since life cannot tolerate a standstill, a damming up of vital energy results, and this would lead to an insupportable condition did not the tension of the opposites produce a new, uniting function that transcends them. (CW6, par. 825)

This achievement culminates in what Jung called "a middle ground" where:

the energy created by the tension of opposites... flows into the mediatory product and protects it from the conflict,... for both the opposites are striving to get the new product on their side. (CW6, par. 825)

Despite the highly abstract nature of Jung's concept, his language is dramatic, energetic, and alive with immediacy: "living," "pregnant," "anticipatory," "dead," "flows," "highest," "deepest," "violent disunion," "damming up," "conflict," "striving," "energy." The dramatic and immediate quality of the language no doubt attests to the drama of Jung's personal experience as the contents of his unconscious burst upon his consciousness. It may reflect also Jung's deeply buried internalization of his reading of Hegel (1807) – the living and violent nature of the dialectical engagement; the life and death struggle when opposites meet, clash and war, risk dissolution and disintegration; the possibility of which constitutes the only authentic prelude to the resolution of the conflict within. If Jung conceived his notions of libido, symbol and transcendent function in a psychological life-and-death struggle of his own, so Hegel – although we do not know his mental state at the time – conceived his dialectical model, writing the *Phenomenology* as he heard the sounds of Napoleon's canons during the Battle of Jena.

From Self to Symbol

The symbol of the Self was for Jung the central unifier of the containment of opposites. Much of his writing is devoted to the discovery and elaboration of representations of the Self. Hegel contributed to the dialectical process that spanned original unity, to differentiation, and finally to an ordered sense of wholeness. So, too, Jung's notion of the Self and its symbols not only express potential integration or order; they also contribute to it.

We think of the archetype of the Self as spanning an early primitive state or core identity through to an individuated state, via the combination and differentiation of opposites. When the Self is expressed through the symbol of the Divine Child, we may be dealing with a state of the primary, undifferentiated core identity of the Self – a primary self. Jung wrote, "The 'child' paves the way for future change of personality. In the individuation process, it anticipates the figure that comes from the synthesis of conscious and unconscious elements" (CW9-I, par. 278).

When, however, the Self is expressed through the mandala, we may be dealing (albeit as an abstract idea) with the end product of the process in which all the differentiations have occurred, all the steps toward individuation have taken place, where an integrating, unified wholeness is achieved. Hegel's idea of the Perfect Man, fully individuated and conscious of himself, is similar to Jung's idea of the Self. Jung wrote, "Psychologically the self... stands for the psychic totality.... Empirically, however, the self appears spontaneously in the shape of specific symbols, and its totality is discernible above all in the mandala and its countless variants" (CW9-II, par. 426).

Fordham's work (1979) offers a further dialectical view of the processes in the development of the Self. In postulating two forms of the self, the whole Self and part selves, he has developed the idea of two kinds of Self functioning – integration and deintegration.

> A symbolic expression can never represent the whole self because in order to form, the self has to divide up to produce two part-systems, the one that creates the imagery (this is rather loosely called the

unconscious) and another (the ego) that records and interacts with
it.... It is the images referring to the self... that become numinous...
when... they come close to representing the whole self. (Fordham,
1979, p. 23)

Fordham's dynamic twofold model of deintegration and reintegration provides a view of the primal self in relation to its
experiences, internal and external: a vision of relating that is
dynamic and synthesizing, like that ascribed to the dialectical
vision and offered in the image he used – drawn from Freud – of
the amoeba with pseudopodia that extends from the central area
to incorporate elements from the outside world. In so doing, both
the Self and the deintegrate undergo a change – a synthesis –
within the central area.

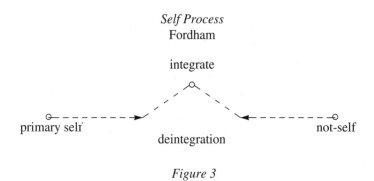

Self Process
Fordham

integrate

primary self   not-self

deintegration

Figure 3

Just as deintegration is the action of the primary self as it
relates to its objects, so the dialectical process is the action of
being-in-the-world. Both describe the dynamic of change and
both use a twofold model, in psychological terms, of "I" and
"not-I." The interaction between them produces a new element,
which is reincorporated into and transforms each element in the
process.

Applied to the evolution of the personality, the dialectical
model can be used to explain how incremental steps take place as
a result of the collision of, and play between, opposite experiences (good/bad, separate/merged, through a practically infinite list
of polarities) and how they gradually may achieve an internal

synthesis. Implied in the model is an explanation of a failure to develop when breakdown or a rigid defensiveness arises through a conflict of opposites with too great pressure on the system and with no means of synthesis. At the same time, it could explain how internal part objects – experienced as opposites – eventually might combine in such a way that a capacity for whole-object perception is achieved, assuming a good enough containing environment, inching toward moments in the depressive position (Klein), the capacity to be alone in the presence of another (Winnicott) or the more individuated personality (Jung).

A pivotal issue in theory-building concerns the question whether there is a primary self, existing prior to any influences from the external environment, or whether the inter-relating function is so primary that, in Winnicott's phrase, "there is no such thing as a baby but rather a nursing couple" (Winnicott, 1952, p. 99). However, if we call the starting point of the dialectic – the thesis – a "primary self" and its opposite – the antithesis – as the parent or another, then thesis and antithesis require the presence of each other. Thus, the primary self has the capacity to become itself through its capacity for finding and relating to the mother: in Hegel's words, its desire for the desire of another (i.e., the mother). In Winnicott's imagery, the baby invents the breast and the breast arrives (if it is a good enough breast) at that particular moment when the hallucinatory desire has occurred.

Thus two apparently opposing notions – Fordham's notion of a primary self and Winnicott's notion that there is no such thing as a baby, but rather a nursing couple – can be mediated by applying the dialectical model. This model provides that the child build up, over time, experiences of self and others that can be plotted on a spectrum of greater or lesser amounts of fantasy and of reality, of internality and externality.

The dialectical model provides for the possibility of value-free statements about the inability of the infant to perceive both opposite attributes at any one moment. Whether or not this results in pathology (e.g., splitting as defense, as states of envy, hatred and aggression considered to arise from the implications of the death instinct of Kleinian theory), or in further steps toward integration (the deintegration/reintegration process of Fordham), would depend on what had happened at the point where the change from oppositional to synthesizing processes occur. Either the resolution is creative and achieves a forward-moving progression in the psyche, or the conditions within and without the conflictual situation have led to disintegration or a defensive rigidity maintaining the status quo.

From Self to Coniunctio

For Jungians, the coniunctio is an alchemical symbol of central psychological importance, denoting the union or marriage of opposites resulting in the birth of a new element. Jung considered that many primal fantasies of adult patients did not arise from actual childhood experiences of the primal scene – as traditionally understood by psychoanalytic theory – but were projected. The sources of these projected "memories" are the bipolar archetypal images of the collective unconscious, for example, images of the anima and animus in coniunctio.

Melanie Klein may be thought of as having developed "archetypal" imagery concerning the coniunctio. For Klein, the infant's unconscious fantasy is imbued with the image of the parents in an almost continuous state of intercourse. ("The infant will phantasy his parents as exchanging oral, urethral, anal or genital [gratifications,] precisely those... which the infant wishes for himself" [Segal, 1964, p. 173]). In Analytical Psychology, the central archetypal image of the primal scene is the coupling parents in all their vicissitudes. Both images provide a series of representations of couplings imbued with negative, dangerous, sundering aspects, as well as with unifying, containing and mediating aspects. The union and opposition of the couple produce the third, the child: an actual child, or the contents of the child's mind, including its capacity for coniunctio or some other creation. The language in which this is expressed is dialectical.

Jung used alchemy to explore elements in the psyche that can be observed in the special analytic coniunctio contained within the transference/countertransference. Much of the alchemical metaphor centered around the coniunctio image – a meeting within the *vas hermeticum* of the primitive psychic elements and those processes they undergo in a series of transformations from base (instinctual) to precious (psychological) substances. We can see the alchemical vessel as the analytic or therapeutic setting, and the elements to be transformed as aspects of the conscious and the unconscious of both the analysand and the analyst. In alchemy, the elements to be combined are conceived of as opposites, the combination leading the alchemist to the production of the "third not given" or the interactive field. The new condition is "against nature," as Jung said.

The alchemical metaphor is rich in its potential for viewing the processes that occur within any relationship, including that within the transference/countertransference, because it is concerned (in a similar way to the dialectical model) with individuals' influence on each other and the internalizing and synthesizing of their experiences: the various modes of projection, introjection, identification, and projective identification.

The interrelation of analyst and analysand, the openness of each to changes in the other, are valued by Jung. It is through the ongoing, changing analytic relationship that the vicissitudes of treatment take place. Indeed, the concepts of complementary, concordant and syntonic countertransference can be understood in dialectical terms as forms of mutual relatedness, contained by the analytic relationship, which allow for subtle communication through projective identification. An "approximate union or identity between the various parts (experiences, impulses, defences), of the subject and the object" (Racker, 1968, p. 136) are achieved. Instead of Racker's idea of a straight-forward exchange producing unity or identity, we could envisage an amalgam of shared projected and introjected elements. For the stuff of the projected or introjected material must find a space in the recipient's psyche, where the material continues to act. Hegel's words are eloquent:

> [Self-consciousness] must supersede this otherness of itself…. First, it must proceed to supersede the other independent being in order thereby to become certain of itself as the essential being; secondly,

in so doing it proceeds to supersede its own self, for this other is itself. (1807, p. 111)

The subjective experience of the transference is "determined by the infantile situations and archaic objects of the patient" (Racker, 1968, p. 152), the understanding of which the analyst can approximate only through a capacity to allow the analysand enough access to the his or her unconscious: what Racker calls "an intensified vibration" of one's infantile situations and archaic objects. The understanding achieved by this subjective experience is then translated into an interpretation, which becomes part of the shared history-making between analysand and analyst. The experience may be repeated at the conscious or unconscious level with each subsequent interpretation. The quality of the resonating constitutes an important therapeutic factor in the analysis.

Jung referred to the centrality of the relationship between analyst and analysand in dialectical terms. Because both personalities are equally involved in the process, change occurs for both: "For two personalities to meet is like mixing two different chemical substances: if there is any combination at all, both are transformed: in any effective psychological treatment the doctor is bound to influence the patient; but this influence can only take place if the patient has a reciprocal influence on the doctor" (CW 16, par. 163).

In the transference, the analysand may project an internal image onto the analyst; in consequence, in the countertransference the analyst may be identified with this object. The analyst's experience of the projected object will depend on the quality of the projection as well as of the analyst's inner world. The building of conscious understanding of this subtle and complex process forms the context of the analysis.

Another way of envisaging the phenomenon of the hierosgamos or archetypal coniunctio, in the minds of the analyst-analysand couple, is to refer to Hegel's formulation of the interaction of the dialectic between two people as the "ambiguous supersession [their] ambiguous otherness" (Hegel, 1807).

Summary

In the work of analytic reconstruction, a history of the internal image building is recreated – a real process of Self-consciousness. This paper proposes a way of understanding the intricate and subtle processes of change and development described in Jung's idea of the transcendent function in terms of Hegel's dialectical model. Any model of psychological change must grapple with core issues concerning the relation between the primary self and its objects.

This paper proposes a way of understanding the intricate and subtle processes of change and development described in Jung's idea of the transcendent function in terms of Hegel's dialectical model. Any model of psychological change must grapple with core issues concerning the relation between the primary self and its objects.

Overall, we could view the basic differences between the philosophical stances taken by Freud and Jung as characterized by the reductionist method of Freud (the archeology of mind) and the synthetic method of Jung (the teleology of mind). Seen together, they constitute a complementary system of opposites that form a whole – a dialectical system in itself.

It is possible that the dialectical model can help us to understand why these two lines of analytic enquiry, the archeology and the teleology of mind, lead to potential conflict. It is also possible to use the dialectical model to understand how they are complementary. If we strive toward a mediation of the two positions, which does not deny differences but rather seeks to understand them as existing within a larger whole, then we would be adding to the work that brings forward the general development and evolution of our theoretical understanding and clinical work.

Throughout our lives there is a constant dialectical process that enables our essential self and our personal, special inner and outer capacities for coniunctio to elaborate and grow. If we allow that there is both a primal self and an innate predisposition for interrelating, then we are in a position to understand that the development of the personality is due to both and necessitates both. The transcendent function of Jung and the dialectical model of Hegel both seek to address similar understandings of psychic reality and as such demonstrate a remarkable similarity of structure.

References

Fordham, M. (1979). The Self as an imaginative construct. *Journal of Analytical Psychology*, *24*-1, 18-30.

Hegel, G.W.F. (1807). *Phenomenology of the Spirit* (A.V. Miller, Trans.). Oxford, England: Oxford University Press.

Hegel, G.W.F. (1812-16/1969). *Science of Logic*. (A. V. Miller, Trans.). London: Allen & Unwin.

Hegel, G.W.F. (1817/1990). *Encyclopedia of the Philosophical Sciences*. New York: Continuum.

Hegel, G.W.F. (1820). *Outline of the Philosophy of Right*.

Hubback, J. (1966). VII Sermones ad Mortuos. *Journal of Analytical Psychology*. *11*-2, 95-112.

Meltzer, D. (1967). *The Psycho-Analytical Process*. U.K.

Racker, H. (1968). *Transference and Counter-Transference*. London: Hogarth Press.

Segal, H. (1964). *Introduction to the Work of Melanie Klein*. London: Hogarth.

Stepelevich, L. (1990). Editor's Introduction to G.W.F. Hagel, *Phenomenology of the Spirit*.

Winnicott, D.W. (1952). Anxiety associated with insecurity. *Through Paediatrics to Psycho-Analysis*. London, England: The Hogarth Press and Institute of Psycho-Analysis, 1982.

Response

Sherry Salman
New York, New York, USA
New York Association for Analytical
Psychology

The theme of my response is "Fermenting the Dialectic into Psychological Process."

Solomon has suggested that both Jung's concept of the transcendent function and fundamental notions of the psychoanalytic object relations school derive their philosophical basis from Hegel's idea of dialectical change. Such a common philosophical origin could reconcile tensions between archetypal psychology and psychoanalysis.

As a counterpoint, I suggest that when Jung wrote his essay "The Transcendent Function" (CW8), he was attempting to formulate answers to a specific question: how does one come to terms with the unconscious – in practice? His answer was: through a dialogue with it. The significance of this answer is that, although the transcendent function has a dialectical motion, it is an "opus contra naturam" (work against nature), involving qualities of ego participation that separate it from instinctual developmental and dialectical processes.

There are similarities between dialectics and the transcendent function, and many developmental processes involving the primal self and its interaction with others may be dialectic. Nevertheless, these processes proceed relatively unconsciously. I suggest that the transcendent function goes beyond dialectics into conscious dialogue by introducing creativity, suffering and ethical integrity to the interaction of opposites. These additions act as the alchemical *ferment* which transforms the dialectical process.

Jung's focus in 1916 was essentially a clinical one, he himself was the anxious and disoriented subject. The situation was urgent, exemplified by Jung's experience when his house became haunted by a crowd of disgruntled spirits who cried out to him: "We have come back from Jerusalem where we found not what we sought" (MDR, p. 191). This weird parapsychological constellation of the objective psyche was one of the seminal events in Jung's life and immediately gave rise to his visionary piece of prose, "The Seven Sermons to the Dead" (MDR). Jung stated: "These conversations with the dead formed a kind of prelude to what I had to communicate to the world about the unconscious: a kind of pattern of order and interpretation of its general contents" (MDR, p. 192).

Jung could have taken the mystical revelations contained in the "Seven Sermons" at face value and published it as an occult piece; such pieces were not unheard of at the time. Instead, he chose to suffer them psychologically, not metaphysically or philosophically. Jung's struggle with these raw products of the unconscious was the experiential basis of "The Transcendent Function." Jung wrote about this period:

> The essential thing is to differentiate oneself from these unconscious contents by personifying them, and at the same time to bring them into relationship with consciousness. That is the technique for stripping them of their power. It is not too difficult to personify them, as they always possess a certain degree of autonomy, a separate identity of their own. Their autonomy is a most uncomfortable thing to reconcile oneself to, and yet the very fact that the unconscious presents itself in that way gives us the best means of handling it. (MDR, p. 187)

The connection between the two essays takes more than one form. The "Seven Sermons" is an explicitly Gnostic text; I suggest that the transcendent function is a gnostic process. By this I mean a psychological process which has as its goal immediate, direct, and personal understanding of one's experience. The gnostic heresy was that personal illumination of existence is accessible, not mediated through the collective, and that realizing this condition is the purpose of each human life. Similarly, Jung's notion of the transcendent function has a "cash value": It is concerned with realizing individual meaning and changing one's psychological attitude. When Jung was working on "The

Transcendent Function" he was evolving a new method of treating psychological material such as dreams and fantasies, quite heretical vis a vis the Freudian school. It was a synthetic and constructive method designed to illuminate the prospective aspects of unconscious material, to make its meaning explicit and immediately useful, as well as contain the disorientation and anxiety it produces.

Before returning to the gnostic derivations of the transcendent function, it is important to review the process itself and how it differs from a dialectical process. Jung defined the transcendent function as both an instinctive process and as something requiring conscious development. It is considered a manifestation of the energy generated from the opposites: a dynamic of related and relating opposites which, through their tension, achieve a synthetic resolution. It represents a link between rational and nonrational data, expressed through a symbol that transcends the tendency to be pulled into one or the other of the opposites.

Jung considered the transcendent function to be the most significant factor in psychological process. Even the purpose of the transference, the archetypal core buried within the analytic relationship, is mediation of the transcendent function and the promise of change implicit in its activation. The transcendent function avoids one-sidedness and meaningless conflict and serves to stimulate "conscience," not just increase consciousness.

This issue of conscience – suffering the ethical demands which increased consciousness necessitates – suggests that the transcendent function is also a non-instinctive process. Conscious and unconscious contents need to be united because in the naive state they exist only in a compensatory relationship to one another. Their union is not a foregone conclusion, but is part of the *opus contra naturam*. Jung stated, "Through constructive treatment of the unconscious the foundation is laid for the transcendent function" (CW8, par. 147).

The rational and the nonrational have to be brought together; Jung introduced the method of active imagination to facilitate this dialogue. In this method unconscious material is objectified, creative energy is applied to it and the product is assimilated partially by the ego. Through such a dialogue unconscious material can exert its regulating influence on the conscious attitude. However, this assimilation is in part an act of conscience and usually involves suffering. Thus, the transcendent function is a process involving more than the laws of compensation involved in dialectics and is actually a corrective to the dialectical movements of the psyche. The compensation of the unconscious has to be made conscious, not just left to its own devices, because the self-regulating systems of the psyche can easily become chaotic.

Thus, the transcendent function is a way to help regulate the interaction between various aspects of the psyche in order to minimize splitting and to escalate development. This function is the epitome of a psychological process, not an instinctive one, because it requires the intervention of consciousness. We cannot take it for granted that self-regulation proceeds autonomously. Without conscious intervention there can be one-sidedness which continues to the point of damage. Witness our current environmental and industrial crisis. Activation of the transcendent function is a way of influencing psychological and collective balance and avoiding large scale enantiodromia and acting-out.

On the other hand, for Hegel reality is constructed historically in pairs of opposites in dynamic relationship to one another. As these opposites interact they achieve a synthesis, the result of their relationship. The process is collective, the synthesis only implicit. For example, in the famous master/slave dialectic: after a very long period of time this interaction of opposites may resolve into a synthesis of mutuality or what Hegel proposed as "Universal Love." According to Kojeve (1977), this absolute knowledge and definitive truth which reveals the totality of Being can be realized only at the end of history.

It seems to me that the dialectical process as Hegel envisioned it does not necessarily work; it needs the intervention of the transcendent function in order to bring the master and slave into conscious dialogue with one another. Only in this way can dominance and submission be integrated psychologically.

There are other significant discrepancies. For example, the dialectical process doesn't require creativity or the sufferings of conscience, which are both integral to the transcendent function. Also, for Jung, the "opposites" are not symmetrical in the Hegelian sense, because the unconscious is always much larger than consciousness. This means that synthesis is by no means assured, as we know clinically. Then also, for Hegel, inanimate things are just objects to be appropriated; there is no dialectic with them. Only other persons are objects capable of interacting in a dialectic process. This is not so for Jung, who endows images, essences, and spirits with an Otherness and seeks to incarnate them. This process of objectification is an essential part of the technique of active imagination, which activates the transcendent function. One might argue that we now have to endow the animal and vegetable kingdoms with Otherness and engage with them in imaginal dialogue in order to avoid catastrophe. We could wait for dialectic processes to right the balance, but the transcendent function is Jung's solution to the sometimes reductive and depressing effects of both Hegel and classical psychoanalysis: that we are not hostage to the dialectic of history.

Although a teleological process is implicit in Hegel, it doesn't manifest for a long time, while the purpose of the transcendent function is to make meaning explicit and accessible. A dialectical process is not the same as a conscious dialogue which encourages shadow integration, crucial to psychic wholeness. The dialectical process is developmental, a description of the natural history of collective consciousness through an inexorable clash of opposites. Jung's process is *contra naturam*: Individual conscience, creativity and suffering must be added into the mix of opposites; a synthetic resolution does not necessarily develop by itself. Hegel (1820/1967) wrote:

> One word more about giving instruction as to what the world ought to be. Philosophy… always comes on the scene too late to give it. It appears only when actuality is already there… after its process of formation has been completed. The owl of Minerva spreads its wings only with the falling of dusk. (p. 13)

Jung considered conscious activation of the transcendent function to be a necessary "way of life," out of concern with the split nature of the modern psyche and the consequent growing problem of the Shadow. In her article on *The Seven Sermons to the Dead*, Judith Hubback (1966) wrote:

> Jung's view of the unconscious, distinct from the then Freudian view of it as the dangerous repository for unacceptable, and therefore repressed contents, was beginning clearly to emerge as a *result of Jung himself* discovering some of the historical and philosophical antecedents of his inner experiences, the gnostics' deliberations on the problem of evil. (p. 109)

Jung said (MDR) that alchemy was the bridge for him back to Gnosticism and forward to depth psychology. In Gnosticism knowledge is based on a dialogue with the numinous, an inner experience of an immediate kind, which includes shadow experience. Jung referred to the confrontation with the shadow as a "gnostic process," namely, a process about knowing not scientifically or philosophically, but from the heart. It is a psychological process based on experience and internal recognition, oriented toward wholeness not perfection, unlike Hegel's dialectical process. In the "Seven Sermons," the dead are taught that only the human ego capable of discrimination, is able to differentiate God and the Devil out of the original pleroma. This is in large part the purpose of the transcendent function; unconscious contents not brought forth into conscious dialogue, into gnosis, live themselves out compulsively. The transcendent function, in addition to representing a synthetic dialogue between conscious and unconscious contents, is the experience of gnosis.

Solomon has suggested that Michael Fordham's notion of a primal self with its defenses and deintegrates is related to Jung's idea of the Self as it arises from the transcendent function. The dialectical processes of deintegration/reintegration are likened to the thesis/antithesis of Subject/Object in Hegel. The primal self, as it deintegrates and reintegrates goes through a dialectical process. The synthesis after the conflict of opposites is expressed in a symbol which unites them, such as the Self. Inch by inch, as the primal self encounters the object and achieves a subsequent reintegration, a synthetic personality evolves.

This image evokes interesting questions. How actually is the integration achieved? How do oppositional processes change to synthesizing ones? Clinically we observe that, if left alone, the resolution of oppositional processes can be either creative, destructive or result in a rigid defense of the original opposition. The question seems to return to a practical one: how is the *coniunctio* achieved? Is the image of Hegel's synthesis the same as the alchemical "coniunctio oppositorum" (union of the opposites)?

I have suggested that there is a dialectical developmental process which leads to a synthesis of opposites. But this is not enough. Interestingly, the alchemists considered the product of the *coniunctio* to be "unnatural," distinct from the conjunction of base opposites, which is more like an amalgam. So also the product of the transcendent function is unusual, more than a combination of opposites: it involves an alchemical "fermenting copulation" adding shadow awareness, creativity, and the ethical imperative to suffer the opposites in conscious dialogue. This process is much like the analyst's creative interpretations of the intersubjective experience in the transference field followed, one hopes, by activation of the transcendent function in the analysand, which allows integration. These factors are crucial and differentiate our analytic work from collective and dialectical developmental processes.

Jung (MDR) recorded a strange dream from the period 1912 to 1916. While seated at a green table – like the Emerald Table in the alchemical legend of Hermes Trismegistos – a dove appeared, changed into a little girl, back into a dove, then spoke: "Only in the first hours of the night can I transform myself into a human being, while the male dove is busy with the twelve dead" (p. 172). This dream seems a prelude to the "Seven Sermons" and "The Transcendent Function;" a differentiation has begun between the collective and objective psyche, and the human soul is capable of dialogue and transformation. Perhaps both Hegel's dialectics and object relations theory describe one aspect of development, the transcendent function another: one, an instinctive and collective developmental process, the other an aspect of the individuation process.

References

Hegel, G.W.F. (1820/1967). Preface to *Philosophy of Right* (T.M. Knox, Trans.) New York: Oxford University Press.

Hubback, J. (1966). VII Sermones ad Mortuos. *Journal of Analytical Psychology*, *11*-2, 95-111.

Kojeve, A. (1947). *Introduction to the Reading of Hegel: Lectures on the Phenomenology of Spirit*. Ithaca, NY: Cornell University Press.

Locating the Transcendent:
Inference, Rupture, Irony

Polly Young-Eisendrath
Philadelphia, Pennsylvania, USA
Philadelphia Association of Jungian
Analysts

Currently, I am taking a strong "constructivist" position in understanding Analytical Psychology as a contemporary depth psychology. Constructivism views human beings as active meaning-makers and pattern-matchers, throughout life. Interacting with a fluctuating environment we impose perception and meaning. Much of this imposition is conservative: We bring old patterns to new experiences. Occasionally the fit between old and new breaks down; we have to change old patterns or we fail to develop.

Many contemporary Jungian analysts and therapists speak from a quite different premise, dubbed philosophically as "essentialism" or "foundationalism." In this view, meaning has its foundation external to a human context. Meaning may arise from the way archetypes organize human consciousness and the physical world. Meaning may reside mostly in physical things themselves, including the human body, to be discovered through immediate intuition. Meaning may arise in eternal forms or categories that reside in our minds or perceptual systems. From a foundationalist perspective, meaning is not primarily a human affair.

My premise here is anti-foundationalist. I believe that our experiences of self and world arise from our own interpretive context and that we have access to different worlds depending on our language and context. As philosopher T. S. Kuhn said at a public lecture a few years ago, the Greeks saw a different sky from the one we see – not because the planets and stars were different but because their concepts were different. I assume that

Jungian concepts such as "archetype" and the transcendental "Self" are products of a particular community of thinkers attempting to come to terms with the unknowable, especially in relation to issues of universality and unity in human experience. Within the constructivist model, concepts that refer to the unknowable are developed by people making inferences about what they cannot experience directly.

In my view, constructivism is consistent with Jung's later work, after 1944. In 1958 he wrote a brief commentary for the publication of his 1916 essay "The Transcendent Function" that states succinctly what I will be saying. Jung said that this function is "identical with the universal question: How does one come to terms in practice with the unconscious?... For the unconscious is not this thing or that; it is the Unknown as it immediately affects us" (CW8, pp. 67-68). The Unknown's being capitalized seems to mean a kind of unconsciousness that is unknowable. This kind of unconsciousness is what psychoanalyst Jacques Lacan calls the "real" and what objection relations theorist Thomas Ogden (1989) describes as lying beyond the "primitive edge of experience." These theorists specify that the Unknown, the real, and what is beyond the primitive edge cannot be captured in language, images or even dreams. The Unknown is incoherent and unrevealed to human consciousness, although we infer it from our experiences. In the remainder of my paper I will use the term "the Unknown" to refer to this type of unconsciousness, whose meaning is inferred in a variety of human contexts, but cannot be known directly even through our dreams and visions.

I shall discuss the Unknown and the transcendent function in two ways. First, I will discuss the role of inference and the interpretive context in our theorizing about the Unknown. Our claims for the unknowable archetype and the transcendental Self (with a capital S) are inferences made within an interpretive context. They are not knowledge of the Unknown. If we forget that these concepts are based on hypotheses and inferences and speak as though they represent direct experiences, we lose the transcendent function in theoretical discourse among ourselves and with others.

My second discussion involves those occasions, especially in psychotherapy or analysis, when our sense of containment or coherence is disrupted. These are moments of horror, pain, fear or irritation that intrude into our apparent control. Such moments are ruptures in the analyst's and/or analysand's belief that analysis can come to terms with the Unknown. In such a moment the transcendent function may be lost or restored depending on how the analyst responds. It is an opportunity to come to terms with the Unknown.

Jung nowhere gave an exact definition of the transcendent function. In his 1916 essay, he said that "There is nothing mysterious or metaphysical about the term," which refers to a "union of conscious and unconscious contents" (CW8, par. 131). In a 1920 explanation he said it is "a complex function... that facilitates a transition from one attitude to another. The raw material shaped by thesis and antithesis... is the living symbol" (CW6, par. 828). I see this function as a capacity to move back and forth between layers of meaning, in a manner that psychoanalyst D. W. Winnicott described as inhabiting "potential space" or "play space." Author and Jungian candidate Carol Savitz (1990) gives the following clinical description of the transcendent function: it is "a bridge to help cross the abyss between affects, between affect and memory, between self and ego, between analyst and patient" (p. 243). This bridge, in whatever form it may emerge, becomes the symbol of the psyche transcending dissolution – and ultimately coming to terms with the Unknown.

Inference and Experience

My response to much contemporary Jungian theorizing and commentary on the Self is to remember Jung's repeated assertions that his concept of the Self as empty center is neither knowledge nor experience of the Unknown. In a 1955 letter, for example, he said of the Self: "Here the limit of possible experience is reached: the ego dissolves as the reference point of cognition" (Let-II, p. 259). In the same letter he said, "If I call the 'ultimate' the self and you call it the 'absolute ultimate,' its ultimateness is not changed one whit.... I see many God-images of various kinds... but I know that none of them expresses or captures the immeasurable Other" (p. 261). Implicitly Jung was stressing the transcendent function in recognizing the role of inference in our speculations about the Unknown. We cannot know this Otherness; we can only infer and attempt to understand it in context.

Jung wrote a great deal about the dialectic in a Hegelian sense of thesis and antithesis; we often describe the transcendent function as "holding the tension of opposites." I discovered the term "dialectical space" in Ogden's work (1990) and have come to see it as the basis for maintaining the transcendent function in both theory and practice. His dialectical process is one in which two opposing concepts inform, create and oppose each other in a dynamic relationship. So far, no different from Jung. Ogden emphasizes, however, that the creative dialectic of human development takes place primarily in the "space" between symbol (image or word) and symbolized (experience) mediated by an interpreting self. In this dialectical space we are creative rather than simply reactive. We are "free" to invent or discover new meaning from old patterns. More emphatically than Jung, Ogden stresses the importance of our awareness of ourselves as thinking subjects – as interpreters within a context. If we lose this awareness, we invite a "pathology of the dialectic" that Ogden describes as follows:

> The subject becomes tightly imprisoned in the realm of fantasy objects as things in themselves. This is a two-dimensional world which is experienced as a collection of facts. The hallucination does not sound like a voice, it *is* a voice. One's husband does not simply behave coldly, he *is* ice. One does not feel like one's father, one's father *is* in one's blood... (p. 216).

 In Jungian discussions of the archetype or the Self, I find us frequently collapsing the space between the symbol (our concept) and the symbolized (the Unknown), and then forgetting that we do not directly experience these unknowables. For example, if we claim that some dreams are "archetypal" and others are "ordinary" without attending to the context of why this claim is made for a particular dream, but instead act as though this knowledge is immediately accessible either to the dreamer or the analyst, we have collapsed the dialectical space around the Unknown. In theorizing about the Self, we have a tendency to describe the Self as a human subject. In such a case, the Self is described as a subject with views, ideas, or guidelines that can be known by us. Here is a randomly chosen example from a contemporary Jungian text: "A man dreamt 'I am a lion.' This presented his Self's view of a potential lion force." If the Self is a concept inferred from a principle of unity, like an empty center, the Self cannot have a view. It is not a perceiving self like a human subject. If we want to infer that the Self is a perceiving subject, then we need to give an account in our theory to defend this assumption.

[margin handwritten note: Not necessarily]

When we collapse the dialectical space around our theorizing about the Unknown, and seem to imply that we experience the Unknown directly, we forget to defend our assumptions. This tends to hamper us in dialogues with our colleagues in depth psychology or other fields. We sound as if we are making truth claims about experiences of the unknowable. Jung was a critic of such truth claims made by theologians. In 1955 he wrote, "If theologians think that whenever they say 'God' then god is, they are deifying anthropomorphisms, psychic structures and myths. This is exactly what I don't do…. Who talks of divine knowledge and divine revelation? Certainly not me" (Let-II, p. 261).

If we lose the transcendent function in our theorizing about the Unknown, there is no space to explore how our interpretive context affects our views. (In Jung's words, the "name means far less… than the view associated with it" [Let-II, p. 261]). What does an analyst's pronouncement about an analysand's Self mean within the therapeutic relationship at any moment? What is its purpose? Defensive? Loving? Aggressive? Why do some Jungians collapse the dialectical space around the concept of Self in Jungian discourse? What does this mean?

All inferences about the Unknown are made within a context. Holding the tension of the transcendent function can produce a new synthesis of meaning about the Unknown from differing contexts. As Jung said: When confronted with the Unknown "the ego can merely affirm that something vitally important is happening to it. It may conjecture that it has come up against something greater, that it feels powerless against this greater power.... The ego has to acknowledge many gods before it attains the centre where no god helps it any longer against another god" (Let-II, p. 259). Context and purpose in confronting the Unknown produce configurations of meaning that guide us in coming to terms with a moment or a larger theoretical issue.

Claims about the Unknown are made in many different languages: scientific, philosophical, mathematical, psychological, religious. These claims are not readily interchangeable because of the different viewpoints of the communities of speakers. Jungian speakers sometimes collapse the dialectical space between different languages and assume that concepts like the archetype or the Self encompass concepts from other disciplines (for example, anthropology, physics or mathematics) in a way that is disagreeable to theorists in those disciplines. When this happens, we tend to subsume divergent assumptions about the Unknown under our concepts without adequate dialogue with the other side. As scholar Wendy Doniger (1992) said recently of Joseph Campbell's tendency to collapse the dialectical space: "He made the myths he retold his myths, instead of letting them tell their own story" (p. 8). Respecting the dialectical space means living within the transcendent function, allowing for the emergence of new meaning from differing views of the Unknown.

I would like to see a new emphasis on the transcendent function in Jungian discourse about the Unknown. If we claim to hear the voice of the Unknown directly or know the view from the empty center, we have collapsed the transcendent function into a pathology of the dialectic. This leads to theoretical dogmatism with no potential space for moving back and forth between levels of meaning in coming to terms with ourselves and our reason for making this or that inference about the Unknown.

Crisis and Intersubjectivity in Analysis

Although inferences about the Unknown are "experience-far," certain disruptive experiences are "close encounters" with the unspeakable. Ogden uses the metaphor of the "primitive edge" to allude to the "surface" or edge of our containment, particularly the containment we feel within a body. The primitive edge is the outermost surface of what seems under our control. Rupture of this edge leads to "unthinkable agonies" (falling forever, having no relation to the body, complete alienation, etc.), as Winnicott called them. The intrusion of the chaotic into the orderly may seem horrific or awesome depending on the context.

In therapy and in life, our close encounters with the Unknown are often shocking. A term for this encounter is "crisis" and Jungian analyst Verena Kast (1990) gives a useful description of it when she says,

> The term 'crisis' describes a very decisive moment… wherein… we can no longer solve a problem with known ways and means at a time when it matters a great deal to us that the problem be solved. (p. 11)

Kast uses crisis to talk about a "creative process" in which we are faced with a gap, barrier or difficulty that we cannot overcome using ordinary solutions.

The particular crisis I want to discuss here is a rupture in the therapeutic relationship. This is a serious disruption in which the analysand doubts the analyst's ability to help and wants to quit therapy. At this point the analyst is faced with an intersubjective disorganization, a break in the trust on which analysis is based.

A woman in her late forties has seen me in analytically-oriented therapy (with periods of crisis intervention) over almost five years, once a week. She had a chaotic, disruptive childhood: She was physically and sexually abused by her step-father, lost her own father through desertion, was repeatedly misperceived by her mother who failed to protect her from the step-father's cruelties, and was socially ostracized because of her mixed racial background. Had I heard her personal history out of context of her present life, I would have predicted that she would have a disabling borderline personality syndrome with overwhelming impulses to mutilate herself.

As it is, she is a very successful psychotherapist who works in a large metropolitan clinic as both a general practitioner and a drug and alcohol counselor. She has been married and divorced twice, has two grown daughters who live on their own and a preadolescent son who does well in school. She has great difficulty trusting the regard and love people feel for her. She also has a tendency to vomit when she feels out of control. Otherwise she now has no serious symptoms. Her symptoms were more disruptive when she began treatment with me.

She came because she wanted "Jungian analysis," with hopes that she might train as an analyst herself some day. During the first year, she was a homemaker (having temporarily "retired" as a therapist) who made a comfortable home for her husband, son and one teenage daughter. (This was prior to her husband's leaving her "for another woman," someone she knew.) She had many dreams with frightening psychotic images: people being ripped apart, body parts fused with machines, deadly animals and weapons, her own violence and others' violence against her. She became afraid to tell me such dreams because she feared they were "true" in the way of prophecy. There had been events in her life that she felt had been prophesied by her dreams. Although I was deeply concerned about the psychotic images in her dreams, I was also convinced that she was a woman of complex development who could hold different meanings simultaneously and reflect on her inner states. I saw her literal interpretations of her dreams as a defense against her self-hatred. I placed my bets on this view.

Many months passed during which we were in a crisis mode after her husband left. I gave much advice – not my usual style. Her conduct with her divorcing husband benefited from my advice, her son benefited from her conduct, and so on. We were all quite contained. After most of the crisis had passed and her son was in treatment with a good psychiatrist and she was making a solid income and could see new possibilities, she lost faith in the treatment.

She complained that although she had followed my advice, was doing what she "needed to live," and had long since given up literal interpretations of her dreams (which had also become more humanized), she felt no better, especially in her body. Everything seemed "driven" from the outside with no personal satisfaction for her. She could see no future for herself and she was distractedly envious of her ex-husband. She worried that I had idealized her, believing she could transcend so many difficulties and develop herself into – something. We both felt a heavy depression and fear, and I was unsure about the paths I had taken with her.

This situation existed at the time of the Christmas holidays. For two years I had warmly accepted small gifts from her during the holidays and believed that she was symbolically putting parts of herself into me as the container. Because of the disintegration in her daily life I had decided to say nothing interpretive about the gifts. This third year she gave me a larger gift. It was a little stained glass window, a delightful design with colors that matched perfectly the stained glass I already had in my office. In the previous session she had expressed frustration that I "wouldn't just let her leave" therapy. The gift was presented with a sort of "here it is" gesture, and when I opened its wrapping and exclaimed how beautiful it was, she said that she had felt very "lucky" to find it. Because of my uncertainty and the size of the gift, I made an interpretive remark about it. I said something like "There is a reason why you keep giving me gifts?" She was enraged. She said that she didn't want her gifts to be analyzed, and I had not done that before. I felt a huge anxiety arise in me. I couldn't make out in my own thoughts anything except how much I cared about this woman and how stupid I felt. I remarked stupidly that sometimes people offer me gifts when they are angry with me; she was nonplused. Then I said that perhaps she "wanted to leave parts of herself in me." She looked puzzled and angry. She announced that this was her last session. I responded emphatically that this was not a good time to quit. She agreed to come for another session and we finished this one in a daze.

In my reflection after the session, I knew my actions were contradictory and wrong. I had accepted the gift and destroyed the "magic" of it through an interpretation. Her faith in me had been wearing thin anyway and now I had destroyed something and hurt her badly. We spent the next session talking about her reactions to my statement. I opened by asking her why my words had hurt so much. She said she felt betrayed by my speaking about her gift. In that moment I had changed into someone who wanted to examine her motives for giving. I had become like her mother who could never simply accept her love, but always had to correct it. Movingly she told me how much she enjoyed choosing and giving me these gifts as a recognition of what I had given her during the crisis. She rejected the idea that she "was putting parts" of herself into me. With relief, I understood. I could see how I seemed like her mother who was never simply pleased by her. I said I believed in her capacity to continue developing, but recognized also that she did not believe in it. She felt relieved. She recommitted herself to therapy. The stained glass remains on my window sill and no further mention of it has been made.

The transcendent function is fostered by the "idealizing transference" to the analyst during analysis. In the words of psychotherapy researcher Hans Strupp (1989), this kind of transference can be understood as the "overriding significance of the interpersonal relationship between patient and therapist as the vehicle for therapeutic change" (p. 723). When I interpreted her gift, my analysand felt belittled. We lost the transcendent function and I became the Terrible Mother. She lost hope in me and was flooded with unspeakable agonies she had experienced with enraged and unpredictable childhood caregivers. In reflecting on the session afterward, I remembered a statement from a self psychologist: In a therapeutic rupture, attune yourself to the analysand's subjective experience.

Attuning to the analysand's subjectivity restores the idealizing transference and with it the transcendent function. After this is re-established, together the analysand and I can examine the conscious and unconscious meanings of what happened. I now take this as a new "basic rule" for analysis: When an analysand threatens to quit and accuses me of being at fault, first I empathize and explore the analysand's subjective state. Then I examine the meaning that has emerged to see how it fits the narrative of our analytic work. A therapist who feels accused may unconsciously handle guilt and shame through projective identification. Reductive or genetic interpretations of the rupture imply "you caused this impasse" to the other person and tend to evoke guilt and shame in the other.

In 1916 Jung described the transcendent function of the idealizing transference. At this early date he observed that the process of transformation is rooted in the idealization of the analyst. The idealizing transference allows an analysand to encounter powerful unconscious material with the belief that the analyst embodies the transcendent function, the capacity to come to terms with the Unknown. Jung said:

> For the patient... the analyst has the character of an indispensable figure absolutely necessary for life. However infantile this dependence may appear to be, it expresses an extremely important demand which, if disappointed, often turns to bitter hatred of the analyst. (CW8, par. 146)

When the idealizing transference is lost the analysand is at the primitive edge. On the other side is the Unknown, the unspeakable, the incoherent and chaotic. The analysand experiences the analyst as having evoked this chaos, and wants to escape the relationship in which the chaos is occurring. When the therapist empathizes and accepts the analysand's experience as valid, for example, "I seem to be causing you overwhelming pain and you feel as though I cannot be trusted," the analysand can begin to re-establish trust in the therapeutic relationship.

In general, the idealizing transference should not be interpreted, unless the analysand requests it, but should be understood by the analyst as necessary for transformation to occur. If an idealizing transference never takes place, there is no possibility of transformation through the therapy. If the idealizing transference is lost, the possibility for transformation dies. The analysand will never again risk much with the analyst because they went to the edge and the analyst failed. If idealization is restored after a rupture, together the two witness the living symbol of their relationship as a means for coming to terms with the Unknown: bridging the most chaotic unconsciousness with conscious meaning.

Irritation and Irony

A therapeutic rupture is a crisis that brings us face to face with the unspeakable Unknown. Smaller moments of irritation, as when an analysand blames us for a mistake or forgets a session, face us with similar but less critical disruptions. Irritating remarks and assaults, aggression, rage and humiliation are opportunities enacted by the analysand for creative transformation, occasionally for feeling the transcendent function. Sometimes a negative transference is interpreted reductively in terms of unconscious projections and images, parts of a psychological complex. Sometimes a negative transference is interpreted interpersonally in terms of a difficulty arising in the therapeutic relationship. With the hope of understanding conscious and unconscious meanings, analysand and analyst come to know how to speak about the various levels of meaning of negative emotions in a context of trust. I am a great believer in the value of negative emotions in analysis, provided that neither analyst nor analysand destroys the idealizing transference. There are few intimate relationships in life in which envy, rage, or hatred can be spoken, acknowledged and understood without serious threat or danger. Allowing myself to be seen and experienced as hated, demanding, aloof and unloving have been moments of grace – when they can be transformed through empathic understanding, followed by a collaborative interpretation of what happened.

Understanding the transcendent function has led me gradually to an ironic view of therapy, development, and even human life. Psychoanalyst Roy Schafer (1976) defined the ironic as a readi-

ness "to seek out internal contradictions, ambiguities, and para-
doxes" (p. 50) without the momentous implications of the tragic.
I tend to see the classical Jungian view as romantic and the
classical Freudian view as tragic. My own approach to Jungian
analysis has been colored by irony through years of struggling to
sustain the transcendent function in my life and work. Here is
Schafer's full description of the ironic vision that describes what
I have learned about holding the tension of opposites:

> The ironic vision... aims at detachment, keeping things in perspec-
> tive, taking nothing for granted, and readily spotting the antithesis to
> any thesis so as to reduce the claim of that thesis upon us. In this
> respect the ironic vision tends to limit (not minimize) the scale of
> involvement in human difficulty while continuing to insist on the
> inherent difficulties of human existence. (p. 51)

I read the term "detachment" here in line with Buddhist teachings about it. It is an attitude in which we let go of our own
egocentrism and get a bigger perspective.

Concluding Remarks

Theory and practice go hand in hand. In the first section, I
suggested that a pathology of the dialectic may collapse the
potential space in Jungian theory-making, especially in regard to
our concepts of the Unknown, most especially about our principle of unity, the Self. In the second section, I suggested that the
analyst must attune closely to the analysand's subjective experience in a therapeutic rupture, or the transcendent function of the
therapy will be lost. I went on to connect the transcendent function to an idealizing transference in which the analyst is seen as
someone who offers the hope of containing and eventually coming to terms with the Unknown.

The perspective of irony, taking nothing for granted, enlivens
our work. If we remain alert to the dialectical space of our own
theorizing, I believe we are better able to attend to the subjectivity of the analysand on the primitive edge of experience. It is not
our theory about the Unknown that will awaken us to the meanings of disruption, chaos, or unity. It is rather our capacity to

remain attuned to the meanings that emerge. I close my remarks with a few verses from poet Howard Nemerov's (1977) poem about the paradox of imposing meaning on "The Blue Swallows."

> Across the millstream below the bridge
> Seven blue swallows divide the air
> In shapes invisible and evanescent,
> Kaleidoscopic beyond the mind's
> Or memory's power to keep them there.
> . . . .
>
> Poor mind, what would you have them write?
> Some cabalistic history
> Whose authorship you might ascribe
> To God? to Nature? Ah, poor ghost,
> You've capitalized your Self enough.
> . . . .
>
> Fully awakened, I shall show you
> A new thing: even the water
> Flowing away beneath those birds
> Will fail to reflect their flying forms,
> And the eyes that see become as stones
> Whence never tears shall fall again.
>
> O swallows, swallows, poems are not
> The point. Finding again the world,
> That is the point, where loveliness
> Adorns intelligible things
> Because the mind's eye lit the sun. (pp. 379-98)

References

Doniger, W. (1992). A very strange enchanted boy. *The New York Times Book Review*, Feb. 2.

Kast, V. (1990). *The Creative Leap: Psychological Transformation through Crisis* (D. Whitcher, Trans.). Wilmette, IL.: Chiron Publications.

Nemerov, H. (1977). *The Collected Poems of Howard Nemerov.* Chicago, IL.: University of Chicago Press.

Ogden, T. (1989). *The Primitive Edge of Experience.* Northvale, NJ: Jason Aronson.

Ogden, T. (1990). *The Matrix of the Mind.* Northvale, NJ: Jason Aronson.

Savitz, C. (1990). The double death. *The Journal of Analytical Psychology*, 35, 241-260.

Schafer, R. (1976). *A New Language for Psychoanalysis.* New Haven, CT: Yale University Press.

Strupp, H. (1989). Psychotherapy: Can the practitioner learn from the researcher? *American Psychologist, 44*-4, 714-717.

Note: For a variety of understandable definitions of Jacques Lacan's concept of "the real," see J.H. Smith and W. Kerrigan (Eds.), *Interpreting Lacan* (1983). New Haven, CT: Yale University Press.

Response

Andreas Wöhrle
St. Gallen, Switzerland
Swiss Society for Analytical
Psychology

Polly Young-Eisendrath's stimulating exposition is committed to liberality in analytic theory and practice. Her work speaks to my apprehension about socio-political changes and tendencies that less and less allow our participation in that which is unfamiliar and strange to us. These developments once more open the doors to an illusionary, security-providing positivist philosophy of life and to its determining social conditions. Therefore it seems necessary even in our circles to keep pointing out the danger of theories' being dogmatically converted into practice, legitimizing political reality without reflection. In a letter to Breuer in 1892, Freud already pointed to the difficulties in using theory dialectically when he wrote: "The main question probably is, do we represent it historically... or rather dogmatically with the theories we found as explanations?" (SE2, Appendix B).

Young-Eisendrath's approach to Jung's theory of the transcendent function is a point of view that is to be understood hermeneutically. From this perspective, the human being is an individual with a personal history in a world that is shaped by oneself and others. The manifestations of this approach emerge in the context of the respective inner and outer reality. The comment that the archetype, which cannot be experienced, is an assumption and therefore not a truth. Thus, the meaning of an image must be put into context.

Jung was of the opinion that the basis of the transcendent function was archetypal. He wrote: "From the conscious elaboration of this material the transcendent function reveals itself as a mode of apprehension mediated by the archetypes and capable of uniting the opposites. By 'apprehension' I do not mean simply intellectual understanding but understanding through experience" (CW7, par. 184). From this quotation it is clear that specific experiences of the ego, in this case the conscious processing of archetypal images, activate the transcendent function. There exists therefore an inner, archetypally-conveyed readiness that must be activated by inner or outer events. The interpretation of the fantasies that can be seen and experienced, however, has to do with the emotional state of the interpreters, with their personal history and its associated conflicts and activated complexes.

At the same time the process of interpretation is influenced by an interest in cognition, the norms and the sense categories of a society. Thus, a continuing analytic reflection concerning the collective is necessary. A directed interest in cognition can prevent those taking part in the therapeutic process from meeting and influencing each other in a way that is still experienced as unfamiliar and therefore often sinister.

Young-Eisendrath focuses on the unreflected, implicit theoretical assumptions of analysts and not on those of the analysands. She points out that the ability to symbolize – the psychological representation of the transcendent function – can be impaired and the imaginative and transitional character of theoretical assumptions get lost in the process. In such cases we can run the risk of reducing the Unknown – that which is non-identical with symbols that have become visible – to known signs and conscious images. The dialectical encounter between the participants of the therapeutic process then is paralyzed.

In such a case fantasies and symbols are treated by analysts as "pure facts" and no longer as imagination. Morgenthaler (1986) points out that "the world of imagination of the analyst replaces reality" when the analytic relationship no longer exists. He further writes: "Once the analytical process is in this track, the analyst easily reaches for role interpretation. Rationalizing and intellectualizing… hinder the further course of analysis" (p. 28). Transferring this into our context: The lively argument between two people in a specific relationship could be warded off less by role interpretations than by a wrongly interpreted concept of transference and countertransference.

For Jungians the warding off is probably less transparent if we adhere to the central idea of our theory of a process of individuation that is induced and maintained by a Self. An interpretation such as the one depicted by Young-Eisendrath can seem as one adjusted to reality in the sense of the acquired, unreflected analytic ideal, without inner and necessary contradiction. Without being aware of this or even consciously wanting it, the attempt at individuation falls under the control of the analyst. Thus, the possibilities for the analysand to be able to feel autonomous and develop in the analytic setting are strongly reduced.

The foregoing is only one side. On the other side, analysands that are working with us can now only unilaterally comprehend how we feel. A therapeutic behavior that is connected too little with the context fosters poorly the psychological process of integration that is at the basis of the feelings of a personal identity and that allow one's own history to be interpreted. Young-Eisendrath points out that "respecting the dialectic space means living with the transcendent function, and in this way a new meaning can be gained through the different interpretations of the Unknown." She seems to make a plea for meeting the Unknown in every relationship, with as much openness as possible.

An example from literature sheds light on the difficulty of facing up to the Strange and to that which goes beyond the ego, without having omnipotent control. Saint Exupéry has left us an example of a feeling of abandonment and fear out of which the dialectic space can collapse. The Little Prince says that above all he loves the sunsets, especially when he is sad, and asks Saint Exupéry to look at one of them with him. Saint Exupéry replies that they would have to wait until the sun sets and draws his attention to the role of time and their own location which determine the appearance and the experience of the sunset. Then he notices that the earthly realities of waiting and of boundaries do not play a role on the small planet of the Little Prince. He can move by merely a few feet in order to see the sunset over and over. "And you experience dusk as often as you like."

What then are the effects of theoretical exposition on everyday practice? Young-Eisendrath has demonstrated that during crises such as transitions from one phase of life to another, the Unknown that is usually only comprehensible by metaphors can be experienced directly. In the course of this she has differentiated between developmental crises and the symptoms that are to be attributed to the warding off of a psychological collapse.

We know from experience that impending termination of an advanced therapeutic relationship can affect us. Even if the personal narcissism has been worked through fairly well in one's own analysis, we can get into a crisis of the way we see ourselves therapeutically. Young-Eisendrath has described the insecurities that suddenly come into existence and has pointed out how difficult it is in such a situation to remain empathetically related to the other.

The first of her two central theses is: "The transcendent function is supported by the 'ideal transference' during analysis." I find that the conditions that are "created" by an "ideal transference" may indeed be the ideal ones for an analysis. The mutual "love" and enhancement of status, and the feeling of working on something wonderful together, make the work of the analysands as well as that of the analysts easier.

The fusion with the object of the Self that is fantasized as ideal and omnipotent becomes a potential for change. The empathy that is associated with the idealized transference "heightens the capabilities of the analysand for self-observation which, however, does not inevitably have to go along with a change of his/her experience and behavior" (Mertens, 1983, p. 197). This objection qualifies the effect of empathy in view of a change or restructuring of personality. This seems to be comprehensible when we remember the work with severely ill people, psychotics, borderline or severely traumatized men and women. More than anything else, a possibility for creating and using the analyst as a new object must be presented to those affected. This is also the reason that transference interpretations are rejected; the required traces of remembrance and the related symbolization are missing as a consequence of splitting. Therefore the feeling of being affected by an interpretation cannot occur.

Furthermore I am not as confident as Young-Eisendrath that, after a severe crisis, the idealization could be restored with the same intensity as before. I rather believe that often we can only hope that the therapeutic bond that comes into existence through the "idealized transference" holds long enough to allow the analysand to withstand ambivalent feelings toward the previous objects, fantasized as omnipotent.

Young-Eisendrath's second thesis is: "If we succeed once again in attuning to the subjective experience of the analysands, the 'idealized transference' and thus the transcendent function is restored." I believe that the "idealized transference" has to do with the fact that it was possible for the person to whom the child related most closely and, later, for the analyst to convey a feeling of mutual harmony. At the same time, however, this is not always possible for reasons that lie with the analyst. The counter-transference feelings that are, for instance, linked to the transference of omnipotence are often hard to withstand, due to the associated pressure toward action. I do not believe that analysts necessarily are ready to identify with the reactivated magnitude of the Self without a second thought. They rather seem to face its representation with great ambivalence, conscious or unconscious. The need to liberate oneself from the demands that are awakened in the therapeutic interaction by the magnitude of the Self can lead to the possibility that the analysands are pushed from their required container earlier than is bearable to them.

In such situations, all we can do is try to remain empathic toward ourselves. Only in this manner can we succeed in adapting once more to our analysands. Thus the ongoing analysis of countertransference seems important. In addition to this predominantly inner dialogue, we should grant the possibility of opening the container toward the outside. As Carpy (1989) explains, by doing this we let the analysands take part in our experience and in the digestion of that which is still comprehensible only in part and with difficulty. It is to be hoped that by this transparency we allow the analysands to become familiar and identify with the aspects of our approach to the difficulties that have surfaced.

Finally, I question Young-Eisendrath's thesis that connects the transcendent function with the idealized transference. Relevant is a case vignette in which the center of attention is the surfacing of visually perceived images in the analyst's presence. As described by Zimmermann (1989), this phenomenon seems to be connected to the restoration of the therapeutic relationship and therefore to an understanding of the event, that occurs after a crisis. They contain aspects of the current dynamism of transference and countertransference and of associated conflicting parts from analysts and analysands. Furthermore, unconscious or preconscious possibilities of development seem to be indicated. This image, which can be called a symbol, serves the further process of symbolization of the analysand as container, and during the process it can be superseded by a single symbol that provides meaning.

During therapy with a 36-year-old music teacher we reached a point where we both felt that nothing was moving anymore. We discussed the possibility of playing in the sand instead of talking. During this talk I saw between the eyebrows of the person opposite me a small, brown eagle that came in to land with stretched-out talons. At the sandbox an intensive game developed that seemed associated with erotic feelings of us both. At the end of this game, in which I was included only as an observer and sympathizer, the analysand modeled a butterfly out of sand. During the next session he referred once more to his game but without being able to take it up properly. In the following session he brought up a dream in which he was instructed by a man unknown to him to introduce his class to a lesson that he was not to give. Thereupon the class started a piece that they were familiar with and that the analysand was supposed to have accompanied on the piano. He realized, however, that he was playing a considerably more swinging piece while he kept looking at his hands that did not want to follow the song started by the class but continued to interpret the livelier canon.

The symbol of the eagle seems to have reflected my rather authoritarian attitude toward the analysand. His awareness of my countertransference appeared once again in the figure of the unknown man. At the same time the eagle seemed to symbolize the severity of the early environment as the personal internalized one as well. As I noticed after the first sandtray session this severity seemed already somewhat changed through the "containing" of the appearance of my image; there was room for the finer and lighter butterfly. In the dream a further personal symbol came into existence which could take over this container-function, show new possibilities of development and enliven the analysand and the therapeutic relationship. However, what seems to have been decisive is the circumstance that my resistance to countertransference, which had been expressed in an authoritarian attitude towards the analysand, suddenly ceased to obstruct further work. With that, communication of the unconscious of both of us seemed to have become possible again, and the "dialectic space" could once more develop on the other side of the personally-tinted dynamism of transference/countertransference.

Roy Schafer's implied criticism of a linear model of development and of an illusionary therapeutic concept is committed to an integral whole. History and identity take place within the personal conditions which include splitting and limitations. However, it can be not only a matter of limiting these within therapeutic analysis, but also to subject them to political reflection and in this way to let them become effectively socially.

Translated from German by
Yvonne Cherne

References

Carpy, D.V. (1989). Tolerating the countertransference: A mutative process. *International Journal of Psychoanalysis, 70*, 287-294.

Mertens, W. (1983/1992). *Einführung in die psychoanalytische Therapie (Band 3)*. Stuttgart/Berlin/Köln: Kohlhammer.

Morgenthaler, F. (1986). *Technik. zur Dialektik der Psychoanalytischen Praxis*. Frankfurt a.Main: Syndikat.

Zimmerman, F. (1989). Optische Anschauungsbilder als Gegenübertragungsphänomene. *Forum der Psychoanalyse, 5*, 237-248.

The Transcendent Function and Psychodrama

Helmut Barz
Zumikon, Switzerland
Swiss Society for Analytical
Psychology

A "very clever young man" suffering from "a psychogenic depression" that had brought him to the conviction that "he is no good, that he has some hopeless hereditary taint, that his brain is degenerating, etc." was "intellectually enlightened as to the cause of his neurosis by a lengthy analysis." Nevertheless, "intellectual understanding made no difference to his depression." His analyst spared himself the "trouble of delving still further into the causality of the case," for he knew that "when a more or less exhaustive understanding is of no avail, the discovery of yet another little bit of causality will be of no avail either" (CW7, par. 344). Instead, the analyst instructed the young man to "accept" the acute mood of "his depression and give it a hearing" (CW7, par. 347). "His mood must tell him all about itself and show him through what kind of fantastic analogies it is expressing itself" (CW7, par. 348).

The young man actually produced "a long and very intricate series of fantasy images" (CW7, par. 345), one of which has been preserved for us.

> He sees his fiancee running down the road towards the river. It is winter, and the river is frozen. She runs out onto the ice, and he follows her. She goes right out, and then the ice breaks, a dark fissure appears, and he is afraid she is going to jump in. And that is what happens: she jumps into the crack, and he watches her sadly. (CW7, par. 343)

The analyst thought to himself:

> The patient really does have a fiancee; for him she represents the one emotional link with the world. Snap that link, and it would be the end of his relation to the world…. But his fiancee is also a

symbol for his anima, that is, for his relation to the unconscious. Hence the fantasy simultaneously expresses the fact that, without any hindrance on his part, his anima is disappearing again into the unconscious.... Once again his mood is stronger than he is. It throws everything to the winds, while he looks on without lifting a hand. But he could easily step in and arrest the anima. (CW7, par. 355).

The analyst did not believe that much would be gained by such an interpretation alone. On the contrary, he maintained that a helpful confrontation with the unconscious would be possible only if the patient experienced the fantasies to the full. By this he meant that "the person of the author should not just be included passively in the vision, but that he should face the figures of the vision actively and reactively, with full consciousness" (CW7, par. 342). Thus, the analyst considered the following:

> The patient would comply with this demand if he conducted himself in the fantasy as he would doubtlessly conduct himself in reality. He would never remain an idle spectator while his fiancee tried to drown herself; he would leap up and stop her.... [Thus,] he would prove that he was taking the fantasy seriously, i.e., assigning absolute reality value to the unconscious. In this way he would have won a victory over his one-sided intellectualism and, indirectly, would have asserted the validity of the irrational standpoint of the unconscious.
> That would be the complete experience of the unconscious demanded of him. But one must not underestimate what that actually means: your whole world is menaced by fantastic irreality. It is almost insuperably difficult to forget, even for a moment, that all this is only fantasy, a figment of the imagination that must strike one as altogether arbitrary and artificial. How can one assert that anything of this kind is "real" and take it seriously? (CW7, pars. 350-51)

The analyst knew of means by which he could help his analysands take their inner fantasy and dream images seriously, for his experience had shown that even affects which are not tied to actions could be shaped by certain techniques: "Patients who possess some talent for drawing or painting can give expression to their mood by means of a *picture*" (CW16, par. 168). "Visual types should concentrate on the *expectation* that an inner image will be produced.... Audio-verbal types usually hear inner words.... Others at such times simply hear their 'other' voice" (CW8, par. 170). "There are others, again, who neither see nor hear anything inside themselves but whose hands have the knack of giving expression to the contents of the unconscious. Such people can profitably work with plastic materials. Those who are able to express the unconscious by means of bodily movements are rather rare.... Still rarer, but equally valuable, is automatic writing, direct or with the planchette" (CW8, par. 171).

The analyst recommended that his analysands sensually shape the material from the unconscious, be it feelings, fantasies or dreams, into the form appropriate to themselves. Thus, they could step out of the role of someone who was passively suffering the influence of the unconscious and into an active participation in the world of images through conscious fantasizing.

Concerning a female analysand who handled her fantasies in this way, the analyst said, "Through her active participation the patient merges herself in the unconscious processes, and she gains possession of them by allowing them to possess her. In this way she joins the conscious to the unconscious.... That is the transcendent function born of the union of opposites" (CW7, par. 368).

The analyst I have been speaking of, of course, is Jung. And all of Jung's quotations that I have used circle around the concept of the transcendent function.

For Jung's analysand who had these fantasies about his fiancee, the transcendent function is practically inaccessible. His conscious attitude is "one-sidedly intellectual and rational" (CW7, par. 347) and "he cannot de-intellectualize himself and make himself dependent on another function, e.g. feeling, for the very simple reason that he has not got it. The unconscious has it" (CW7, par. 347). It is important that he "has" fantasies but, once again, how should he succeed in becoming actively involved in them and in reaching a holistic experience of connection between the conscious and the unconscious? How should he let his feeling, his sensation, even his intuition participate in this experience?

At this point I shall abandon Jung's report and imagine that the young man has the opportunity to participate in a psychodrama session. "Jonathan" finds himself one evening in a group of some ten persons who are sitting on chairs in a relaxed circle: persons of various ages, roughly as many men as women. They appear to know each other quite well and Jonathan feels himself rather inhibited amid the chatting and joking. The leader, an older man, requests that the other members introduce themselves briefly and then asks Jonathan if he would like to tell a bit about himself. Jonathan declines, claiming that he would rather just listen, although he is already feeling more comfortable among these people, who are acting quite natural with one another.

When a young man tells a dream – about his girl friend – from the night before, the non-intrusive response of the others stirs something in Jonathan. He suddenly feels himself called upon to reveal something about himself after all, and – to his own surprise – he tells his fantasy about his fiancee. "The worst thing is that I am so passive. I know that, of course, but it would be artificial if I were to think up a happy ending. That's just the way I am. And besides, the whole thing, thank goodness, is not real."

The leader asks him if he would like to enter into the fantasy again here, but now in as real a way as possible. "In front of all these people?" asks Jonathan, glancing around anxiously. "You will quickly forget the others," replies the leader, "and they will try to be helpful to you."

Indeed, as Jonathan walks around inside the circle with the leader – the others have all moved their chairs as far from each other as possible – he has soon lost sight of the others. The room is filled with a lively tension, but he sees only the wooden paneling of the walls and the carpet on the floor. The leader points out that he doesn't have to say or do anything that he doesn't want to or anything that is unpleasant for him, and that he can break off at any time he chooses.

Jonathan is surprised at how easy it is for him, during the somewhat odd walking in circles, to speak about his life and especially about his depression. The words come nearly all by themselves; it is actually easier than it sometimes is in the analytic hour. He returns to his fantasy: "I know that my analyst is waiting for me finally to actively intervene. But should I pretend to do now in fantasy what I can't do in reality?"

"Let's run through the whole scene – and then see what happens." Jonathan notices that the leader is speaking rather suggestively, but he doesn't feel overpowered. He stops and looks inquisitively at the leader, who then continues, "All right. Where is the street? Where is the river?"

"What do you mean?"

"We want to have the street and the river here in the room, and you are supposed to create it."

Jonathan proceeds and notices how much more credible, more sensual the fantasized scenery becomes, even for himself, when he makes use of the room for it: "Here is the street, it goes somewhat downhill, back there you can see the river, to the left is a bridge." He sees for the first time the attentive faces on the others, but he also sees with increasing clarity the street with the low houses and the slope toward the river.

He starts walking slowly down the street with small uncertain steps. Now he feels two hands on his shoulders and a woman's quiet voice asks, "What do my feet feel?" The leader quickly explains to him that the woman behind him is his auxiliary ego and is more or less speaking out of Jonathan. "What do my feet feel?"

"Oh, yes, those are cobblestones, I'm not used to them." "Where do you know them from?" asks the leader.

"Yes, we had those years ago near our house, this kind of an old cobblestone street. Uncomfortable. My mother called them 'Kitten-heads.' I haven't thought of that since back then." Pause. Then the hands on his shoulders again and the quiet voice of the woman, which he now accepts easily as his auxiliary ego. "What is the weather like now?"

Jonathan: "It is winter. Quite dark. Almost evening already. And not very cold. It could snow tonight. Yes, the air smells of snow." The atmosphere of the wintry street becomes more dense. Jonathan feels cold.

He is somewhat surprised when the leader now asks him to select one of the group members to play his fiancee. "Do I have to?" He looks hesitantly at the woman. That young pretty one there? No, not her. He approaches an older heavy-set woman. "Would you – ?" Then, following the leader's directions, he stands behind her chair while she remains seated. He places his hands on her shoulders, waits awhile, and then says very softly, "I am Miriam, Jonathan's fiancee. I am nineteen years old." Slowly an image of Miriam comes alive; Jonathan almost seems to disappear, so intensely is he speaking out of her and not about her. Thus he can answer as Miriam when the auxiliary ego asks, "What is Jonathan like?" "Ah, Jonathan, he is so far away. I love him. But he…"

The leader asks him to finish "warming up" Miriam: The auxiliary ego carefully leads him out from behind the woman's chair and back onto the wintry street. The auxiliary ego asks, "How do I, Jonathan, feel now?"

"I am sad. I want to stop here. There is no sense in continuing."

The leader asks him if he wouldn't like to run through the fantasized scene after all.

Jonathan is immediately ready and appears grateful. The leader has the lights in the room turned down and vividly repeats some of the descriptions of the street and the river. "And there, to the left, there is someone walking!" Miriam walks in slow motion toward the river and steps onto the ice. Jonathan stares after her and follows her very slowly, as if numbed. Miriam stands before the crack in the ice, and peers into it. Auxiliary ego: "But that's Miriam! What am I going to do?"

Jonathan, tormented: "I can't, I can't." Miriam takes a step in the direction of the crack and then lets herself fall flat on the ground. She has effectively vanished.

Jonathan's face is hard. He doesn't look away. Auxiliary ego: "My shoulders are as stiff as a board. I'm sweating. What do I want?"

Jonathan stares at the crack in the ice. "I don't know, I can't." At this point the young man who had told his dream earlier gets up, goes behind Jonathan, affectionately places his hands on Jonathan's shoulders and, speaking as Jonathan, says, "I want to play through the scene once more."

Jonathan is silent, his face twitches. Auxiliary ego: "Possible?" Jonathan, very softly but earnestly: "Yes, please. Please, if that is possible."

The scene is repeated. The leader insures that Miriam approaches the crack even more slowly than she did the first time. The woman playing Miriam shivers. She lifts her head and looks at Jonathan in desperation. Then she bends over to let herself fall. "No! Miriam! Stay here! Come to me!" Jonathan presses the words out but remains rooted to the spot.

Carefully the leader steps between the two of them and has Jonathan and Miriam exchange places. "Jonathan, you are now Miriam. Miriam, you are now Jonathan." Jonathan stands as Miriam before the crack in the ice; the woman playing Miriam repeats Jonathan's words in his tone of voice: "No! Miriam! Stay here! Come to me!"

Jonathan has completely taken over the gestures of Miriam, turns his head slowly toward the figure of "Jonathan" and says calmly, "No. Jonathan, if you don't come I'll have to jump.

"The leader asks them to change back. Jonathan is again himself. Miriam repeats: "No. Jonathan, if you don't come I'll have to jump." Very slowly Jonathan moves towards Miriam, pulls her one step back from the crack, puts his arm around her shoulders and says, "I'm here. I want to stay with you. No one can hold me back." After a pause, the auxiliary ego asks, "Who is holding me back?"

Jonathan: "Now I know. My mother."

Here I break off my fantasy about the depressive young man's psychodrama and ask briefly what has happened in this symbolic portrayal. I have not embellished the scene in any way. The young man was given an opportunity through the simple technique of psychodrama to create the scene of his fantasy. By really stepping onto the imagined street with his feet and not just in his mind, an actual memory of his childhood (the cobblestones) was triggered, and with this a memory of his mother ("she called them 'kitten-heads'"). Unconsciously, his choice of a woman to play his fiancee was influenced by this memory of his mother; he selected a rather motherly woman, although an outwardly more appropriate person was present.

By warming up the fiancee in the first person, he was not only able to experience her from "within" for the first time, but also to see himself through her eyes: "Ah, Jonathan. I love him. But he is so far away." After playing through the scene and letting his fiancee sink out of sight, he gets to experience an increase of libido, which he cannot produce by himself, through the intervention of the other young man, who in place of him and yet for him expressed the wish to repeat the scene. He would not have been able to stand up for this wish by himself but the auxiliary ego supports him by inquiring, "Possible?" Now he gathers the courage for a second run-through. Although this carries him substantially further – to the request that his fiancee not jump but instead come to him – his body is still stuck in depressive passivity. The step in the direction of his fiancee is beyond him. By means of the role reversal, he then experiences with greatest intensity the difference between word and gesture. He can say to himself – as fiancee and anima – "If you don't come, if you don't make a move toward me, then I have to jump." Thus it is he who provides the decisive push. Yet it comes not from his conscious intellect but from his unconscious feeling, from the anima. This demand is one that he is able to follow, after stepping back into his own role; he does so with a simple gesture.

At the same time he vaguely feels that something wants to keep him from making this gesture. With the help of the auxiliary ego who now asks, "Who is holding me back?" the largely unconscious emotional leap suddenly gives way to a leap into conscious recognition: What is keeping me from grabbing hold of life is not the depression; it is my mother.

I have a suspicion that this intellectual insight alone is nothing new to the young man; probably it has been brought up by his analyst. But the insight gained in the analysis remains abstract, an airy thought which one can hold to be true, or reject. It is not sensual, has no body, is two-dimensional; its comprehensibility stands and falls with the acknowledgment of the underlying theory.

In contrast, the insight gained in psychodrama is manifest. It results from the bodily perceptions of the cobblestones, of the snowy air, of the cold. It presumes no theory but only the ability to empathize. It arises out of the temporary return to the unitary reality in which ego, fiancee, mother, anima are all one and the same.

The insight that it is the mother sitting at the base of the depression and that it is she who is holding the anima prisoner naturally requires introspection and an influx of theory. This means that psychodrama cannot replace analysis, but it can give analysis the dimension of concrete bodily experience of symbolic processes in a way that no other procedure could ever achieve – not even the subtlest processing of transference and countertransference.

The combination of shaping in psychodrama and understanding in analysis enables the unconscious material to be dealt with in the holistic manner described by Jung in his essay, "The Transcendent Function" (CW8). As he put it, "Aesthetic formulation needs understanding of the meaning, and understanding needs aesthetic formulation. The two supplement each other to form the transcendent function" (par. 177).

In his preface to "The Transcendent Function," Jung declared the following question to be the fundamental issue of the essay: "How does one come to terms in practice with the unconscious?" (CW8, p. 67). He holds this to be, in an indirect way, "the fundamental question, in practice, of all religions and all philosophies" (p. 68). Farther on in the essay, he formulated statements that seem to refer to psychodrama. "How am I affected by this sign? This Faustian question can call forth an illuminating answer. The more direct and natural the answer is, the more valuable it will be, for directness and naturalness guarantee a more or less total reaction.... The shuttling to and fro of arguments and affects represents the transcendent function of opposites. The confrontation of the two positions generates a tension charged with energy and creates a living, third thing: not a logical stillbirth... but a movement out of the suspension between opposites, a living birth that leads to a new level of being, a new situation" (CW8, pars. 188-189).

And now, in view of Jung's use of the concepts directness, naturalness, the shuttling to and fro of arguments and affects, picture an average Jungian analytic hour today!

How much argument, how much cleverness, how much knowledge, how much appeal to understanding, how much amplification, how much interpretation, how much good will – and how little "directness," how little affect. Naturally, one asks about feelings (And how did you feel when you woke up?). There are even times when feelings are discussed at length (particularly when they cause a disturbance). But it is true for most analysts as well as analysands that they "try to understand with their brains only, and want to skip the purely practical stage.... Intellectual understanding and aestheticism both produce the deceptive, treacherous sense of liberation and superiority which is liable to collapse if feeling intervenes. Feeling always binds one to the reality and meaning of symbolic contents, and these in turn impose binding standards of ethical behavior" (CW16, par. 489).

Why might it be that all of us in our work again and again tend "to skip the purely practical stage" and take flight into abstract understanding or purely esthetic shaping? Whence comes our fear of letting feeling intervene? What makes it so difficult for us to put the transcendent function to use in its full right?

I suspect that there is more at hand than merely the dispute between literary intelligence and scientific intelligence which C.P. Snow pointed out more than 30 years ago, and more than the repeatedly warmed-over dispute between Zurich and North America. Yes, even more than the discrepancy between extraverted and introverted attitudes toward the unconscious. I suggest that we try in a mythological way to understand our difficulty with letting the transcendent function be at work, even if by this I reveal myself to be hopelessly "Zurich-oriented."

In our confrontation with the unconscious, are we not – in spite of all the theoretical references to polytheism that we hear –

all too fixed upon that one god who loves distance, clarity and analysis: Apollo? Doesn't the training at our institutes, the climate and themes of our Congresses, yes, probably even the methodology of our day-to-day analytic work stand all too exclusively under the auspices of that pure Apollo, whose arrows strike from a distance and who brings about healing precisely by not becoming involved in closeness? And who, unnaturally isolated from the rest of the Pantheon by us, must soon turn from youth to senex?

We have sufficient indications that Jung was no one-sided admirer of an isolated Apollo but rather that, as someone who strove for the union of opposites at all levels, he gave equal significance to Dionysus: ravishing, overpowering, and always concerned with sensual proximity.

All right, you will say, Jung was a genius. But what about us? We have had to put up long enough with being suspect as Jungians: with being mystics, esoterics, naive enthusiasts. We finally want to be recognized as scientists, esteemed by colleagues, respected by patients, reimbursed by the providers of health insurance. What good can Dionysus be to us in these matters?

Thus the Apollonian Jungian comes into being, apparently well-balanced but, behind the scenes, an apprehensive person – unafraid, to be sure, of the ethics committee but just as surely afraid of falling into the grip of what in psychology is called affect and among the gods, Dionysus. Such a person might be perceptive as an analyst, and even helpful, yet unable to activate in analysands something that, as Jung explains, is the decisive factor in the confrontation with the unconscious: the transcendent function.

Jung wrote: "But the confrontation with the unconscious must be a many-sided one, for the transcendent function is not a partial process running a conditioned course; it is a total and integral event in which all aspects are... included. The affect must therefore be deployed in its full strength" (CW8, par. 183). In practice this means, "The unconscious contents want first of all to be seen clearly, which can only be done by giving them shape, and to be judged only when everything they have to say is tangibly present" (CW8, par. 179).

All previously-known possibilities of shaping unconscious contents can be brought together in psychodrama, where thinking and feeling, perception and intuition are brought into play as much as are body and soul, individual and group, outer and inner world, subject and object, Apollonian form and Dionysian emotional involvement.

For those who are unfamiliar with psychodrama: Some of its elements are significant in our present context. I refer to the "protagonist-centered" psychodrama, which is the form that my wife and I have been working with for the past 15 years. It was conceived by J. L. Moreno and further developed by our teachers, Dean and Doreen Elefthery.

Our psychodrama groups, which meet once a week for two and a half hours, are composed of eight to twelve participants who are mixed according to age and sex. They remain together for at least a year and often much longer. All participants are required either to be or to have been in analysis, not necessarily with either of us. Strict confidentiality concerning the group is maintained. At each meeting only one protagonist may enact a psychodrama. Everyone in the group cooperates in being useful to this protagonist – which does not mean being "nice" to the person.

There is no theme that cannot be treated in psychodrama. Whether marriage or occupational problems, finding a place to live, addiction, illness, vague anxieties, phobias or dreams: anything that stirs a protagonist. The topic is not discussed, analyzed or interpreted; it is acted out in the form of one or more scenes. The leader's task initially is to conduct conversation with the protagonist to find an actual or imagined scene, one that both portrays the problem to be treated and possesses enough intensity to insure a dramatic tension. This tension can arise equally well through an epic calm as through "action."

With enough talent for theater – without this one should not be a psychodrama leader – the leader will always seek a scene that contains an archetypal constellation, with or without having heard of the concept of "archetype." Good theater is always archetypal and every psychodrama strives to be good theater.

The protagonist chooses the players in the scene from among the group members and warms them up to their roles one at a time. This is not done with objective descriptions ("You are my fiancee...") but from an attempted identification with the person who is to be warmed up. That is, the protagonist lays hands on that person's shoulders from behind and attempts to speak from out of the role-player in the first person (e.g., "I am Miriam, Jonathan's fiancee"). The protagonist turns the role-player into a projection carrier. In this case he assigns her the role of Miriam, furnishing the role-player with objective information about Miriam and also with elements of his anima.

Thus the role-player, by the time the action of the scene begins, is a symbolic figure in several regards: She is herself as the person on whom the protagonist carries out his transference. She is the one who, with the help of the information received in the warm-up, will consciously "play" the fiancee. She is involved unconsciously when, thanks to her affective participation, she reacts with her countertransference to the behavior of the protagonist.

Yet the protagonist and role-player are far from reflecting upon these connections or even from seeing through them. They are entirely bound into the scene they are playing. That is, they are concerned only with the conscious shaping of the material without paying attention to its unconscious implications.

The elevation of the enacted scene to the symbolic level becomes apparent through an ingenious invention of Moreno's: At a significant point in the dialogue between protagonist and role-player, the leader can call for a role-reversal. The protagonist and role-player exchange places. The role-player then repeats the last sentence of the protagonist so that the protagonist (in our example, Jonathan) experiences himself through the eyes and ears of his vis-a-vis. This exchange of viewpoints, often employed suddenly and unexpectedly, can shake up the protagonist quite severely. At the conscious level he experiences the reality of his conversation partner and the affect that goes out to this person from himself. Yet unconsciously, he apprehends through the symbolic act the reality of what we call the subjective interpretation. For once, he doesn't need to be requested to experience the fiancee as part of himself or to see her as the inner fiancee. Rather, at this moment he is the fiancee as well as himself – not through theoretical reflection but through emotional experience.

There is a further technique through which the role of the body in psychodrama can be seen more clearly. If a significant difference or contradiction is perceived between the protagonist's conscious intention and unconscious gestures, facial expressions or language, the leader lets the protagonist be mirrored through another group member. The protagonist is taken out of the current scene and a group member (if possible, one with a talent for acting) is asked to imitate the protagonist's previous bearing as precisely as possible, without turning it into a caricature. If the protagonist sees and hears himself or herself, say, in a declaration of love, appearing noticeably bland and non-erotic, one can become aware abruptly of an unconscious attitude – sometimes in a shattering way, sometimes in an enlivening way but, above all, in a way that could never be achieved in individual analysis.

These few examples of psychodrama techniques are intended to show what a powerful instrument this invention by the brilliant Moreno represents. This means also, of course, that it is a dangerous instrument, thoroughly comparable to the dangers represented by individual analysis. We are therefore immeasurably grateful to our teachers, Dean and Doreen Elefthery, for their introduction of the auxiliary ego. Throughout the psychodrama this co-therapist accompanies by walking and standing behind, as well as speaking out of, the protagonist. The leader makes suggestions, confronts, demands and challenges; the auxiliary ego, in trying to express the protagonist's unconscious feelings and thoughts, has the function of a "guardian angel" who prevents injuries and occasionally makes the shadow more visible. The auxiliary ego can therefore be supportive and protective at one moment and in another situation either question or spur on the protagonist.

But it is not only the leader and the co-therapist, along with the protagonist, who are responsible for the course of the psychodrama; each member of the group can intervene to help shape the course of symbolic events by "doubling" either the protagonist or one of the role-players. That is, each group member at any time can step behind the protagonist or role-player, place hands upon that person's shoulders and give voice to what the group member feels the player might want to say or is thinking or feeling.

To the extent that the group members have learned not to let detached psychological observations or moralistic thoughts guide them, but instead speak from an empathic involvement, doubling can provide an astonishing enrichment of the personal happenings. Spontaneous ideas and inspirations come not only from the individual but often enough from the group unconscious or even from the collective unconscious. Thus the group is not only a participating witness and a reservoir of players, but is even comparable to the chorus of ancient drama, which embodied the collective conscious as well as the collective unconscious.

I have attempted to show how we, as Jungian analysts, might engage the transcendent function as holistically as possible. Our difficulties in dealing with unconscious material, as I see them, lie less on the side of intellectual understanding and interpretation, but far more in the realm of shaping it, where shaping means more than mere esthetic objectification. If the effect of the transcendent function is to allow something new to emerge, a living third thing, then it requires the union of all the opposites: collaboration of conscious and unconscious, of interpretation and formulation, of reason and emotion. With many of us the aspect of emotional formulation does not receive its due. Consequently, I have introduced you to an approach that has directly enriched my work as an analyst.

You will seek or have already found your own paths. If you happen to be dissatisfied with what you have tried up until now, and as long as you have a talent for theater and no insurmountable fears of that gripping god of theater, Dionysus, then go learn psychodrama!

Translated from German by
David Oswald

Response

Elizabeth Strahan
Fullerton, California, USA
Society of Jungian Analysts of
Southern California

This enlightening, provocative and enjoyable paper presents psychodrama as a tool for engaging the transcendent function. Barz's imaginative trickery in the introduction engaged us in a fantasy/memory of an analytic encounter constructed from a composite of Jung's work. I deeply appreciate the position that psychodrama can be a valid and powerful tool for healing. But most of all the paper set off in me some important though subtle effects: I found myself feeling more light-hearted in my work: more interested, more daring to do or say what came to me in the hour, more playful.

I studied drama in undergraduate school and used psychodrama techniques quite extensively in my work with children early in my practice as a psychotherapist. I have felt sad to notice how much of my own spirit I have dampened in my efforts to be extremely attentive to "tightening up boundaries" in my work. Barz's paper made me aware that I had become heavy and too careful. No wonder I was so tired!

I have been inspired to bring more of myself into the work; I have responded to those pertinent moments in which role-playing ("now I'll be you and you be the stranger in the dream") facilitates a visceral experience of an archetypal image or an affect. I have felt freer to insert moments of dialoguing with an affect or an image, to invite the analysand to draw the "disfigured tree" or to shape in clay the tension she feels in her stomach. I have found myself able to shuttle back and forth between a classical analytic style of quiet holding, listening attentively, and intervening with suggestions for more interaction with images and/or affects: through a kind of in-the-hour active imagination using roleplaying, dialoguing and creative formation – as well as making transference/countertransference interpretations. I have been inspired to "loosen up" and experiment more freely and more deeply while holding to the boundaries of the analysand's own process. I feel reinspired to be myself in the analytic container while facilitating an atmosphere in which the analysand can be also. This is the essence of what it is to be a Jungian analyst. It is this mysterious art which we try to draw forth from candidates in our training programs and for which we search in our examining committees.

Barz has dared to confess his own art as an analyst. He has told us candidly how he works. I think that one of our greatest collegial problems is in sharing with each other what we actually say and do. Out of that gap (which is enhanced by fancy theoretical footwork of both developmental and archetypal tunes) creeps a dark shadow of secrecy and competitiveness, veiling our personal anxieties about the worth of our work – maybe even about ourselves – as well as our collective doubt about the value of analysis itself. We all share in the existential secret that we know nothing about what we are doing. As Barz pointed out, we try hard to be a science. But the psyche is so elusive, so paradoxical and so unknowable that we are constantly dumbfounded.

I hope that we can follow Barz's example and tell each other more often and more plainly about our everyday work: what our own idiosyncratic approaches to the psyche are, how we coax people into a relationship with the unconscious or into some kind of relationship with us. We may have theoretical differences that bear examining, but I expect that the integrity of our work rests with our willingness to honor the richness and variety of our individual differences in expressing the Self. Perhaps Jung's willingness to be truly who he was (however obnoxious, unshamedly intrusive, overbearing, incisive, unconsciously entangled, brilliant, uncannily wise, loving, etc. that was) and to tell us about it was his gift and his challenge to us. He met the Unknown without claiming to know it.

Jung's seminal essay, "The Transcendent Function" (CW8), presents the fundamental issue of our healing art: "How does one come to terms with the unconscious?" Barz has added psychodrama to the list of approaches to "active imagination" identified by

Jung. Both Jung and Barz stress the element of "actively" engaging the unconscious. Traditionally active imagination, whether drawing or painting, or dialoguing and recording it, molding in clay or dancing was done outside the analytic hour, either alone or with such guides as art therapists and dance therapists. Even sand-tray work sometimes is outside the analytic hour with a person other than the analyst. We now question the "work" done outside the session as a possible defense; and we worry about the "split transference" inherent in the second relationship. In Los Angeles, we are still rather paranoid about group work of any kind, creating what I consider to be one of our primary shadow issues: the unconscious formation of little cliques which arise out of the archetypal need for group or community.

As I remember my own early analysis, 20 or so years ago, it was primarily an experience of reporting on my dreams and the active imagination I had done with them, sometimes experiencing affect in the telling and sometimes receiving interpretation and amplification from my analyst. There was little talk about transference in those days. Even worse, amplification often included being read to from one of the esoteric volumes in the analyst's library (pretty Apollonian) or being told stories from the analyst's own life (pretty Dionysian).

It was not all bad. In fact, it was very helpful in many ways: I felt better, I knew myself and my complexes better and I even changed some. Upon reflection I think what probably worked, even then, was the peculiar mix between the two of us, especially when my analyst allowed his own eccentricities to show, when he allowed his own Unknowingness to be in the process. He was a second generation Jungian; that is, his analyst had worked with Jung.

Most of those first and second generation Jungians are gone from our Los Angeles group now. We, third generation practitioners, are the elders now. We are a more eclectic group, I think. We have had to do some soul searching, even some outside-the-fold-analysis, to find our way in the modern general psychoanalytic community. We have had to live with our anger at not feeling very well analyzed, our frustration at trying to find a good analytic situation for ourselves as well as trying to provide better training for the next generation. Some of us have had to suffer greatly through the moral, ethical and legal difficulties of acting out sexually with a patient when such incestuous behavior was accepted practice by our predecessors. We, in the United States, have been (and are) in a tumultuous transitional stage. Every examining committee on which I have sat has spent a great deal of time trying to define "What is a Jungian analyst?" What do we consider to be effective Jungian analysis? This question is everywhere present. For example, one may hear such comments about Barz's paper as: "Well, it is very interesting and perhaps helpful, but it is not Jungian analysis."

We scrupulously examine our colleagues' comments in meetings and conferences for hints of whether they are developmental or archetypal, Kleinian, Kohutian and so on. Out of lack of real dialogue about what we do in practice we entertain fantasies about each other. Then, if we are not careful, we carry those fantasies to our candidates. On the more positive side we are becoming more openly challenging to each other about how we work. This openness, I think, will alleviate much of the feeling of anxiety and splitting in our institutes. We are always hard-pressed, however, to define exactly what is a Jungian analysis. I dare say that each of us thinks we are doing Jungian analysis and that we also have deep questions about whether we are doing it right.

Barz makes a disclaimer for psychodrama's being Jungian analysis: "Psychodrama naturally cannot replace analysis, but it can give analysis the dimension of concrete bodily experience of symbolic processes in a way that no other procedure could ever achieve." Again, he separates the active imagination experience from the analytic experience. He points out that all participating members of a psychodrama either are or have been in analysis. We need to consider how we function differently in analytic hours from psychodrama sessions and how, as Jungians, we differ from psychodrama leaders of other orientations.

I appreciate Barz's suggestion that the mythological underpinnings of differences in the way we practice could be described by Apollo and Dionysus. I agree with him that the splits within our institutes are not primarily along lines of developmental and archetypal, reductive and synthetic/constructive, masculine and feminine, or extraverted and introverted. These opposites are inherent in the practice of each analyst, inviting the enlivening and transformative energy of the transcendent function.

Barz's image of the healing gods – Apollo and Dionysus – as the mythological backdrop behind our differences is a very interesting and pertinent concept. In the United States Dionysus is purged from our consciousness as thoroughly as possible. Consequently, he bursts forth in the madness of cults, sexual promiscuity, divorce, "gang-banging" and so on. Dionysus shows up in our consulting rooms in compulsive sexual involvements with analysands, usually by male analysts. Culturally we are devoted to Apollo while Dionysus continues to impinge on us from the unconscious.

The transcendent function can be engaged in both an Apollonian and a Dionysian way; our differences arise out of projective identifications of our split-off parts as analysts. Perhaps we are at a new stage of development in our work in which another of the elements from Jung's shadow must be carried by us into consciousness. Are we now at the place where we can bear the tension of Jung's concern whether our work is science or art? (Remember that fateful question he reported from his mother about one of his sketches, "Is it science or is it art?") Jung makes too many proclamations about not being a mystic and demonstrates far too much talent as an artist, both in his temperament and in personal drawings in his "Red Book," for us to ignore his rather obvious fear of his genius as an artist who wants to be a scientist. There is also his continual struggle between psychology and religion, which we carry forward. Ann Ulanov speaks eloquently and often about that pair of opposites and how they are united through the transcendent function in analysis. And John Beebe in his new book, *Integrity and Depth*, challenges us to look into the shadow of Jung's work which we have inherited along with its brilliance.

While holding Apollo and Dionysus as opposites in my imagination, I have found myself wishing for a goddess to emerge as the transcendent function. But instead came Eros, that sharpshooter from afar who, with his self-inflicted wound, succumbed to the realm of Dionysus when he fell in love with Psyche and went with her to his underworld realm. Might the "third" in our split be Eros, that son of Aphrodite, our great mother, who marries the human Psyche and thus enthrones her in the Olympian realm? Might the tale of Eros and Psyche be re-viewed as a paradigm of the analytic process itself? In our work we certainly fall in love with Psyche. And like Psyche we catch a glimpse of the beauty of Eros and must suffer many tasks in order to win his union in marriage. It would be interesting to follow the tale along those lines.

I have thought it would be healing and enlivening to bring such myths into consciousness through a kind of "performance" psychodrama, acting out the story in groups such as analytical psychology clubs. It seems to me we need such community rituals. I have had at least two powerful experiences of the validity of such dramatization. Betty Meador, a San Francisco analyst, put together a small troupe to enact the Sumerian story of Inanna. I asked to play a small part because I was so touched by a performance I had seen. I was surprised at the intensity of the experience of the acting. At a seminar I led last year, I invited participants to read parts in A.C. Gurney's play "Love Letters." That experience brought considerable depth to the seminar and was remembered by most as the highlight of our week's work about relationship. I wish we had opportunity for acting such stories as an adjunct to analysis.

Barz's presentation of psychodrama as a powerful tool for engaging the transcendent function is inspiring and convincing. He has given us a clear description of how it works and why. I conclude with some rather obvious questions about the work. What are some of the dangers we may encounter? How may we experience our participation with the analysand in terms of the transference? Does psychodrama interfere with the formation of a necessary transference? Does it intensify the transference? How can we deal with the dependencies which may be created by assuming such an active role in the analysand's process? And, finally, how do we find people conscious enough to participate in such a group effectively? And what can we do with the rivalries, projections, and other archetypal dynamics of group interactions which are bound to occur?

Living, Ignoring, and Regressing: Transcendent Moments in the Lives of a Child, a Transsexual, and a Sexually Regressed Adult

Lee Roloff

Evanston, Illinois, USA

C.G. Jung Institute of Chicago

Differentiated and primitive, conscious and unconscious are united in the symbol, as well as all other possible psychic contents. Whenever such a symbol comes spontaneously to light from the unconscious, it is a content that dominates the whole personality, "forcing the energy of the opposites into a common channel," so that "life can flow on... towards new goals." Jung called that unknown activity of the unconscious which produces the real, life-giving symbols the *transcendent function*, because this process facilitates a transition from one attitude to another. A still-living, genuine symbol can thus never be "resolved" (that is, analyzed, understood) by a rational interpretation, but can only be circumscribed and amplified by conscious associations; its nucleus, which is pregnant with meaning, remains unconscious as long as it is living and can only be divined. If one interprets it intellectually one "kills" the symbol, thus preventing any further unfolding of its content. (von Franz, 1980, p. 83)

Todd

When Todd first appeared in the sandplay room he was almost four years old: bright dancing brown eyes, a curious twinge of a smile and a sturdy agile physique that was at his complete command for climbing, crawling, moving quickly. Todd was the older of two siblings. His brother came into Todd's life when he was two and a half years of age. Before his brother's birth, however, Todd had experienced serious and invasive surgical procedures in his anus and lower intestines, an experience that his parents knew had been traumatic for Todd. Experiencing the sudden appearance of a brother had not been easy, though by every observable and historical evaluation, his parents had given

careful attention to Todd and his needs. They gave a report of
two presenting symptoms: an inability to control bowel movement and an unwillingness to allow others to touch or hold him.

Todd's play world was a complex amalgam of electronic and
reactive playthings, an interest in sports and sports figures and a
keen interest in music and musical expression through an electronic keyboard. Both parents are brilliant professionals in a
highly demanding field of endeavor but, since the second child,
the mother has temporarily forsaken her career to be mother and
nurturer. The most immediately obvious characteristic of both
parents is that they are highly verbal, engagingly articulate and
committed to the lives of the two children.

Todd had a shyness, however, and a rich interiority of discourse to which few outside the family were admitted. In the
sandplay room he spent most of the early sessions searching for
the toys of his choice: a miniature word processor, toy soldiers
and motion picture and television figures of the Ninja Turtles.
Once the toys had been placed in the sandtray elaborate games of
divide and conquer would begin. As he progressed, however, he
raised the level of articulation so that he might be overheard and
his play shared with his observers, who had become parental
figures of another kind: silent and permissive overhearers of
psyche's stories. A woman child analyst and I were his observers. Always observant, always caring, always watchful, we became symbolic parents to the child searching for the boundaries
of permission and containment.

A precise moment in the life of Todd at age four brought the
power and presence of the transcendent function into our lives as
a living reality. In a move that has no rational accountability, and
drawing only upon the observation that Todd played with sword-
wielding figures, I withdrew from a container in the playroom a
bamboo stick about one meter long. I also withdrew one for Todd
and gave it to him, and holding the bamboo stick thrust forward
said, *"En garde*, Todd!" Todd, knowing just what to do, matched
his bamboo sword to mine, touched it gently and repeated the
phrase, *"En garde!"* In the middle of the playroom, then, was an
adult man and his small charge poised for fencing. I said, "Todd,

I want you to hit my sword as hard as you are able." He gently tapped my stick. "Harder," I said. Todd allowed a little more striking power, but not much. "Todd," I said, "I want you to hit my sword as hard as you can!" Finally, swinging his sword as hard as he could, he knocked the sword from my hand. A most engaging, full, and satisfied smile crossed his face. He stood facing me with his arms akimbo and said, "I really did it, didn't I, Lee?" And I said, joined by my colleague, "You were wonderful, Todd; you are really strong and powerful." There the session ended.

Before the next session Todd's father, as it happened, took Todd to a swimming lesson and, because the parental conference had not taken place for that week, Todd's father had no knowledge of the "sword incident." The swimming lesson was a diving lesson. The children were asked to walk to the end of the low board and simply tumble into the water. Todd walked to the end of the board and, according to the father's report, froze. His father urged him to fall into the water. There was no movement from Todd. After what seemed an agonizingly long time, Todd uttered something incomprehensible to his father, who asked Todd to repeat it. Todd, looking directly at his father said, "*I have lost my sword!*"

We ask ourselves, "At what age does the symbolic process begin? At what age does the life-giving symbol become a living reality for a child? At what age can a symbol become a facilitating transition from one attitude to another?" The answer is – from one case, at least – by age four. By that age the living transcendence can be experienced. The degree to which it is assimilated by a developing ego remains to be tested. What I do know is this. Sometime later, it became necessary for Todd to undergo another invasive, though less serious, surgical procedure. I promised Todd that I would be with him prior to surgery at the hospital, a promise which I kept. As we sat together on his bed playing with things he had brought to the hospital, I said, "Have you brought your sword? You will need to be strong today." "Oh sure," he said, "I brought it." He went with a tense bravado to surgery and his recovery was quick and swift.

The sword was only a bamboo stick; it became a psychological necessity as well as inner reality. "Ego consciousness seems
to depend upon the capacity to differentiate one thing from
another and to make value distinctions between them," observe
Moore and Gillette (1992). "This idea," they continue, "is related
to the 'masculine' principle of discernment. Though not an exclusively male preserve, the mythic image of discrimination is of
the sword that cuts through confusion" (p. 141). What, in a four-
year-old boy, is the consciousness that knows when a sword is
"lost" and "when he has it with him"? It is true that his father and
mother were working diligently to empower Todd, and that another "father" (his male therapist) and his biological father were
empowering Todd symbolically. But it is Todd who must know
the sword, believe in the sword, and hold the sword – acts of
considerable psychological complexity, but available, it seems,
to a four-year-old.

In assessing the incident of the sword play and its assimilative
symbolic presence in Todd's life I consulted another psychologist and child analyst familiar with symbolic development in
children. What happened between Todd and me was in pure play,
in an intense moment, in which "playing being strong and powerful" constellated the *kairos* of the appropriate mythologem, a
moment of pure assimilation in which everything became sub-
sumed to "play" necessities. So strong was his sense of safety
that Todd could tell his father that he had lost his sword, mitigat-
ing the power of the father, at the same time helping the father in
a transformative attitude toward his son. In defeat, Todd, at four,
made a valiant attempt to claim his own authority. It takes
strength to de-integrate; it is play, the ludic moment, that gives
the imaginative symbolic power of an assimilative truth. Todd is
living a transcendent moment, a life-giving symbolic intensity
uncontaminated by rational interpretation.

As Todd matures he will need and gather other "swords" –
penetrating intelligence, a capacity to break through confusions,
a sensitive "phallic nature" and the discovery of a king within.
As Moore and Gillette remind us it is the sword of the masculine
that is the sword of gnosis, the knowledge that began one sum-

mer's afternoon at the end of a diving board for one little boy, age four.

Abbey

Abbey is a tall, blond, stunning woman who was born a gendered male. I knew her briefly as a male during high school years when mother referred her son to my office for "emotional reasons." As it turned out, the son was an active homosexual teenager – attracted to much older men – who, even at that time, loathed his maleness and his genitals. Somehow, things became stabilized enough, and because financial pressures were so great for the family, this teenager left therapy to pursue a college career and sexual life. Two years later, I again received a call, but this time from a young woman, Abbey. The voice I recognized; the name I did not. Abbey informed me that I had known her by a male name, but that now she was in the process of changing her sexual identity and anxious for me to see her. The decision to see Abbey was a fateful one for me.

Nothing in my training prepared me for the challenges I had to face. I was entering into a process that had not been initiated in an analytic setting; I found little understanding regarding trans-sexuality in the literature of Analytical Psychology; and, finally, I found myself cast upon a journey into a post-modern sensibility augmented by medical and surgical procedures that could be had, in various parts of the world, merely for a price. The case of Abbey precipitated a moral crisis in my soul that I had not anticipated nor, obviously, desired; a phenomenon that is so often the case in working with transsexuals.

In the case of Todd, the epiphanic, living reality of the intangible symbolic potential had a healing and deeply reassuring quality. While the history of Todd's invasive surgeries could evoke an empathic resonance, the surgeries of Abbey's journey became nightmarish and disturbing of my own inner equilibrium. There were times my body would become racked with a sympathetic pain, even nausea. Of all these countertransferential somatic responses, not one occurred in a session. My neural nightmares occurred only in reflecting on the case, of reading the surgical procedures to be involved. At one point, I recall, I wondered if I had ever dreamt of a transsexual, if there were a symbolic presence of the case Abbey was presenting in my own personal history. It took going through dream journals for the past 30 years, but I did find a dream that I had met Christine Jorgensen, possibly the best known public personality of the 1950s to make the transsexual journey. I cannot explain why that dream was so re-assuring, but it has helped me in dark recessive ways to grapple with the case of Abbey.

It is the vocabulary of the post-modern era that I want to point out: destruction, reconstruction and deconstruction. These inflected forms of *construction* provide an understanding of the forces of post-modern cultural consciousness and unconsciousness. For what seems to be true of culture is all too true of the human body: The destruction of one gendered body for the reconstruction of another gender is a frequent occurrence. There is the additional assumption that inner psychological processes lead to this deconstructive/reconstructive process. If there be a facile manner in which to encapsulate the post-modern sensibility, it might be summed up as follows: Gender is not destiny. Everything about the body can be deconstructed and reconstructed through chemistry and surgery. With research currently investigating the possibility of male bodies carrying a fetus, the topsy-turvy world is an ordinary deconstructive imagining. The sex act is no longer a necessity for the fertilization of the ovum. The tacitly assumed world of investigation that Freud and Jung explored for the formulation of their shaping of interiorities no longer exists.

What the post-modern world view seems to state in psychological terms, at least, is something like this: *Where ego is, id shall be.* And that, when all the complexities of Abbey's case are put aside, is precisely what she posited in my consulting room. Transsexuality begins with a conundrum: "I am gendered male, but inwardly I am a woman in a male body." The reverse pertains likewise: "I am gendered female, but I am a male trapped in a female body." Transsexuals and transvestites are more concerned with maleness and femaleness than anyone else. The dichotomy is a severe one, and "androgyny" or "unisex" or "bi-sexuality" are of no interest in the deconstructive movement of transsexuals.

One further observation: in this post-modern world and its sensibilities, it is not psychology that is immutable in its pre-mises against a changing and chaotic world. It is, rather, psychol-ogy that becomes mutable, changing and variable in response to the mutability of the collective. Or, in a mode I have come to learn all too well: It is not psychology that changes persons; it is persons who change psychology. Jung taught this and we must learn from it.

Did Abbey ignore the promptings of her inner life, and did I function in such a way that did not adequately mirror and reflect the "promptings of the Self?" "To ignore" suggests "to refrain from noticing, to disregard the nature of something." This was Abbey's strong and insistent ego position: "Everyone simply ignored the fact of my true self, that I played with dolls, that as a child I wore girls' clothing whenever possible and that I had no interest in anything masculine, except attracting the male sexual-ly." In an autobiography Abbey had to write for her surgeon, she observed:

My sister [younger than Abbey] and I always dressed up in my mother's clothes. We had several friends from the area whom my sister and I would play with. One of our favorite games was playing "house." We would all pretend to be members of a family, and I always played the female roles. I wanted to be the mommy, or the sister, or the aunt, or the grandmother. When our father saw me dressed up this way, he would tell me I should be playing in his old clothes and not in my mother's. I always tried to humor him, because I enjoyed having his approval, but it was not fun. My mother was much more tolerant, although she never encouraged me to cross-dress in play. I also spent many hours playing with Barbie dolls. I wanted to grow up to look just like Barbie, tall, blonde, and beautiful. My mother perceived my "different" behavior as an artis-tic quality and kept me quite busy after school and on weekends at home with various art projects. The thing I enjoyed most about these times was being given approval to wear an apron.

I mentioned that Abbey is a tall, blond, stunning woman. At that moment I had no awareness that she had, in fact, become the living representation of a Barbie doll. This widely popular doll appeals to pre-pubescent and pubescent girls. As the "baby doll" awakens the mother archetype in the child, Barbie awakens the goddess Aphrodite, a love doll concerned solely with seductiveness, appearance and her beloved opposite, Ken. Together these two inhabit a never-never land of magical weekends, resorts, and "situations," including marriage. Can one ignore her fascination with the love goddess? Can one ignore the fact that in choosing Barbie over Ken, Abbey might be telling the truth about the viable and living presence of the feminine within her personality at a very early age?

I can report the psychological facts, and I have not ignored them, but I do not know if they are true; I know that they are true for Abbey. If there are archetypes of life, meaning, and transformation, who is to determine what the archetypal forces will become, particularly in a post-modern society when the ego can purchase virtually any transformation of the physical body it desires? With already achieved and maintained levels of estrogen hormone, with already the process of the male body's deconstruction into the constructed female presence, and with already implanted presences of silicone in the body to augment and emphasize female configurations, what, in truth, can be ignored? Virtually anything but murder.

Abbey spoke often of killing the male she had been. While it was not casual talk it verged, it seemed to me, upon a certain carelessness, of an unwillingness to confront what was being destroyed, a destruction of her past and her birth gender identity. Where, in point of fact, was the so-called transcendent function that would lead her into a consciousness of her new situation? Two important dreams occurred, approximately two months apart, that led her into "accidental" and "injected" awareness.

Dream 1: I am driving south on the drive next to Lake Michigan. I come to a tunnel, a tunnel that does not exist, but in my dream is a part of the drive. I enter the tunnel and I discover that the police are there blocking traffic. A policeman waves me by. At the very center of the tunnel where it reaches its lowest point, I find a small car smashed up, but I drive on. I then know that I must go back to the accident. Behind the wheel of the crashed car is a man. The man has a horrified look on his face. "My god," I think, "he's dead!"

Dream 2: I am in a wooded area. I see a low modern building, one story, and the walls are all of glass, a lightly tinted glass. I hear over a loud speaker, "We're about to make the injection." I know what this means; it means that there is going to be an execution by means of injection. I look into the building. A man in a white coat injects another man lying upon a table. The man groans. A lab technician asks, Do you need another injection? He's almost dead, but groaning." I look at the man on the table and I think, "How attractive he is. He is my Ideal Man."

These dreams of accidental death and execution by injection brought to memory a recurrent dream that Abbey experienced between the ages of eight and ten, as a young boy living in terror of the father.

I am at the end of a bowling alley lane. I feel that I am a part of the pins. I hear a ball rolling down the alley. I am terrified. At the "thump" of the ball on the bowling alley lane, my terror begins. As the ball rolls towards the pins my terror increases and increases until I awaken with my heart pounding.

To observe that Abbey was resistant to the images of the murder she was engaging in is to understate the matter. "I hated him, I did not want to live in his body, and I did all that I could to change my life and body," she would state again and again. "I suppose that you want me to grieve for him? I suppose that you expect me to be sorry for what I am doing?" she would rhetorically ask me. My answer: a steady gaze into her eyes. And then an astonishing thing occurred unexpectedly and dramatically. She said, "What I have killed, I will love. What I saw in the car and what I saw on the table is my ideal man."

This much she said. But I would like to put my interpretation into a fictive dialogue that Abbey did not utter, but of which she eventually had some degree of consciousness. What I would have her say is this, "Because I could not become the idealized boy/man my father wanted me to become, I can do that now by having an actual relationship with him." Or, in the language of Analytical Psychology: Only by crossing over into the body of the feminine can the ideal masculine become the animus energy of my new feminine. This is nothing else but a total and post-modern deconstruction and reconstruction of Jungian psychology. In the old Freudian world, you may recall, men have perversions and women have neuroses (Garber, 1992). Moreover, perversions concern having something and neuroses have something to do with not having something. In the physicalization of transformation, of surgically surrendering the male body, including the penis, Abbey's task was and is to love what she had ignored, what she had turned away from and turned toward. Something very tender was killed by male balls thundering down her ally in childhood and by being, it would appear, only "a sitting pin" for a destructive and voracious father.

Clearly I have reserved the greater part of Abbey's personal history in the interest of a specific point: That we can be led to the transcendent moment of the meaningful symbol even by choosing at some level to ignore it. Transsexuality is one of many post-modern elements that causes the profoundest "cultural anxiety," to borrow Lopez-Pedraza's (1990) trenchant phrase. "Cultural anxiety," he suggests, acts us out because "our deepest conflicts are cultural, something that psychology cannot evade" (p. 34). Currently, those most articulate in the social phenomenon of transsexuality are sociologists, behaviorial psychologists, ethnologists and a few medical ethicists. The literature often has what I would describe as an omniscient detachment, of little or no help to the soul.

Fleming and Ruck (1979) have concerned themselves with what they term "a mythic search for identity" in a case of a transsexual, though the case they note is a female-to-male transsexual. They observe, "Some people... do not seem at home in the world in which they were born, and seem to be deviants or anomalies... [inventing] their own private mythology, an idiosyncratic system of beliefs and myths which play as dominant a formative role in their lives as does the traditional mythology in the lives of those from whom they are alienated" (p. 298). For

Abbey, the myth is Aphrodite in the banalized form of Barbie; her dread is her Ares father. The children of Aphrodite and Ares are Fear (Deimus), Panic (Phobos), Harmonia and Eros. Abbey has known the extremities of fear and panic; she is finding a measure of harmony in her own nature and, one hopes, love. After a prolonged period of alienation and absence from her biological father she visited him, not without fear and panic. Astonishingly, the boy the father never knew, and who died both an accidental and irrevocable psychic death, appeared to him as a tall and beautiful woman; he accepted her and told her he loved her.

The purpose of Sufi discipline is to prepare oneself for a gift of incalculable value. In preparation for this gift, the searcher becomes a female saint, a *waliyeh* who, we are told, sits among the women because he is, for the moment, "changed into a woman." So powerful is this moment that there is a desire to transform the soul into poetry, a soul which is expressed with the feminine pronoun. A concluding line from such a poem reads, "Through her I went forth from myself to her and came not back to myself: one like me does not hold the doctrine of return" (quoted in Bullough, 1976, p. 235). Abbey is far beyond the point of return; in her own fashion she holds to the "doctrine of no return." After reporting the dreams of the beautiful young man, at the end of that hour of ignoring and facing, Abbey cried. She is not completely unaware.

David

David is 39 years old, a mental health professional with solid educational and professional credentials, including a doctorate. He is respected by his peers. He is openly gay; he would specialize in the treatment of gay and lesbian persons if the opportunity presented itself. He has studied and written on the topic of sexual infantilism or, more precisely, "the adult baby," and he is obviously familiar with all the clinical languages and discourse surrounding his interests and passions: fetishism, paraphilia, sexual dysfunction, fixation and regression.

He came to a Jungian analyst because (1) the power of his interest – meaning the symbolic power – would be understood best by a Jungian; (2) a Jungian might be more disposed to deal with his issues and be free of the "rant and cant" of clinical language and diagnosis; and (3) he was looking for the "father" he had never had. His statements were, in short, a "no nonsense" approach to me and I could "take him on," as he put it, or refer him to someone else. After several days of soul-searching, I agreed to meet with him. At the time he began work, he had not completed his degree and monograph on the topic of "the adult baby"; the completion occurred during the time that I saw him.

Though I have been confronted with virtually every aspect of his performed infantilism, I was impressed at our first meeting, as I am presently, by the power and authority of his adult male visage, an almost hallucinatory transposition of image when I am in his presence. And it has been David, perhaps more than any other recent analysand, who has presented me with the analytical conundrum that haunts my speculations: What is it in the lives of persons that absolutely insists that that which might be psychological and hence mental, must be literalized, concretized, behaved, enfleshed, acted out, presented? Even more importantly, what is it when that which is being concretized carries within its enactment the very nature of the transcendent function, and a symbolic possibility becomes actualized? Why is it that a child, Todd, who lives in the unfolding development of play, has the ability to psychologize an inner symbolic reality while astonishingly brilliant and sensitive individuals such as Abbey and David must become what cannot be psychologized?

A child's play, a physical transformation, and an adult's enactment of infantilism suggest radically different modes of psychic discourse and behavior; in a post-modern sensibility that culturally condones and provides the services necessary for physical transformations and enactments, the familiar ground of cultural continuity has been replaced by crossing-overs and discontinuities. It is important before reflecting further on these concerns to place David's "adult child" in a cultural and personal context.

"The adult child" is a performance event, highly charged with sexual overtones and enactments. Through computer networks worldwide, individuals can communicate with other "adult children" 24 hours a day, from Bangkok to Berlin, Chicago to Manila, San Francisco to Haifa. These individuals are not pedophiliacs nor are they interested in sexualizing relationships with children. The obsession is the helpless child, alone in a crib or playpen, diapers wet or soiled, waiting and desiring to be bathed, held, loved, stroked, kissed, fondled. The fixation then moves to a literalizing and a physicalizing. The adult then becomes the child, discarding adult clothing for diapers, plastic pants, adult made-to-order infant clothing. Once contacts are made, meetings are arranged for periods of time suitable to both, perhaps a day to a week to a month in which the adult baby is cared for, fed, nurtured, held, loved. All aspects of life become regressive, including feedings with bottles and specially prepared foods. After periods of extended play, the roles are abandoned and adult sexual contact occurs.

The hallucinatory response that I experienced in being with David can be understood better now. During various sessions, though not all, there have been presentations of the "the adult baby." In the intensity of the analytic hour the child becomes a *mysterium tremendum* in psychological power and presence. Like a thin steel wire, the pull of the undifferentiated and abused child archetype lures both analyst and analysand to a paradoxical moment of differentiation and non-differentiation. Like a colossus, the adult child strides the borders of consciousness and unconsciousness.

Jung noted: "In the individual, the archetypes appear as involuntary manifestations of unconscious processes whose existence and meaning can only be inferred" (CW, 9-I, par. 260). When the transcendent function has become an obsession, when it has become lodged in *materia*, when it has been an ego-compulsive necessity to investigate and to write regarding it, when the ego has virtually exhausted its ratiocinations; then the archetypal manifestation that is clearly beyond the individual's choice becomes like "being hit by a projectile sent by an overpowering being that transfixes us and brings us into its power. At the same time we are assailed by fantasies and imaginary images experienced either as proceeding directly from the inner world... or, more often, as caused by an outer object" (von Franz, 1980, p. 24). Yet, it is, I believe, precisely the ratiocinations, the elaborations and the endless defenses that have lodged the archetype of the "adult baby" into the relentless physicalization it demands.

> The archetype... is a psychic organ present in all of us. A bad explanation means a correspondingly bad attitude to this organ, which thus may be injured. But the ultimate sufferer is the bad interpreter... Hence, the "explanation" should always be such that the functional significance of the archetype remains unimpaired, so that an adequate and meaningful connection between the conscious mind and the archetypes is assured. For the archetype is an element of our psychic structure and thus a vital and necessary component in our psychic economy. It represents or personifies certain instinctive data of the dark, primitive psyche, the real but invisible roots of consciousness. (CW9-I, par. 271)

The function of the child archetype, the form in this case being "the adult baby," is (1) a fragmentary part of a cultural malaise that has seriously endangered the child and the archetypal foundations of the child; (2) a revelation that certain phases of an individual's life can become autonomous, and actually result in a vision of oneself; (3) an image and symbol functioning in the present to compensate or correct the one-sidedness of the conscious mind.

The meaning of the child for David remained beyond the sophisticated and articulated research and comment submitted for his degree. Yes, there had been childhood deprivations, humiliations and abandonments; their recall was accessible and communicable. For Abbey what psyche materialized and incarnated that might have been psychologized, or transmuted into psychological insight, or relieved from the incarnational, simply no longer was an option. The physical enantiodromia is an irreversible reality in Abbey's case at this writing. Such is and was not the case for David, but so long as the power of the archetype persisted there could be no change. Then, in a development that was spontaneous and synchronistic, the analysis itself became transmuted by the alchemy of discourse.

The moment of dialogue developed over David's terrible pain and loneliness that his own "adult child" created.

David: It's my goddamn naiveness that hurts.

Analyst: What do you mean?

David: Just that. No one likes it when a person is naive. Its just too fucking difficult in a fucking adult world.

Analyst: [pause] I do not know what has happened, but I think we ought to check what the word, *naive*, carries in its history. What are you saying about yourself that is really important?

David: Yeah. Go ahead. Look it up.

Analyst: Well, it says that to be "naive" is to have an unaffected simplicity, to be untaught, to be unsophisticated, to be frank, to be simple.

David: [begins to cry] I have never been allowed to be that. Only baby can be that way.

A simple word, *naive*, spontaneously erupting and interrupting – that is "rupturing" a moment's duress – became an emotional affordance and functioned, in all of its poignancy and affect – as the archetypal presence of truth, healing, possibility. David has not abandoned "the adult baby," indeed, he must not; he is learning, however, a new candor, frankness, simplicity, and openness in language that is a "baby talk" of an "adult kind." Through regression, in an astonishing and important way, came the possibility of relief and pursuit of adult relationships based not on dominance and passivity but, rather, mutuality and respect.

Epilogue

Four-year-old Todd, in the miraculous phenomenon that is the development of consciousness and the ability to think, feel, and know the symbolic power of the symbol, is already equipped with some of the "powers of nature and instinct." He is living for the future. Abbey, who at a crucial point in her own transformation began to dream with a female dream ego, is attempting to transform agonies of the past, self-hatreds, and narcissistic wounds into something altogether different: a post-modern woman in a post-modern world in which aspects of a physical body can be deconstructed and reconstructed in something of her own image, a modern Aphrodite whose knowledge of fear, panic and physical and psychological harmony might be merged with love. The physically completed transsexual is a reality in our post-modern world: their presence creates anxieties whether they write (Jan Morris), compete at tennis (Renée Richards), haunt dreams (Christine Jorgensen) or sit opposite analysts in consulting rooms. David's sexually regressed "adult baby" is linked with other "adult babies" on all the continents of this globe, in instantaneous communication with each other, and parenting each other in ways that cannot help but, for some, cause extreme cultural anxieties. David found his own "baby talk" and perhaps his new-found language will lead him, as it led Todd, to a moment of consciousness. Death is not usually an immediate association with the words "transcendent" and "function." And as Abbey discovered, and as we discover from Abbey, we sometimes "kill the thing we love, the thing we shouldn't kill at all." Abbey is a beautiful woman originally gendered male. That she has had to ignore, turn away from and kill a part of herself is the story telling her, injecting what once was him; creating what now is her (the objective pronouns the only viable ones to employ). David is a handsome, aging man who knows more about regression than I, though I thought I knew something. It is a new language of the soul that he is learning.

References

Bullough, Vern L. (1976). *Sexual Variance in Society and History*. Chicago: University of Chicago Press.

Fleming, M; Ruck, C. (1979). A mythic search for identity in a female to male transsexual. *Journal of Analytical Psychology* 24-4, 298-313.

Garber, M. (1992). *Vested Interests, Cross-Dressing and Cultural Anxiety*. New York: Routledge.

López-Pedraza, R. (1990). *Cultural Anxiety*. Zurich: Daimon.

Moore, R.; Gillette, D. (1992). *The King Within: Accessing the King in the Male Psyche*. New York: Morrow.

von Franz, M.-L. (1980). *Projection and Re-Collection in Jungian Psychology: Reflections of the Soul*. LaSalle, IL: Open Court Press.

The Perverse and the Transcendent

Ann Belford Ulanov
New York, NY. USA
New York Association for Analytical
Psychology

A man of 76, Helmut, seeks analysis. "What brings you?" I ask. "I have suffered from a perversion for 70 years," he answers. Was he sure he wanted to be rid of it? Consciously yes, very much, he said, but unconsciously he did not know. Had he sought treatment before? Once, briefly, years ago, with a Freudian who reduced his perversion to a congenital foot injury corrected after birth. That made no deep sense to him so he stopped therapy. Later he had conversations with a Jungian, conversations which introduced him to Jung, whom he had read ever since, but the discussion of archetypes was too general, never reaching to the core of his complex. Why me? I asked. Because of my dual profession in religion and analysis, he said; the religious part was essential.

This case shows, I believe, that the transcendent function works to loosen the grip of well-entrenched perversion, that it builds up the ego at the same time it constructs the Self and that the transcendent function working within the psyche connects us to the Transcendent itself in whatever ways we experience it. The opening conversation told me that a purely reductive approach would not work, an archetypal approach that omitted the guts and gore of addictive compulsions would not work, and that whatever he meant by religion, it was going to be central.

What he called his perversion turned out to be a complex with many facets. A gripping fantasy – no longer acted out with prostitutes – of domination and degradation by an all-powerful female dressed in black, often with whip or boot, compelled his prostration in complete self-abnegation. "I want to become nothing, to disappear," he said. In one version he saw himself tightly encased in black leather, including his face, nailed to a cross with silver nails, not able to move an inch, like a parody crucifixion. A compulsive fascination with wide, shiny, black patent leather belts – their smell, taste and touch, their tightness around a woman's waist or his own – lured him to purchase them and to spend hours fingering them. Donning a woman's dress and standing before a mirror, he cruelly tortured his nipples and climaxed in orgasm through masturbation.

Maps of Masochism

Various schools of depth psychology map the territory of masochism, fetishism and transvestism in ways that proved helpful in unraveling this man's vast suffering. For Freud and his followers the erotogenic transformation of pain into pleasure springs from reversal of the oedipal drama. The parent we desire becomes the dispenser of punishment instead of caresses. We disavow our genital inadequacy to satisfy our parent sexually, by exalting pre-oedipal parts, procedures and body zones, thus obliterating at one stroke the differences between the sexes and the generations. The aggression of the death instinct makes one the pleased victim of another person's power and authority. By fetishistic devices we avoid the oedipal conflict and threat of castration, insisting that we alone are the object of our mother's desire, thus disqualifying the father. A man in woman's dress simultaneously displays and defeats his identification with the phallic female because his penis under the dress is real and achieves orgasm. By eroticizing a frightening sense of deadness, we seek control in the theatrics of being controlled.

Berliner (1947), Horney (1939) and Menaker (1979) map masochism as a defensive ego-strategy to survive overwhelming anxiety about being annihilated. Relinquishing ego-autonomy in order to avoid such anxiety, we stay at a preambivalent early stage of development and cling helplessly and dependently to the person who makes us suffer. We introject the other's disparaging attitude toward us and become unlovable. Neglecting to build other relationships that reflect our worth, we know only experiences of self-depreciation to which we add self-condemnation. Terror of being abandoned stirs our aggression toward our love object; we feel guilty, deserving punishment. Yet we seek secret control of others by relentlessly positioning them in a superior role.

Object-relations theorists see masochism as an expression of psychic pain experienced before the self clearly emerges from the other. Winnicott (1951, 1984) finds the fetish a transitional object that gets stuck in a delusion of an impinging maternal phallus. Instead of the creative living found in the illusory transitional space, the fetish confines us to addictive literalizing of what should be symbolic.

Khan (1979) says that we sexualize events as our way of remembering before an object relationship develops. We build up a collated internal object out of archaic body experience, undifferentiated from bits of mother and father, primarily to cope with a dissociated unconscious element in our parent. We idealize this created object, surround it with intensified fantasy, and substitute it for the more ordinary initiation of experience with a caring parent into an imaginative play space and a developing symbolic life. Hiding in our compulsive routines is psychic pain we have lived and lost in dissociation. We dread total collapse and hold ourselves together against the threat of annihilation by fetish rituals, cross-dressing and libidinized pain that remains under our ego control.

The Self Psychology theorists see masochism as arising from desperate attempts to foster the rudimentary self in a desert of isolation. Kohut (1979) sees such fantasies and activities as feeble attempts to provide a "feeling of aliveness" and to separate in a healthy way from engulfment in the mother. Thus we maintain psychic structural cohesion.

Jung and Jungians

For Jung, neurosis is "a defense against the objective inner activity of the psyche,... to escape from the inner voice and hence from the vocation.... Behind the neurotic perversion is concealed [our] vocation" (CW17, par. 313). To reconnect with our lost vocation takes a double move: reduction to instinct that leads back to reality and its overvaluation, thus necessitating sacrifice; and synthesis of symbolic fantasies that result from sacrifice. "This produces a new attitude toward the world,... a new potential. I have called this transition to a new attitude the transcendent function" (CW6, par. 427).

We engage in a continual process of "getting to know the counter position in the unconscious" (CW14, par. 257). We admit the other and engage our differences with it; in turn, it engages us with its views, expressed in image, emotion or behavior pattern. Out of this conversation – which is often a struggle – emerges a symbol, a third point of view that formulates a uniting of the two, conscious and unconscious. It is "a creative solution... which is... not unjustly characterized as the voice of God. The nature of the solution is in accord with the deepest foundation of the personality as well as with its wholeness" (CW10, par. 856). The "transcendent function is not something one does oneself;... it cannot be invented.... The experience of it does not depend on our will" (Let-I, p. 269). It is "equivalent to a renewal of life;... the soul is born again in God" (CW14, par. 427). But this involves a perilous "descent to the *deus absconditus*" (CW6, par. 427).

When caught in perversion, we treat this renewal with disrespect instead of loyalty, getting caught in the shadow side of our psychic need to venerate something beyond ourselves. Connecting to the transcendent function, working within our psyche, opens us to the hidden god in the midst of the opposites and transcendent to our whole psyche. We listen through the perversions to receive a bulletin from the Self to our self. Only thus do we find our vocation, what Jung called living according to the will of God. We break down false organizations of self and other to break through to joyous knowledge that we are known.

History

Helmut had three histories: his life, his perversion, and the unfolding narrative of his analysis which – intertwined with the other two and the transference – produced symbols that brought him home, deep down inside himself and into relation to the Transcendent far outside himself. Work with him had to go backward to the origins of his long-standing masochism and, simultaneously, forward to the purpose it was trying to accomplish.

Born and raised in Germany into an upper-middle-class family, Helmut arrived as the unexpected twin of a sister who was eagerly awaited. He was "found" in the womb after her birth and became the favorite of both his parents. His left foot, originally turned backward, making his left leg weaker and slightly shorter, was corrected early by a cast. He remembers no teasing or fuss made about his leg, and it did not come up in unconscious material. He and his twin sister were the third and fourth of eight children.

He remembers being fascinated with shiny belts at the age of five, and at seven wanting to be beaten. He remembers wanting to be his sister and to dress in female clothes. At six he nearly died from attacks of influenza and meningitis. His next older brother, who was his mother's original favorite and his own, did die, but Helmut was so ill his parents did not tell him for some weeks.

At the end of our first year of work, many years after the events, he learned crucial facts from his nephew, his sister's child. (The nephew had been raised by Helmut's mother after her sister died.) Helmut's mother, the nephew revealed, had felt very guilty about Helmut's brother's death. She felt she had not given him enough food even though, because of rationing at the end of World War I, there was simply not enough to go around. The nephew also described Helmut's mother as so overwhelming in her display of motherly affection that she ruined life for her brother-in-law, the nephew's father. He never dared marry again for fear of greater hurt to the already wounded maternity of his sister-in-law, Helmut's mother.

At puberty Helmut remained utterly naive sexually until he saw dogs copulating and a friend enlightened him. Then masturbatory fantasies of submitting to a dominatrix came to possess him. At the same time he had an ardent crush on a girl his age which he did not live out. In his twenties he had two long affairs with older women, one with a golf pro in Germany, one in Asia. These he described as normal in feeling and sexuality. He remembers his childhood as happy, his mother as beautiful and loving, his father as wanting him to succeed him in business – which he longed to do to emulate his parent. His twin sister, who like his younger sister died in her thirties from stomach cancer, was the aggressive one; Helmut was a gentle, dreamy boy. When his twin grew up she too became another powerful mother. His religion was calm enough; conventional Protestant. Though interested in spiritual matters he felt no connection to God or Christ.

Helmut felt business was the wrong occupation for him and that he had wrecked many opportunities because so much energy had been detoured into fetish and prostitute activities. He felt inferior to other men and, though he had some male friends, never felt himself "one of the boys." He was often cheated by partners because he lacked ruthless force. In analysis he came to mourn what his perversion cost him: in money, in business failure, in wasted life. "I used so much of my life in pursuit of my complexes which produce nothing."

An immensely happy, steady part of his life was meeting, marrying, and living for over 50 years with his beloved wife.

Falling in love with her and standing up for her in a courageous way made one of the first bridges between his dissociated life and his ordinary life in business and with his family. He spoke simply and ardently about her and their life together, of their daughter and granddaughter. He said loving his wife had been the most important aspect of his life. She knew about his obsessions but not their extent or their power. Her common-sense attitude, seeing them as nonsense he should conquer, was upset when he entered analysis. Equal to it he now rated the investigation and healing of his perversion.

Just as the Nazis began to rise to power, he fell in love with a beautiful, talented painter from a prominent Jewish family. His parents were not pleased and sent him to Asia on business to get over her. When he returned to Germany, Hitler was in power. It was 1937; Helmut was 26. He saw clearly that the Nazi movement would destroy his country; his opposition to it put him in opposition to both his parents. His father even suggested that Helmut join the Brown Shirts. Stunned, Helmut exclaimed, "I would not dream of it!" The new racial laws which banned marriage with Jews intensified Helmut's struggle with his parents. His father said, "Oh, forget about her. You've had affairs before. Don't let her determine your life." Helmut replied firmly: "It exactly does determine my life and it is the greatest injustice to me and to her to say that. It is insulting to her family, which is a great family, not to care what happens to them."

Helmut told his mother he would marry. His mother said, "You are no longer my son," and left the room. "I wept bitterly," he said, "like a primal scream, for five minutes. Then I finished with it, went downstairs and joined the ongoing dinner party. I never had a warm feeling toward my mother and father after that. I left the country." After the war he returned to see his parents, who were "extremely nice," but cool when he spoke of Hitler and the terrible camps. Helmut said he felt he went wrong there: "I was righteous and not forgiving."

He told this tale in a matter-of-fact way, as if it revealed nothing unusual about his behavior. Yet the theologian, Paul Tillich, said that he had to get out of Germany because, though consciously he knew it was wrong, unconsciously he was not sure he could resist the tremendous pressure and danger of the Nazi environment. And here was Helmut, wracked by psychic illness and chronic inferiority feelings, simply standing up to everyone he loved, to his government and to his culture, saying, "No, it's wrong and I won't do it!" His capacity for love and his wife's connecting with his true self opened a deep channel. The energy usually locked up in his perversion flowed together with his love for his wife and enabled him to begin life anew in another land, another language, another culture.

The Work

Helmut's history made clear that a whole quadrant of his sexual life occupied itself with libidinizing pain. We found that he reversed his oedipal desire for his mother into being punished for his oedipal strivings and his pre-oedipal incestuous wishes. He was conscious of wanting to disappear into the womb and to become female, thus avoiding oedipal conflict. Helmut received scant support to use his aggression to separate and individuate; instead he detoured it into a fantasy loop enacted in belt and submissive rituals where he projected his aggression onto a dominating female.

In persisting over months in this retrospective analysis, we came upon a live bit of Helmut's true self, a small boy hiding and surviving in the perverse fantasies. This discovery initiated his awareness of the transcendent function. The masochistic rituals and fetish routines told the story of this lost boy in the only way possible, preverbally and preconceptually. It could not be told in words, but only in symbolic facts. Helmut and I listened again to the perverse fantasies. We found something crucial in this little boy. The man felt deeply touched and his obsession with belts loosened its power. Energy formerly detoured into the loop of masochistic fancy Helmut now used to receive this part of himself. He claimed his ego.

Helmut had been a dreamy little boy, unlike the conventional masculine figures of his family and culture. Imaginative, sweet, speculative, feeling-centered, meaning-preoccupied, he was not a rough and ready boy. His introversion was surely heightened by the confinement in a cast to correct his foot. Full of feminine sensibilities and passion, loving his mother and father, loved by them as their favorite, he was captured by love. How could he disappoint them? Hurt them by being different from what they wanted? Abandon their plans for him in business by pursuing the arts instead? Part of his self-punishment grew from this wish to go another way and thus hurt his parents. This boy of imagination degenerated into a boy of compulsive fantasy centered on punishment.

In therapy Helmut wept for this boy and felt finally that he could love him. Second to meeting his wife, he said, this was the greatest event of his life, to enter into relationship with this lost part of himself. Indeed, it was this boy that his wife – with her artistic sensibilities – touched in the grown-up man, that enabled him to stand against the pressures of family, society, and government.

With his claiming of this boy, a new impetus entered our investigation of Helmut's repetitive fantasies that featured two archetypal females: a white and a black fairy. Lilith, the black fairy, claimed him at birth as her plaything, mixing a dreadful brew of incestuous love for his mother, transvestite desires for his sister's dresses, jealousy of his father. Prostrate at her feet, he lusted to be her slave. In thrall to Thanatos he wished to destroy himself. Then the white fairy, Sophia-like, banished her sister by changing her into a snake. But the black fairy revenged herself with a curse: He would see in every shiny black patent leather belt a symbol of her serpentine power over him. The white fairy countered with a promise to aid him by bringing a wife whose deep love would help overcome the temptations against which he must strive with all his might.

With the boy in mind, Helmut now entered into active dialogues with the black and white fairies, thus engaging the transcendent function. Instead of submitting to the fantasies Helmut took on the fantasy figures in conversation, making his will felt. He no longer wished just to banish the black one and dismiss all his complexes. He looked to see their view of things, perhaps because they had functioned as the hiding place of the boy. Rapprochement grew between the two fairies and one day the resultant fantasy surprised him. The two fairy women decided to exchange belts, so that the one all in black now wore the white belt, and the one all in white now wore the black. This lessened his wish simply to kill off Lilith and live happily forever after with Sophia. I stressed the integration of the split between the two images of the feminine and this led us to the awe-inspiring mother figure behind the split.

Helmut called his mother-image Gaia: lovely, loving and huge in power. She never displayed aggression openly; none of her children did either. The violent aggressivity of Helmut's fantasies, we came to see, reflected his mother's dissociated, undifferentiated aggression that lay all about him. Her genuine lovingness frightened anyone who loved and depended on her into stifling any aggression they felt toward her for fear of hurting her. We concluded that the mother's undifferentiated aggression hindered Helmut's differentiating his own. She remained in his unconscious as the original phallic mother. In wearing women's clothes but clearly remaining a functioning male with erection and ejaculation underneath, he was displaying in action something he experienced before words came to him: his mother's power there under her soft dresses, her phallic aggression under her lovely femininity. He thus showed that his masculinity survived under his feminine identification with her.

It was as if his mother were only the "good breast," and he lacked a personification of the "bad breast" (Klein, 1948, p. 34). Helmut felt a phobic dislike of rubber nipples and pacifiers. We speculated that his twin sister, as the first daughter, more often got the breast and he – the third son – got the bottle, and that he coped with his rage by detouring his aggression into a loop of punishment fantasies. The little boy took on the task of differentiating mother, not just for himself but, we suspected, for her undifferentiated and impinging aggression.

But Helmut was stuck there. No environmental provision encouraged his differentiation into his own self, different from his family. His aggression stayed primordial, archetypal. I risked the interpretation that when his brother died and his mother felt swamped with guilt, Helmut identified with her, taking on her suffering as his own. I believe that his mother identified with the earth-mother archetype; to lose a child was the worst possible sin. Helmut's punishment rituals were in part to expiate his mother's guilt. Still more darkly, he may have felt that here was a female who felt herself in charge of life and death, blaming

herself for his brother's death. Helmut may have been struck
with terror at her power, thus reinforcing the ban against any
show of his own aggression to challenge it. He too might be
killed!

The Unfolding

Our reductive analysis opened into synthetic work; we uncovered purposes toward which Helmut's complexes were striving.
The transference figured centrally. Three months into the work
Helmut felt he had fallen in love with me, and in his writings
called me Athena, as a symbol of an intelligence that allowed
him to reflect on the Gorgon-like power of his complexes. His
love sprang from his catharsis of confiding in detail secrets he
had kept for 70 years, from what he found to be my warm interest
and my taking his problem seriously without judging him and
from our discovery and care of the little boy together. In addition,
I came to link the opposing archetypal white and black fairies for
him by refusing to let him spiritualize his problem as a way of
getting rid of the perversions. I insisted instead that we engage
them and penetrate their meaning.

He also felt power in me; when we had to work out the
schedule, he started to position himself submissively, apologiz-
ing for pushing me too much and was astonished when I said not
to worry, I would push back. That remark broke up any incipient
masochism in the transference and brought the dark feminine
into the room for Helmut. He could make use of me to carry
some of the Lilith power. For the first time, Helmut felt himself
in relation to a woman holding both the black and white powers.
It was at this time in active imagination that the "exchange of the
belts" occurred. During the next month his obsessions decreased
so markedly that he declared himself cured. I was touched by his
relief but kept to myself the fact that this was a transference cure.

From my side, I respected Helmut, recognizing how much he
had suffered and how much effort he was putting into his analysis. I found it hard work to figure so centrally in the transference
– to find how to confront without hurting, and to analyze the hot

passion without insulting him. At one point I said, "To be obsessed with me is not much better than to be obsessed with the old rituals." He said, "Oh, but it is because it is more normal." "You have a point," I agreed. He said, "I see what you mean: it is not the goal." "Exactly," I replied; "the goal is to live that energy, to see what it brings you and wants from you when it is no longer dissociated but part of you."

The belt fetish gobbled up a lot of energy. It expressed the intrusion into his psyche of his mother's unconscious dissociated aggression. Helmut pulled the belt tight to create a woman's waist, as if to hold himself together against the disintegration of his fledging masculinity. The belt also linked him to the mother he loved and his feeling of being in thrall to her power which he could now control in her surrogate. The belt joined him to the feminine side of himself, which did not accord with any conventional masculine role and had had little chance to be mirrored and grow. Altogether, the belt functioned as a link to the boy who was the lost true self and to the unintegrated aggression belonging to him.

After the April exchange of belts between the black and white fairies, in July Helmut prayed to Sophia, offering her the patent leather belt and all it stood for. In August, he dreamt that he tried to give me the belt but found half of it grown into his skin. In December he did something dramatic that followed on our fall work. He bought a belt, brought it to the session, asked me to put it on, saying, "This is a sacrifice. I give the whole thing up to you with a prayer to God to be freed and to give it all to God." I stood up and put on the belt, saying, "I receive and accept it." After a few minutes I took it off, to Helmut's distress and said, "This belt is symbolic, an important part of our analytic work. I cannot wear it as a personal gift." Helmut said, "You take the belt and the perversions. I get the link to Sophia, who loves the boy as he is." In April of the following year, Helmut threw away his entire belt collection, accumulated over 60 years.

During the previous fall Helmut had been dreaming the sadistic side of the masochistic adaptation of his aggression. He was shocked, but I was encouraged. First, and harmlessly, he dreamt

I was teaching him to play tennis. To this he associated his tennis pro's telling him his game was too defensive; he ought to go on the attack. But then a series of dream images alarmed him. He was looking behind a curtain for murdered children, he was strangling a mouse that would not stay dead, he saw across a gulf between Palestine and Israel a man mercilessly beating a horse, he was being chased by storm troopers. What stood out in all these images was the horrific pain he felt; it was no longer libidinized into pleasure.

His unconscious also punctured his idealization of me, first in an October dream where he and his wife are lying on the ground watching the rise of a giant moon. It suddenly falls and he sees that it is a paper moon, a lamp on a pole which sticks in the ground as if to light the way. He said of the dream, "It shows my love for you is illusion, lighting the way, but not real and ground-ed as is my love for my wife."

The second dream came the day after he gave me the belt. We have a session in a hospital, but therapy with a young woman goes on in the same room. Helmut protests, but I say nothing can be done. I look sweaty, grubby from the hard work.

Following this dream he wanted to stop analysis. He said that I had fallen, like Sophia, into matter, where he found how hard it was to attain the treasure, namely, his whole self. In addition to his resistance, the dream also showed a new feminine part quite outside his perversions, one fully occupied with her own treat-ment.

In the winter his wife's objections to his analysis intensified and Helmut felt caught. I stood firm against the struggle's being described as wife versus analyst. That would only preserve the split Helmut suffered, now once again a struggle between two powerful women. He must decide his course and stand for what he believed. So he entered into another dialogue of opposites – love for his wife and love for the self he was finding in analysis. This opposition was a striking replay of his early conflict be-tween either following his soul and hurting the woman he loved, whether mother or wife, or pleasing her at the cost of his soul. The aggression once detoured into perversion was now much more available to Helmut and he used it to differentiate his mother projection from his wife, and consciously to relate to her distress. With conscious psychic suffering, as opposed to sexualized pain, he decided to give up his analysis at the end of June. "This is real suffering," he said, "not masochism." This was a sacrifice, born of his love for his wife.

I watched my countertransference closely for I felt vulnerable, not in sexual but in analytic passion. I had added hours to my schedule to work with Helmut because his problem fascinated me psychically and because I felt he really wanted to settle this lifelong complex to live more freely before he died. I was afraid he was once more sacrificing his soul to please the woman he loved, but I remained firm that he must decide and follow his own way. In my way I felt the pain of sacrifice too, because our work was being stopped in the middle.

The next fall Helmut contacted me but I had no free hours and I felt I had to wait on the Self, so to speak, to open up hours if we were to continue. Early winter that happened and we worked again through June. He returned, saying his transference had quieted down but was still there. He had read Jung's work on transference and apologized for breaking off treatment. He saw now how much the analyst was involved. He also had persisted in telling his wife what understanding his perversion meant to him, to be himself and not just a persona. She grasped this, yet also criticized his tendency to give too much power over to the other – in this case, the analyst.

In the previous year's work, Helmut had told me of praying to an unknown god for forgiveness for wasting so much of his life. In one prayer he felt no audible answer but knew that "the slate was wiped clean." In our final spring's work, he said he had felt a conscious longing to worship something bigger than himself rather than to submit and be punished. He felt that the erotic longing concealed veneration. Reading Willa Cather's *Death Comes for the Archbishop*, these words struck him: "Where there is great love, there are always miracles." He said, "Feeling great love for Athena, I prayed for a miracle and the love turned into a blue flower which grew in my heart, a symbol of God's love."

This image shifted the transference in a major way. Helmut thought of me now as a messenger, a link, not a goal. A theological change also occurred. Before, he had asked God to take care of him – wipe the slate clean, forgive him, free him from his complexes. Now he felt he must take care of God – to tend this blue flower within.

Jung's remarks on the symbol of the blue flower addressed Helmut's estrangement from any established religion, his longing for connection to the transcendent, and his idiosyncratic sexuality that mixed feminine and masculine. Jung wrote, "the 'blue flower' of the Romantics looks back to the medievalism of the ruined cloisters, yet… modestly proclaims something new in earthly loveliness…. A friendly sign, a numinous emanation from the unconscious," shows the "modern man… robbed of security… where he can find the seed that wants to sprout in him too…. For the 'golden flower of alchemy'… can sometimes be a blue flower: 'the sapphire blue flower of the hermaphrodite.'" (CW12, pars. 99, 101).

This sprouting happened in mid-March when Helmut dreamt of visiting a hospital nursery where a baby girl lies critically ill. Small and starving, she may die at any minute. He asks a doctor her chances of survival. Maybe, is the reply, but only if the child is very well cared for.

About his dream Helmut said, "The dying baby is my newly born faith in God, that precious little thing I had felt inside me that I did not take care of." He felt that I, too, was stern with him for neglecting what had been given him.

He imagined feeding the baby regularly, but in the fantasy it was clearly not enough. Then a series of synchronistic events strengthened his confidence. He remembered suddenly all the paintings of Mary feeding the Christ child; he prayed that she would help him. Then a librarian returned to him a postcard from his daughter, found in a book he had returned. On it was a reproduction of the angel of the Annunciation foretelling to Mary her coming motherhood. He went home to a nap. When he awoke, a vision of the heavens opened to show Mary nursing his baby. Then a blinding light came toward him. When it vanished, he found his baby lying in a cradle, now strong and healthy. Full of gratitude, Helmut also noticed that this baby got the breast, not a rubber nipple.

A dream two weeks later carried the theme further. Here a blue hyacinth in full bloom stood before Helmut and a small pinkish hyacinth grew next to it in the soil, like a daughter of the blue flower. He felt the new life was now grounded, planted in soil. I noted the interchange of the pink and blue flowers, like a new born anima and a faith in something beyond himself.

But, like most of us, Helmut's road was up and down, off as well as on. In late April he dreamt again of the baby girl, again neglected but now older, about four. This child stands naked and alone on a dangerous subway platform. She enters a train, and curls up in a corner and sleeps. No one pays her any attention. Helmut kneels, full of pity, to care for her and sees that she has vomited in her sleep. What should he do? He worries, then decides to take her to a nearby hospital. He picks her up in her arms, knowing she is his own baby.

Thinking about the dream, he realized she had grown and was strong now, sure of herself, healthy. She was somewhat androgynous, he felt, and reminded him of his early desires to be a girl, though he never really wanted female genitals. How had she been nourished, despite his neglect, he wondered? Who had been taking care of her? He did not feel so guilty as in the first baby dream. He felt this child was his, inside him, and not really his but connected to something outside him. He felt Sophia in the wings.

In May, several dreams recalled young women on whom he had crushes when a youth. He likened his transference to me to that kind of falling in love, a "bolt of lightning" but now these actual women from his life carried that emotion. In these dreams his wife has gone off to the Fiji islands. We talked about the differentiation of this anima part of him as his own, adding unmistakable zest to his life. A final dream, before we ended in June, featured Helmut in bed asleep. His wife enters. "She kisses me and says she loves me. I glimpse Athena in the next room reading peacefully in bed and tell my wife to close the door and lock it."

Summary

The transcendent function working in a man's psyche loosened the grip of what he called his life-long perversions. They told the coded story of his effort to keep his true self alive by detouring his aggression into a loop of fantasied masochistic submission, fetishistic compulsion and transvestism.

He entered that inner conversation between opposites – of conscious revulsion and unconscious thralldom, of struggle to free himself from belts and obsession with them, of dialogue between black and white feminine powers, of conflict between analysis and wife, of suffered versus libidinized pain. When he entered it, a solution occurred "in accord with the deepest foundations of the personality, as well as its wholeness; it embraces conscious and unconscious and therefore transcends the ego" (CW10, par. 856). The little boy, the blue flower, the baby girl who began to grow up – all symbolize life outside the loop of perversion and link Helmut to life beyond himself.

Through this inner conversation of the transcendent function within the psyche Helmut gained access, as we all may, to conversation between the psyche and what lives beyond it. It is as if we thought we were conducting a two-way conversation only to discover that it was in fact at least three-way. For Helmut this was symbolized by his feeling that some small piece of God had taken up residence within him, which he needed to keep caring for and relating to. Consistent with his love for his mother, and difficulties with her, his love for his wife, his transference and working it through, his image of God was feminine – the divine Sophia.

The November following his June termination, Helmut sent me a dream: "A young female student shows me a postcard she received from Athena who did a little drawing in the left corner in red ink. Suddenly Athena is across the table from me.... I looked long and closely into her face and deeply into her gray eyes and was so overcome by her earnest expression, I had to look away to suppress my tears."

His immediate association, he said, was that of an encounter with the unconscious. The little-girl anima continues to grow up and is linked to the work of analysis as she receives word – or images – from the analyst. Helmut was most struck by the unforgettable expression in Athena's eyes – visible compassion and admonishment for the future. It was not the real Athena, he said, because of the gray eyes instead of my own actual blue and brown ones. "What moved me so much," he concluded, "was that this was an encounter with my unconscious and this new part of me, the anima."

Helmut had reached a new attitude toward his life and his perversions. This attitude enables him to live more fully before he dies.

References

Berliner, B. (1947). On some psychodynamics of masochism. *Psychoanalytic Quarterly, 16*, 459-71.

Horney, K. (1939). *New Ways in Psychoanalysis*. New York: Norton.

Khan, M. (1979). *Alienation in Perversions*. New York: International Universities Press.

Klein, M. (1948/1975). *Envy and Gratitude and Other Works 1946-1963*. New York: Delacorte Press/Seymour Lawrence.

Kohut. H. (1979/1991). The two analyses of Mr. Z. In P. Ornstein (Ed.), *The Search for the Self* (Vol. 4). Madison, N.J.: International Universities Press.

Menaker, E. (1979). Aspects of masochism. In L. Lerner (Ed.), *Masochism and the Emergent Ego: Selected Papers of Esther Menaker*. New York: Human Sciences Press.

Winnicott, D. W. (1951/1975). *Through Paediatrics to Psycho-Analysis*. New York: Basic Books.

Winnicott, D. W. (1984). Aggression and its roots. In D. W. Winnicott, R. Shepherd, M. Davis; *Deprivation and Delinquency*. London: Tavistock.

Wisdom, J. O. (1988). The perversions: A philosopher reflects. *Journal of Analytical Psychology, 33-3*, 229-249.

Aspects of the Person

Decoding the Diamond Body: The Structure of the Self and the Transcendent Function

Robert L. Moore
Chicago, Illinois, USA
Chicago Society of Jungian Analysts

In recent decades there has been a puzzling tendency in Jungian circles to move away from the fundamental metatheoretical assumption that Jungian analysis is a psychology of deep structures and from their implications for human life and behavior. There has been a decreasing emphasis in Jungian conferences and publications on the concepts and phenomenology of the collective unconscious/objective psyche. An accompanying trend is an uncritical acceptance of the hyper-modern influences of "postmodernism," "poststructuralism," and "deconstructionism." Related to these influences is a tendency to miss the significance of what I consider to be a crypto-Adlerian deconstruction of Jungian theory by the Archetypal Psychologists. A second trend is the increasing influence of a crypto-Freudian reading of Jungian theory; it involves the uncritical acceptance of models and methods from the Freudian tradition, leading to an increasing and unbalanced emphasis on reductive analysis and the personal unconscious.

Rediscovering Jungian Psychology

These trends – which of course have made positive contributions to our communal discourse – are grounded, I believe, in a well-founded reaction against popular Jungianism as a cult, one which treats the *Collected Works* as "the Black Bible." There is, however a better alternative – that of working to move Analytical Psychology forward, building on Jung's most fundamental insights, but correcting his errors as we find them and using current scientific and cultural research to deepen, elaborate, and extend the reach of our distinct school of psychoanalysis. Theory matters, and we need to expand the research of Jungian hermeneutics without unwittingly regressing into more truncated paradigms. The model I outline in this brief paper is an attempt to follow this latter course.

Into the Labyrinth: A Sketch of My Research Journey

Elsewhere (Moore, 1992) I have discussed more extensively the research journey which led me into a realization that I was engaged in an attempt to decode the Diamond Body (CW9-I, par. 637), the quaternio and double-quaternio. My early studies of the archetype of the magician in occult practice led me into studies in comparative mythology which focused in turn on the mythologies of kingship, the warrior (or knight), and the lover. I slowly came to realize that these four figures were constantly presented in dynamic interrelationship in the mythologies of masculine selfhood from around the world. Collaboration with mythologist Douglas Gillette enabled me to sharpen my understanding of these structures in the mythic imagination and their psychological dynamics and implications. Our series of five books (Moore and Gillette, 1990, 1991, 1992, 1993, in press) explicate these findings.

It was relatively late in this research journey that I began to realize that there are four parallel feminine figures that, together with the masculine structures, constitute the structural forms of the archetypal Self. At this point I began to realize that Jung's fascination with inner couples reflected intuitions into the structural dynamics of the Self that have been intuited only vaguely by most researchers, including Jung himself. This new view of the structure and dynamics of the Self – focusing on four couples within – while confirming many of Jung's most basic theoretical assertions, took me in a direction intuited, but not fully developed, by Toni Wolff (1956). Let me now turn to a brief summary of this alternative decoding of the quaternio and double-quaternio.

Decoding the Diamond Body: Beyond Jung

Given contemporary tendencies in the Jungian community to either crypto-Adlerian deconstructionist formulations of psyche or of ill-disguised crypto-Freudian ones, many Jungians today seem to have forgotten the nature and depth of Jung's commitment to the idea that the human Self was structured in a way that reflected both a quaternio and a double-quaternio (imaged in octahedral form). That is to say, Jung believed that the human preoccupation with quadration reflects a structural reality in the collective unconscious. His best-known attempt to understand this quadration has come to us through his typology, in its concept of the four functions: intuition, thinking, feeling, and sensation. Less well known is his idea that the totality of the archetypal Self is imaged clearly in the octahedron. His most extensive attempt to understand this double-quaternio in the Self was presented in his essay, "The Structure and Dynamics of the Self" (CW9-II). In that essay Jung seemed determined to articulate the various ways in which an octahedral image of the Self may be shown to contain important insight into the structure and dynamics of the psyche. While he struggled mightily to ground his intuitions about the importance of the octahedral image, his exposition there remains frustratingly opaque. Nevertheless, other prominent Jungians, also fascinated with the octahedral image as a representation of the inner "Diamond Body" (CW9-I, par. 637), have continued to search for a key that might unlock reasons for Jung's fascination with the image. Some have followed him in asserting the octahedral structure of the Self, while presenting alternative interpretations of the structure and meaning of the various facets and planes of the image.

Notable among these interpreters was John Layard (1975) with his presentation of an alternative decoding of the diamond body. He follows Jung's suggestion that the Self is octahedral, but he finds that an analysis of Celtic mythology offers a different explanation of the facets of the octahedron. He offers an interpretation of the octahedron that locates the archetypal Self in the lower pyramid of the octahedron and the human individuating ego in the upper pyramid. Mother and father images are placed on opposite sides of the octahedron. The archetypal feminine joins the Self in the lower pyramid.

While somewhat more intelligible than Jung's own treatment of the dynamic meaning of the octahedron, Layard's ingenious interpretation of the Diamond Body has not become widely known for either its value in understanding Jungian metatheory or for its clinical applications. Jungians have tended to follow Jung's lead in turning to the theory of types to offer clinical explanations of Jung's preoccupations with the quaternio and have more or less ignored the double-quaternio.

A key exception to this is Toni Wolff's (1956) exposition of the "Structural Forms of the Feminine Psyche." Wolff demonstrated the way in which the quadration of the psyche is expressed in more than typological distinctions. She delineated the four major structural forms of the feminine as the mother, the amazon, the medial woman, and the hetaira. Her work comes closest to anticipating the structural decoding of the present model. While she saw these four forms as important structural forms of the feminine, she did not perceive the fullness of the archetypal realities of queen, warrior, magician and lover that lie behind them. She discerned aspects of these archetypes, but described, for the most part, traits that I would call aspects of the feminine bipolar shadow – ones that do not highlight the positive aspects of these energies as they manifest in an integrated and cohesive way in a mature feminine self. A major limitation of her model, therefore, includes her lack of sufficient emphasis on the necessity of balancing these four aspects of the feminine in the movement toward individuation, as well as her apparent inability to comprehend the dialectical tensions that can be discerned between the structural forms of mother and the medial woman and those of amazon and hetaira.

Fairness to Wolff, however, demands that we wonder whether she may have intuited four parallel structural forms in the male psyche which correspond to those which she has discerned in the feminine. It seems likely that she raised this rather obvious question, one which would have led to an alternative and more promising interpretation of the eightfold structure of the double-quaternio than that offered by Jung. One can only speculate not only why such a line of questioning does not seem to have been followed, but also why Wolff – as far as we know – never developed and deepened the significant insights shared in an all-too-brief paper to the Students' Association in Zurich. Perhaps it is too much to hope that one day a thorough researcher will uncover a dusty, unpublished manuscript by Wolff on this topic.

With regard to my own research on this topic, there is some irony in the fact that I did not approach this topic deductively, reasoning from an a priori fourfold or eightfold structure in order to further Jung's interest in these ideas. Rather, I came to this model inductively, seeking a geometric model to aid in understanding the shape of my research findings. Later I was both astounded and gratified to find that others, most notably Jung himself, had struggled to decode an octahedral image of the Self. The model presented in this brief report is based on over 20 years of cross-cultural study and psychoanalytic clinical research utilizing resources from Freudian, Adlerian and Jungian traditions. If one examines this model of the decoding of an octahedral structure of the archetypal Self, a number of important dimensions of deep structure can be seen in visual representation. The following is an outline of key structural and dynamic implications.

Decoding the Diamond Body: The Double Quaternio

1) The Four Foundational Powers Potential in the Self

The astounding human obsession with the quaternio (fourfold structures in cognitive mapping) has been based, I suggest, on an intuition of these four powers within. Each of the quadrants represents, I believe, a distinct "biogram": with encoded potentials necessary for integration into the structure of a cohesive and fully functioning human self. The king/queen biogram contains the ordering and nurturing potentials; the warrior biogram contains the potentials for boundary formation and maintenance, effective organization and action, vocation and fidelity; the magician biogram, the potentials for cognitive functioning, understanding, deconstruction and reconstructive healing (death and rebirth); and the lover biogram the potentials for receptiveness, empathy, and intimacy, healthy dependency, affiliation and embodied sexuality.

2) Fundamental Oppositions in Deep Structure

An examination of the octahedral structure of the Self reveals that there are two fundamental oppositions built into the deep structure of the Self: between eros (lover) and aggression (warrior); and between ruler (king/queen) and prophetic rebel/sage/healer (magician). Freud, of course, had focused on the lover/warrior dialectic and Adler on the ruler/magician dialectic (see Adler's work on superiority and social interest). Thus Jung was not entirely correct in ascribing the conflict between Freud and Adler to their typological differences. In my view, they were focusing on different dialectical structural dynamics discernible on different axes of the deep structure of the Self. For fully mature human selfhood, each of these biograms must be accessed adequately and balanced against the others in a healthy tension analogous to the tension between muscle systems in a healthy human body. Individuation and wholeness, then, are not just vague esoteric concepts. Viewed from the point of view of this model of the structure of the archetypal Self they have clear contents and discernible components, requiring deliberate sustained efforts to attain, to consolidate and to maintain. Thus, the shape of psychopathology can be understood, not only as a lack of development and maturation of the four powers, but as an inability to recognize and redress imbalances in developmental attainments in the four powers.

3) Four Lines of Development

On the basis of this model, then, individuation proceeds along four lines of development corresponding to the four powers. Development toward maturity and cohesiveness of the personality counteracts the dialectical tensions and tendencies to split which are built into the foundational deep structures of the Self. It is probably not just an accident of history that over 50 cultures built pyramids at some point in their development. These structures were probably an externalization and projection of the intuited blueprint for individuation lying deep in the psyche. Indeed, the shape of the pyramid most graphically illustrates the individual struggle involved in the individuation process. There are four faces of the pyramid which must be traversed successfully. In my view these represent lines of development for aggression, cognition, affiliation and nurturance.

Wholeness and cohesiveness of the individuated personality can be seen in the capstone of the pyramid. Images in human mythological traditions have long reflected intuitions regarding the accuracy of this model of the psychological and spiritual quest. From the eye of illumination on the capstone as imaged on an American one-dollar bill to the temple on the top of Mayan pyramids, to the human preoccupation with climbing sacred mountains – all illustrate our intuition of the stressful, nonquietist nature of the true developmental quest. This model, I believe, is an accurate decoding of the psychological contents behind these traditions in human mythological images.

4) Shadow, Anima, and Animus

Space does not permit me to elaborate the way in which our decoding of the octahedral structure of the Self supports Jung's assertion that shadow work must precede the deeper and more difficult confrontation with the contrasexual aspects of the unconscious (see Moore and Gillette, 1993, pp. 247-255). The deep pyramid of the contrasexual code not only images the greater difficulty in working with the contrasexual – but it also offers much more sense of the richness and parallel structures of the contrasexual than do previous theoretical formulations. There are, in effect, four archetypal couples in the structure of the Self: King and Queen, the Warrior couple, the Magician couple, and the Lover couple.

I am currently in the process of delineating how this deep structure influences couple relationships in the form of predict-

able archetypal dyads with accompanying predictable intersubjective fields. Also deserving of a more comprehensive discussion is the way in which an understanding of the dynamic code of
the octahedral structure helps us understand the ubiquity of bipolar expressions of the shadow (imaged in the base of the pyramidal structures). A preliminary discussion of this (Moore and
Gillette, 1990, pp. 16-17) will be elaborated in subsequent publications.

Conclusion: The Diamond Body and the Transcendent Function

While some Jungian analysts have followed Jung in emphasizing the importance of the ego-Self axis in the individuation
process, there has not been a consistent emphasis on the structure
of the Self as the blueprint for individual development and individuation and the structural ground for the actual regulative
process of the transcendent function. While today even the cutting edge of Freudian self psychology is proclaiming the existence of such a blueprint which serves as a regulator of the
schemas unfolding in self-development, many Jungians are moving away from serious structural analysis of the collective unconscious. Under the guise of "post-structuralist" ideology they are
abandoning the task of developing Jungian analysis as a serious
scientific psychology. Whether this avoidance of attempts to
decode deep structure is a result of the deification of the Self
characteristic of Jungian pietists or the uncritical embrace of the
magician inflation of the contemporary deconstructionist "post-
structuralists," the result is a turning away from the scientific
challenge of Jungian analysis: that of continuing to investigate
the grammar of the deep structures of the unconscious encoded in
the DNA of the two-million-year-old human species that we are.

If we are to understand the transcendent function in a way that
is grounded in a metatheoretical treatment of the collective unconscious, I am convinced that we must understand the way in
which the octahedral structure of the archetypal Self is a clear
code: 1) for what lines of development and resulting potentials
must be evoked, developed, and balanced; 2) for mapping the

bipolar shadow dynamics built into psychic structure; 3) and for the richness of and proper relation to the contrasexual. This octahedral structure in the deep Self is not passive but numinous, evoking the canalization of libido toward wholeness in structuralization of the individual psyche. Given adequate containment in the vessel of analysis, its luminous structure is the basis for the manifestation of the transcendent function.

References

Layard, J. (1975). *A Celtic Quest: Sexuality and Soul in Individuation.* Dallas: Spring Publications.

Moore, R. (1992). Decoding the diamond body. In F. Halligan & J. Shea (Eds.). New York: Crossroads.

Moore, R. and Gillette, D. (1990). *King, Warrior, Magician, Lover: Rediscovering the Archetypes of the Mature Masculine.* San Francisco: Harper Collins.

Moore, R. and Gillette, D. (1991). *The King Within: Accessing the King in the Male Psyche.* New York: William Morrow.

Moore, R. and Gillette, D. (1992). *The Warrior Within: Accessing the Knight in the Male Psyche.* New York: William Morrow.

Moore, R. and Gillette, D. (1993). *The Magician Within: Accessing the Shaman in the Male Psyche.* New York: William Morrow.

Moore R. and Gillette, D. (in press). *The Lover Within: Accessing the Lover in the Male Psyche.* New York: William Morrow.

Shea, J. & Halligan, F. (1992). *Fires of Desire: Erotic Energies and the Spiritual Quest.* New York: Crossroads.

Wolff, T. (1956). Structural forms of the feminine psyche. Zurich: Privately printed for the Students' Association, C. G. Jung Institute, Zurich.

The Body as Container for the Transcendent Function: Thoughts on its Genesis

Gustav Bovensiepen
Berlin, Germany
German Society for Analytical
Psychology

Jung considered the transcendent function to be the most important psychological function. He described it as a "complex function made up of other functions" (CW6, par. 828), represented by the "living symbol." It is notable that such a central concept of Analytical Psychology, containing a hypothesis on mental/psychic functioning, has been so little explored and theoretically expanded. Especially, it has not been related to ideas on emotional or mental activity, as has been done by other sciences. My main question is: When does the transcendent function begin to be realized and where in the psychosomatic spectrum are its roots?

If we talk about the transcendent function only by referring to manifest images and symbols, not much is explained about the structure and dynamic of this function. Symbols and images are usually complicated mental representations and expressions of differentiated ego performances that reveal little about their underlying mechanisms. To gain insight into the genesis of the transcendent function, I will consider "primitive" symbolic material as it may be expressed by body language, body experience and in the primal affects, as it appears in infants or in infantile states of mind.

My thesis is that the transcendent function integrates in the ego the realizations of experiences that are organized and lived around the instinctive pole of the archetypes. The second part of my thesis is that the unfolding of the transcendent function is coupled tightly with the development of early interpersonal relationship in infancy. The early infant-mother relationship is primarily a psychosomatic relationship; thus I focus on the body as a containing representation for psychic contents such as fantasies or internal object relations.

Clinical illustration

Two short excerpts from adult analyses are illustrative of infantile states of mind where adult analysands experience in a session severe bodily sensations such as headaches, dizziness, nausea, muscle cramps or abdominal pains. In such situations I may feel little rapport with the analysands; they talk about one thing or another and I am neither emotionally involved nor do their stories stimulate me to fantasies; my capacity to develop a symbolic attitude (as an expression of an operating transcendent function) seems to be disturbed. My attempts mostly fail to use a feeling, a dream or symptoms to establish a relationship to the experiences of the analysand. With one woman, for example, dealing with her "stomach-ache" led to her feeling that she required extreme effort to hold herself together during the sessions. She remembered that her first menstruation was accompanied by heavy attacks from her father. During the menstruation she felt drained, that her body was falling apart. This analysand reacted to interpretations always with great sensitivity and narcissistic anger. She experienced me as an aggressive and intruding part of her mother. Then she reacted with great relief and happiness to my statement that she might not be required to accomplish the strength-sapping "holding together" by herself, but the two of us together, might do it.

In another situation, a man in his forties suffered from constantly changing bodily complaints and hypochondriacal fears and, when he came to me, found himself in a deep professional and personal crisis. His compulsive brooding, his self-doubts, his desire for "limitless appreciation" and his fears of annihilation brought him frequently to the brink of suicide. Moreover, his creativity appeared to have been extinguished. Although he often spoke of his wild destruction fantasies, I could only understand that intellectually, without feeling that I was ever being attacked by him. This allowed me only to perceive his defense – and mine – against it, while feeling that I was sitting separated, in helplessness, boredom or resignation. There were sessions in which he discharged his total despair, crying and repeating. However, this had more the character of an affective abreaction; relief occurred rarely or only for a short time and left me in a helpless, gloomy, resigned mood.

When his large, massive body was lying on the couch, always appearing somewhat rigid, with his face turned away, he reminded me of an infant who, after a period of overpowering malaise, cannot stop crying. Although with his mother, the child is in powerless loneliness, no longer able to accept the bottle or breast. The man could not receive my words or my attempts to make contact with him. He brooded by himself, as if empty and dull, with a somber look. I felt left alone, possibly as he had felt alone as an infant in the presence of his mother.

This became apparent in a session to which he brought a picture that he had painted, showing himself as a small boy standing next to his mother. Both are looking at a human-sized sculpture of a Greek mask that consists almost entirely of a wide-open mouth. His mother, smoking a cigarette, looks petrified. The boy – desperately looking at his mother – points with the finger at the mask. The analysand cried severely as he laid the picture on the table and complained that I could not help him either, that mother never stood by him, never perceived his fear. Consequently, he is very angry at her. He remembered situations at ages two and three, during World War II, sitting in an air-raid shelter during bombing raids. Although his mother was present, he would feel abandoned. He said: "You have to get angry and fearful, experience panic; only then will you feel how it looks inside of me."

This man appeared in his defense against fears of destruction and depressive anxieties to be identified more with the shelter than with a protective mother. He "bunkered" himself into his body and developed a defensive "bunker introject" that I connected with his mother's severe depressions suffered since his birth. I did not reach him; he used me and the analysis to show me that his mother could not mother him and I could do nothing for him.

For both analysands, a connection was missing between the bodily, affective experience and the psychic experience; this unconnectedness at times characterized our relationship. These tormenting conditions interfered with my ability to maintain a symbolic attitude; at times, the transcendent function seemed not to operate or was damaged.

The Transcendent Function as Development Function and the Affects

The transcendent function expresses itself as "the peculiar capacity for change of the human soul" (CW7, par. 360), as Jung wrote; it mediates also between body and psyche: "The symbol is thus a living body, *corpus et anima*" (CW9-I, par. 291). Jung viewed it as a function that was supplied by the archetypes, leading not only to intellectual understanding but also to an understanding through experience. The realization of the transcendent function occurs in the transference. Indeed, he sees the unfolding of the transcendent function with the parent-child transferences.

> The patient clings... to the person who seems to promise him a renewal of attitude;... he seeks this change which is vital to him even though he may not be conscious of doing so. (CW8, par. 146)

In his description of active imagination, Jung stressed that, if no fantasies are flowing, the first goal is to look for the affect, before attempting to provide it with an expression, for example, through an image:

> The purpose of the initial procedure is to discover the feeling-toned contents, for in these cases we are always dealing with situations where the one-sidedness of consciousness meets with the resistance of the instinctual sphere. (CW8, par. 178)

Thus, the archetypal structure of an affect is rooted in the physical realm which, with the aid of the transcendent function, is to be integrated and prepared for consciousness. Indeed, I find that there are many situations in analysis, where affects or bodily manifestations stand in the foreground without images.

Although the transcendent function belongs structurally to the ego complex, in its rudimentary form it is already effective in the infant or in the mother-infant relationship. According to Piontelli (1992), evidences of this are the differences in intrauterine behavior of identical twin fetuses: including individual, sensory and motor adaptation reactions to physical and psychic trauma during the pregnancy.

In analysis the transcendent function is likely to unfold as a two-step process: The search for, or the recognition of, the affect is the first step. The description of the affect in images or symbols is a second step; it has received much more attention than the first. I am devoting myself primarily to the first step.

At the end of his essay on the transcendent function (CW8), Jung emphasized once more how he saw the role of the affects in the conflict between the ego and the unconscious:

> The shuttling to and fro of arguments and affects represents the transcendent function of opposites. The confrontation of the two positions generates a tension charged with energy and that generates creates a living, third thing – not a logical stillbirth... but... a living birth that leads to a new level of being. (CW8, par. 189).

At the same time it becomes apparent how the danger of separation of affects from consciousness can lead to physical manifestations, which exist as foreign objects in the psychic experience. In connection with the amplification of the child motif as Self symbol, Jung pointed out that fantasies and symbols, especially primitive archaic symbols, are rooted in materiality.

> The symbols of the self arise in the depths of the body and they express its materiality... as much as the structure of the perceiving consciousness. The symbol is thus a living body, *corpus et anima.* (CW9-I, par. 291)

Fordham (1969, 1971) has worked out the developmental aspect of the Self. He assumed an original or primal Self that existed prenatally as a psychosomatic unity and, after birth, a deintegrating and re-integrating activity of the Self. These processes are not purely intra-psychic but rather are tied to the interpersonal relationship, perhaps expressing an archetypal readiness and urge for relationship. The empirical and experimental research on the psychology of development confirmed particularly one aspect, which Fordham emphasized in his theory of the primal Self: From the beginning of life the infant is an active being who has a biologically preformed urge to seek a provider.

In order to understand the transcendent function within this theory of deintegration/reintegration of the Self, development of the ego must be considered. Through the experiences of the child with the inner and outer world – by way of the deintegration/reintegration of the primal Self – the child's perception, control and memory of bodily, affective and sensory stimuli ripens. These experiences and the gradually developing consciousness form the ego complex. Out of the inner processing of these primarily bodily and affective elements, the psychic representations develop which, in the preverbal phase, are visible primarily through projection. But awareness is helped by the infant's ability to express affects through facial expressions, gestures and vocalization, the capacity to tune in affectively to its providers and to monitor them affectively.

So develops the ego in the service of the Self. The question now is what causes the transformation or expression of bodily, sensory and emotional experiences into representations, and how does it occur. The transcendent function may arrange the connection between the archetypal expectancy and the ego. I assume that the spiritual pole of the archetype is as much in need of activation or realization as the bodily even if the poles are two sides of the same structural element. The activation and development of the transcendent function which unfolds between Self and ego is, in my view, as a preformed readiness. It is constructed as archetypal and must be activated by corresponding experiences.

Another aspect is that the mother/child relationship assumes an especially important role. The effectiveness of the transcendent function in the mother, in the form of the symbolic attitude, is essential. Noticing the bodily and psychic signals of the infant, she absorbs them into herself, assigns meaning to them and converts it into emotional images, fantasies, words and actions. All that is a transformation and translation achievement and requires in the mother the effectiveness of a symbolic attitude and brings her into contact with the inner world of her infant.

Looked at in this way, I understand "giving of meaning" not only as an autonomous archetypal need of the psyche, but I define it as repeatedly lived emotional experience of the meaningful relationship, interaction and connection between psychic parts of two human beings. In addition, through internalization and memory, this experience leads to inner representations that may manifest themselves later in symbols. For this process to occur, the infant must internalize the symbolic attitude of the mother. Thus, the effectiveness of the transcendent function provides the mother with a knowledge about her child; this knowledge strengthens her emotional ties with the child.

Bion (1962) developed this aspect from another theoretical perspective in his theory of thinking, which he derived from primitive emotional experiences and his opinion of the container/contained relationship. Bion's alpha function is akin to Jung's transcendent function, and Bion's beta elements may be viewed as the psychoid elements of Analytical Psychology.

Summary

For Jung the symbol creates a connection between two different or contrasting elements, for example, between body and soul, which can be experienced as a new third element. However, he left open the question how the symbol is formed and especially what may interfere with the symbolizing process. This becomes clearer if we understand the development of infantile relationships with the aid of the deintegration and reintegration processes of the Self and consider the transcendent function as effective within an object relationship from the beginning. The beginning of object relationship lies in a close psychosomatic exchange of mother and infant. The patterns of primitive affect and of emotional interaction play an important role in this process and are – according to modern research on infants and affects – innate, archetypal patterns. In this process the transcendent function seems to moderate between the instinctual pole of the archetypes and the integration of psychic contents and images in the ego.

Translated from German

Note: An extended and revised version of this paper, with infant observation and research results, will be published in the *Zeitschrift für Analytische Psychologie*.

References

Bion, W. R. (1962/1984). *Learning From Experience*. London: Karnac.
Fordham, M. (1969). *Children as Individuals*. London: Hodder & Stoughton.
Fordham, M. (1971). *The Self and Autism*. Library of Analytical Psychology (Vol. 3). London: Heinemann.
Piontelli, A. (1992). *From Fetus to Child. An Observation and Psychoanalytic Study*. New Library of Psychoanalysis (Vol. 15). London: Tavistock/Routledge.

Turning Inside Out:
Disguise as a Transition to Homecoming

Henry Hanoch Abramovitch
Jerusalem, Israel
Israel Association of Analytical
Psychology

The transformation of identity through disguise is part of the individuation process. We must appear as we are not in order to become more truly who we are.

I begin with a text from a great Indian epic, *The Mahabharata* (Van Buitenen, 1978). The story of a conflict over succession to the kingdom between two sets of cousins: the usurping Kauravas and the displaced Pandavas. Knowing the weakness for gambling of the eldest Pandava brother, Yudhisthira, his rivals challenge him to a game of dice that has been "fixed." In an epic gambling spree, Yudhisthira loses all his wealth, his brothers, even himself and finally the common wife of all five brothers. By terms of the game the brothers are forced to spend a dozen years in exile and then a further year in disguise. If they are recognized during the thirteenth year, they must repeat an additional 13-year cycle of exile and disguise until they can pass a full year incognito.

During this year of disguise, each brother takes on a new persona. Yudhisthira, former pathological gambler, takes on a disguise as a Brahman dice master. Arjuna, the world's greatest warrior – subsequently hero of the Bhagavat Gita – becomes a transvestite dancing master in the king's harem. After a full year, they are finally ready to return home.

The symbolism is rich. Indeed, the epic says of itself: "What is here is also elsewhere, but what is not here, is not anywhere." Similar themes of danger and disguise as a prelude to the archetypal experience of homecoming may be found in the *Odyssey*

(Books 13, 18, 19); the Bible (Genesis 20, 27, 37, 45; I Samuel 21) and elsewhere. The appearance of such common motifs also in Indian, Greek and Hebrew epics suggests that we are dealing with an archetypal pattern.

Disguise is better known through the pattern of the trickster: symbolized in Biblical lore, for example, by the young Jacob, stealing his brother's identity; or the fleeing David, feigning madness at the court of his former enemy. Such a "trickster persona," part of a dangerous flight from father anger, initiates the young hero into his symbolic quest. Such flights in disguise at the outset of the quest, as at the beginning of analysis, are expressions of persona anxiety.

Jung defined the persona as the "outward face" of the psyche, that which mediates our relation to the external social world just as the anima/animus is our "inward face," mediating ego and unconscious. The persona "is that which in reality one is not but which oneself as well as others think one is" (CW9, par. 221). It has been called the "archetype of conformity" (Hall & Nordby, 1973, p. 44), a compromise between what we wish to be and what the surrounding world will allow us to be. Identification with a specific persona inhibits psychological development since each persona, "the professor with his textbook, the tenor with his voice" (CW9, par. 221) is dominated by a single function.

Although Jung emphasized that the persona is necessary and in itself neither positive nor negative, most writers have emphasized pathologies of persona. Only a few writers argue that the confusion between genuine identity and social role can act as a vehicle for transformation.

Within analysis Jung noted that psychic material is usually dealt with in a predictable order: persona, shadow, animus/anima and ultimately Self. From this perspective, persona issues are dealt with early in analysis, as a necessary prelude to the "deeper stuff." The archetypal pattern suggested by the epic material indicates that within the motif of exile and return, persona issues may surface again, with a life and death ferocity, toward the end of the quest or analytic process, when we are truly on our way Home.

Jung often compared the individuation process to the arche-typal pattern of hero quest, in which the hero or heroine is forced to leave home to search for identity. Implicit in this conception is the need to leave the person you seem to be at the outset of the quest -- the roles ascribed by family and society – in order, after a series of trials, to earn a new identity and return home to reclaim your own (inner) kingdom. Such a "progress model" of the hero quest does not always fit the perturbations of analysis. Like the heroes of Mahabharata, analysands may have a more unsteady, chaotic path: one involving conscious use of persona manipulations, disguise in the service of individuation. In a phase I call "turning inside out" the repressed irreconcilable aspects of the personality are temporarily but knowingly taken on as an outward identity or "transitional persona." Wearing these formerly repressed identities on the outside, displaying them to oneself and others not only protects the individual from the danger latent in any transition but also sets the stage for their integration.

In the early phase, one comes to understand that one is not who one seems. In the later stages, as in the *Mahabharata*, the analysand may become the Other, externalizing previously un-conscious aspects of the personality. Some individuals must be-hold this otherness on the outside before being able to take it back inside. As a result, "persona play" may allow surface to touch depth.

In this way one can differentiate two developmental lines toward individuation. One is the gradual expansion of awareness, as ego becomes painfully aware of the complexes and their archetypal depth, the nitty-gritty and daily bread of analysis. The other is the more dramatic embracing of the not-me, a leap to the depth, with all the attendant dangers of inflation, psychosis and impulsive chaos, a kind of personal equivalent of the collective cultural masquerades such as Fastnacht, Carnival or Purim. While it is often a rift in the public persona which brings a person to treatment, I suspect that in some cases the order is reversed: slow steady progress seemingly destroyed in some outrageous persona play, only to give way again to a renewed sense of depth and wholeness. In that sense, such a turning inside out may be a disturbing but necessary prelude to coming Home.

Two brief examples illustrate the importance of a transitional persona. The first concerns a young man in his late twenties. As an adolescent he had been sent to Israel where, under the influence of drugs, he had a kind of breakdown. Ten years later he still had not developed an adequate social role, moving from job to job, city to city, woman to woman, even citizenship to citizenship, without an inner center. He had an unusual symptom; on occasion he was overwhelmed with existential panic, fearing that he did not exist. Only by seeing himself reflected physically in the mirror could he regain a sense of his own identity. Such a literal mirroring undoubtedly was connected to the lack of good mirroring in the primary relationship but also reflected his use of persona as a container for the personality as a whole. In one session the young man brought the final passage from Philip Roth's *The Counterlife* which glorifies a postmodernist persona and no authentic sense of self: "a variety of impersonations... that I can call upon when a self is required.... It's *all* impersonation – in the absence of a self."

In the absence of a living ego-Self axis, the persona is alienated from the Self and takes on its central organizing role. Such a pattern is akin to the trickster persona of young Jacob or David who must disguise himself to avoid imminent psychic or physical danger: the destructive paranoid attacks from the father. It is not surprising that the analysand's dream life was full of ferocious, frightening black muggers. Significantly, the analysis was broken off at the point when he felt he must return to the land of his birth and, in that way, find his way back home.

The need for "turning inside out" may function, in contrast, as part of individuation. A woman training in a helping profession came for analysis with symptoms of depression and identity confusion. All her life she had done what people expected of her, so successfully that she was no longer aware of what she wanted. Such excessive development of persona led to inner emptiness and a long-standing fear that analysis would reveal her to be truly empty. She expressed her anger, passively, by going blank during sessions; the analysis was punctuated by long silences.

One key area of distress concerned gender issues and interpersonal relationships. Although outwardly attractive, she lacked an inner relation to the feminine. This lack expressed itself in persona issues. She never felt comfortable in any feminine clothing and "dressed down." Her relations with men were intense and stormy, after an initial "honeymoon" tendency to fusion. There followed horrendous quarrels and hostility but she was unable to disengage. After an abrupt breaking-off, she would feel entirely unconnected with her former lover.

The family background to this persona/animus turmoil was a hypercritical mother who constellated an inner negative self which the analysand experienced as an idealized but overwhelmingly critical inner voice. In contrast she spoke of her father as warm but seductive; he treated her as she felt herself to be: a child uninitiated into the adult world. In therapy she had a dream in which a woman from her mother's country of origin gave her new and colorful clothes to wear. The dream clothing – new personal possibilities – reflected a new inner experience of a good mother.

As the analysis progressed she became involved in a lesbian relationship. In this relation too, after the honeymoon phase, the familiar cycle of fusion-separation returned, but with a difference. In the midst of deciding whether to break off the relationship, she had her hair cut very short, like a man's, or indeed like the persona look of some lesbians. "All the women and none of the men liked it." But, for her, it was a time of turning inside out, allowing her to see and be seen as a different kind of woman: the unfeminine inner woman she felt herself to be, yet a woman able to receive a woman's love, which she had never received from her own mother. The haircut was also playful since, as she said, she did not feel herself to be lesbian but rather enjoyed the freedom to act the role.

As with the Pandavas, the "disguise" was protective; it protected her from men and so allowed her a secure feminine inner space, without having to deal with masculine intrusiveness. The changes brought about by her new look were impressive. Within her family of origin, a distancing from father allowed a new closeness with her mother and a corresponding development of inner mothering.

When the romantic relationship ended, on her initiative, she was able to mourn it. She displayed new investment in her growing professional identity. The playfulness she had brought to persona, consciously displaying these aspects of not-me – the unfeminine, the undesired, the unlovable – allowed her to experience an altered sense of her own fate: one of the hallmarks of a successful analysis.

Finally, we return to Mahabharata. Arjuna, like my analysand, was over-identified with his social role. He too was turned inside out and spent the year in feminine disguise, teaching dance instead of war.

How does a man contact his feminine side? Through his relationship with a woman, projecting his anima outward and by encountering her in dreams, fantasy and amplification. But there is a third way: by "becoming a woman," thus role-playing the anima. The subsequent effect of Arjuna's experience with and as a woman bursts out dramatically. Arjuna was a general of a vast army about to fight his cousins for the kingdom. Instead of sounding the charge, he announced that he would not fight and kill his kinsmen and his mentor, who were arrayed opposite. Krishna, his charioteer, spoke to him and taught him the way of detachment in action. Even though he felt the compassion – presumably the result of his feminine experience as part of the world of women (in Hebrew compassion, "rakhamin," is literally the plural of womb, "rekhem") – he must still act and do what his duty called upon him to do.

The danger of turning inside out, then, is to be frozen in the other or lose a sense of balance – in this case, between the aggressive and the compassionate. The person may be deprived of the ability to act. Having turned inside out, one must still turn outside in, allowing disguise to be the prelude to Homecoming.

References

Hall, C. & Nordby, G. (1973). *A Primer of Jungian Psychology*. New York: Mentor.

Van Buitenen, J. (1978). *The Mahabharata* (Vol. 3). Chicago: University of Chicago Press.

The Transcendent Function
in *A Midsummer Night's Dream*

William Willeford
Dover, New Hampshire, USA
New England Society of Jungian
Analysts

In adopting the term "transcendent function," Jung related it to mathematical transcendent numbers existing in an ideal realm. The term suggests that whatever one hopes to name by it does what it does necessarily, going about its urgent business of transcending. And so one may relate this transcendence to the culminating moment in the dialectical scheme of the German idealist philosopher Hegel, for whom there was a relentless cosmic and historical progression of thesis, antithesis, and synthesis (see Solomon's paper, in this volume). But such symmetry, necessarily culminating in synthesis, is remote from the immense personal turmoil in which Jung discerned the pattern he was trying to describe. And his description of it included attention to aspects not so neatly formalized as Hegel might have wished, while implying others Jung did not spell out though he knew them to be important: the messiness of the process, its rootedness in the instinctual and emotional body, and the uncertainty with which we grasp – or sometimes merely grasp after – its products.

A recent version of Shakespeare's *A Midsummer Night's Dream*, by The Acting Company of New York, included a moment that beautifully illustrates the process with which Jung was concerned, while highlighting aspects of it that are intensely problematic in lived experience, and that deserve further attention.

In the play Theseus, Duke of Athens – the Theseus who killed the Minotaur – is to marry Hippolyta, Queen of the Amazons. Two pairs of lovers (Demetrius and Helena, Lysander and Hermia) become lost in a wood near Athens, where they are acted upon by the Mercurius-trickster figure Puck. In the course of the action the men and women of this quartet become paired and unpaired in all possible ways, partly because Puck puts love-magic in the eyes of some of them. Also in the woods, the foolish Bottom and his friends are rehearsing a play. Puck plays a prank on Bottom by putting an ass's head on him, and also puts love-magic in the eyes of Titania, the Fairy Queen, with the result that when she awakens, she falls in love with the ass-headed Bottom. All of these complications are resolved by the close.

A speech early in the play sums up the issues I want to raise. Lysander has spoken of true love as unfolding "both heaven and earth" but adds:

> And ere a man hath power to say "Behold!"
> The jaws of darkness do devour it up:
> So quick bright things come to confusion. (I.i.146-49)

"Confusion" thus annuls "quick bright things." If all such things are thus foredoomed, the chaos from which the world, in one view, originated will prevail as its ultimate reality. Indeed, the sense of opposites interacting in this sinister way is pronounced enough to give the play, despite its farcical elements, a fitfully perceptible undertone of near-tragedy.

The dramatic moment to which I call attention occurred when the lovers lost in the woods are arranged in one of the ballet-like configurations of love and hate they assume in the course of the action. Demetrius and Lysander, both in love with Helena, are kneeling on each side of her, Demetrius holding her right hand, Lysander her left. In the background the betrayed Hermia is distraught. Demetrius and Lysander have each begun to kiss one of Helena's hands, engaged in identical projects of kissing their way upward – hand, wrist, forearm – toward her face. Her attention is totally on Demetrius (Fig. 1). Finally, when Lysander has kissed his way almost to her shoulder, she notices him, appalled at his intrusion, and the whole situation disintegrates (Fig. 2).

*Figure 1. Demetrius (left) and Lysander (second from right) court
Helena (between them), as Hermia (far right) looks on in anguish.
Enthralled by Demetrius's attentions to her,
Helena is oblivious to Lysander's.*

*Demetrius is played by Rainn Wilson, Lysander by Mark Stewart
Guinn, Helena by Angie Phillips, and Hermia by Terra Vandergaw,
in a 1991 production directed by Joe Dowling.*

*Figure 2. It dawns on Helena that something ominous is happening to
her left. In an instant she will be aghast at Lysander's presumed
intrusion, though he has been kissing her passionately all along.*

Helena's attention has served as a barrier to hold beloved
Demetrius in and hated Lysander out. But attention implies a
process of judgment: Is it safe and in my best interest to attend to
this and not to that? When there is a shift in this judgment –
when, for example, it suddenly seems prudent to look at a threat
squarely – what has been disattended from may be admitted to
attention. And so Lysander, who can be ignored no longer, crosses the threshold of Helena's attention, and she responds with a
rush of indignation.

Helena is already erotically aroused – by Demetrius – and it is
in an erotic way that Lysander breaks into her attention. (Note
that the lovers are in their undergarments, close to nudity, sexual
intimacy, and the unconscious.) Suddenly Lysander has pushed
his way into her presence, as though from nowhere. As the
audience has followed them, Lysander's advances have accorded
with decorum, despite his eagerness. But Helena has noticed
them only when they reached a degree of intensity that makes her
experience them as an assault akin to rape.

It is easy to imagine that Helena feels some responsibility for
having been compromised. After all, Lysander has done what he
has done without her explicit prohibition. And forgetting to lock
the door lessens one's right to outrage at whatever unwelcome
thing comes through it, though awareness of one's forgetfulness
may enhance the urge to demonstrate one's outrage.

In any case, Helena experiences Lysander and Demetrius as
being as unlike as black and white, though to the audience they
are more or less interchangeable. And owing to her inattention to
Lysander's erotic advances, the audience sees a leakage, a befud-
dlement in the devotion to Demetrius that she assumes to be
simple and clear. Attending not to one but to both suitors, the
audience sees Helena as deluding herself until her self-delusion
becomes insupportable. Psychoanalysts speak of patches of reality beginning to show through someone's habitually unconscious
view of things: Lysander is suddenly to her a large patch of this
kind.

Helena's horrified recognition that Lysander is in a position of
intimacy that she had assumed to be exclusively Demetrius' is an

instance of what Jung called *enantiodromia*, a "running counter to" that is part of "the play of opposites in the course of events" and that leads to "the emergence of the unconscious opposite in the course of time" (CW6, pars. 708-709). Its emergence may result in the creation of a symbol mediating the conflicting opposites. Such a symbol, Jung observes, "cannot be a onesided product of the most highly differentiated mental functions but must derive equally from the lowest and most primitive levels of the psyche" (CW6, par. 824). The dramatic moment we have been considering explores the tension between the higher and lower levels with which Jung was concerned and does so, more specifically, with respect to the ethos of romantic love.

At the beginning of this moment, Demetrius and Lysander are kneeling in an attitude of supplication implying the elevation of the beloved to the level of the ideal. But romantic love has a physically erotic component. Hence the ambiguities figuring in the debate about the chivalric tradition in which romantic love developed. Was chivalry primarily spiritual? What did chivalric lovers do, or not do, with their bodies? Did chivalric love legitimate adultery?

One boon that the chivalric lover desires is recognition that the beloved sees his love and at least will not dissuade him from it. Her acknowledgment of his suit implies that his love is not egocentric, that it is respectful, placing her well-being first, that it can wait, and that it aspires to a form of mutuality in which the spiritual element is vivid. Helena seemingly grants such recognition to Demetrius and, in welcoming him into intimacy, she is granting him a foretaste of that mutuality. But the foretaste is charged with erotic urgency: the dilemma of romantic love hovers near these two, quite apart from Lysander.

Lysander's interaction with Helena, further, is an outright parody of romantic love in its spiritual aspect. Far from acknowledging his suit, Helena is oblivious to it. And far from waiting for this acknowledgment, Lysander is impetuously trying to avail himself of her intimacy. Moreover, far from putting her well-being first and aspiring to mutuality, he is blindly egocentric. Indeed, he is fundamentally deluded, owing to the love-magic Puck has put in his eyes.

Yet Lysander's parody of romantic love brings into operation "the lowest and most primitive levels of the psyche," which must be engaged if there is to be the tension necessary for a reconciling symbol to appear. And since the attitude expressed by Lysander is one term of the conflict requiring resolution – let us call it the conflict of body and soul – that term, the body, must be at hand as part of the material to be transformed.

The issues I have been discussing are amply present elsewhere in the play, notably in the interaction between Titania and Bottom. When Titania falls in love with Bottom wearing his ass's head, she promises him, "And I will purge thy mortal grossness so, / That thou shalt like an airy spirit go" (III.i.161-2). These words parody not only romantic love but, more broadly, the whole human enterprise of finding an accommodation between the natural and the spiritual. This particular attempt is all the more grotesque since "From antiquity up to the Renaissance the ass was credited with the strongest sexual potency and among quadrupeds was supposed to have the longest and hardest phallus" (Kott, 1964, p. 220).

Religions often present a vision of human perfectibility with the implication that the perfection to be achieved can be made into a steady state. This play implies rather that there is no such steady state. Thus, as the lovers come out of the woods, Hermia remarks, "Methinks I see these things with parted eye, / When everything seems double." Helena concurs, saying that she has "found Demetrius like a jewel, / Mine own, and not mine own," and Demetrius wonders, "Are you sure / That we are awake? It seems to me / That yet we sleep, we dream" (IV.i.192-97).

The double vision of the lovers leaving the woods and of the audience is, on the one hand, of an imaginative reconciliation of the higher and lower, the spiritual and the natural – or if not a reconciliation, at least a recognition that both exist and are interrelated in a partly patterned way. But this double vision is also, on the other hand, of "confusion" as threatening "quick bright things."

The ambiguity to which I am calling attention can be seen in the character of Theseus. He shows himself to be of uncommon imaginative vision. Yet the Theseus of classical lore is a partly duplicitous figure, whose betrayal of women is an important part of his legend. Indeed, Shakespeare's play names some of the women he has wooed and abandoned (McAlindon, 1991, pp. 51-53). Moreover, he courted Hippolyta only after he had faced her in armed confrontation. Thus we are uneasily aware that this ruler, teacher, and exemplar has within him inclinations to the lechery, sneakiness and aggressiveness that Helena sensed in Lysander.

Enantiodromia is generally most obvious when the previously hidden opposite is revealed as contradictory and incompatible, for example, when Helena is shocked by Lysander's erotic designs. But in and around such opposition – and quite apart from it – we may sense that the interplay of opposites is coherent, and that it fosters harmonious development of various kinds, though the class of opposites is easier to talk about. (One must remain aware, however, that the mind creates both false unities and false dualities and that we may be mistaken in regarding some things as coherent.) The imaginatively gifted Theseus is thinking of the coherence of opposites and taking it to be genuine when he plans to let his hounds loose and, from the mountain top, "mark the musical confusion / Of hounds and echo in conjunction" (IV.i.113-4). He knows – a hard thing to know – that the "confusion" that threatens quick bright things can also have the harmony of music. And despite the many mishaps in it, Shakespeare's play is harmonious in having a highly formal overall pattern bringing the action to a comic resolution.

As the play makes clear in its treatment of romantic love, many forms of quickness, brightness and harmony are illusory. Not all of them are; here I can only assert my agreement with Theseus about this. But the enterprise of discriminating between illusory and real forms of them is uncertain. Certain, in contrast, is our subjection to "confusion" and "the jaws of death" looming in the background of whatever quickness, brightness, and harmony we are able to experience. It is in relation to this dark background that we know them and their value.

References

Kott, J. (1964). *Shakespeare Our Contemporary.* Garden City, NY: Doubleday.

McAlindon. T. (1991). *Shakespeare's Tragic Cosmos.* Cambridge: Cambridge University Press.

Narcissistic Disorder and the Transcendent Function

Rushi Ledermann
Hove, Sussex, England
Society of Analytical Psychology

In his synthetic view of the psyche, Jung saw the transcendent function "as a quality of conjoined opposites" (CW8, par. 189). He stated that it leads to "the production and unfolding of the original potential wholeness," which he called the "individuation process" (CW7, par. 186). This process foreshadows Michael Fordham's theory of the deintegration of the primary self. Jung said also that "the suitably trained analyst mediates the transcendent function for the patient" and thus enables the person to "arrive at a new attitude" (CW8, par. 146).

In applying Jung's concept to the treatment of narcissistic disorder I shall use the term "transcendent function" as bridging opposites in a wide sense: not only the unconscious with the conscious but also opposites which are constellated in the psyche from the very beginning of life; for example, good and evil, omnipotence and powerlessness, love and hate, creativity and destructiveness.

People who suffer from narcissistic disorder manifest an almost complete lack of this function, a lack that appears in the transference relationship. Thus, it is important for the analyst to work toward the eliciting of this function.

Pathological narcissism needs to be distinguished from narcissism in ordinary parlance, namely "the tendency to self-worship, absorption in one's own personal perfection" (Oxford English Dictionary). That definition seems to describe the defense or façade in people who suffer from narcissistic disorder. The actual disorder is in fact the opposite of self-worship. Kernberg (1974), the eminent psychoanalyst, holds that the disorder is the inability to love oneself and hence the inability to love another person and the appearance of self-absorption. These defects coincide with a superficially smooth and effective social adaptation. Narcissistic persons occupy a borderline area between neurosis and psychosis and are fixated on an early defense structure from disturbances in early object relations. Their self-regard is threatened, yet they frequently suffer from grandiose ideas about themselves. Coupled with serious deficiencies in their capacity to love is their exploitativeness and ruthlessness toward other persons.

Kernberg's view accords with my clinical observations, especially that narcissistic persons are unable to love themselves. They tend to develop pathological defenses: (a) defenses of the self, (b) power and control in place of eros, (c) splitting off instinctual impulses, which may lead to the formation of the "robot personality," (d) head-ego in place of body-ego. I have described these defenses in previous papers (Ledermann, 1979, 1981).

Narcissistic persons may seek help because they are overwhelmed by archetypal experiences that were unmodulated by their mothers in infancy and which they are unable to integrate. Owing to the pathological defenses mentioned, they suffer from unbridged splits in their personalities and they cannot form symbols. They are devoid of viable relationships and cannot find meaning in life. Feelings of love and hate for the analyst or anyone in the outside world will be denied. They will be split off from their unconscious shadow because they lack the transcendent function, which links consciousness with the shadow. They keep the inner child separate from their adult personality, tucked away and unreachable. In the transference, such persons will erect an almost unbridgable gap and utterly resist any dependence. They will strive for power over, and control of, the analyst, as they lack eros, which would enable them to link with another person. They will experience the analyst as non-human, archetypal and therefore alternatively all good and all powerful, or all bad, impotent and useless, if not outright evil. This renders the countertransference very painful.

The analyst must try to humanize these archetypal experiences, as the healthy mother does for her baby. This process takes place gradually and over a long period of time. The analyst constantly needs to handle his/her own hate and create an empathic and containing environment in which analysands feel safe to experience the stark opposites inside them and feel understood. The trust for the analyst develops only gradually, eventually enabling the analyst to penetrate the barrier between him/her and the analysand, thus facilitating the deintegrative processes which could not take place in infancy. Then the transcendent function can emerge.

The analyst will work toward reducing the pathological defenses which have left the opposites in the analysand's psyche unbridged. Archetypal libidinal as well as destructive impulses frequently are fused or totally split and not humanized owing to impeded deintegration in infancy. Now they can separate out, become modified and brought together and become humanized and symbolized. Little by little, the analysand may be able to experience love and hate for the analyst. Impulses gradually lessen in their absoluteness. Love is tempered by frustration and disappointment. Hate and destructive impulses become detoxified by the analyst and, because the analyst survives them, they will lose their terror of absoluteness.

The transcendent function will be activated: love and hate, creative and destructive impulses will be bridged. There will come a time in the treatment when the analyst can interpret the shadow in the analysand and enable him or her to integrate it in due course. But I have found that if this is done too early, the analysand will widen the distance from the analyst and may leave treatment.

Clinical Illustrations

My first and principal illustration concerns Mrs. B., an extreme case of narcissistic disorder. She was 38 at the beginning of the analysis, married with three young children. The analytic work with her – 12 years, five times a week for much of the time

– helped me enormously to understand the defenses of narcissistic disorder which prevent the emergence of the transcendent function. Mrs. B. described her mother as utterly useless, in fact psychotic and hospitalized three times during my analysand's childhood. Mrs. B. idealized her father as strong, earthy and powerful, although he beat her when she did not come up to his expectations. He abandoned his family when Mrs. B. was nine years old. No healthy deintegration could have taken place in her infancy. This left her with a deep split: the useless mother and the idealized father. The internal image of the united parents could not become constellated. Needless to say, the transcendent function could not become activated.

When I knew her first, she felt powerful in her murderousness. At the same time she experienced herself as non-existing and "dead." For a whole year she called me a useless stupid monster; yet she hardly ever missed a session. She threatened to kill me if I did not help her.

Her feeling of being a "lily-white robot" alternated with the terrible feeling of being evil. These experiences were quite unconnected in her as she lacked the transcendent function. Before the first holiday separation she brought this gruesome picture which she called the dead thing (Fig. 1). The picture speaks for itself: her inner child which cannot link with anybody as it has no mouth, no nostrils, no ears, no arms and no legs. It is precariously suspended on a broken string. She also used the robot defense which I mentioned earlier; she called herself a steely hard robot who powerfully presides over the tangle of split-off instincts (Fig. 2).

Mrs. B.'s denial of her mother's body and of her own instinctual life produced the delusion that all her instincts had been sent off into space in her infancy (Fig. 3). She claimed that women had no three-dimensional bodies. She explained her two miscarriages by saying: "I am flat and babies just drop out of me."

For years she drew only heads and never a body. She denied having a shadow and could not admit that she had destructive impulses nor that she suffered from enormous envy. Years later, as she discovered that she had an inner life, she began to link

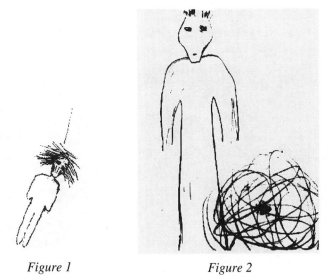

Figure 1   Figure 2

Figure 3   Figure 4

Figure 5   *Figure 6*

with her instinctual urges (Fig. 4): split-off urges as heads only with hungry open mouths, now beginning to escape from the domination of the robot and coming down to earth. At that time she felt that her Self was beginning to emerge from the darkness that enveloped her: a faint white mandala-like ring (Fig. 5).

During many years of analysis she manifested another pair of unbridged opposites in her psyche: the Apollonian and Dionysian principles. For many years she liked only Apollonian music. When, after long painstaking analytic work, she connected with her instinctual life, she fell victim to the Dionysian principle in herself; dissolution and abandonment to her destructive drives took her over. She became a heavy drinker and made three serious suicide attempts. I could no longer reach her with analytic work. She agreed to enter a drying-out unit. After several months she was weaned from alcohol and we resumed once a week sessions for a further two years. She now rejoined her husband whom she had left and began to repair her difficult marriage.

The transcendent function began to emerge and with it her capacity to symbolize. In the early days of the analysis she simply declared her murderous feelings for me. After some further years of treatment she was able to express these feelings by a symbolic equivalent: a baking tin which she brought to the session. When held upside down the molds of the baking tin looked like breasts. With a hammer she proceeded to bash in all the buns/breasts, screaming with rage while she did it. She understood my interpretation: This action was the symbolic equivalent of furiously bashing me in, as I stood for the breast-mother. Some years later she experienced the more developed "as-if" quality, relating now to her positive feelings for me. She brought a packet of candies and deposited them with me. Every time she came, I was to give her a candy to take home so that she could keep me alive inside her until the next session.

At this time she had a recurrent dream: A fat powerful man dismembered a thin man, gouged his eyes out and killed him. She identified with the victim and projected the sadistic man onto people in the outside world, including me.

Several years after we had ended the analysis she came back for a short spell of post-analytic work. She was now leading a creative life and trained for a helping profession. But she had great difficulty in discussions with her co-trainees. She always experienced herself as the victim and the others as the aggressors. She felt unable to continue with her training unless she got some further analytic help from me.

She returned to the dream from many years ago. Interpretation now made it possible for her to bring the opposites in herself together and recognize the symbolic meaning of the dream: The two men were both aspects of herself, which needed to be bridged. She had kept them apart by projecting the cruel man into the outside world. At that time also her extreme view of her father and mother modified considerably; another pair of opposites became reconciled.

Another narcissistic analysand drew a picture (Fig. 6) after many years of analysis. It depicts his grandiose view of himself, as the crucified Christ, but at the same time as a helpless baby imprisoned in a womb and gnashing his teeth. Producing this symbol helped him to bridge the opposites of grandiosity and powerlessness he carried in himself. This picture seems to show the transcendent function at work.

Of course I have not been able to help all narcissistic analysands to develop the transcendent function. For example, I failed sadly with a young man who had large psychotic areas and was tyrannized by obsessional rituals.

Even people of great genius struggle with bridging opposites within themselves. The great pianist Claudio Arrau described how often, when he had won first prize in a demanding piano competition, he felt tormented by the idea that he played worse than anyone else. At other times he thought he played better than everyone else. He was delivered from this painful contradiction through treatment by a Jungian analyst who helped him enormously to bridge this and other contradictions in his nature. Arrau said: "Analysis... does not do away with conflicts and suffering. It is the finding of a *modus vivendi...* of how to deal with them and live with them that matters. For the artist... tensions need not be erased, for it is these very tensions that give the creative process its intensity and are a vital source of creative powers" (Horowitz, 1984, p. 247). Arrau was helped to develop the transcendent function in his psyche. He expresses his deep gratitude to his analyst and thinks that all aspiring artists would benefit greatly from access to Jungian analysis.

References

Horowitz, J. (1984). *Conversations with Arrau*. New York: Lime Editions.

Kernberg, O. (1974). Further contributions to the treatment of narcissistic personalties. *International Journal of Psycho-Analysis*, *55*, 215-240.

Ledermann, R. (1979). The infantile roots of narcissistic personality disorder. *Journal of Analytical Psychology*, *24*, 107-126.

Ledermann, R. (1981). The robot personality in narcissistic disorder. *Journal of Analytical Psychology*, *26*, 329-344.

The Chaotic Dynamics
of the Transcendent Function

John R. Van Eenwyk
Olympia, Washington, USA
Chicago Society of Jungian Analysts

The psychological mechanism that transforms energy is the symbol.
C. G. Jung

Jung described the psychodynamics of symbols by images and mechanics. His investigations using images are recorded throughout his writings, for he felt that images capture most graphically the complexity of intra-psychic dynamics. His accounts of their actual mechanics, however, are far less extensive. See, for example, "On Psychic Energy" (CW8).

Symbolic images transcend not only categories, but themselves as well, challenging the perceptions and assumptions of those who encounter them. By expanding awareness beyond the immediately apparent, symbols and metaphors exert a compelling effect. Like discourse, which "refers back to its speaker at the same time that it refers to the world" (Ricoeur, 1976, p. 22), they also come to life on the interface between individual and world. Thus, the act of interpretation reactivates the relationship between individual and the world that generated their meaning. This meaning may not be discerned easily, however.

While all symbols transcend categories, a certain type of symbol integrates them into new amalgamations that, in a synergetic manner, become more than the sum of their parts. That is, each amalgamation incorporates greater realms of meaning than can any simple conglomeration of the original images. Jung called the process by which such symbols are generated the "transcendent function." Although it is a complicated phenomenon, the transcendent function is "a natural process, a manifestation of the energy that springs from the tension of opposites, and it consists in a series of fantasy occurrences which appear spontaneously in dreams and visions" (CW7, par. 121). "Transcendent" refers not to the metaphysical but to the ability to create transitions from one attitude to another.

The "uniting symbols" by which this transition is achieved bring together diverse elements, some of which are mutually contradictory. They compel the attention and transform the perspective of the ego, establishing new directions and patterns for growth. Formed from the fabric of everyday life, uniting symbols are the essence of transformation, through which polarization becomes potential.

The Mechanics of the Transcendent Function

Jung's description of the transcendent function is entirely consistent with his metapsychology, fundamental to which is the idea that conflict – tensions of opposites – is essential for psychological growth. "Man needs difficulties; they are necessary for health" (CW8, par. 143). Tensions and conflicts, however, often feel like stalemate and deadlock. Nevertheless, if these are allowed to persist, said Jung, they can activate the transcendent function. The inherent conflict between consciousness and the unconscious, for example, constitutes the most basic dynamic of this process, which "makes the transition from one attitude to another organically possible" (CW8, par. 145).

When this tension focuses on a particular issue,

> the shuttling to and fro of arguments and affects represents the transcendent function of opposites. The confrontation of the two positions generates a tension charged with energy and creates a living, third thing – not a logical stillbirth but a movement out of the suspension between opposites, a living birth that leads to a new level of being, a new situation. The transcendent function manifests itself as an operation of conjoined opposites. So long as these are kept apart – naturally for the purpose of avoiding conflict – they do not function and remain inert. (CW8, par. 189)

In short, seemingly irreconcilable conflict – if incubated – can activate the transcendent function and lead to growth.

While Jung described the prerequisites for the appearance of the transcendent function and referred to the images that it produces, he also noted that some may not be satisfied with descriptions of processes that exclude accounts of their mechanics. He wrote: "I have unfortunately had the experience that the scientific public are not everywhere in a position to follow a purely psychological argument." Nevertheless, he added, "I must content myself here with a description of the outward forms and possibilities of the transcendent function" (CW8, par. 191).

Strangely enough, there are those who argue that a "scientific" account of the transcendent function is neither necessary nor desirable. But scientific – or even mechanistic – explanations help not only to communicate Jung's ideas to the larger psychological community, but to clarify the phenomenon (and thus its utility in analysis) as well. Meanwhile, the sciences themselves, particularly contemporary physics and mathematics, are proposing models of complex dynamic processes that utilize metaphors very similar to those of Jung. In fact, one of these new theories, sometimes called "chaos theory," reveals much that can be useful for expanding on Jung's accounts of the dynamics of the psyche, particularly those of the transcendent function. (See Van Eenwyk, 1991.)

Chaos Theory

"Chaos is a mathematical concept that is somewhat difficult to define precisely, but it is probably best described as deterministic randomness" (Pool, 1989, pp. 25-28). While a chaotic system is deterministic, obeying certain equations that can seem quite simple, its behavior is so complicated as to look random. Predicting the long-term behavior of a chaotic system is virtually impossible, for any differences in the initial conditions of such a system, even when its dynamics are identical to another, will increase exponentially over time, leading to enormous differences in outcome between the two systems.

Chaotic dynamics "iterate" – work on themselves in such a way that every aspect of their dynamics becomes the basis on which further dynamics occur. Such feedback allows chaotic processes to achieve major transformations during very brief time periods. Moreover, their iterative dynamics lead them to be exquisitely sensitive to the initial conditions from which they arise. For example, if a dynamic system is defined by the equation $y \rightarrow y^2$, wherein each result of the equation is substituted back into the equation as the next value of y, and if the value of y to be computed begins at 2, then after only five iterations of the equation y = 4,294,967,296.

This in itself is a rather extraordinary result. But consider what happens if the initial value of y is 2.001. After five iterations (rounding off each iteration to three decimal places for simplicity) the new value is 4,364,168,157.546. So, a starting value that is larger by only 1/1000 yields a result that is larger by 64,200,861.546 after only five iterations!

Iteration and sensitive dependence on initial conditions can lead to chaotic dynamics when the system they characterize begins to oscillate, leading to bifurcations and period-doubling (the geometric multiplication of frequencies of oscillation). Furthermore, if the system is *fractal*, the resulting chaos is not entropic (leading to greater disorganization), but deterministic (order resurfaces in different dimensions at different times during the process). This is a crucial distinction among dynamic processes, and one that bears important implications for the analytic process.

Some of the crucial terms of chaos theory may require explanation. Coined by Benoit Mandelbrot, "fractal" refers to dynamic systems that demonstrate three characteristics. Their dynamics are self-similar (as they change, they continue to resemble themselves); are scale-invariant (the self-similarity persists across carrying scale) and transcend categories.

For example, to measure the length of a coastline is to discover very quickly not only that length varies with scale, but that there actually is no "line" to the coast at all! Measuring the length of a coastline on a map requires progressively smaller measuring devices to fit around all the protruberances and indentations – peninsulas and bays – of the coastline. Obviously a one-millimeter measure can fit around and into more of the irregularities in the coastline than can a one-centimeter measure. Actually walking the coastline itself reveals that each peninsula and bay is comprised of more peninsulas and bays at ever smaller scale. These progressively smaller versions of the same thing require correspondingly smaller measuring devices, presumably down to the molecular and subatomic level. Indeed, the smaller the measuring device, the longer the coastline turns out to be, for smaller measuring devices can fit around (and thus measure) correspondingly smaller irregularities *ad infinitum*.

Consequently, using length as a means of discriminating between coastlines is an unwieldy and imprecise means of comparison. The coastline of Argentina, for instance, has many more peninsulas and bays than the coastline of Florida. Yet the length of each increases with each smaller scale. In an attempt to solve this dilemma, Mandelbrot proposed a measure based on irregularity rather than on length.

To illustrate fractal dimension, consider a line and a plane. The line has one dimension, length; the plane, two – length and width. But if we draw the line on the plane, ranging over its surface and around its perimeter, filling most of the available space, what do we have then? Certainly we have a line, which has a dimension of one. But it fills virtually all of the surface of the plane, which has a dimension of two. So what is the dimension of our configuration? One, or two?

Fractal dimension provides a solution. By assigning a numerical value between one and two to our configuration, we can calculate the degree to which it approximates a line or a plane. A line that covers virtually all of the planar surface would have a fractal dimension close to two, whereas a line that had few convolutions would be closer to one. Thus, fractal dimension provides a basis for comparing structures that otherwise elude the grasp of traditional logic. Like a coastline, fractal dimension transcends categories.

It is here that the dialogue between fractal geometry and Jung's metapsychology comes alive. The science of chaotic dynamics, which are both deterministic (self-similar and scale-invariant) and representable – although not reducible – (through images that are characterized by fractal dimension), provides yet another tool for the analyst who wishes to decipher the convoluted world of unconscious processes.

Chaos Theory and the Transcendent Function

That the mind is a unique relationship between energy and matter, both of which are to some extent measurable, is undeniable. Elaborating its exact structure and mechanics, however, is another question. Nevertheless, there are some clues. For one thing, nerve impulses oscillate. Jung's metapsychology, which is grounded in the idea that tensions of opposites generate psychic energy and regulate psychological growth, is essentially a theory of oscillators. When such oscillatory dynamics become deterministically chaotic, moreover, they demonstrate self-similarity, scale-invariance, and fractal dimension. For example, when certain neurological inputs to the brain are visualized graphically – in the olfactory bulb, for example – inputs from similar stimuli form patterns that resemble one another across scale, and are fractal. (See Freeman, 1991, pp. 78-85.)

Thus, combining Jung's language with that of chaos theory leads to an interesting description of the process of individuation: When tensions of opposites generate oscillations between consciousness and the unconscious, chaos enters the psychic realm. If the chaos is allowed to continue (and the tension of opposites maintained), recognizable patterns (symbols/fractal attractors) eventually appear. An attractor is the pattern into which the dynamics of a system settle, like the point under a pendulum at rest, or the orbit of a planet. Fractal attractors are characterized by self-similarity, scale invariance and fractal dimension. These patterns represent the emergence of order from chaos and, if correctly interpreted, give insight into the status of the process.

Tensions of opposites, then, function as oscillators. When a tension of opposites is contained (as opposed to arbitrarily siding with one pole of the conflict), the intensity of the conflict escalates. In the terminology of chaos theory, as the oscillations intensify they bifurcate, leading to new tensions. As these bifurcations themselves bifurcate, all becomes confusion. The original order dissolves, and chaos ensues.

As the chaos continues (if the original tension of opposites is contained further), fractal attractors begin to coalesce, permeated by whatever order persists within the chaos. Their self-similarity across scale and fractal dimension reproduces the salient characteristic of the transcendent function: The symbols it produces are "uniting" in both their content and influence. Combining the two metaphors suggests that uniting symbols are fractal attractors.

Thus, chaos theory helps us to understand how the transcendent function operates. Chaotic dynamics must be allowed to permeate the conflict that seems to keep the patient stuck. In order for such chaos to be deterministic, analysts must allow themselves to be drawn into the bifurcations that permeate the oscillations between dimensions of the conflict. On the individual level, consciousness must incubate the conflict, allowing as many of its dimensions as possible to emerge into consciousness. In conformity with the compensatory nature of the unconscious, once consciousness becomes permeated by the conflict, the unconscious can provide the uniting symbol.

My hypothesis is that interpretation, on the interface between symbol and interpreter, recapitulates the dynamics between the symbol and the symbol-generating event. This hypothesis demonstrates self-similarity and scale-invariance. That the process of interpretation is fractal as well is suggested by the manner symbols open to the realm of the unconscious, where categories are blurred. "Man needs difficulties," said Jung (CW8, par. 143). "Healthy systems don't want homeostasis. They want chaos," say the chaos researchers (Pool, 1989, p. 604). Both maintain that the blurring of categories often leads to greater definition, and thus to greater potentials for development.

References

Freeman, W. (1991). The physiology of perception. *Scientific American, 264*-2, 78-85.

Pool, R. (1989). Is it chaos, or is it just noise? *Science, 243*-4887, 25-28.

Pool, R. (1989). Is it healthy to be chaotic? *Science, 243*-4891, 604-607.

Ricoeur, P. (1976). *Interpretation Theory.* Forth Worth, TX: Texas Christian Press.

Van Eenwyk, J. (1991). Archetypes: the strange attractors of the psyche. *Journal of Analytical Psychology,. 36*-1, 1-25.

Illness as Oracle: Psychosomatic Symptoms as Synchronistic Occurrences

Kaspar Kiepenheuer
Zurich, Switzerland
Swiss Society for Analytical
Psychology

I dare to speak about something unspeakable. Much has been said and written about the physical and spiritual background of psychosomatic manifestations, and yet the question whether they are synchronistic occurrences is unspeakable.

For some valuable suggestions that led me to my point of view I am indebted to Susan Bach (1990), Aniela Jaffé (1990), C.A. Meier (1986) and H.K. Fierz (1980). The most impressive insights, however, I received from my everyday teachers: the children and teenagers with whom I have worked, either as a doctor in the children's clinic, as a psychiatrist in the child-psychiatry clinic or today in my child- and teenage-psychiatry practice (where I also treat some adults).

Characteristics of Psychosomatic Illness

Psychosomatic sufferings are distress signals, expressing what cannot be expressed in any other way: hidden emotions breaking through. Rational measures of orthodox medicine are usually of little value in the treatment of psychosomatic suffering, at least for the total well-being of the ill person.

Psychosomatic symptoms seem to be an intensification of a psychological energy to the point of physical manifestation.

These illnesses can mean a bridge between body and soul, offering the affected person an approach to wholeness. Unfortunately, this bridge to a new orientation does not offer itself immediately and quickly. Rather, these physical messages are ambiguous, to be compared with answers of the I Ching.

The connections between body and psyche are not subject to a one-sided direction of cause and effect in which a specific emotional situation would call up a specific symptom. Rather we are faced with the typical question of "the chicken or the egg": psychophysical parallelism. When I see a child laughing I am not sure the laughter is because the child is cheerful, or if the laughter causes the child to be cheerful.

When a psychophysical symptom comes into existence a symbol is born. As a catalyst, the symbol can bring about a transformation in the spiritual as well as the physical area, if the meaning is understood. The literal understanding of symptom (from Greek) is "it falls together": coincidence, chance. If this falling together is connected with a symbol we have approached synchronicity.

Synchronicity

Synchronicity describes a subjectively significant coincidence, in time or space, of two or more separate occurrences or situations. Intellect may doubt a connection but, on a feeling level, even the confirmed rationalist is strangely touched and may recognize that transcendent powers are involved. Such situations tend to happen during borderline experiences: illness, nearness of death, depression or other critical situations.

I do not wish to pursue the question whether these phenomena can be understood scientifically, except for the rather vague explanation that spiritual energies – emanating from a strong complex – become so intense that they influence the physical circumstances. Parapsychology has coined the term psychokinesis for comparable phenomena. Perhaps psychokinesis is very ordinary, although surprising. Immanuel Kant said: "That my willpower moves my arm is no more comprehensible to me than if someone were to say that the same would also be able to hold back the moon in its orbit." Is it outrageous to assume such long-distance effects? Those who believe in astrology recognize powers that are able to transcend vast spaces and times.

Figure 1

An example occurred for me during a study visit in London. While celebrating my birthday with a friend, an indescribable physical unrest grabbed me. I hurried back to my apartment where I received a telephone message that my father had died: a heart attack during a visit to a sun observatory high in the mountains of Mexico. He was a sun astronomer and had always talked of "his sun" with visible passion. Later, at home, I discovered next to his bed a 1947 booklet entitled "The Sun," by Franz Masereel; it contained pictures of numerous wood engravings. One page was specially marked (Fig. 1). The picture on it seemed to indicate my father's premonition of death. Only later did I learn about an old Mexican myth in which those dying are thought to unite with the sun. Apart from this collective aspect, I sensed my father's death as a personal message to me, since he "chose" my birthday as his "return home to his sun." Thereafter we often met in dreams, where he developed a kind, fatherly tenderness toward me that had never existed during his lifetime.

From the estate of Aniela Jaffé a wonderful booklet from 1796 with the title *Ghost Appearances and Prophesies* came into my hands. I was astonished at the conjectures of the time: "If besides us there could not exist creatures that have such a subtle body that it could not be seen by our eyes in its natural form but that this merry body could be capable of giving itself more consistency from time to time, whereby it could be seen."

I think also about ghost stories, preferably English reports about ghostly apparitions. These ghosts seem to want to tell the living that they wander around unredeemed because something was not taken to a proper ending. For instance, there is the ghost that one could deliver by freeing the corpse from a wall. Thus, ghosts and related apparitions are to be perceived and taken seriously so that they can be freed from their boxed-in existence and buried properly, whether it be concretely or metaphorically.

What is the Common Factor?

The "subtle body" seems to approach a solution to the puzzle of psychosomatic and synchronistic events. In psychosomatic cases this subtle body corresponds to the symptom with its power of symbolism. The symptom represents a bridge between the unconscious and the ego through an unconscious content's choosing an expression that may become comprehensible to the ego. In synchronicity the meaning confronts us (see Fig. 2). Here we experience a link, this time between the outer world and the inner. In both cases does this "subtle body" not approach that which Jung called the transcendent function?

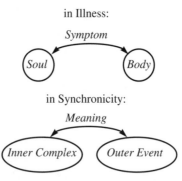

Figure 2: The Catalyzing Function of a Symptom and of Meaning

A subtle medicine and psychology is needed to enable healing persons to make room for the transcendent function and to obtain a hearing for the "subtle body." All too often, this "subtle body" seems neglected in encounters with the ill, and there seems to be too little room for the work of the transcendent function. A free and yet protected place is needed for such qualities to constellate. I think of this place concretely in the therapeutic setting but also in a transcendent sense, in that we cultivate a setting that leaves room for mysteries in the therapeutic process and the therapeutic relationship.

Charlotte

An experience with a girl's illness was valuable to me in becoming respectful toward the indescribable laws that I have tried to describe.

The girl's mother telephoned me. She was looking for help for her 12-year-old daughter Charlotte who was awkward, plump, lazy, an underachiever in school. Everything slid off her like raindrops off a taut umbrella. Among children she cut herself off in her own dreamworld. In school her sitting there "like a pudding" provoked the teacher. Already as an infant Charlotte was always hungry, while all others in the family – the parents and the three siblings – were slim, athletic and successful.

With me the slightly adipose girl seemed passive at first, but expectant. In the sandbox she stroked through the sand with her hands, mixed it, smoothed it and then cast a deep, questioning look at me. In the sand she created a peaceful scene with a farmyard, rural animals, a shepherd in the middle. "Like in paradise," she said. Then very suddenly, as if by magic, she held an enormous rubber monster over it: "With that it would not be so peaceful!" It was meant jokingly but we were both affected by this dark hint. At the parting after this first hour she pressed my hand for a long moment as if grateful.

Later she wrote a spontaneous composition that described her situation in a sympathetic way. Here is a shortened version:

The girl had been locked up with a mean woman for many years, because mother and father had died. She received bad food and all the mean woman did was scold the girl. The windows were barred. But one day the key was in the lock. With a smile on her face the girl quietly opened the door. The church clock struck and she knew she would soon be free. But she became very afraid of the cars outside because she did not know them. Briefly she thought: if only I had stayed inside the house! She lived on scraps. One day she met an artist who saw her pictures and invited her to live and paint with her. This is how she became a well-known painter. THE END!

At home, the sadder and quieter she became, the more the mother would scold her. She was imprisoned in a vicious circle. It was odd to learn that during pregnancy her mother had fungus poisoning and at the time of delivery had typhoid fever. Both left their marks on Charlotte's entrance into life. Did the prison stand for the connection with the "poisonous" mother in the physical as well as spiritual sense? I understood her cry for help for a place where a door opens, the church clock strikes and she can develop her true gifts. After her story it was understandable to me that the road to this goal was laborious. She said that it was so "terribly far" to my practice; in fact it was about 3 minutes.

In sessions with me, she was always all "there," involved and grateful for my being "there." In one sand-tray is a conical island (Fig. 3); on top and in the middle is a man with a "loudspeaker" in his hand, "but it had no people" (that would listen); "maybe it was to lure the fish!" Behind him stands Tarzan with his hand raised (moral support?). Two waiters bring him something to drink; two women bring him something to eat. A policeman takes care of "the boats docking correctly."

Did Charlotte have to stuff herself because no one was really aware of her? Or the other way around: Was she not more perceptible because she was shielding herself in this manner? It was as if ghostly apparitions were screaming for deliverance. The strengthening of this scream did not come from me as much as from her inner depth. Tarzan – expression of a primitive elemental force in her – supports the voice of the unheard singer. The first hint appears that she has found "her center." At that time she had an angina accompanied by high fever. After that she

Figure 3

Figure 4

seemed totally changed, as if she had incubated something in the warmth of the fever and the regression that was linked to it, and had blossomed out into an individual core of essence.

A tissue-paper collage (Fig. 4) gives an impression of her outer as well as inner development of the time: a tender-fluffy flower with a dark sky and green ground. Just like the flower her face blossomed out. It was as if the mist in front of her eyes had lifted. In this way she could reach new horizons:

"Now we will make a holy landscape." She introduces her new sand-tray: the stable of Bethlehem. From there hay would be brought across two bridges to feed the sheep. The bell on the right would announce each time the arrival of the feed. This image gave me an insight into the true character of her hunger: a hunger for spiritual orientation.

In a later sand-tray (Fig. 5), the strict separation of two contra-dictory worlds impressed me. On the left a tightly constructed town; on the right once again the stable of Bethlehem, this time with animals of different genera walking in a radiating formation toward the Christ-child. In between is a fence that "separates the two sides so that they will not disturb each other."

In school Charlotte had changed "like night and day," the teacher said. Her handwriting had improved in a striking way. The parents now took a totally different attitude toward the child; it remained unclear if it was the cause or result of Charlotte's changes. For all of us concerned, the connection remained as mysterious as the sound of the clock in Charlotte's story.

Our sessions became more comfortable. She chopped wood; I made a fire. She seemed to feel in good hands with me. She became more daring with the sand-trays; all of a sudden there is a monster "that surfaces there!" as if it belonged quite obviously into her life. I was glad to hear that she began a course in rock 'n roll and could make contacts spontaneously.

One last image in the sand (Fig. 6) gave me a reassuring image of her soul. In the middle is a round lake; various animals come from all directions. "They are all thirsty" and drink from the lake. No animal seems disadvantaged; they are peaceful together. Contemplated as a whole, the image in the sand looks like a radiating sun – a convincing manifestation of the Self. And I felt a confirmation that therapy (after a year at this point) could now stop, as she urgently desired.

At a final conversation with the parents I wanted to share these impressive images. As if by a miracle, however, the slide projector "refused" several times. Synchronistically the projector

Figure 5

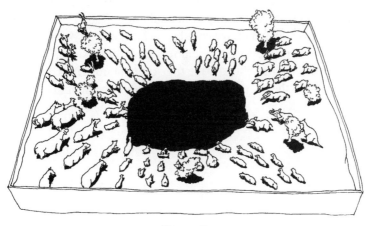

Figure 6

gave me a sign: The secrets of the girl are to remain her own and she is to free herself from the influence of the parents. Simultaneously the parents were developing a respect, a stepping back from the Self of their daughter.

In a later composition Charlotte remembers the time of therapy: "I used to think that no one loved me,… that I was a dumb little girl.… Then I had to go to a psychiatrist.… During that time it was as if I was born a second time. It was as if the scales fell from my eyes."

These words summarize her history of suffering and healing. The recognition of her own values meant a new birth for her, comparable to a fish losing its scales, becoming a being of broad daylight.

To what degree did Charlotte's illness have synchronistic characteristics? 1) There was a physical and social illness on the outside and a suffering searching on the inside that pointed beyond the earthly "captivity" of the girl. 2) In the parents there was simultaneously a deviation of attitude that was associated (synchronistically?) with the illness of the child (Kiepenheuer, 1990). With the dissolution of the "ghostly apparitions" of the daughter the parents simultaneously gained a new attitude without my having to intervene – which would have created new feelings of guilt. 3) A conventional attitude of cause and effect did not do justice to the girl in her situation. Rather a space had to be provided in which we could forget rational associations and let ourselves be surprised by entirely new dimensions. These at first seemed bizarre but later the transcendent, religious character emerged – in the holy birth and the sound of the church clock.

References

Bach, S. (1990). *Life Paints Its Own Span*. Zurich: Daimon.

Fierz, H. K. (1980). *Jungian Psychiatry*. Zurich: Daimon.

Jaffé, A. (1990). *Death, Dreams and Ghosts*. Zurich: Daimon.

Kiepenheuer, K. (1990). *Crossing the Bridge*. La Salle, IL: Open Court.

Meier, C. A. (1986). *Soul and Body*. Santa Monica, CA: Lapis.

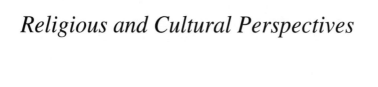

Religious and Cultural Perspectives

Reflections on Self as Internalized Value: Ancient and Modern Techniques

Marilyn Nagy
Palo Alto, California, USA
Society of Jungian Analysts of
Northern California

Every theory comes to life in a particular cultural situation; it must be tested in other cultures and in other time periods. The historical reading tends to free us from identification with doctrine. Thus a historical and cultural reading of Jung's essay on the transcendent function relativizes the theory to a certain extent. We can examine the theoretical language and think anew about how the theory accords or fails to accord with professional experience at the present time, in our present situation.

Insight widened by the historical method may have an exhilarating effect. But it may be experienced also as a painful loss of spiritual object, for we seek the reassurance of the unchanging and the secure in the language terms of our deep value commitments. Like the rhythmic systole and diastole of the living organism, we require in our study of Jungian psychology not only steady allegiance to objects and values that endure, but also a flexible response to the conditions of changing culture.

My goal here is a better understanding of Jung's idea of the Self, and of what we might mean when we speak of a mode of identity consisting of individualized values. Although Jung did not codify his theory of the Self until 1929 (CW13, par. 67), 13 years after writing his long-unpublished 1916 essay on "The Transcendent Function" (now in CW8), the essay describes a technique for developing a Self. How did Jung's technique reflect his cultural situation? Can we validate, by discovering common factors, the experience of the Self in other cultures? What terms and images might be common to Western experience of the Self?

Jung began this essay by admitting that fantasies, affect and forbidden desires coming from the unconscious can be disturbing. But those fantasies may actually present moral demands: a call to action or a challenge to one's conscious attitude, which is usually society's attitude. In order to achieve a creative widening of the personality it is important to get rid of the separation between conscious and unconscious, to see the significance of both; together they equal the transcendent function.

In the second part of his essay, Jung turned his argument around and headed back in the other direction. If it is indeed good, often productive and creative, for the person to integrate strange, until now unconscious ideas, the psyche itself may be not so much at war with itself (as in Freud's *id* and Christianity's dualism between good and evil) as it may be a self-regulating system, with compensatory responses emerging out of any point of view which becomes too one-sided. If one is "stuck" one can try to produce fantasies artificially, so that compensatory and renewing responses enable one to find a new direction in life. Instead of suppressing the troubling effects of emotion we can view emotion as a moral impetus to change and growth. Jung then described his new technique of "active imagination," followed by a little sermon: Although we may deny the value or the truth of a point of view not our own, it may nevertheless be valid. The widening of consciousness by including more and more of these previously excluded contents has moral value in itself. Those who deny it may be morally or mentally too lazy or too cowardly to make the effort.

We can imagine the conditions of personal and cultural experience by way of which Jung reached this remarkable thesis. Jung is 41 years old; he has long suffered being "out of step" with others. It is barely three years since his last, exquisitely painful appearance at the 1913 International Psychoanalytic Association meeting in Munich and his subsequent resignation as editor of the *Jahrbuch* and as president of the Association. His embrace of Freud's insights 15 years before, his decision to become a psychiatrist, his nocturnal reading of philosophy as a medical student, his abrasive relationships with his professors – these were the pattern and not the exception in his life. As a child he was teased by the boys of his village until he got big enough to beat them up, he read books in his father's and uncle's libraries that were too adult for him, he wondered at the stiff propriety of dark suits and proper words at church services on Sundays and dreamt forbidden and shocking dreams of turds falling on the Basel cathedral and of underground gods with penile erections.

Now Jung is confronting the impossible dilemmas of his life. He has been married since 1903 and has five children. Emma, the youngest, is just two years old. But he has been carrying on an affair with Toni Wolff at least since 1912 and will soon begin to build his tower house at Bollingen, partly – according to Brome (1981) – in order to have a place where he can spend time on weekends with Toni. He is building villages on the beach, keeping records of his fantasies and has just completed his strange little book, *Seven Sermons to the Dead* (MDR). Jung cannot believe in the religion taught by his father but he does have a deeply religious sincerity about his attempt to make sense of his own obstreperous and impassioned behavior and feelings. In his essay on "The Transcendent Function" Jung came to terms with his dilemma by proposing, over against the moral authority of the prevailing social order, a higher level of moral authority, one that inheres in the individual and accepts the value of every kind of human potential.

A number of factors peculiar to the early twentieth century post-Reformation German culture in which Jung lived assisted his ability to make this counter-cultural formulation. Jung's middle-class intellectual society was a homogeneous culture of Sunday morning church goers with tight moral proprieties, who paraded their scientific skepticism as professors on weekdays. (See Jung's *Zofingia lectures* CW Supp. Vol. A.) It was a culture of sexual and social repression. It was in some ways a secure society, but one whose security involved a deadening weight of parental/societal authority. Hermann Hesse's 1919 novel *Demian* reflected the upsurge of the forbidden "dark" side of God (the Abraxas of the *Seven Sermons*) and Jung wrote eagerly to Hesse: "Your book came at a time when, once again, I was oppressed by the darkened consciousness of modern man, and by his hopeless bigotry" (Let-I, p. 573). The Romantic tradition of individualism in Rousseau and Goethe had its late flowering in Hesse and in Thomas Mann, who, together with Jung and others, provided an ideational gradient into a new cultural period.

The new technique of individual development as a joining of the conscious and the unconscious perspective was at the leading edge of social movement in 1916, when Jung was about to come into his full strength. His concept thus had a heroic quality, because it showed the way for a society which was not yet – but would soon be – evolving into a more open culture. Counter-cultural ideas which are not merely aberrant have a heroic, superior character; they pull ahead, intimating in advance of the larger course of events the direction that is being chosen.

This emphasis on the counter-cultural attitude and on the value of the individual is the main glue binding together those of us who call ourselves Jungians. Those who have been deeply wounded in their families of origin or in the institutions of society – usually both – feel understood by Jung, who dignified the suffering inherent in standing alone by giving it a higher value than that of successful adaptation.

But different cultures have different concepts of identity, different hierarchies of value and different techniques for attaining the high value. An interesting example of such contrasts is Nyantiloka, the Ceylonese/Buddhist monk who pioneered Buddhist monastic reform in Sri Lanka. He was born in 1878 in Wiesbaden, Germany, as Anton Walther Gueth, in cultural circumstances strikingly similar to those of Jung. Both men faced the supreme problems in life and sought a solution for the individual based on moral values. Both moved toward the high value of their culture by turning away from the parents who represent, at least in projection, the lower or inferior values.

Nyantiloka's life exemplified the Buddhist solution to achieving the value being sought; doing away with the self by discrediting narcissistic emotional involvements and concentrating on making the complex moral code of the *Vinaya* come alive within. This is a practical, down-to-earth task which requires a lifetime to achieve. Jung sought to achieve a self by overcoming the split between good and evil, the stiff but shallow proprieties and the sexual repressions which he found in his culture, by widening the range of morally allowable emotional contents.

Possibly the best example of a counter-cultural attitude that is inimical to parents and domestic interests, while expressing the high value of the culture in symbolic parental images, is that of fourth-century Christian culture. Great ascetic heroes retreated to the outer desert in Egypt in order to glorify God and ensure their salvation – an old word for what we now frequently call "the experience of the Self." The use of both terms implies achieving a) a sense of relative autonomy and b) a sense of freedom from excessive anxiety.

Christianity began as a tiny counter-cultural fragment in the Roman Empire, with a group of people following the command of Christ, who said, "Whoever has left houses or brothers or sisters or father or mother or children or lands, for my sake, will receive a hundredfold, and inherit eternal life" (Matthew 19:29). In the first years after Jesus' death on the cross Christian followers awaited the imminent end of the world. In the world to come there would be no marriages, no families. For some years the question of accommodation to life that would go on in *this* world did not arise. But as the years went by and it became apparent that the Kingdom of God would not arrive immediately, the question of what it really meant to "follow Christ" – to espouse the high value – became urgent.

The French anthropologist Louis Dumont (1970) observed that in India, at least since 500 B.C., there is a division between the "inworldly" majority of householders and an "outworldly" minority of mendicant and monastic renouncers. There are also, correspondingly, two classes of virtue. For the Buddhist lay householder the only occasion for acquiring virtue is through generosity and support of the monastic *sangha*. To the monk belongs the responsibility for moral action and for meditation. Only the monk is given the task of solving *dukka*, the problem of the human condition. Dumont thought that the outworldly/inworldly division of moral classes which he had observed in India might apply also to the picture of emerging Christian culture in the Roman Empire. But there is a crucial difference.

The division of classes in India into a higher and a lower path is institutionalized in a stable society. Early Christian culture, by contrast, was destabilized by the Christians' having to obey two opposing commandments. Christ had said, "If anyone comes to me and does not hate his own father and mother and wife and children and brothers and sisters, yes, and even his own life, he cannot be my disciple" (Luke 14:26). Yet the Bible contains a contradictory and equally clear commandment to "honor your father and mother." Christianity collapsed social differences by placing the same ethical requirements on *all* its adherents. The new religion thus created crisis among its members, at the level of parent-child relationships.

Christians were confused about how they were supposed to achieve the high value in their intra-Christian culture. But so long as the great persecutions lasted – about 250 years – the possibility of vocation as a martyr ensured a vehicle for an individual, counter-cultural identity following the high value, Christ. The prospect of martyrdom provided a *technique*, a clearly envisionable path – namely suffering and death – toward salvation, or toward the Self. This experience cannot be co-opted by any collective, politicized uses that are made of it. Christians fervently believed that if they died as martyrs they would go directly to God. In second and third century culture the sacrifice of the martyr was thus a completely valid, ethical internalizing of the self-object.

With the peace of Constantine in 313 A.D. Christians were no longer persecuted. They were not yet in the majority in the Roman Empire but they surely became part of the "inworldly" group. Martyrdom could no longer serve as carrier of the *technique* of salvation – of achieving the high value of the culture. A new type of Christian saint began to appear: Christian ascetics who were the direct inheritors of the tradition of the martyrs in their search for salvation. They prepared the way for Augustine, whom history generally accords the honor of first having achieved a full sense of interiority of substantive mental and emotional contents.

The ascetics set the pattern for development of the idea of the individual in Western culture. They were men (and women too, though fewer in number and little-recorded) who wandered out into the Egyptian desert, beyond the villages, beyond the cultivated land, sometimes to live an eremitic life and sometimes to live in strict monastic communities. They survived with primitive handwork, usually weaving mats which sold at the village markets for a few pennies, which bought the barest necessary food. They contested with each other to serve God by sacrificing food, sleep, and sexuality. In passionate devotion to their goal they abandoned every domestic relationship; they prayed constantly and fought devils who appeared in the air.

John Cassian, who spent some years late in the fourth century visiting the various hermitages in the Egyptian desert, has Abbot Abraham tell the inquirer:

> You may leave your family and go on a pilgrimage in the flesh. But until you have endured the separation with your heart, and have given up every memory of those in your past, you have not understood the principle of renunciation, nor the main reason for a life of solitude in the desert. Not until you no longer feel either joy or sorrow at the fortunes and misfortunes of family members can you feel safe that your exertions will receive their due reward. (Cassian, 1978, pp. 532, 536-537.)

But the ascetics did discover the path to an internalized parent image. Less than 50 years after it became politically safe for Christians in the Roman Empire, Bishop Athanasius of Alexandria was writing the probably part fictionalized, part true-to-life biography of St. Antony, destined to become the paradigmatic ascetic saintly life story. Born about 251, Antony's parents died while he was in late adolescence. In church, not long after that, he heard texts being read which seemed to him to be a call to a new home in the desert. From then on he determined not to "look back on things of his parents, nor call his relatives to memory." And if in future he should indeed call to mind his old home and its comforts, or his sister in the place where she now lived among the virgins of his village, or any of the relatives with whom he used to feel close, then it was only the devil crashing around and making noise in the night – a devil who, if possible, would keep him from the good and destroy his salvation.

Living in the tombs outside his village, Antony felt that he was completely beaten up by the devil, enough that he might die of the pain. Finally the roof opened and a beam of light descended. Antony felt the presence of God and the pains were relieved, but Antony reproached God for leaving him alone and allowing him to suffer. Then the voice of God came to him: "I was here, Antony, but I waited to watch your struggle. And now since you persevered and were not defeated, I will be your helper forever." The parents whose memory Antony left behind with his first decision for the ascetic path had now been internalized as a parenting God, as a result of Antony's lonely struggle with himself and of painful impositions on the body.

During the second stage of Antony's discipline, hidden in the fortress of the outer mountain, he was persecuted again by devils, but he was no longer physically injured and he felt support through his beneficient visions. When at last he was forced to come forth and show himself, because so many would-be ascetics sought his teaching, his body seemed perfect and unchanged by the rigors of his ascesis:

> The state of his soul was pure, for it was neither contracted by grief, nor dissipated by pleasure nor pervaded by jollity or dejection. He was not embarrassed when he saw the crowd, nor was he elated at seeing so many others there to receive him. No, he had himself completely under control – a man guided by reason and stable in his character.

The language being used in this text is the Stoic vocabulary describing the state of the "wise man." Although this is the only language available at that time, we can easily follow the stages through which the ascetic hero internalizes the parental images and develops finally a counter-cultural identity which Jungians might call "being in the Self."

The point of doing history and of making comparative studies is always to better understand better ourselves in our own time.

Differing techniques to reach the Self appear in different cultures, partly because the "high values" of the society vary. The individual's *experience* of the Self, however – of a sense of relative autonomy and of relative freedom from excessive anxiety – seems similar even in widely separated cultures. Our own culture of the late twentieth century is already profoundly different from the homogeneous culture in which Jung lived. We now live in a radically pluralistic society. The compensatory activity of the unconscious psyche, insofar as it may offer response to the outer cultural milieu, surely has changed also. Relying on Jung's basic commitment to individual values, it is important to discover the techniques and the images which belong to our own time.

References

Athanasius (1980). *The Life of Antony and the Letter to Marcellinus* (R. Gregg, Trans. & Ed.). New York: Paulist.

Brome, V. (1981). *Jung, Man and Myth*. New York: Atheneum.

Cassian, J. (1978). The Conferences (E. Gibson, Trans.) *In Sulpitius Severus: Vincent of Lerins*. Grand Rapids, MI: Eerdmanns.

Dumont, L. (1970). World renunciation in Indian religions. In L. Dumont (Ed.), *Religion, Politics and History in India*. Paris: Mouton.

Heaven's Decree:
Confucian Contributions to Individuation

Bou-Young Rhi

Seoul, Korea
Association of Graduate Analytical
Psychologists
(Zurich Institute)

At fifteen I set my heart on learning; at thirty I took my stand; at forty I came to be free from doubts: at fifty I understood the Decree of Heaven; at sixty my ear was attuned; at seventy I followed my heart's desire without overstepping the line.

Confucius

Heaven's Decree, *Tien-ming* is interpreted usually as destiny or the mission given by Heaven. For Confucius, the most important preconditions to becoming a "gentleman," the ideal mature person, were to understand Destiny and to stand in awe of the Decree of Heaven. But actually Confucius, except for a few occasions, had rarely mentioned Heaven, Destiny or Benevolence – which were essential concepts in his thought. Confucius' concepts of Destiny and Heaven and his reactions to them were different in each situation he encountered. When one of his disciples, Po-niu, was ill Confucius visited him, held his hand through the window and said:

We are going to lose him. It must be Destiny. Why else should such a man be stricken with such a disease? (Confucius, 1979, Bk. VI, par. 10)

Confucius mourned deeply the death of his disciple, Yen Yuan, saying:

Alas! Heaven has bereft me! Heaven has bereft me! (1979, Bk. XI, par. 9)

Popular thought in the time of Confucius seems to have regarded Destiny as related to natural affairs such as death and life,
and Heaven to be concerned with social values such as wealth
and honor. But for Confucius, when we consider some of his
words, *Ming*, Destiny, was Heaven's Decree. As he heard of a
slanderous affair that might interfere with his political intentions,
he said;

> It is Destiny if the Way prevails; it is equally Destiny if the Way
> falls into disuse. What can Kung-po Liao do in defiance of Destiny?
> (Confucius, 1979, Bk. XIV, par. 36)

Huan T'ui, an officer of the Sung dynasty, bore a grudge
against Confucius and secretly attempted to kill him. When one
of his disciples warned him of the danger, Confucius said;

> Heaven is author of the virtue that is in me. What can Huan T'ui do
> to me? (Confucius, 1979, Bk. VII, par. 23).

It is impressive to see in these words what certitude Confucius
had and how tremendous was his trust in Heaven and Heaven's
Decree. Heaven was to Confucius a personified existence like a
benevolent and righteous father; also the primordial source of
virtues and a powerful, ultimate principle of justice. It provided a
strong sense of self-confidence to those who were convinced of
the existence of Heaven. Consequently, to question whether
Heaven was thought to exist within or outside one's mind is
futile. In Confucian terms there was no clear distinction between
the outside and inside of the human mind.

Historians hold the opinion that, in the time of Confucius, the
old belief in a deified emperor in Heaven had started to waver.
The idea that human intention reflects that of Heaven also appeared at that period.

In a later publication of Confucius' thought, we find these
very important words:

> What Heaven has conferred is called The Nature. (Confucius, 1933,
> Ch. I, par. 1).

Hsing, Nature, indicates the primordial human nature, a term
comparable to Jung's concept of Self. Everyone is endowed by

Heaven with Hsing but the original nature of each person can be distorted according to the various influences after birth. Xiu Ji (*Shuki*), Confucian way of Self-cultivation, is focused on the discovery and development of original human nature. Thus, *Chung-Yung* (1933) mentions:

> We may say therefore that he who is greatly virtuous will be sure to receive appointment of Heaven. (Confucius, 1933, Ch. XVII, par. 5)

A greatly virtuous man should be one who actualizes *Jen(In)*, the most perfect virtue rendered by Heaven.

Not only *Hsing* (Song), the Original Human Nature, but also *Cheng* (Sung), Sincerity, belongs to Heaven's way:

> Sincerity is the way of Heaven. The attainment of sincerity is the way of men. He who possesses sincerity, is he who, without an effort, hits what is right, and apprehends, without the exercise of thought; he is the sage who naturally and easily embodies the *right* way. (Confucius, 1933, Ch. XX, par. 18).

Cheng means to be truthful, to be steady and without falsehood. It also means incessant effort, constancy, concentration of mind. Instability, easy change of mind without effort, falseness, artificiality, discrepancy between the inner mind and outer behavior are the opposites of Sincerity. *Cheng* (Sung) is a primordial dynamic force of cosmos. Therefore, it belongs to the Way of Heaven and at the same time to every life. Everyone has the potentiality of Sincerity, but some actualize it while others do not. Therefore, *Hsing* and *Cheng* are synonymous; the potentiality of Sincerity belongs to the primordial human nature.

> The doings of the supreme Heaven have neither sound nor smell! That is perfect virtue (Confucius, 1933, Ch. XXIII, par. 6).

The absolute neutrality of Heaven and of the great virtue expressed in citation from the *Book of Poetry* (Shi-Kyung, 1951) remind us of the concepts of *Chung* – the Mean – and *He*, Equilibrium, the final goal of life according to *Chung-Yung* (1933).

> While there are no stirrings of pleasure, anger, sorrow or joy, the mind may be said to be in the state of Equilibrium. When those

feelings have been stirred, and they act in their due degree, there ensues what may be called the state of Harmony *He(Hwa)*. This Equilibrium (*Chung*) is the great root from which grow all the human acts in the world, and this HARMONY is the universal path which they all should pursue (Confucius, 1933, Chs. 1, 4)

Chung-Yung is, according to the commentary by *Chu Hsi (Chu-Hui*; 1130-1200 A.D.) – the famous neo-Confucianist of the Sung Period – neither deviated nor one-sided, neither excessive nor deficient; it is the principle of ordinary things (Chu Hsi, 1976). It is the natural consequence of Heaven's Decree and the ultimate of the subtle and the minute. *Chung*, the Mean, is neither a rigid collective norm, nor a compromise with reality, but a state of true inner equilibrium, Jung's "the middle" of psychic opposites. The state of Chung might be achieved by being free from the four troubles (Confucius, 1933, Bk. IX, par. 4): prejudice, insisting on a certainty, stubbornness and selfishness. With this attitude, the state of the Mean can be achieved and the mind becomes pure, free, insightful, simple. This state is also *Cheng*, Sincerity. Since *Cheng* is the Way of Heaven, the zenith of *Chung Yung* (the Mean) should be the state of oneness of human with Heaven. It is a long hard way to reach the state of *Chung Yung*.

Heaven in Confucian terms can be regarded from the Jungian viewpoint as the archetype of the Self. *Hsing, Cheng, Jen* and *Chung* are all derivatives of the Self, revealing various aspects or manifestations of the Self archetype. Heaven's Decree should be regarded as the teleological meaning of the Self and the archetypal constellations of individuation. Confucius sought to teach his contemporaries the meaning of the ego-transcendent spiritual world in order to help them actualize it and become mature persons.

Confucius' emphasis on the attitude of great reverence and awe toward Heaven reminds us of the Jungian attitude of "religio" toward the unconscious Self. Thus, the process of individuation may be said to be one of pursuing Heaven's Decree as reflected in one's mind in which the attitude of religio – the careful, sincere observation of that we call the numinosum – is crucial.

The question may arise how one can know the Decree of Heaven, if Heaven is a transcendent source. Confucius did not teach the direct way to elucidate Heaven's intention. The ability to have such transcendent knowledge seems to be acquired only after long self-cultivation until the later stage of life. Rather than teach magical skills to discover the transcendent secret of Self, he tried to show the right attitudes toward self-cultivation.

> Wishing to rectify their hearts, they first sought to be sincere in their thoughts. They first extended to the utmost their knowledge. Such extension of knowledge lay in the investigation of things. (Confucius, 1933, The Great Learning 4)

Only with an attitude of Sincerity free from self-deception, by close watching of one's inner mind *Shen du (Shin-dok)*, and loving other persons without projecting to them, *Shu (Shu)*, one is then expected to learn wisdom from other people and from the classics: history, poetry, music and ethical principles.

For Confucius, everyone is a teacher and human interactions are the source of education. It was realization through life, as Jung (CW11) pointed out, characteristic of Eastern ways of meditation. Nature, such as mountains and water, is also included in the world of experience for a mature person.

As the thoughts of the *I-Ching*, Taoist and Buddhist viewpoints were reflected in the neo-Confucian world-view, the concept of Heaven and Heaven's Decree came to be incorporated into the concept of *Chi* (configurative energy), *Yin-Yang*, and *Li* (primordial principles). Thus, the symbol of Heaven changed into a psychological and metaphysical concept. Humanity, as a microcosm, consists of *Li* and *Chi*.

In this connection, the development of human mind and its relationship to the cosmos were explained through diagrams which were devised by neo-Confucian scholars. For example, the Diagram of the Supreme Ultimate by *Chou Tun-yi* (1017-73) is the Sung dynasty of China; Diagram of the Union between the Nature of Heaven and Human by *Kwon Kun* (1352-1409) and the

New Diagram of Heaven's Decree by *Lee Toe Kye* (1501-1570), both in Korea. Their depiction and explanations are extraordinarily interesting and worthwhile to make comparative investigation, but I do not attempt it here. However, the nature of mind and the goal of maturation in the terms of Confucian and neo-Confucian scholars seem to be the same as Jung's idea of individuation.

Like all other religious doctrines, however, Confucianism in its classical form seems to have neglected some aspects of the ego-transcending realm behind the solemn supremacy of Justice designated as Heaven and Heaven's Decree. It was the world of prodigies, power, disorders and gods which Confucius did not mention (Confucius, 1979, Bk. VII., par. 21). And to these shadows of Confucian consciousness belong sexuality, feminine attractiveness and the images of ordinary men and women. Confucius' avoidance of confrontation with these shadow aspects of the psyche was both his merit and his demerit.

On the other hand, Confucius' emphasis on *Li*, etiquette and other formulations about the moral behaviors of a "gentlemen," has tended to be adopted by the people as collective moral norms. This tendency is found not only in Confucianism but also in other religious doctrines. *Li* might be interpreted, in Jungian terms, as patterns of behaviors derived from the Self archetype, or belonging to persona – an archetypal aspect of the Self. The basic spirit of Confucius' thoughts does not lie in rigid collective moral doctrines, but in a central teaching of the actualization of the great virtue *Jen*, Benevolence, the love of fellow humans.

In a time of moral confusion of modern industrialized society, the Confucian approach of self-cultivation may be helpful, especially for young people establishing their personas, which are rooted in the unconscious ethos.

To know Heaven's Decree is not the final step of self-cultivation. It is a precondition for a further maturation process when we consider Confucius' (1979) statement. To know Heaven's Decree is again the indispensable condition for reaching the state of absolute harmony and freedom, *Chung He*.

But Heaven is ultimately an ego-transcending existence, though it is closely related to mind. Here we can see why Confucius rarely mentioned Destiny, Benevolence or Heaven: because Heaven's Decree cannot be explained with words.

The same attitude can be recognized when, asked about Benevolence by his disciple, Ssu-ma Niu, Confucius replied:

> The mark of the benevolent man is that he is loath to speak!....
> In that case, can a man be said to be benevolent simply because he is loath to speak?
> The Master said, When to act is difficult, is it any wonder that one is loath to speak? (1979, Bk. XIII, par. 33)

Like Lao-tzu, Confucius appreciated unyielding strength, resoluteness, simplicity and reticence, which he regarded as "close to Benevolence" (1979, Bk. XIII, par. 27) He disliked the use of "cunning words and ingratiating face" (1979, Bk. I, par. 3). In a time of commercialism, where strategies, political showoffs, and skillful flattering expressions dominate, Confucius' simplicity of the "gentleman" can perhaps play a role as a catalyst for the maturation process of the human community.

The insight that there exists something which is too awesome and mysterious to be explained with human speech is well reflected in Confucius' statement when he considered giving up speech:

> Tzu-kung said, "If you did not speak, what would there be for us, your disciples, to transmit?" The Master said, "What does Heaven ever say? Yet there are the four seasons going round and there are the hundred things coming into being. What does Heaven ever say?" (1979, Bk. XVII, par. 19)

Here Confucius sought to illustrate the importance of nonverbal teaching through deeds.

Modern psychology went beyond the old philosopher and began to elucidate the secret intention of the Self. An attitude of reverence and awe toward the world of the unconscious numinosum, however, should be maintained as a basic Jungian attitude in the process of individuation.

References

Chu Hsi (1976). *Non-o Chip-chu: Commentaries to Lun yü* (Vol. 6). Seoul: Myung Moon-dang.

Confucius, (1979). *The Analects: Lun yü* (D.C.Lau, Trans.). Middlesex, England: Penguin Books.

Confucius, (1933). *Chung-Yung: The Great Learning: The Doctrine of the Mean.* (J. Legge, Trans.). Tokyo: Nisanshi-do-sho-ten.

Shi-Kyung (1951). *The Book of Poetry* (W. S. Lee, Trans.). Seoul: Hyon-am-sa.

Culture and the Transcendent Function

Makoto Takeuchi
Kyoto, Japan
Association of Graduate Analytical
Psychologists
(Zurich Institute)

There are two main factors in the individuation process:
1) development of ego and 2) having a proper mutual relationship between ego as the center of consciousness and Self as the deepest center of the human psyche. People in Western culture tend to attach importance to the first factor – being a unique individual. People in Eastern culture tend to attach importance to the second factor; being identical with others has been an almost compulsive need for them. Their loyalty is for their collective centers such as family, employing company and nation. They want to be together and to keep harmony in their groups even if they must sacrifice individual needs.

It is no wonder that modern science, which is based on separation, started in Western culture. In Eastern culture it is important for individuals to move together. There are considerable differences between Western hero images and Eastern hero images. For example, Japanese heroes prefer to sacrifice themselves for the collective purposes with fewer individual rewards.

The meaning of individuation may be the same in both types of culture. However, the process of the individuation is different. For example, we can observe the Mandala-like figure only in the last stage of the sand-play therapy with Western analysands. But it is not rare to observe the Mandala-like figure in early stages of therapy with Eastern analysands.

Contemporary Eastern people are beginning to be dissatisfied with their collectivism. As they meet the Western culture they seek to become more individual. However, it is still difficult for them to do so; they face the pressure of being counted as social disturbances. Indeed, many of them are having mental problems.

On the other hand, many Western people are very lonely. Many of them also suffer from mental problems. They are seeking change too. Perhaps the Western people and the Eastern people are beginning to climb the same mountain from different sides.

A Theoretical Understanding of Western and Eastern Psychic Structure

Self is the center of each human being's psyche, including conscious and unconscious. Ego is a center of each individual's consciousness. Therefore, the structure of the human psyche is something like a sea urchin. Self is the center of the huge sea urchin's body. The individual ego is the center of the sea urchin's feelers.

Ego and Self make a pair, as do a sea urchin's feelers and body. Self has a huge amount of information about reality, gained through the experiences of many egos. Self stores and integrates all this information; it can influence individuals' destiny based on collective information. Destiny is like a closed circuit: If it starts this way, it must be ended that way. The function of both ego and Self is integration. Ego integrates each individual's experience and controls the individual's reaction to reality. Self integrates all human beings' experience throughout history and controls the way they live in the reality.

At the same time, Self desires to know more through egos. If many individuals bring new information with new quality, Self can replace an old closed circuit by a new circuit in order to integrate the new information. Egos can bring new perceptions of reality and how to react to it.

Transformed and highly individuated egos can gather new information about reality. After all, they change not only the reality but also the old integration of Self. Therefore, transformation of each individual changes the destiny of all individuals and the human race as a whole.

All human beings can be seen as a single life from the Self's point of view. Individual egos are sense organs – receptors – and effectors of the larger life. Self is the center of life but without egos it cannot transform itself. Both the Self-oriented view and the ego-oriented view are right; they see the same thing from different directions, complementing each other.

One American astronaut felt himself as a sense organ of a divine whole when he landed on the moon. Since landing on the moon was a new experience for all human beings, it could be clear to him that he represented the species.

If ego is a center of each individual's consciousness and Self is an identical center of all human beings' psyches, a simple diagram (Fig. 1) can suggest the psychic structure of human beings, along with a simple and a rational explanation of the difference between the Western and Eastern psychic structure.

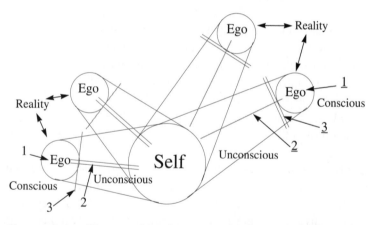

Characteristics of Easterners' Psychic Structure	*Characteristics of Westerners' Psychic Structure*
1. Lower ego development	1. Higher ego development
2. Closer connection with Self	2. More distance from Self
3. Less clear boundary between conscious and unconscious (more open to unconscious)	3. Clearer boundary between conscious and unconscious (less open to unconscious)

Figure 1

The Dominant Archetypes
of Western Culture and Eastern Culture

The dominant archetype of Western culture is more the Father; the dominant archetype of the Eastern culture is more the Mother. The father archetype gives higher ego development, to conquer reality. The mother archetype is more accepting of egos and keeps them more in the Self's collective integration. A father trains his children to go far away from his house to build their houses; a mother prefers to have her children stay around her house to build their houses. Therefore, Westerners are more challenging to nature and destiny; Easterners are more obedient to nature and destiny. The difference in the dominant archetype may be connected with climate, history and religion.

The Transcendent Function in Ego-Oriented Culture
and in Self-Oriented Culture

Archetypes always make a pair: the extremes of any bias. Therefore, it is not enough to say which archetype is dominant in each culture; it is necessary to say which pair of archetypes is dominant. The father-daughter axis is dominant in Western culture. The mother-son axis is dominant in Eastern culture. Western culture and Eastern culture are opposite. It is important to clarify the characteristics of opposites in order for both to integrate and transcend (Table 1).

	Western Culture	*Eastern Culture*
Basic Principle	Individualism	Collectivism
Orientation	Ego	Self
Dominant Archetype	Father-Daughter Axis	Mother-Son Axis
Future dominant Archetype for both	Man-Woman Axis	

Table 1

The dominant archetype-pair influences individuals in families, organizations and societies in both cultures. For example, Western women have a tendency to expect Western men to act more like father. Western men prefer Western women to act like daughter. Eastern women prefer Eastern men to act more like son. Eastern men expect Eastern women to act like mother. They all are starting to complain that their partners imprison them in fixed roles. These expectations are the basic reason for family problems world-wide. Men and women are tiring of the old collective fixed roles, derived from the dominant archetypes in their cultures, because there are always restrictions and a protector-protected relationship. Therefore, the dominant archetype-pair of the future culture for all human beings must be the man-woman axis. There would be no restriction, no protector-protected relationship and no upper-lower relationship. Then human beings will be able to accomplish true equality between men and women: Westerners, Easterners and all races.

Both cultures are facing a new, difficult situation. When the ego-oriented culture faces a difficult situation it makes people more separated and egoistic. When the Self-oriented culture faces a difficult situation it compels people to be more collective and identical. Both situations cause neurosis. Westerners and Easterners are beginning to climb the same difficult mountain from different sides. They have to work on the problem in order to see each other on the top of the mountain. On the way they will bring new information into the deepest center. Then they can change the destiny of all individuals and the human race as a whole, unifying the ego-oriented culture and the Self-oriented culture and finding all human beings as the same species on the same planet.

Eshu-Elegba, Master of Paradox: An African Experience of the Transcendent Function

Pedro Kujawski
London, England
Independent Group of Analytical
Psychologists

The investigation of the Yoruba god Eshu-Elegba, a great figure of African creative imagination, can help us to become more aware of the workings of the transcendent function in our psyches.

Jung equated the transcendent function with "this remarkable capacity of the human soul for change." He even said that "the secret of alchemy was in fact the transcendent function, the transformation of personality through the blending and fusion of the noble with the base components, of the differentiated with the inferior functions, of the conscious with the unconscious" (CW7, par. 360). This mysterious capacity of the human soul for change can be said, also, to constitute the core of the myth of Eshu.

Scholars who study the religion of the Yoruba, a West African people whose ancient culture has spread from native Nigeria to Brazil and Cuba, tend to describe him as a trickster god. Many of his stories and praise names describe him as such but we should be wary of a too-quick classification of Eshu. Whatever one says about him could be reversed and still be true. If Eshu is a troublemaker, irritatingly capricious and provoking disaster, he is also the great donor of gifts in Yoruba religion and is praised as the "road maker," the giver of riches.

The following story, collected by Pierre Verger (1957, p. 113) and quoted by John Pemberton in his excellent paper about Eshu (1975, p. 26), shows the god as a pure trickster:

> Eshu comes upon a queen whose husband had been inattentive. Bring me several hairs from the beard of the king," he says, "and cut them tonight with this knife. I will make an amulet of them which

will restore his passion for you." As the queen makes ready, Eshu goes to the queen's son, heir to the throne, who lives outside the royal compound as required. "The king is leaving for war," Eshu reports. "He wants you to go to the palace this evening with your soldiers." Then off to the king goes Eshu to whisper to his majesty: "Embittered by your coldness to her, the queen wants to kill you to avenge herself. Be on guard this evening!" Night comes. The king goes to bed, feigning sleep. Soon he sees his wife approaching with a knife. He disarms her and they argue loudly. The prince arrives with his soldiers, hears the cries from the king's chambers, and rushes in. Seeing his father with a knife in his hands and fearing an attack on his mother, he accosts the king. The latter, believing his son is attempting a coup, calls the palace guard. A general massacre follows.

It is not easy to understand why Eshu's destructive action in this story is so absolute; the transformation depicted ends in chaos with apparently no redeeming features. The psychological effects associated with the intervention of Eshu are, however, noteworthy. He creates an atmosphere of illusion by weaving a web of misrepresentations and wrong interpretations which lead to a complete falsification of reality. Under his influence powerful feelings of suspicion are generated and violent, destructive impulses are unleashed, resulting in the complete annihilation of the people in the story. Thus, Eshu is called the troublemaker, the one who acts capriciously, the confuser of people.

Nevertheless, at this point of the argument, one can almost hear Eshu rise to his feet to say: "Is that really so?" Is he really deceiving us with all this tangle of intrigues? Or is he revealing the hidden or unconscious motives behind the actions of a jilted queen, a power-driven king, and an over-ambitious heir to the throne?

Another story, collected by Maupoil (1943) in western Africa, amplifies and elucidates the role of Eshu. The main character is a mythological king, Metonlonfin, a paradigmatic figure representing the principle of kingship. He is the king of Ife, a mystical land, the place of origin of the Yoruba people in particular and of humankind in general. A synopsis of the story goes as follows:

Metonlonfin, king of Ife, possessed a he-goat who had four eyes, two in front of the head and two behind. This goat was in fact the sun, which watched over the whole world for the king. One day the king gathered all his subjects and proclaimed that he was omni-scient, that he knew of the actions of all of them, thanks to the ability of the goat to see in all directions at the same time. At these proud words Eshu stood up and challenged the king, saying that he, Eshu, had the power to do whatever pleased him, either before or behind the sun-goat, and the latter would not be able to see it.

To prove that he was able to do what he said, Eshu first made four little heads of clay and covered each of them with a cap of a different color: white, black, blue and red. He placed them at the four cardinal points: East, West, South and North. Next he made a four-colored cap for himself, using the same color scheme. With this strange cap on his head, Eshu entered the kingdom of Ife and attacked, cutting off the head of the king's wife. Although the deed had taken place in broad daylight, to find the culprit turned out to be an impossible task. Some people had seen a man wearing a white cap on it, some said his cap was red, or blue, or black, according to the angle from which they had witnessed the murder. Amidst this tremendous clash of opinions Eshu struck again, killing the prime-minister. And he went on killing people, rotating the cap on his head and spinning… like a whirlwind, creating more and more confusion until the whole country was engulfed in a bloody battle.

When chaos reached its peak Eshu revealed himself as the one who had killed the queen and the prime-minister, as well as many others, thereby proving that his freedom to act unseen and unrestrained was supreme, in spite of the power of the four-eyed goat, the sun. A solemn act followed, in which the king fully acknowledged the power of Eshu to "eat the goat," that is, to obliterate the light of the sun like dark clouds gathering round it, interposing themselves between the star of the day above and the earth below. (p. 190)

This story is a variation on a more common tale of Eshu in which he appears wearing a two-colored cap, either black and white (Bascom, 1969) or white and red (Maupoil, 1943). Walk-ing along the border of two farms, the god provokes a fight between two neighbors because they cannot agree on the color of the cap, each one seeing it from a different angle. Our story is much more elaborated, probably because it was collected in the kingdom of Dahomey (now the Republic of Benin), which was ruled by a powerful monarchy on top of a very complex machin-

ery of State. In my view the story dramatically compensates a
collective historical situation in which state and kingly power
have become too strong.

As in the first story, the intervention of Eshu generates chaos
and destruction. The second story reveals, however, that it was
the king's claim to absolute power that brought Eshu's destruc-
tivity into play. The king proclaims that he possesses all-seeing
consciousness, symbolized by the four-eyed goat, the sun. Eshu
proves him wrong and, as a result, the monarch is forced to
recognize the limitations of his own power. This recognition, as
well as the acknowledgment of Eshu's power, finally brings
peace back to the country. Eshu's action here carries meaning
and purpose; it is not mere capriciousness that compels him to act
the way he does.

In order to counteract this being of four-fold vision, Eshu puts
in motion another quaternio, the four hooded figures with their
specific colors. Representing the four cardinal points, these little
statues also stand for the four major divination signs of the
Yoruba religious system. They constitute what is called "the four
roots of the world and of life," that is, the four basic principles at
the basis of existence, the four pillars upon which the world is
built. The white figure represents East, day and life; the black
one West, night and death. Together they form the axis of "the
great road of life," embracing everything that is alive and perceived by the senses. It is the visible world. The North-South
axis, defined by the blue and red figures, is more difficult to
describe because it constitutes "the place of the unknown beyond," the domain of mystery where the senses cannot penetrate.
It is the spirit world, realm of the ancestors, of the gods (Maupoil,
1943, pp. 187-89).

Eshu confronts the power of the king with an image of all-
embracing totality, representing the mystery of existence. This
image alludes to a powerful and secret symbol of Yoruba religion, the *Igba Odu*, or calabash of existence. The object which
represents it is a calabash cut in halves which are then united and
sealed, thus expressing the eternal and fruitful embrace of the
two aspects of existence, the *aiye* (this world) and the *orun* (the

beyond). Only a few powerful diviners know what is inside the calabash, but among its items are four receptacles, each containing a substance of a different color. These substances are associated with the same major divination signs mentioned above, the "four roots of the world and of life" (Gleason, 1973, p. 188).

It is not difficult to see that Eshu faces the king with a mystery which far surpasses the latter's capacity of understanding, thereby plunging the country into complete chaos. The kingly power is expressed in a totality of what is visible and known, the fourfold vision provided by the sun. Thus, the king embodies the principle of consciousness, which has a quaternary structure given by the four functions. In contrast, Eshu's image of totality adds the dimension of the unknowable, the invisible, the divine – what in Analytical Psychology we call the collective unconscious. Through Eshu, therefore, an entirely different order of being makes itself manifest, which has the power even to obliterate consciousness completely and "eat the goat," as the king says at the end of the story. In the intervention of Eshu, the myth – typically – portrays a dynamic and autonomous factor invading the conscious world from all sides, creating confusion and destruction, but also movement and transformation.

All myths and rites surrounding the image of Eshu make it clear that he stands between the two aspects of reality, the aiye and the orun, and that his function and purpose in the Yoruba conception of the universe is to see that these two levels of existence are in equilibrium and communication with each other. Whenever one sees Eshu displaying his tricks, acting destructively and being a troublemaker, the understanding of the Yoruba is that one must have fallen out of touch with the spirit world or strayed away from the habitus of one's ancestral life. A gesture of reconciliation is needed so that the balance can be restored.

The more one deviates from one's ancestral disposition, the more destructive will be the image of Eshu. If one makes a comparative study of the image of Eshu in the various geographical areas of Yoruba culture one finds that the areas which retained more African cultural values show an image of Eshu that is complex, richer in contrast and creative. Conversely, in the areas where the African culture has been disrupted by either forced Christianization or the repression of the original forms of religious expression, the image of Eshu tends to lose its creativity and take on predominantly fearsome and demonic traits. As his multicolored cap suggests, Eshu can be seen from different angles. As a rule, however, the first manifestation of the god is disruptive, negative. One sees one's intentions crossed by a contrary will which at first one cannot understand: One fails just when one most wants to succeed, an accident prevents the realization of one's most cherished dreams, or one is driven to a dangerous spot against one's will, only to be killed there, or crippled for life, or involved in an unexpected conflict. All these phenomena are associated with Eshu in the divination stories of the Yoruba. Whenever one makes a bold assertion, saying with utter conviction, "This is so," Eshu says, "Is it really?"; and goes on to prove how wrong one is.

A divination poem is about "head" and "legs." The Yoruba believe that the head is the seat of individual destiny. A good head gives luck in life; a bad one brings misfortune. The danger involved in this conception is that one can become either too fatalistic or too confident in one's talents and neglect any idea of work. The story aims to correct this view. It runs as follows:

> The flat one, Ifa priest of *ese*
> Performed divination for *ese*
> On the day he was coming from heaven to earth.
> All *ori* gathered themselves to deliberate,
> But they did not invite *ese*.
> Eshu said "You do not invite *ese*,
> We will see how you would be able to achieve success."
> The meeting ended in a quarrel.
> They then sent for *ese*.
> It was then that their deliberations were successful.
> They said, "that was exactly
> What their Ifa priests had predicted"
> The flat one, priest of *ese*
> Performed divination for *ese*
> On the day he was coming from heaven to earth.
> The flat one has surely come,
> Ifa priest of *ese*.

Nobody makes a plan
And leaves out *ese*.
The flat one has surely come,
Ifa priest of *ese*. (Abimbola 1973)

The idea here is that without "legs" there is nobody to carry the heads about! "Legs" are associated with the hard work that is needed to bring to fruition the potentiality for success contained in the *ori*.

For the Yoruba, *ori* and *ese* are two basic components of the human personality. They constitute a pair of opposites which must work together if anything is to be accomplished in an individual's life. Eshu's role is to challenge the one-sided self-sufficiency of "head" and bring "legs" into play. Again typically, a quarrel follows his intervention. Eshu precipitates the conflict, which leads to a solution at the end.

If one is brought up in an environment in which the stories about Eshu are part of the general knowledge and are told again and again through generations, the perception of one's inner contrariness sharpens. One finally realizes that a spirit at times full of pranks, exasperating and malicious, at times funny, benevolent and inspiring, seems to be the true master of one's fate. Eshu adds an element of unpredictability that is always worth considering. This awareness of the unexpected stimulates "careful consideration" of ever-present unconscious forces which, as Jung said, we neglect at our peril.

From the stories discussed so far it is easy to see that Eshu always acts toward the recognition of the full parity of the opposites. This very African attitude of constant observation of the contrary will of Eshu is equivalent to the process of getting to know the counterposition of the unconscious, a process which Jung called the transcendent function. Speaking of psychic dissociation, for example, he said: "In order to abolish the dissociation either nature herself or medical intervention precipitates the conflict of opposites, without which no union is possible. This means not only bringing the conflict to consciousness; it also involves an experience of a special kind, namely, the recognition of an alien 'other' in oneself, or the objective presence of another will" (CW13, par. 481). For the Yoruba, this "other" is Eshu. When the will of Eshu is not taken into consideration he causes all accidents.

Psychologically, the trickster tales of Eshu are descriptions of situations in which the unconscious fails to cooperate. To quote Jung's words, "a failure of memory, of coordinated action, of interest, of concentration, can well be the cause of a serious annoyance, or of a fatal accident, a professional disaster, or a moral collapse" (CW11, par. 784).

When a person of Yoruba culture is plagued by the unpleasant forces unleashed by Eshu – a true nigredo, in alchemical language – the person goes to the master of divination, the Ifa priest. Through the casting of 16 palm nuts, divination produces a particular sign – rather like the I Ching – among the 256 possible signs. This sign depicts a typical pattern composed by the forces which came into play in the creation and development of the person's fate. As the divination proceeds, the priest diviner recites the verses and mythological stories associated with the sign, which he sees as relevant for the understanding of the person's life situation. In these myths the wisdom of Ifa, the god of divination, is manifested.

As much as Eshu makes one sweat, the experience of Ifa is like a cooling breeze. All difficulties calm down in contact with Ifa. The moment of divination is a moment of quiet illumination where one has a glimpse into a pattern which gives a sense of order and meaning to one's life. As Pemberton (1975) puts it, divination corresponds to a psychological reordering of the client's affective and cognitive situation. One contemplates one's life vis-a-vis an eternal myth; this has a liberating and vivifying effect.

During the moment of divination Eshu is present, but quiet. As the 16 palm nuts are handled by the diviner, Eshu places himself in front of him, as the seventeenth. His face is carved in the divination tray where the sign is inscribed. As communication between Ifa and his human counterpart takes place, Eshu observes. He is the guardian of this process because he regulates the relationship between the two levels of existence, the divine and the human.

Thus, after having pushed the individual to the brink of destruction with his tricks, Eshu now leads the person to Ifa, who imparts knowledge of the powers that shape his or her life. Divination imparts knowledge of hidden potentialities. However, this knowledge alone does not make such possibilities real. In the Yoruba view of the world one needs an act of sacrifice to activate these hidden powers and make them effective. Thus, each divination story is complemented by a prescription of such a sacrifice.

At this state, Eshu becomes active again, as the Lord of Sacrifice. In the act of sacrifice the *ashe* – the mana or life principle which animates the offering – is transported by Eshu from this world to the other world. The *ashe* enhances the powers of the gods, creating higher energetic potential in the beyond. As a result, the creative energy of the gods flows back to the human world in the form of a healing gift, brought by Eshu. This exchange and transformation of energy is controlled and symbolized by Eshu.

As we can see, there are two distinct moments in the divination process. The first one, divination proper, is quiet, receptive, characterized by insight, illumination and sense of meaning. The second one is active. Through the sacrificial act the insight gained becomes effective; part of one's actual life. During the first stage Eshu sits and observes, as a perceiving eye. The madness, the restless and chaotic activity which he had induced gives way to reflection. At the second stage Eshu moves to and fro between the two worlds and becomes that instance which leads to the realization of one's potentials. These two moments in divination are analogous to the two main phases of the alchemical work, the *opus ad album* (*albedo*) and the *opus ad rubeum* (*rubedo*). According to Jung (CW14) psychologically they correspond to the constellation of unconscious contents in the first part of the analytic process and to the integration of these contents in actual life. This passage of contents from a potential into an actual state is, for the Yoruba, promoted by Eshu.

Because it involves the destruction of the offering, the sacrifice is a movement toward death, which opens a yawning gap into the beyond. However, thanks to the specific power of Eshu in the order of the universe, this movement into death, once fulfilled by the symbolic act of sacrifice, is reversed; a new situation is created, in which new gifts come true and new beings are generated. Eshu is then praised as the donor of gifts, as a child full of riches.

Thus, what Goethe termed this "strange son of chaos," who has the uncanny power to dissolve fixed structures and plunge the world into confusion, has also the power to bring into reality a new birth, born out of the confrontation of the individual with the divine forces. He is a Master of Paradox; as such he is praised by the Yoruba in songs full of contrasts and reversals: "Eshu," they say, "turns right into wrong and wrong into right."

> He killed a bird yesterday
> With a stone he has thrown today.
> He slept in the house
> But the house was too small for him.
> He slept in the veranda,
> But the veranda was too small for him.
> He slept in a nut,
> At last he could stretch himself!
> Lying down his head hits the roof,
> Standing up he cannot look into the cooking pot.
> He buys palm oil in the market,
> and carries it off in a sieve,
> But the oil does not leak
> From this strange vessel."
>
> (Verger, 1981, p. 78; Pemberton, 1975, p. 25)

For the Yoruba this most paradoxical being is present in each individual unit of life as a mysterious agent which triggers its life processes into action. He is that active force in the core of the living being which promotes its growth and development so that it can fulfill its individual destiny. One could well describe him with the words Paracelsus uses to describe Mercurius: "that occult virtue in nature, by which all things increase, are nourished, multiply and quicken." (CW13, par. 171)

Jung has said that "we need to find our way back to the original, living spirit, which, because of its ambivalence, is also a mediator and a uniter of opposites" (CW9-II, par. 141). Eshu, the Master of Paradox, is a superb African formulation of this true spirit of human nature. Among the gifts he carries is the transcendent function, that unknown activity of the human psyche which produces new syntheses by creating real, life-giving symbols.

References

Abimbola, W. (1973). The Yoruba concept of human personality. *La Notion de Personne en Afrique Noire.* Paris: Centre National de la Recherche Scientifique (C.N.R.S.).

Bascom, W. (1969). *Ifa Divination: Communication Between Gods and Men in West Africa.* Bloomington: Indiana University Press.

Gleason, J. (1973). *A Recitation of Ifa, Oracle of the Yoruba.* New York: Grossman.

Maupoil, B. (1943). *La Géomancie à l'Ancienne Côte des Esclaves.* Travaux et memoires de l'Institut d'Ethnologie (Vol. 42). Paris: Institut d' Ethnologie.

Pemberton, J. (1975). Eshu-Elegba, the Yoruba trickster god. *African Arts, IX-*1; 21-27, 66-70.

Verger, P. (1957). *Notes sur le Culte des Orisa et Vodun à Bahia, la Baie de Tous les Saints, au Brésil et à l'Ancienne Côte des Esclaves en Afrique.* Memoires de l'Institut Français d'Afrique Noire (Vol. 51). Dakar: Institut Français d'Afrique Noire (IFAN).

Verger, P. (1981). *Os Orixás.* Bahia: Corrupio.

Beyond the Dreamtime

Leon Petchkovsky
Hazelbrook, New South Wales,
Australia
Australian and New Zealand
Society of Jungian Analysts

This work consists of notes on a video presentation by Leon Petchkovsky from John Lind's film essay on the life and works of Ainslie Roberts, Australian painter of Aboriginal myths. Its time frame, 1950 to 1992, was a period which began with the seemingly inevitable demise of the Aboriginal people but gave way to a resurgence of Aboriginal culture, whose power and scope Australia and, indeed, the global village, have yet to experience fully.

Ainslie Roberts was born in England in 1911. As a child, he came to Australia with his parents. He became a highly successful commercial artist and partner in an advertising agency in Adelaide but, at the age of 39, experienced a paralyzing mid-life crisis which led him to Alice Springs and the deserts of central Australia. There he found a healing environment and met Charles Mountford, a renowned Australian anthropologist and ethnographic film-maker. This encounter was to be Roberts' entrée into Aboriginal myth and culture. Together, the two men journeyed into remote landscapes and met and lived with the traditional owners and caretakers.

The leaven of these experiences worked on Roberts for almost a decade, erupting finally in an awareness that his artistic destiny lay in re-evoking and illustrating the myths and stories of Aboriginal Australians and communicating something of their meaning and beauty to non-Aboriginal people. He began to paint the myths and produced a body of remarkable works, a wealth of haunting imagery and resonance. In collaboration with Charles Mountford, he produced a series of "Dreamtime" books of myths and paintings, which have sold over 750,000 copies in Australia alone.

My focus is on three key paintings of Roberts' later years, (ages 66 and 67), the time of another major creative block: "Yulu's Charcoal" (January 1976), "Wungala and the Evil Big-Eyed One" (June 1977) and "The Moon-Woman" (November 1977). These works are of particular interest to psychologists; they illustrate the intersection between creative block and private and collective mythic imagery.

John Lind is an Australian film maker, born in Calcutta in 1944 of a Russian mother and an English father. In 1965, a vivid dream drove him into film-making. In 1969, he won a cultural exchange scholarship at the Moscow All-Union State Institute of Cinematography and was strongly influenced by film-makers Grigori Kozintsev (*Hamlet* and *King Lear*) and Andrei Tarkovsky (*Solaris*). Lind was at the British National Film School from 1971 to 1974. He directed two 35mm period piece dramas on czarist themes; one of them received a Director's award at the Melbourne International Film Festival. He has produced, directed and written for many films, including co-writing an adaptation of Ibsen's "The Wild Duck" in 1982; it starred Liv Ullman and Jeremy Irons. Lind is working currently on a series of films on artists devoted to other cultures. These include "Beyond the Dreamtime" and "A Celebration Of Life," the latter on Bobby Holcomb, an American Hawaiian artist and musician devoted to Tahitian mythology.

In 1985, Lind was co-writer for "When The Snake Bites The Sun," a documentary for Film Australia about the return of a small group of Aboriginals to their spiritual homeland in the Kimberley mountains in Western Australia. In 1991 Lind participated in intensive seminar workshops in Sydney led by me and Andrew Japaljari – an elder, teacher, and healer of the Pintubi tribe – on Aboriginal ways of working with dream processes and Kurunpa (life energy). A collaborative process evolved between me and Lind.

Charles Hulley, Ainslie Roberts' biographer, was born in Australia in 1928 and is an alumnus of the Harvard School of

Business. Though interested in writing from an early age, Hulley became a senior executive for a major American corporation. In the mid-1970s, on a visit to Australia, he first saw the paintings and Robert's Dreamtime books and became his close friend and a collector of his work. Having developed a deep interest in Jung's work, Hulley – on his retirement – brought to his writing his love of Aboriginal mythology, Jungian psychology and Ainslie Roberts' art.

Creative Block, Cultural Block, Developmental Block: Three Paintings and a Myth

The Australian painter-sculptor Owen Shaw has produced three line-drawings after the three paintings under consideration, taking excerpts – under my instructions – of the components of significance to depth psychology and mythography. Color reproductions of the originals can be found in Hulley (1988).

Yulu's Charcoal

In early 1976, Charles Hulley's empathic eye, informed in part by his Jungian perspective, fell with dark concern on this painting (Fig. 1), one of Roberts' latest works. He said of it:

> There had been a violent bushfire, and at the bottom of the picture the trunks and branches of the fallen timber are already beginning to harden into coal. The air is hazy with the smoke, and the mountains are just visible against a remote green sky. On the left of the picture hovers a great insectile shape, its legs touching a pile of blackened rocks. It seems to be an empty bark shell, hollowed and burnt out, with a glowing red eye and a single black hand supporting itself on one of the charred spars.... I was disturbed by it.... I found it a constellation of illness and waning life-force, with nothing psychically positive about it, save that the coal might store and transform the energy that had been lost (Hulley, p. 116).

Hulley's pessimistic prognostication proved all too accurate; a prolonged spell of ill-health and artistic dryness followed for Roberts. Hulley suggested to Roberts that he might return to a

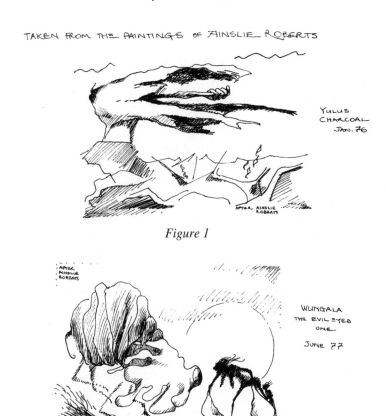

Figure 1

Figure 2

project on a Moon-Woman myth which had been abandoned in the 1960s because of viewers' objections to its strong sexual theme. At first the suggestion sparked no response. Then in June 1977, Roberts wrote to Hulley:

> My "artistic roadblock," as you dub it, Charles, is now being dismantled... but only piece by piece. I tried to sneak under it unobserved about six weeks ago, using humour as a cloak, with a myth entitled "Wungala and the Evil Big-Eyed One"... but I plead guilty to avoiding the depth and scope of the myth, settling instead for the comic-opera climax. Frivolity can be used as skates so often, but if the ice is thin and you go through, it's just that much more weight on your feet to take you down. (Hulley, 1988, pp. 117-118).

Wungala and the Evil Big-Eyed One

This painting (Fig. 2) shows a woman ancestor throwing hot dough into the eye and face of a monster that looks like a transformation of the menacing shape in Yulu's Charcoal, as Hulley points out. Her little boy clings to her leg. What have we here?

Holding the wracking tension of the opposites in order for the transcendent function to emerge is all very well if you can manage it. But what if the current blows your fuses, cooks your circuits? As with so many things in life, the art lies in judging just how much pressure you can get away with. The Buddha called it "Right Effort," the optimal pressure of application of blade against grinding wheel. Too little, and it will never get sharp; too much, and the edge buckles. This picture, then, is in praise of dissociation, maligned but necessary brother of relationship. Or more precisely, of the dance between association and dissociation.

As analysts, we sing the praises of consciousness, Inshallah! (Arabic for "Amen" or "God willing"). But who can see the face of God and live? Consciousness heals, consciousness fries. Even though consciousness is ultimately the goal, were we to be hit with it all at once, we would surely fry. Birth is a process of gradual dilatation. This was well-known to Aboriginal Australians.

The Waddaman (South Western Arnhem Land) myth of Wungala shows one way of dealing with this predicament. The version here was told to Bill Harney, an Australian writer on Aboriginal culture, who lived at Ayer's Rock among indigenous people for many years. He was a close friend of Irene Rix-Weaver, Australia's first Jungian analyst.

> An Aboriginal mother, Wungala, is seed-gatherer with her little son, Bulla. She grinds the seeds to flour, and adds water to make dough. When the clouds throw their shadows across the earth, she tells Bulla to stay close and not to wander, because with the shadows, the Evil Big-Eyed One comes out of his cave in the hills. As the clouds thicken, the Evil Big-Eyed One, roaring and full of menace, appears on cue; but Wungala knows from her tribal elders that she and Bulla

are safe as long as she pretends the monster is not there. The penalty for taking notice of it is to be eaten up. Wungala goes on making more and more dough to keep her son near her and interested, and finally puts it on the coals of the fire to bake. The Evil Big-Eyed One, baffled by this show of indifference, and wondering why it seems to be invisible to the woman, creeps up curiously behind her. This is Wungala's moment. Picking up a great mass of hot dough in both hands, she hurls the sticky mass in the monster's face, picks up her son, and runs back to the safety of the camp, leaving the Evil Big-Eyed One roaring in agony. (Hulley 1988, p. 118)

The Australian Robert Gardner (Zurich-trained Jungian analyst practicing in Canada) argues convincingly in his book (1990) that Aboriginal culture resolves the Oedipal conflict by identification with – co-optation of – the mother, particularly her nurturer aspects. Hence the spiritual care-giver tradition permeates Aboriginal life, along with the ahistoricity, absence of cults of the Great Man, obliteration of the names of the dead and distaste for focused and exploitative technologies and attitudes. We Westerners, children of Yahweh – the ruling masculine principle – find these phenomena hard to understand.

Roberts' painting of Wungala in the moment of hurling a mass of hot sticky dough onto the monster's single phallic eye can thus be read as the tracks left by the artist in breaking a severe creative drought which had many of the features of a major clinical depression. Hulley (1988) conjectured that "whatever the malignant shapes of Yulu and the Evil Big-Eyed One represent, Ainslie could not bring himself to confront its full intensity. His art showed him the way out, and his creative feminine side, also incarnated in the Moon-Woman, carried out the rescue" (pp. 118-119). We could say also that the painting and the myth are about one way of dealing with a phallic aggressive focused consciousness that threatens to devour the nurturing process in a culture.

Pre-Oedipal processes – malign maternal animus or abuse by the father – threaten to devour the matrix of creative vitality in the infant. The child's response is dissociation. Nevertheless, without the interplay of masculine and feminine principles – focused and diffuse consciousness – certain kinds of develop-

ment are frustrated. They manifest characterologically as personalities typical to Aboriginal and Western cultures, with their
advantages and deficits. Perhaps the next ground-swell in human
culture needs to be an androgynous resolution of the Oedipal
predicament, identification neither with mother nor father, but
with the dancing couple. The third painting in this series seems to
be a partly successful attempt in this direction.

The Moon-Woman

In many Aboriginal moon-myths, the moon is envisaged as a
male. This painting (Fig. 3) is one of the few in which it is a
woman. "When the Moon sets, the Moon-Woman joins the tribes
on earth for an orgy so intense she wastes away and dies. After
three moonless nights a new moon is born and the cycle begins
again." Hulley goes on to describe the painting: "The naked body
of the Moon-Woman lies on a gray ridge about the contours of a
silver lake. The dim blue night sky is lit by the white glow from
her pelvis, and her torso is grossly attenuated and wasted away.
Below the bare fibrous undulations of the lake shore, the satiated
tribe is encamped. The men, gross and swollen, but retaining a
suggestion of human shape, have become boulders" (1988, p.
120).

The sated boulder-men, clear homomorphs of Yulu and the
Evil Big-Eyed One, the sated Moon-Woman and Roberts' reso-

Figure 3

lution of the Wungala form, lie in post-coital slumber, united by a lake. Spermatic? Galactic? But where is the little boy? Is he awake, contemplating the pregnant calm after the primal scene? Is he Ainslie Roberts, acknowledging the return of his creative powers after a long struggle? I finish with a quote from Roberts:

> I must consider myself as the agent only, the communicator,... stay personally as anonymous as I can be,... let the basic myth come through without being clouded or overlaid by what the public shows a preference for in the way of colour, mood, or subject matter. I must let the myth itself dictate all these things.... I must always keep in mind my debt to the aborigines who created these myths.... If my paintings continue to be accepted as readily as the first exhibition, I have the opportunity (and responsibility) of communicating to my fellow whites that here, under their noses, is a rich culture that deserves to be noticed, respected, and explored. (Hulley, 1988, p. 86)

References

Gardner, R. (1990). *The Rainbow Serpent*. Toronto: Inner City.

Hulley, C. (1988). *Ainslie Roberts and the Dreamtime*. Melbourne: J.M. Dent.

Viewing Typology from the Star Maiden Circle

Mary Loomis
Grosse Point, Michigan, USA
Chicago Society of Jungian Analysts

Jung's theory of psychological types has been popular with Jungians and non-Jungians alike because it can explain human interactions in understandable, non-judgmental terms. This practical application of Jung's theory validates typology's worth but it clouds and diminishes the full potential Jung envisioned for his theory. Jung viewed typology as a road map for the individuation process, a road map that would point out where one-sidedness in the personality existed if the individual took the time to look. It may be that a different perspective, including certain Native American teachings, could revitalize the interest in typology as a "map" of the transcendent function.

When Jung wrote about typology he described the inferior, neglected functions as residing in the shadow and stated that the dominant functions are aspects of the persona (CW7, par. 487). The persona, in turn, would be aligned with the myth the individual was living. The four functions – thinking, feeling, sensation, and intuition – exist *in potential* in archetypal form within each personality and combine with introversion or extraversion when each is *in action*. Since the functions exist in potential as psychoid realities, I prefer to use the term "cognitive mode" in discussing any of the eight interactions that result when function and orientation combine. Paraphrasing Jung, we can say that the neglected cognitive modes reside in the shadow and the preferred cognitive modes are integral to the persona.

The undeveloped cognitive modes reside in the shadow along with the individual's unacknowledged complexes. Together, these are the hidden determiners of behavior. This situation begins in childhood and the hidden determiners continue to exert their influence until the individual begins the laborious task of becoming conscious.

How do these complexes begin? Why does an individual develop certain cognitive modes and not others? Jung addressed these questions by speaking in general terms about the influence of biology and environment on the individual's personality. However, certain Native American teachings, called "The Teachings of the Twisted Hairs," also detail how complexes are formed and suggest different answers to these questions.

The Twisted Hair teachings come from many tribes. I was taught by a modern Twisted Hair, Harley Swiftdeer Reagan. The teachings that I find particularly helpful in the context of typology are called the Star Maiden Circle, the infinity movement and Sun Bear's earth astrology. When these teachings are combined in a particular way, they describe the formation of complexes and shed light on the myth that is being lived, the persona that is being worn and the cognitive modes one habitually has used. They also suggest where the inferior cognitive modes lie. The development of these inferior modes can lead to the birthing of the transcendent function. The descriptions of these teachings here are necessarily brief, but a fuller discussion of the Star Maiden Circle may be found in an earlier work (Loomis, 1991).

The Star Maiden Circle

The Star Maiden Circle (Fig. 1) depicts the cycling of life and delineates eight major areas. The movement begins in the south with the myth that the individual is living and spirals clockwise, moving through the symbols encountered during the process of life (southwest) to what is being actualized (west). The myth one is living underlies the persona being worn and determines the cognitive modes one will develop.

As one cycles through the process of life the myth establishes the perspective for understanding what is being experienced and provides the parameters for what will be actualized. The northwest of the circle depicts the rules and laws to which the individual adheres. These rules and laws govern the individual's behav-

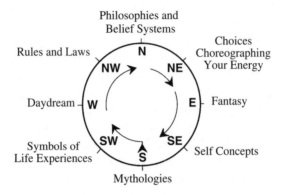

Figure 1. The Star Maiden Circle

ior by inducing guilt and shame; again, they are in accord with the myth being lived. The rules and laws the individual holds are then generalized to philosophies and belief systems that clarify how the individual expects others to behave (north).

The spiral of life then moves to the choices that are made (northeast) and here again, although the individual believes he/she has free will, the choices are pre-determined by one's myth. The movement of the Star Maiden Circle then goes to the east, the place of fantasy, the place of unlimited imagination. The myth being lived determines what can be imagined. The unconscious individual, caught in an illusion, is living a life in accordance with another person's expectations. One's self-concepts (southeast), determined by one's childhood myth, are dominated by a sense of insufficiency, the insufficiency of the needy, abandoned, wounded child.

The spiraling of life depicted by the Star Maiden Circle is continuous. For the child and the unconscious adult, the endless cycling on the Star Maiden Circle is called "The Circle of Foxes" because the individual is going around and around, repeating the old patterns like a fox chasing its tail. When an individual begins the process of individuation, the movement on the Star Maiden Circle becomes the Dance of the Coyote. The Coyote is the trickster and the individual must choose, willingly, to become a trickster to instigate change.

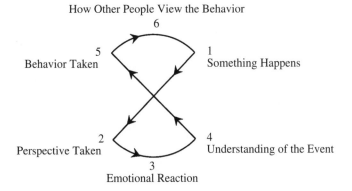

Figure 2. Steps on the Infinity Movement

The unconscious myth controlling the cycling of life on the Circle of Foxes, is established in childhood in response to events that happened in one's environment. The pattern of responses involved with one's myth may be examined by overlaying the infinity movement on the Star Maiden Circle and aligning the infinity movement with one's starting place on the wheel.

The Infinity Movement

The infinity movement (Fig. 2), comprised of six steps, is drawn like a figure eight. These steps occur in milliseconds and outline a behavioral pattern fundamental to the individual's myth. The pattern, begun in childhood, involves the cognitive modes which will be developed. In almost all cases, the pattern is ingrained in the individual to such an extent that it occurs automatically. The sequential steps of the infinity movement are these:

1. An external event over which the individual has no control. In the initial occurrence, the child is the observer.

2. The frame of reference from which the event is perceived. The selective perception of the child focuses on and records a single, particular aspect of what was observed.

3. The individual's emotional, affective reaction to what was perceived. Almost always, the child experiences fear. As the

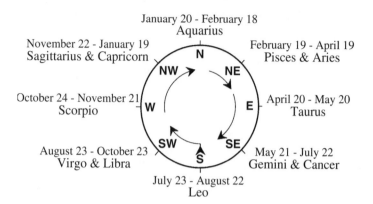

Figure 3. Birth Place According to Sun Bear's Earth Astrology

pattern becomes habitual, the fear is masked, repressed into the unconscious.

4. The individual's understanding of what has transpired. Here, decisions are made about what needs to be done.

5. The behavior by which the individual actualizes or implements her or his understanding.

6. Other people's view of the individual.

To discover the basic pattern integral to one's myth, the infinity movement is overlaid on the Star Maiden Circle with the numeral three located at the individual's starting place on the medicine wheel, as determined by Sun Bear's earth astrology.

Sun Bear, a Chippewa medicine man, has written about a vision in which he saw all the people on earth coming together (Sun Bear and Wabun, 1980). He saw the spirit guides of all the people: their animal helpers, their plant and mineral totems. His vision revealed that one's starting place on the medicine wheel is determined by the moon sign under which one was born: the Earth Renewal Moon, for example, or the Long Snows Moon. Although Sun Bear uses moon signs, the moons correspond to the astrological sun signs. The Earth Renewal Moon at the winter solstice, for example, corresponds to Capricorn embracing the dates from December 22 to January 19.

Sun Bear's Earth Astrology

Sun Bear begins with the three winter moons and arranges them around the medicine wheel (Fig. 3). These moons correspond to Capricorn, Aquarius, and Pisces; they are located in the northwest, the north and the northeast, respectively. He continues with the spring moons – corresponding to Aries, Taurus, and Gemini – and arranges them around the east of the medicine wheel. Because there are 12 moons, or signs, and only eight positions on the medicine wheel, two signs are placed in each non-cardinal position. Thus, Aries becomes the second sign placed in the northeast, joining Pisces in that location; Taurus is placed in the east and Gemini becomes the first sign placed in the southeast. The three summer moons – corresponding to Cancer, Leo, and Virgo – are placed around the south of the medicine wheel. This puts Cancer in the southeast, Leo in the south and Virgo in the southwest. The remaining three moons, the moons of fall, are arranged around the west of the medicine wheel. These correspond to Libra in the southwest, Scorpio in the west, and Sagittarius in the northwest. The pattern revealed by the infinity movement, when it is overlaid on the Star Maiden Circle, is the pattern underlying one's myth when one is caught on the Circle of Foxes.

Let us look at an example (Fig. 4). Someone born under the sign of Taurus (April 20 to May 20) would place the infinity movement so that three is in the east and six is in the west. The particulars of this movement would then be one-northwest, two-southeast, three-east, four-northeast, five-southwest, six-west. Translated into the language of the Star Maiden Circle, the infinity movement for this particular alignment could be read this way. When this person was a very small child, something happened in the realm of rules and laws (one-northwest) which the child observed. What the child focused on was colored by the child's dependency and neediness (two-southeast). The fear that was engendered immediately impacted the child's imaginative capacity, limiting the possibilities that could be entertained (three-east). The child decided to behave in a way that would

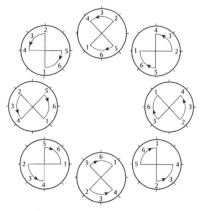

Figure 4. Infinity Movements for One's Birthplace

allow her or him to handle guilt and shame (four-northeast). This decision may have resulted in the child's becoming perfectionistic, not wanting to make any mistakes or refusing to make any decisions, in order to avoid blame. Another option the child might have chosen would be a decision to rebel against any and all rules. Life would be lived according to those decisions (five-southwest). The perfectionist would be striving constantly to be perfect by monitoring or analyzing his or her behavior. The non-choice maker, refusing to discriminate, would lack boundaries and could move into co-dependent relationships. The rebel probably would react against authority figures. When other individuals observe the child, they may see a fighter or they may see the other extreme, a victim (six-west).

Spiralling through life on the Circle of Foxes, the pattern of the infinity movement is repeated, again and again. From the child's viewpoint, this pattern is the only one possible. The child is shocked to learn that other people act differently. A further shock results when, usually as an adult, one learns that others' perceptions of oneself are not consistent with one's own.

The first occurrence of this basic pattern probably will not be remembered unless trauma was associated with the event. But why did one choose that particular pattern? The Twisted Hairs teach that we have come to this life, at this time, in order to learn a lesson; the pattern which has been our habitual way of respond-ing is the one best suited to help us learn that lesson. One may reach the point of saying "I've learned that lesson," and then ask, "Where do I begin if I want to change the pattern?" The answer is that one could change anywhere, but often the easiest place to begin is where the numeral five, for your particular infinity movement, lies on the Star Maiden Circle.

The reason for choosing the area where the numeral five falls has to do with the numerology associated with these teachings. Simply put, the infinity movement is a figure eight; eight sym-bolizes karma and the cycling of life. The number three, the starting place on the medicine wheel, symbolizes the child in trust and innocence. The number five symbolizes the conscious human being, speaking with open heart-to-heart communication and seeing all people as members of one family. Three plus five makes eight; this symbolizes the child becoming an adult, seeing the pattern and changing karma to dharma.

In the example given above, the numeral five lies in the southwest, the area specified as the process of living. When life is being lived fully, the individual can be engaged totally yet maintain a reflective capacity to analyze all experiences. In order to give birth to the transcendent function one person may be required to work on establishing boundaries and not being co-dependent; another person may be required to balance having an observing ego without being too distant. It is the individual's responsibility to determine how the balancing required in the process of living will be accomplished.

Having the knowledge of one's myth and its underlying pat-tern helps the individual recognize the aspects of the personality that need to be developed. This will always include acknowledg-ment of the neglected cognitive modes. If the individual chooses to begin developing the unlived side, then typology will fulfill the promise Jung envisioned for it by becoming a map indicating where the transcendent function may be birthed.

References

Loomis, M. (1991). *Dancing the Wheel of Psychological Types*.
     Wilmette, IL: Chiron.

Sun Bear & Wabun (1980). *The Medicine Wheel: Earth Astrology*.
     New York: Prentice Hall.

African Healers: Called to Be Isangoma or Prophet

Margaret P. Johnson
Ventura, California
Society of Jungian Analysts of
Southern California

In Durban, South Africa I was introduced (in 1987) to two kinds of healers in the Zulu culture, the isangomas – who are the traditional healers – and the prophets: new kinds of healers who heal within the context of one of the African Independent Churches (AIC). The prophet's role can be seen as an evolving form of the traditional healer's, a form that is coming into being as a result of cross-cultural change. These two worlds or cultures have been described as: "The Western world, which is primarily scientific, rational and ego-oriented, versus the world of the Black healer, which is non-rational, intuitive and human instead of object-oriented" (Bührmann, 1986, p. 15). When two such powerful opposites meet, something is bound to happen. Often it is chaos. What impressed me was that there was not complete chaos.

I planned a study partly supported by NERMIC (Research Unit for Indigenous Independent Churches and New Religious Movements), that would focus on the similarities and differences between these two kinds of healers: a study of changes in the archetype of the healer, which is intimately related to the archetype of the Self, as a way of understanding cross-cultural change. In both groups the call to become a healer comes from the unconscious, usually in the form of a physical and/or mental illness.

Background

The Zulu people total some 6.4 million and live primarily in the northeastern part of South Africa. Half of them live inside their self-governing territory of Kwa Zulu, which is one and a half times the size of Israel. It is estimated that over half the Zulus still observe the customs and practices of their traditional society.

The Zulu culture is patrilineal and patrilocal. The extended family lives in huts built in a circle, with the headman's hut facing east overlooking the rest. In the center is the cattle kraal where the family treasures are kept, the cattle, the grain (stored in underground pits) and the Ancestor Spirits. One could say that the cattle kraal is the Zulu church or temple where the most important religious rituals take place. It is believed that the Ancestor Spirits have the power to protect or to punish their living kin. Therefore it is a matter of great importance for the Zulus to maintain a good relationship with them.

When things go wrong, a Zulu may decide to consult an isangoma. About 80 percent of all patients visit the isangoma before they go to a hospital. The isangoma plays a role in the Zulu culture that is a combination of doctor, priest, family counselor, psychologist and psychic. The isangoma is able to mediate between the ego of the patient and the patient's unconscious by entering the realm of the Ancestor Spirits to determine what the problem is, why it exists, and what can be done about it.

The AIC is a movement that has been growing slowly in South Africa since the turn of the century. Many of these churches have the word Zion in their church name. Many are small – 50 or 60 members. Some are large, with as many as 200,000 members. They have broken away from established Christian churches to form their own combination of Christian and African beliefs. The AIC movement had grown to 4000 denominations in 1985, eight and a half million members, representing 35 percent of the Black population of South Africa.

Within the AIC churches there is a great emphasis on healing, laying on of hands, prayer, speaking in tongues and cleansing through repeated baptisms in the sea or rivers. Many Zulus join one of these churches because they are ill. The prophets divine and heal through a special connection with the Holy Spirit, using prayer, singing, candles, holy robes and giving the patient holy water to drink. The congregations constitute a well organized social and economic system that gives comfort and help to their members.

The Study

I first designed a field questionnaire with 15 questions relating to the personal history of the healers. A field worker, a young Zulu woman, located a group of 20 isangomas and 20 prophets in Kwa Mashu, a township near Durban, to participate in the study. Their responses were translated into English and mailed to me in the United States. After careful analysis I could find no real differences between the two groups on any of the major variables.

In 1988 I returned to Durban and arranged to go into the field myself to conduct in-depth interviews with the healers. I was accompanied by the same field worker, as guide and translator, and by my husband who managed the technical part of the interviewing task. Again in 1989, 1990 and 1991 the three of us returned to gather more in-depth interviews with healers in black townships around Durban and the more rural areas in Kwa Zulu. The interviews, usually an hour or more in length, were tape-recorded and later transcribed by two independent translators to insure the validity of the translations. This present study is based on information gathered from 36 healers – 23 females and 13 males.

A Model for Analysis

The questionnaire results revealed that the two groups, isangomas and prophets, were not discrete as I had expected. Rather, the healers combine the Ancestor Spirits and the Holy Spirit in different degrees. I developed a model to describe the different combinations I found. The model is a five-step continuum designated by arbitrarily numbered categories. Category I is the pure isangoma. Category V is the pure prophet group. The criterion that determines into which category the subject is placed is the mediating archetype between the ego of the healer and his or her connection with the Self. That is, I ask them to whom do they pray or who gives them their visions, dreams and power to heal. In Category I the isangomas are helped by the Ancestor Spirits. In Category V the prophets are helped by the Holy Spirit. In the middle categories the healers are helped by both spirits but to different degrees. Healers in Category II, the isangoma/prophets, say that for them the Ancestor Spirits are more powerful than the Holy Spirit. Subjects in Category IV, the prophet/isangomas, say that the Holy Spirit has more power than the Ancestor Spirits. In Category III, equal, the healers say that for them the Ancestor Spirits and the Holy Spirit are equal in power.

Analysis of Results

Most of the healers interviewed received their call to become healers when they were in either Category I or in Categories IV and V. Categories II and III seem to be positions that the healers come to after experience in other categories.

In this sample 55 percent of the healers moved out of the category of their calling and into another category. Thirty percent moved into one other category and 25 percent moved through two or three categories over time.

Category I is the most frequented category; 77 percent have had experience in Category I. Of those moving through and out of Category I, 76 percent ended up in Category II, 24 percent in Category III.

There appear to be two general patterns in the histories of the healers who move from one category to another. The first pattern is to be called in Category I and then to move one step to Category II. The second is to be called in Category IV or V, to move to Category I and then to Category II or III. The percentage in each pattern is about equal, 25 percent of the sample.

Discussion

The first pattern seems to be typical of isangomas in urban areas who join or found their own AIC churches. The second is more complex. One case history helps to explore this pattern.

Robert is a 53-year-old business man. The call to become an isangoma began in 1979 when he survived a serious automobile accident. After this he began to have strange dreams in which his deceased grandmother appeared. He suffered some business failures and went to an AIC church for help. Then he dreamed:

> "In this dream a voice asks me if I am ready to be baptized. I say yes. The voice tells me I must get four strong men to baptize me because should I slip while in the water, I would not come out of it again. So I find four strong men, but in the process I slip out of their hands and go past the water into a dry area beneath the river. There I see a room made of rocks and at the entrance is an ox with red eyes which keeps on gazing down, not looking at me. Ahead of the ox are people busy cultivating the fields. The voice then tells me to return to the surface of the water because if I were to go closer, I might recognize some of the people and no longer wish to return to the earth. The voice tells me that the ox is no real ox. It is a person who is stopping me from meeting with the people on the other side. The voice tells me to hold on to the water, which then throws me outside onto the dry land.

When he awoke he was speaking in tongues. For a year he was a prophet and healer in his church. Then the Holy Spirit left him. His bad dreams and bad luck in business returned. He consulted more prophets and isangomas. They all told him he was called by the Ancestor Spirits. He finally went for training to become an isangoma. He was a student isangoma when I first met him. Since then, he has returned home and is practicing as an isangoma/prophet, Category II.

Since the majority of healers are called in either Category I or in Categories IV and V, this suggests that these categories are the most powerful activators of the collective unconscious. The fact that 55 percent of the healers change categories suggests a psychic restlessness, a looking for a container that better fits the demands of the psyche. The direction of the movement of the healers is toward the center categories, suggesting a collective need to integrate both spirits, the Holy Spirit and the Ancestor Spirits.

Many of the healers who are called in another category are forced to move into Category I for healing and training. This suggests that the call to become a healer comes from a deep level of the psyche, or the Zulu cultural unconscious, which is best contained by the traditional isangoma training. Robert's dream of failing to be contained in the waters of the AIC baptism and slipping away into the realm of the Ancestor Spirits is particularly instructive.

The curriculum of an unusual school for isangomas, the Canaan School, supports this hypothesis. The curriculum begins with basic and traditional isangoma training given by an isangoma, of Category I, along with her student, who is also her niece, of Category II. Once the call from the Ancestor Spirits has been answered properly, the students are introduced to church services by a prophet and church leader, Category IV. The students are then taught to divine and heal through the Holy Spirit also, if their Ancestor Spirits permit. Students who graduate from this school return to their communities prepared to practice as healers in any of the categories except Category V, depending on what suits them best.

Currently there is resistance to the call of the Ancestor Spirits. One subject resisted his call for a long time because he thought "isangomas are retarded people." Others have said that isangoma training is "too expensive and time consuming; you have to sit on the floor, wear animal skins, can't wear beautiful (modern) clothes, and educated people can't accept that." The younger people in the urban townships are ridiculed by their peer groups if they appear in isangoma clothes. On the other hand, healing in the AIC churches is considered to be "the modern way." It is cheaper. It is cleaner because it "adheres to the modern standards of sanitation." One prophet said, "Very few people in our days have the Ancestor Spirit because we have rejected our customs and rituals. The modern generation takes it as prestigious to possess the Holy Spirit." In addition the prophets in Category V tend to look on the isangomas as deriving their power from "an evil source" or from an inferior source, and they exclude from their churches isangomas or members of their churches who visit isangomas.

With this movement toward the center, one could ask whether there has been a transformation of the God image. My answer is that it is still in process. In the center categories there is an honoring of both spirits, but still as separate spirits with separate kinds of rituals. Perhaps the Shembe Church comes the closest of the churches to offering a mixture of two God images, hence its great popularity. Shembe, the deceased founder of this church, could be seen as both an Ancestor Spirit and a black Moses. A church member explained to me that he prays to Shembe in order to reach God. "The Ancestor Spirits don't go far enough. We pray to Shembe to reach God. Praying to Shembe is like dialing the correct area code."

Finally one could ask: If there is a change in the Self or God image occurring here, what is the change supporting or moving toward? It does appear that the AIC churches, with their strong work ethics and moral codes, are providing containers for their members that support a social and psychological shift toward the requirements of life in an urban environment. Perhaps that is why they call themselves "the modern way." The ritual of baptism is the most important sacrament of most of the AIC churches. Jung said, "Baptism endows the individual with a living soul.... The idea of baptism lifts man out of his archaic identification with the world and transforms him into a being who stands above it" (CW10, par. 136). On the other hand, the roots of the call to become a healer come from the realm of the Ancestor Spirits, the Zulu cultural unconscious; it is important to retain and to integrate this spirit as well.

Reference

Bührmann, M.V. (1986). *Living in Two Worlds*. Wilmette, IL: Chiron.

The Political World

Analytical Psychology and Politics;
the Political Development of the Person

Andrew Samuels
London, England
Society of Analytical Psychology

By "politics" I mean the concerted arrangements and struggles within an institution, in a single society or among the countries of the world for the organization and distribution of power, especially economic power. Economic and political power includes control of processes of information and representation to serve the interests of the powerful as well as the use of physical force and possession of vital resources such as land, food, water and oil.

On a personal level there is a second kind of politics. Here, political power reflects struggles over agency: the ability to choose freely whether to act and what action to take in a given situation. This is feeling-level politics, a politics of subjectivity.

But politics also refers to a crucial interplay between these two dimensions of power, the public and the personal. There are connections between economic power and power as expressed on the domestic, private level. Power is a process or network, demonstrated experientially: in family organization, gender and race relations as well as in religious and artistic assumptions as they affect the lives of individuals.

Where the public and the private, the political and the personal intersect, there is a special role for depth psychology in relation to political change and transformation. The tragicomic crisis of our *fin de siècle* civilization incites us to challenge the boundaries that are accepted conventionally as existing between the external world and the internal, between life and reflection, between extraversion and introversion, between doing and being, between politics and psychology, between the political and psychological development of the person, between the fantasies and the politics of the political world. Subjectivity and inter-subjectivity have some political roots; they are not as "internal" as they seem.

There would be little point in our having worked on the orientation of depth psychology to the world of politics if psychology's basic theories and practices remained completely unaltered. I support the continuing practice of analysis with individuals and small groups; I do not agree that therapy inevitably siphons off rage that might be deployed in relation to social injustices. In fact, I think the reverse often happens: Experiences in therapy act to tone down generalized rage into a more constructive form, hence rendering that emotion more accessible for social action. Even when this transformation does not happen the potential remains for a move from private therapy to public action.

My focus here is on the political development of the person and on public implications of private imagery and experiences. Elsewhere (1989) I have written about other concerns: the politics of the analytic encounter and the politics of the discipline of depth psychology itself.

I see the clinical setting as a bridge between depth psychology and politics rather than as the source of isolation of depth psychology from politics. Critics of depth psychology (e.g. Hillman and Ventura, 1992) have noted the isolation. This is not a totally wrong observation. But there are also potential links; a radical revisioning of clinical work can occur, instead of a simplistic huffing and puffing aimed at its elimination. This paper offers a beginning of a much-needed new language to link depth psychology and politics – a language which will lead, I hope, to the evolution of research techniques, literature, training and monitoring that are informed by it. (See Samuels, 1993, for a fuller account.)

I am not so omnipotent nor so optimistic as to expect major breakthroughs or new paradigm shifts within depth psychology as a result of this new language. The golden age of theorizing is surely past. But every now and then one perceives gaps in the theory, lacunae in the practice of depth psychology. Then one is obliged to plunge into the void to see what lies there.

The Political Development of the Person

One such gap concerns what I have come to call "the political development of the person." Although I have been working on this idea since the early 1980s, I have not felt confident enough to publish before now.

Many would agree that the analysand's material cannot remain linked only to his or her personal situation or to the working through of innate, instinctually-based fantasies. Links have to be made with the person's culture, its traditions and history and to the individual's racial, ethnic, religious and national origins. But how might this linking be done, and what changes in theory and practice will be necessary? What happens if we factor the political into our narratives of the psychological development of the person?

A person leads not only an individual life but also the life of the times and the culture. Jung is said to have remarked that "when you treat the individual, you treat the culture." Acknowledging that there is such a thing as a political history of the person makes us build into our apperception of the person the impact of the political events of his or her life. These events have contributed, over time, to a person's state of political development.

Taking a historical, hermeneutical, or even an old-fashioned etiological approach helps to give the analyst confidence in moving into an area fraught with worries about bias, suggestion and disagreement. I believe that such worries are, to a great extent, delusive. When confronted with a patient whose views are repulsive, an analyst's best course might be to focus on the emergence and origins of such views. Such explorations can take a variety of different forms. We have to consider the politics an individual has "inherited" by reason of family, class, ethnic, religious and national background, not forgetting accidental, constitutional, typological, fateful and inexplicable influences – the nonrational element.

I must admit that it has been very tempting to refer to a "political drive," something innately political in human beings, not a derivative or sublimation of something else. Should we talk of a "political drive"? I am not sure (but see Mattoon, 1978).

However, if political potential is innate, it may be expressed as a quantum: a constitutionally given amount of energy of a political kind. Not all individuals have the same quantum of political potential or political energy. Then one could ask: What happens if a person of innately high political potential/energy has parents with a low level of it? Or vice versa? What is the fate of the political potential in an age that does not value a high level of that kind of energy? What will be the consequences for an individual if the innate level of political-ness is not in tune with that of the society into which that person is born? Situations of this kind may be as likely to produce problems in political development as are specifics such as infantile traumas or maternal and paternal insufficiency.

There are numerous other questions that now can be asked. Did your parents foster or hinder the flowering of your political potential? If they hindered it, what was the destiny of that repressed political energy? Do some people sublimate their political energy in the sexual or aggressive areas of their psychology – turning the usual formulation on its head?

This kind of inquiry indicates that it becomes ever more difficult to render the political into other terms such as those of conventional drive theory or object relations. I do not deny the many articulations between political development and sexuality, spirituality, aggression or object relations. But a partial, limited, focused approach has its advantages. Moreover, working on the political history and the political development of a person might open a wider discovery of unconscious material and processes.

Why do I refer to political *development*? In spite of an ongoing debate about it, the general idea of development – moral, spiritual, religious and "personality" – seems to be in the zeitgeist (See Samuels, 1989, pp. 15-47). The idea of development is intended to be applied as non-normatively and non-judgmentally as possible, though I admit immediately that my own political beliefs and values will enter the picture unavoidably and help to bring a kind of hierarchy into play. But I do not believe that my having beliefs and values of my own makes me any different from theorists in the fields of moral, spiritual, religious and personality development who undoubtedly have moral, spiritual, religious and psychological positions of their own to defend and privilege.

My interest is not in what might be called "political maturity." No such universal exists. My interest is in how people got to where they are politically and, above all, in how they themselves think, feel, explain and communicate about how they arrived where they are politically – a subjective narrative of political development. Moreover, they may turn out not to be where they thought they were politically, or to have come where they are by a route that they did not know about. We ask how a person became a liberal, say, not whether being a liberal is a good thing in itself, but not denying that we have a viewpoint about liberals. Moreover, not all liberals become so in the same way. We want to know how they have experienced their becoming liberals.

When an analysand describes formative or crucial political experiences, an analyst concerned with political development would listen with the same mix of literal and metaphorical understanding applied to any kind of clinical material, but with the idea of political development in mind as a permanent heuristic presence. Sometimes, the analyst would accept as fact the account of the analysand's political history. At other times, the account would be understood as image, symbol and metaphor; as defensive and/or distorted; or as a medley or competition of these ways of understanding.

The idea of development does not have to be used as if it were an exclusively linear, personalistic, causal-deterministic idea, characterized by regularity or predictability. Development is a creative fantasy with extraordinary utility. By fantasy, I do not mean anything pathological or lacking connection to reality. Rather the reverse. Political development is a "professional" fantasy that enables us to look at an aspect of the person that has been relatively neglected. The fantasy of political development helps us to access the politics of the person in the here-and-now, as the warring elements in personality clash and conciliate. For phases of development do not just fade away. Each phase remains active in the psyche in competitive relation to phases which only seem to us to be successive. Therefore, to the concepts of the political history of the person and the political development of the person we should add the concept of the political here-and-now of the person.

The implications for depth psychology of taking in these ideas about political development could be profound. In 1984 I suggested to my fellow members of the training committee of a psychotherapy organization that we should start to explore with candidates something about their political development – history, roots, antecedents, patterns, vicissitudes and current situation – just as we look into sexuality, aggression and spiritual or moral development. At that time, the idea was regarded as a bit far-out but more recently it has evoked a favorable response. Similarly, if political and social factors are part of personality and psychological development, should analysts not explore those areas in initial interviews with prospective analysands?

There are problems with the use of the term "person." To continue to refer to the person does not bring with it a belief in an innate, single viewpoint, arising from a center, as if independent of social institutions, relations and language. In fact, I recognize that the person is indeed constructed, polyvalent and heterogeneous. The deconstruction of the person is not the same as the deconstruction of the political – and the political constellates the person living in the polis.

Thus, in considering the political development of the person, we need to envision a new relationship in clinical practice as well as in theory between the private and the public, the intimate and the crowded, the secret and the open, the vulgar and the numinous. Analysis is a kind of theater; we need a crowd on the stage and a crowd in the audience. On that crowded stage are individuals who offer their most secret truths to individuals within that crowded audience, sharing a collective experience with them. Workshops on "the political development of the person" facilitate such sharing.

Description of a Political Workshop

After an introduction in which the ideas outlined above were presented, I asked the participants to undertake two experiential exercises. In the first exercise, the participants were asked to work in pairs, avoiding working with people they knew well. One person was to fantasize aloud what the other person's political history and development had been – with no factual information on which to base the fantasy. Then the roles were reversed. Finally, a debriefing period took place in which the accuracy and inaccuracy of the fantasies could be checked. A few pairs then shared their experiences with the total group.

The idea was that the use of fantasy, play and irrationality might lead to a deeper level of exploration of the political development of the participants. A more conventional kind of sharing took place in the debriefing period. Many people reported strong and even cathartic experiences during this exercise. None had done anything quite like it before.

The second exercise was rather eccentric, designed to test the possibility of a co-existence of political styles and also to build up faith in the capacity to utilize more than one style at a time.

Each couple was given a roll of toilet paper. They were asked to use the paper it in as many different ways as possible but trying to bear in mind the idea of political styles. Couples used the paper in an extraordinary number of ways. It could be fought over and torn up. It could be used to link people, draped tenderly over bodies. It could be used to communicate between one couple and another. It was even possible to link all the participants in the workshop into a shared social reality by using an entire roll to touch everyone. Rolled into a ball and stuffed down the front of a man's pants, the paper symbolized the potency/power aspects of politics.

Clearly, some ribald responses were to be expected. Also, there were protests from environmental activists over the waste of paper. But the exercise seems to have been enjoyed and the various arguments it can illustrate have had an airing.

References

Hillman, J. & Ventura, M. (1992). We've Had A Hundred Years of Psychotherapy – And the World's Getting Worse. San Francisco: Harper San Francisco.

Mattoon, M. (1978). Politics and individuation. Spring, 77-87.

Samuels, A. (1989). The Plural Psyche: Personality, Morality and The Father. London/New York: Routledge.

Samuels, A. (1993). The Political Psyche. London/New York: Routledge.

Armageddon Next Time: The Los Angeles Riots

William O. Walcott
South Laguna, California, USA
Society of Jungian Analysts of
Southern California

Although my paper is about the place of blacks in white America and the 1992 riots in Los Angeles, make no mistake; from a psychological standpoint, it is also about the plight of racial, ethnic, and religious minorities worldwide: Croats and Bosnians in Yugoslavia, Armenians in Azerbaijan, Azerbis in Armenia, Shiites and Kurds in Iraq, Palestinians in Israel and Jews in the world. I could go on. In other words, I do not believe that we can pass off these Los Angeles riots as something unique to Los Angeles or even the United States. The riots were not just the consequence of unfortunate economic, social, or political conditions.

The story of the violence that newspapers published and television broadcast worldwide was a horrifying spectacle. A few facts must suffice here: During the three days of disorder 45 people died, 2383 people were injured and 9500 were arrested. It was the most deadly civil disturbance in the United States in the twentieth century.

By the 1960s warning signs of rising Black anger were evident but were unnoticed by the society at large. Two years before the Watts riots in Los Angeles James Baldwin (1963) described the Black "hatred for white men [as] so deep that it... made all love, all trust, all joy impossible." He warned that Blacks were ready to retaliate unless they received "total liberation, in the cities... before the law, and in the mind" (p. 109). Only months before the Watts riot Malcolm X, heart and soul a part of African-American frustration, wrote, "You let any of these bitter, seething ghettos all over America receive the right igniting incident, and become really inflamed, [they will] explode, and burst out of their boundaries into where whites live!... you name the city. Black social dynamite is in Cleveland, Philadelphia, San Francisco, Los Angeles... the black man's anger is there, fermenting" (1964, p. 360). On the heels of the Watts uprising were riots in Detroit; Newark and New Brunswick, New Jersey; Washington, D.C.; New York City and other urban centers.

Twenty-seven years later – April 29, 1992 – an all White jury acquitted three of the four police officers who allegedly beat Rodney King, an African-American. The city, the nation, the world was stunned by the verdict. After the violence erupted, Americans of all colors were again stunned, but not surprised.

What is it like to be black in white America? Imagine you are a 17-year-old Richard Wright living in the 1930s – in Jackson, Mississippi, the heart of the black belt. You are spending the summer holding a series of petty jobs for short periods, quitting some to work elsewhere, being driven off others because of your attitude, your speech, the look in your eyes. You are trying to save enough money to get out of the South.

You meet a friend who tries to help. He tells you, "You act around white people as if you didn't know that they were white. and they *see* it.... when you are in front of white people *think* before you act, *think* before you speak. Your way of doing things is all right among *our* people, but not for *white* people. They won't stand for it" (Wright, 1945, pp. 177-78). You hear that it is impossible to calculate, to scheme, to act, to plot all the time. You remember to dissemble for short periods, but then you forget and act straight and human again.

If you are a teenager today living in South Central Los Angeles, you follow informal rules that have evolved for Blacks that seem at times like martial law: "Never drive with more than three in a car, never talk on the street in a group, never drive through white a neighborhood after dark" (Los Angeles Times, July 5, 1992). "If you are a young black man, as you pass by on a city sidewalk, white women clutch their purses tighter; drivers push the automatic door-locking button of their cars; supermarket clerks ask for an extra identification or call the manager before they cash your check" (Los Angeles *Times*, May 31, 1992).

The examples of discrimination I have cited are what Richard Wright, the Black novelist, called "petty grievances." He wrote, "Our anger was like the anger of children, passing quickly from one petty grievance to another, from the memory of one slight wrong to another" (1945, p. 219).

To Wright the frustrations of real consequence were the thwarting of aspirations. He revealed (1945), "I was building up in me a dream which the entire educational system of the south had been rigged to stifle.... I was beginning to dream the dreams that the state had said were wrong, that the schools had said were taboo.... In me [at fifteen years of age] was shaping a yearning for a kind of consciousness, a mode of being that the way of life about me had said could not be, must not be, and upon which the penalty of death had been placed...." (pp. 161-62). Richard Wright's dream: to be a novelist.

While living in the South, Wright (1945) believed, "I had been what my surroundings had demanded,... what the whites had said that I must be. Never fully able to be myself" (p. 288). Most importantly, he had not had a chance to learn who he was.

When in the eighth grade of a Michigan school, Malcolm X's reading skills and interest in knowledge flourished. The school principal patronizingly dismissed his wish to be a lawyer by telling him his goal was unrealistic for a Negro.

It is not just that Blacks object to being humiliated, scorned, beaten, and denigrated – all of which still happens throughout the nation. As Wright says, these are the "petty grievances" that blacks have had over three centuries to accommodate to. Most importantly Blacks want an identity that includes an acceptance of their ambitions and goals. They want to be able to define themselves free of white definitions. Baldwin (1953) said, "The long battle has been for the white man to protect his identity; the black man to establish his identity" (p. 631).

The uncertainty, distrust and fear that for centuries blacks have evoked in white minds are the same emotions elicited by strangers. Thus Blacks, whose past, as Baldwin (1953) wrote, was taken from them, who have never felt a part of white society, feel themselves as strangers. The Stranger seems psychologically to be the appropriate and most explanatory archetype for the relation between Whites and Blacks in America.

Both Baldwin and Wright speak of the Black person's place in Western civilization. Wright (1945) says, "Whenever I thought of the essential bleakness of black life in America, I knew that Negroes had never been allowed to catch the full spirit of western civilization; that they lived somehow in it but not of it" (p. 37). Baldwin (1953) made the point that Whites will never be strangers anywhere in the world because "the most illiterate among them is related, in a way that I am not, to Dante, Shakespeare, Michelangelo, Aeschylus, da Vinci, Rembrandt, and Racine.... Go back a few centuries and they are in their full glory – but I am in Africa, watching the conquerors arrive" (p. 625). "White supremacy," Baldwin (1953) added, "rests simply on the fact that white men are the creators of civilization... and are therefore civilization's guardians and defenders" (p. 630).

From the White standpoint, what does the stranger represent? What do we project upon strangers? For example, the epitome of the ingratiating, evil, invidious stranger is William Faulkner's Flem Snopes in *The Hamlet*. Like a malignant cancer he and his relatives take over a town with their acquisitiveness, their ambition, their greed and their shrewdness. At the same time they destroy the ante bellum value of honor and social respectability of the landed gentry. An opposite stranger is in Robert Nash's movie "The Rainmaker." He is of a different sort: an eccentric, a magician, a mystical man who comes to a Midwestern farming town that is mired in the dust of a blistering drought. He promises to bring rain for a price. The townspeople scoff and laugh at him; only one lonely spinster listens. As in the ancient mysteries it is the sacred marriage of the stranger to the virgin that admits the spirit – and brings rain to the land.

The most striking and profound strangers are to be found in the Bible. Moses was the stranger who redeemed the Israelites from Pharaoh. Jesus, after thirty years in Galilee, was a stranger who came to Israel to redeem humanity. Indeed, it was a stranger, the Holy Ghost, who conceived Jesus in the first place.

In the world psyche the archetype of the Stranger is manifold and powerful. The stranger embodies the dual potentials of change – the promise of good fortune or ruin, of redemption or damnation. It seems human nature to mistrust change rather than to welcome it; thus people exploit every human fear to resist if not repel the stranger – wanton generalizations, unfounded rumors, unbridled imagination.

What is the answer? As followers of Jung, we know that some form of integration is essential. We cannot keep forever outside the stranger who angrily pounds on our door for admittance or the one who meticulously observes all our rules and knocks politely. Already the enraged stranger has burned down some of our homes. Over a century ago Anglo-Saxons grudgingly admitted into their "homes" strangers in the persons of immigrants. The immigrants were assimilated as quickly as they were willing to discard their funny costumes, their unintelligible languages and their morally suspect customs – in other words, as soon as they were able to dress, behave, and think like Anglo-Saxons. They became ingredients in America's prized melting pot.

But the mixing of African-Americans into the melting pot has not worked. However pervasive a complication, I do not believe color is the crucial one. A far more serious impediment is the perception that it is their Black soul that they must give up to be assimilated. With their leaders declaring "Black is Beautiful" or having urged Black Pride or Black Power African-Americans have asserted their unwillingness, as a price of admission, to abandon – even if they could – the deep psychic scars of slavery, discrimination, and subjugation that they have endured.

Of all people, we psychologists are sensitive to the need of any individual to defend his or her own rich cultural, moral, and spiritual character. This notion makes assimilation a two-way street with something required by both groups. So far we may have invited the stranger in, but with certain patronizing and not always explicit conditions. It should be no surprise that the stranger hesitates. Does it occur to anyone to ask the stranger if he or she has any stipulations about accepting our invitation? On the other hand, maybe it is time we whites stopped assuming that our home, our establishment, is the ultimate prize. Has anyone thought of Whites going outdoors to join the strangers, to seek a common, mutually acceptable living space? The Los Angeles violence informs us clearly that African-Americans are no longer waiting hat in hand, they are angrily demanding – not assimilation, but equality and justice and a world that honors diversity.

When we eventually learn how to open our souls to the African-Americans as they are, not according to their similarity to us, we will be opening our hearts to their unique energy and spirit. Asians and Latinos also await our willingness to accept them on their terms – as wholly themselves, not as homogenized Americans.

When will we be able to admit into our souls the disruption and conflict that the diversity of race and culture foretell? The Blacks represent not only that within ourselves that has been enslaved, but that which we have deemed alien, inferior, and beyond salvation. On the other hand, what riches, cultural and spiritual, lie outside awaiting our welcome? Freeing the slaves should have brought redemption to America. Sadly, that promise still awaits in us a new level of consciousness.

If that growth takes too long – next time, not the fire, but Armageddon: the Biblical scene of the final battle between good and evil with the promise of the dawn of a new age. I am not hopeful that the recent disorder was the arrival of a new age. I do not expect a new age to come anytime soon.

No one knows, of course, when or where Armageddon will take place, except that it will be in the souls of all of us, Black and White. If we forget this uprising as quickly as we forgot the Watts disorders of 27 years ago, it will take place sometime, somewhere. If we can't resolve in our souls the battle against blackness, it will happen in the streets.

References

Baldwin, J. (1963). *The Fire Next Time*. Cited in J. Blum (1991), *Years of Discord: American Politics and Society, 1961-1974*. New York: W. W. Norton.

Baldwin, J. (1953/1991). Stranger in the village. In J. Gross (Ed.), *The Oxford Book of Essays*. New York: Oxford University Press.

Malcom X (1964/1992). *The Autobiography of Malcolm X*. As told to Alex Haley. Ballantine Books: New York.

Wright, R. (1945/1991). *Richard Wright: Early Works*. New York: Library of America.

Eastern Europe and Analytical Psychology
(Summary of Forum)

Renos Papadopoulos
London, England
Independent Group of Analytical
Psychologists

An historic event in the life of the IAAP occurred when non-members participated officially in a Congress program, the forum that I am summarizing. Perhaps even more significant is the fact that they were from several countries in Eastern Europe where Jungian psychology had not been studied and practiced openly. Some of these participants were members of the panel in the forum; others were members of its audience.

Leading up to this occasion were events of several years. In May 1991 IAAP president Thomas Kirsch went on an official fact-finding mission to Russia and arranged for the publication of Jung's *Collected Works* in Russian. His second trip was that September, a few days after the attempted coup against Gorbachev, but Kirsch still managed to sign the contract. [Editor's note: The Russian language Volume 15 appeared in early 1993. Volumes 7, 11 and 18 are in process at this writing. The publisher is E-W-Renaissance. The Van Waveren Foundation in New York is helping to support this project.]

In addition, at the request of the Association of Practicing Psychologists (APP) – the main psychotherapy organization in Russia – the IAAP collaborated in a program of block teaching and supervision in Jungian psychotherapy. This course was taught in Moscow by IAAP members. Gradually, the IAAP has established contact, directly or indirectly, with most of the countries in Eastern Europe.

The moving scenes of the breaking down of the Berlin wall have affected the psyche of every person and led to changes in the world order and our images of it. These fundamental changes have deep psychological implications. The 1991 IAAP Newsletter reflected this mood. A poem by Pino G. Bartalotta entitled "The Wall" ended with these words:

> within those blood-red bricks
> each of us
> with hearts full of hope
> we
> keep a brick
> from that wall.

Letters in the same issue addressed the new situation. Robert Bosnak suggested that IAAP members assist in two possible ways: (1) conducting intensive workshops for psychotherapists in Russia and (2) training four to six Soviet therapists in Jungian institutes in the West. Bosnak also proposed that individuals provide financial support to the training of Soviet colleagues.

A second letter, which I wrote, was based on my experiences in Eastern Europe. I identified a "worrying aspect" of the change in attitude of our colleagues in these countries after the collapse of the communist regimes: the hasty rejection of everything associated with the old order and the uncritical importing of Western ideas and goods. I was concerned also about a dangerous phenomenon: Eastern European psychologists seeming to undervalue their own understanding of Jung and perhaps discarding their own applications of Jungian theories. The pattern seemed to be that "we" try to help "them" both materially and professionally. Although I did not object to such help, a broader framework was necessary, of appreciating the situation in its totality, to avoid entanglement with old-time patronizing colonialism. To avoid these traps, I argued for a genuine mutual respect. Our Eastern Europeans colleagues' eagerness to learn our ways must be complemented by an opportunity for us to enrich our own approaches.

This Forum was designed to provide an opportunity for IAAP members and representatives from Eastern Europe to discuss openly the psychological and practical problems of cooperation. As analysts, we should attempt to understand the imagistic context of this exchange, in order to prevent disguised imperialism.

The program was attended by about 60 participants. The panel consisted of Sergei Agrachev (Moscow), Krassimira Beychinska (Sofia), Grazina Gudaite (Vilnius), Thomas Kirsch, Andrew Samuels (London), Ferenc Sule (Budapest) and myself as chair. Julia Aloyshina, also from Moscow, was a participant. Each member of the panel spoke for about ten minutes; open discussion followed.

After welcoming our colleagues from Eastern Europe and all the participants and emphasizing the need for an open exchange of ideas and feelings about this complicated situation, I identified three aims for the forum: (a) to exchange and share information on what is happening in various countries with regard to Analytical Psychology, (b) to consider the relationship between the IAAP and Eastern Europe and (c) to reflect on the psychological dimensions of this exchange, in order to avoid archetypal traps.

Drawing on my own experiences, first as a colonial subject (I was born in Cyprus) and subsequently as a lecturer in Eastern Europe, I outlined some archetypal constellations. These included the interchange between rebellion and imitation, guilt and aggression, deification and vilification, impotence and omnipotence, genuine help and charity. Although the similarities between colonialism and the current situation – which is not coercive – are not apparent, I argued for an appreciation of their imagistic parallels. Moreover, I attempted to convey the likely feelings of a visiting lecturer in these countries in encountering the deep need and deprivation in the hosts. The situation can generate inflated states of omnipotence or despairing deflation.

Agrachev offered a brief historical account of the psychotherapeutic group in Moscow; the core of the group received psychotherapeutic training in the late 1970s and early 1980s from Boris Kravtsov. There has been no official training program for any form of psychotherapy; all psychotherapeutic activities have been underground. "Our teacher was at the same time our analyst, which is, of course, against the rules but in those times, as far as I know, he was the only analytically-oriented psychotherapist in Moscow and maybe in the whole of Russia.... A year ago I attended a psychological conference in Czechoslovakia and one person asked me whether we could freely choose our analyst during our training. I could only answer him with a Russian joke of past times; God calls Adam and tells him 'This is Eve. Now choose yourself a wife!' That's how Soviet democracy was born."

Agrachev stated that psychotherapy in Russia is no longer an underground activity, but there are still no facilities for systematic training. "As for Kravtsov, he had not received any psychotherapeutic training either; he was self-taught. After finishing our training with him, for several years we worked privately. Then Perestroika began. In 1988 Russian psychotherapists, mainly from Moscow, formed an umbrella organization, the APP. Within its framework we organized a Section for Individual Psychotherapy. This Section has about 30 members and its theoretical orientation was and still is not very clear.

"In the course of our training Kravtsov himself underwent significant changes in his professional orientation. At first he was more Freudian but he increasingly tended in a Jungian direction. In 1991 we first came into contact with the IAAP. Andrew Samuels met us during his first brief visit in Moscow and Renos was the first to establish contact with the section as a whole and to conduct a Jungian workshop in Moscow. Then Thomas Kirsch visited us also and conducted a workshop. It was agreed to establish a Foundation Course in Jungian Psychotherapy in collaboration with the IAAP. We have had workshops also with Papadopoulos, Jean Kirsch and Robert Bosnak. In September we are expecting Verena Kast, in November Andrew Samuels and, next year, Papadopoulos again.

"The Foundation Course in Jungian Psychotherapy offered us far more sound theoretical foundations than we had before. It provided a structural base for our rather loosely organized Section, brought us closer to each other and gave us a cohesion as a group."

In his presentation, Thomas Kirsch reflected: "When I became president of the IAAP in 1989 I had no idea I would go to Moscow and stand in the Red Square. This is important not just for me but for the whole concept of communism as the enemy."

He discussed some implications of the lifting of the "Iron Curtain." This division "for 74 years has created an isolation which left parts of Eastern Europe and Russia virgin territory." He spoke about seeing Westerners in Russian hotels acting as "missionaries of various sorts, passing out Bibles by the ton." He warned that "it is very easy to get caught up in a sort of missionary spirit because of the need there." These missionaries included therapists of various persuasions pushing their brands of therapy. He also noted that "it was so wonderful to feel free of the whole history of the conflicts in depth psychology. It didn't matter whether I was a Jungian, a Freudian, a Neuro-linguistic programmer or a Gestalt hypnotist. All goes, all is acceptable and you're not bogged down by transferences and allegiances to this person or that person, this theory or that theory. In a way I thought I was in the garden of Eden! Everything was possible. It was like a high. I can't imagine any other feeling like this."

Kirsch spoke about the APP as "a most serious group." He was struck by the fact that all members were under 40 years of age, and thought that their youth enabled them to be free and not "contaminated" by the ideology of the system. He was overwhelmed by the vastness of the country and impressed by the serious scholarship of the people there. "They are avid readers." That convinced him to concentrate on the publication of the *Collected Works*. Each volume will be published in 100,000 copies; the first volume has sold out before publication.

Sule started with a short history of Analytical Psychology in his country, Hungary. Before World War II there were only a few psychiatrists, psychoanalysts and priests who were "acquainted in a deeper sense" with Jungian ideas. The mainstream of psychotherapy was Freudian. Then, after World War II, interest in Jung began to rise; three books by Jung were translated into Hungarian. However, "after 1949, when the communist regime came to power, every kind of psychotherapy, especially depth psychology, was suppressed." During the communist era some intellectuals – priests and psychiatrists – "kept the Jungian thoughts alive. Disciples came together around senior colleagues in private homes and formed illegal theoretical seminars and case workshops. They taught each other. Regular personal analysis was impossible for political reasons and because we did not have properly trained Jungian analysts." However, during this period, personal analysis went on in the form of pastoral care and self-analysis.

Since the late 1960s group psychotherapy and personal analysis slowly became possible in a semi-legal way, Sule reported. The therapists belonged to different schools of psychoanalysis. Those interested in Jungian psychology underwent training in psychoanalytic group psychotherapy and individual psychoanalysis because nothing Jungian was available. "In the 1970s the interest and the need for training in psychotherapy among the professionals was growing considerably. In 1980 the psychiatrists divided from neurologists and founded an autonomous Hungarian psychiatric association. It created a psychotherapeutic section with 10 subsections for the different schools of psychotherapy; one of them was the 'Jungian, Complex Psychotherapeutic Section'." This was the first time that a Jungian organization was established in Hungary after the war. Late in the 1980s "great political and ideological changes took place. During the early 1990s more than half the psychotherapeutic sections became independent associations."

Thus, the Jungians formed the Hungarian Jungian Association (HJA) in 1991. Sule told us that they had had a "regular education and training" since 1980. "During the first five years, theoretical seminars dominated our activities but some personal analysis had begun before 1980." At this juncture, the Zurich Jung Institute came to their assistance. Since 1986, members of the Hungarian association have been attending regularly the two-week international intensive seminar. We get much useful information and also deep emotional impressions about the surroundings and style of Jungian analysts."

Another milestone in the development of Analytical Psychology in Hungary came in 1987, when "the Hungarian post-graduate medical university accepted our educational program as one of the facultative forms of psychotherapeutic training." At present, they have "five training analysts; among these is Judit

Luif-Magos from Zurich. We keep regular 2-hour long theoretical seminars which deal with the basic Jungian concepts. We keep regular individual and group supervision. We have an analytic training for group psychotherapy as well." In 1992, the HJA had 90 members. Of these, 40 want to be Jungian therapists. Other activities mentioned were the publication of five of Jung's books in Hungarian.

Sule identified three issues which occupy his Association at present. The first concerns "in-patient work, because most of the Hungarian psychiatrists and psychologists work in hospitals or other similar institutional settings." The question is "how to organize a brief psychotherapy or psychiatric department from the Jungian point of view." The second concern is "how to relate, how to be in cooperation with the religious people." In recent years there has been a proliferation in Hungary of different kinds of religious groups. This proliferation has created crucial psychological and psychopathological problems because the upsurge of spirituality lifted everything that had been suppressed. The third, and perhaps their main problem, is how "legally" to be in contact with Jungian organizations in the West. This is an issue because the training has been based on "self-analysis" and therefore is not recognized by the Western Jungian community.

Samuels told about his visit to the Bekhterev Psychiatric Institute in St. Petersburg, to meet some psychoanalysts. He described that meeting, "in a large ornate room, around a large polished wooden table," where people sat in two groups: "On one side of the table was a group of young people who looked rather like post-graduate students from any Western university. They were dressed in attractive woolen sweaters and blue jeans, some had beards or moustaches, all were competent in English and smoked Marlboro cigarettes incessantly." On the other side of the table, the people "were dressed in white coats, the coats were buttoned from throat to knee but one could see from protruding sleeves and trousers somewhat shiny, rather cheap-looking suits. On the whole they did not speak English, they were cleanly shaven and were certainly not smoking Marlboros."

Then, he asked, "Which group do you think were the psychoanalysts? The answer is both."

This story illustrates the difficulty for the IAAP and member-analysts who visit these countries in deciding "where to put our time and in a sense our money.... It is extremely difficult when you are faced with those two groups of psychoanalysts." He hoped that we don't make the mistake that other organizations have made, "following the traditional, hegemonistic tendency of putting all their eggs in one basket and beginning to slander all the other groupings in the region. This would be the colonial error as I understand it."

Samuels' suggestion was to "try to achieve an attitude that values the apparent contradictions of choice regarding psychotherapy that you meet in Russia." In Moscow he asked a psychotherapist the kind of therapy he liked; the reply was "I like Winnicott and Neuro-linguistic programming." Although Samuels was shocked by the response, he now saw that they are "privileged; they really don't have our rigidity" about all our divisions and distinctions. "When we go there to teach we must value that kind of contradiction."

Samuels discussed "snapshots" of Russian therapists that he obtained as part of a larger piece of research, investigating "political material that is brought into the clinical setting." Whereas "all the Jungians in the United States who replied to the survey were over 45 and had more than 10 years experience, the Russians had less than 10 years experience and were under 45. I wonder how that is going to affect our communication."

Next was the question "which political issues your patients or analysands raise most frequently, in order of frequency." I provided a list of 11 or 12 pretty conventionally described categories. The Russian therapists seemed to encounter political issues in this order: economics, violence in society, gender issues. The American Jungians (drawn from Chicago, San Francisco and Los Angeles) reported gender issues, national politics, economics. The Society for Analytical Psychology [SAP] in London reported economics, gender issues, violence in society, national politics; the German Jungians, environment, gender issues, violence;

Israelis national politics, international politics, violence; Brazilians, economics, national politics, violence, world survey, gender issues, economics. These results did not seem to reveal anything unusual about the Russian therapists.

Another question was, "How do you handle and understand overt political material that is brought to the clinical setting?" One category of responses was whether therapists mentioned "the reality of the issue in the description of what they typically do." These results, despite the flaws in the survey, showed an amazing discrepancy. Twenty-four percent of the Russian therapists mentioned reality as a constituent of their interpretation, their handling, their managing of overt political material. Among the United States Jungians, 74 percent and 86 percent of the Society of Analytical Psychology (SAP) in London mentioned reality as something that came to their minds when they were handling, interpreting, understanding political material. The Italian Jungians 75 percent, the Germans 84 percent, the Israelis 100 percent and the Brazilians 71 percent.

The percentages reversed in the next question: "Were political issues as such discussed during your training?" Yes, say 83 percent of Russian therapists as compared to 28 percent in the United States, 3 percent of the SAP, 10 percent of the Italians, 39 percent of the Germans, 30 percent of the Israelis and 58 percent of the Brazilians. We do not know how people understood these questions.

It was possible for survey respondents to reply at length to a question about their current political attitudes and histories. Some of the replies from Russian therapists: (1) "I agree with the democratic changes that are going on in the country but in general I am very far from politics." (2) "The things that are important to me are political freedom, the rights of people, legalism, and a political culture in the country." (3) "I judge myself to be a liberal democrat but for me freedom is more important than social justice." (4) "I was active during the events of 19-21 August 1991. Before that I took part in democratic meetings. I am not interested in politics. I feel myself more conservative than democrats, but more democratic than conservatives. (5) "I am not interested in parties but my orientation is democrat. I took part in the meetings and demonstrations when Perestroika had just started." (6) "We live in a patriarchal society where everything is ruled by force, in society and in the family. Out of that a hierarchy comes into being." (7) "I used to be active in Comsomol. I was a secretary of an organization of the communist party of the Soviet Union." (8) "I am distant from politics, but the best I think is democratic. I was active during 19-21 August 1991. In the former USSR psychoanalytically-oriented work was against official rules so I think that independence of my personal views, the fact that I did such work could itself be considered as evidence of political activity." (9) "I am mildly liberal, but I do not play in political games."

The coordinator of the survey wrote a remarkable statement: "For the time being in our country the term politics means something very special and rather narrow; that is why many of my colleagues who were answering the questions were shocked that political is interpreted as referring to such things as gender issues. For us politics is political struggles which are connected with the discussions in the Supreme Soviet, the falling into pieces of the USSR, the problems between former republics, the fight against communism. While many checked the gender roles or other issues they were smiling, as this was not politics for them. The same thing is connected to the questions devoted to the issues of political activity. We all read newspapers and listen to the radio; the thing that is discussed most often between people is politics, but no one will interpret that as political activity. The level of 'political activity' in our country is much higher than somewhere else. For example, one of my colleagues who spent the night of the 20th of August 1991 near the White House said that she is not politically active, because it was only once that she did something of this kind. She also did not interpret her involvement in meetings and demonstrations in 1990-91 as political activity; as she said, everyone from our circle was there. And to some extent she was right. Looking over the answers of other people, I think that many of them just forgot to

mention this period of politically very active life as it was typical
behavior for well-educated circles of people in this country."

Samuels concluded that "there are questions about who they
are, what they want, the extent to which we can empathize with
them, the extent to which we can be of any use because there is
the missionary fantasy that needs to be dealt with. These 'snapshots' are, as I said, not to be taken as scientific, as 100 percent
empirically valid; they are to be taken, I hope, as a stimulation to
thought and discussion."

Gudaite emphasized the transitional period through which
Lithuania is going. "Chaos and crisis are natural at this time.
Some obstacles in our way are related to the syndrome of Homo
Sovieticus: a low degree of personal integration and lack of
maturity." She mentioned other typical symptoms of the present
time: "personal regression and disintegration, a growing number
of alcoholic psychoses, a large number of suicides, increasing
crime rate." This crisis places many demands on psychologists
and psychotherapists who increasingly find Jungian insights of
great help.

The Lithuanian Jungian Society has about 40 members. Their
activities include seminars, case discussions, publication of articles in professional journals and intellectual magazines. Thomas
Kapacinskas has conducted workshops and other IAAP members
are expected to follow him. Their main problems stem from the
fact that they are also self-taught, without a formal recognized
training, and they now want to organize a training program. They
hope that it will be possible for one or two persons to receive
training in a Western country.

Beychinska, from Bulgaria, remarking on the transcendent
function, found the theme of the Congress "provocative" because
almost everyone in Eastern Europe is facing a very difficult
situation. Many people are in need of psychotherapy in order to
transcend their old identities and find new ones. There are no
trained Jungian therapists in these countries. An increasing number of psychologists, psychiatrists and psychotherapists are interested in Jungian ideas but have no way of actualizing this inter-

est. She made a plea for assistance with training and publication of Jungian books in Bulgarian.

Beychinska said that she graduated in psychology from Moscow State University in 1972 when there was no psychotherapeutic movement. The only avenue open to her and most of her colleagues was academic/research psychology. Currently, she is working in research at the Institute of Psychology in Sofia, including research in Jungian typology. She spoke of her need to understand the transitional situation in Eastern Europe in Jungian terms, and mentioned a paper she wrote to systematize her thinking. (The paper is available to anyone interested.)

Her main point was that socialist society distorted the psyche to a great degree. In 1946 Jung analyzed the psychic distortion caused by fascism in Germany. He wrote that "the psychologist cannot avoid coming to grips with contemporary history, even if his soul shrinks from the political uproar, the lying propaganda, and the jarring speeches of the demagogues" (CW10, p. 177). Her paper, entitled "Man in Socialist and Post-socialist Society," was her attempt not to be swayed by propaganda but to articulate a Jungian approach to the understanding of the psychological dynamics of post-socialist humans in a post-socialist society. She asked those who read her paper to offer her their comments.

Julia Aloyshina spoke briefly. She mentioned the creative possibilities that may arise from problems and from varying psychological theories.

I gave a brief account of Jungian activities in other Eastern European countries. Belgrade has a strong Jungian presence; the local society has been active since long before the collapse of communism. It has regular meetings, both for the general public and for professional therapists. The members have published translations of Jungian books, including their own works, and they have made a significant contribution to the intellectual and professional community in their country. It was regrettable that, due to the tragic events in former Yugoslavia, representatives were unable to attend the Congress.

In Czechoslovakia, too, there is a large psychotherapy society; some members are interested in Jung. Also, some professors in literature and art seem to have Jungian leanings. Although nobody seemed to know of any specific Jungian activities in Prague and Brno, a group from those cities had contacted the German Society for assistance.

Gert Sauer, an analyst from Germany, has assisted colleagues in Eastern Europe and formed the Foundation of Analytical Psychology for this purpose. It aims to help individuals and groups in Eastern Europe in many ways. The most important achievement thus far has been their enabling two Russian psychotherapists to receive training at the C.G. Jung Institute in Zurich.

Patricia de Hoogh-Rowntree, a London-trained analyst who now lives in Holland, spoke of her work in Poland. For many years she maintained professional and personal contact with Polish colleagues, visiting them, organizing conferences and bringing them to Britain and Holland. Last year, she established a foundation with the specific purpose of facilitating this work and subsidizing Eastern European colleagues to visit the West for conferences and workshops so that "we could learn from them and they from us."

De Hoogh-Rowntree informed the workshop of the "tremendous growth in Jungian thinking in Poland. There is a lot of Jungian theoretical work being carried out in the universities and in the medical schools but with the emphasis on theory." She defined the main problem: "People spend a great deal of time thinking, reading and talking; then they call themselves analysts. But there is no training, no basis in clinical work." In addition to the professionals, there is also another group of people, "the grass roots workers," people "working in a Jungian way and sometimes not realizing it." These professionals do not have theoretical background. Thus, there is a tremendous split. De Hoogh-Rowntree also addressed the difficulty in fund-raising, wondering whether the IAAP could facilitate this process.

The possibility of linking the various initiatives in different countries, or sometimes even in the same country and city, was discussed. Among the substantial projects mentioned were those of Laura Dodson and Bosnak. Dodson (from Denver, Colorado) has set up The Institute for International Connections to facilitate exchange programs; she has been active especially in Moscow, St. Petersburg and Vilnius. Some of her projects include arranging for Russian and Lithuanian families to visit the USA and stay with American families.

Bosnak, from Boston, has been involved in exchange projects in Russia for nearly a decade. More recently he organized the event "Dreaming in Russia;" North American and Russian professionals met in joint dream groups.

Also mentioned were names of other IAAP members who visited and/or lectured in various countries of Eastern Europe. These include Judith Hubback, Kathrin Asper, Robert Hinshaw and Paul Brutsche. Several participants mentioned smaller projects such as sending Jungian books to groups in Eastern Europe.

The forum did not wish to create the erroneous impression that only official IAAP activities should take place or that initiatives from individuals or societies were discouraged. Neither did it wish for IAAP to coordinate all initiatives. Rather, we should be sensitive to each situation. Although coordination of these efforts is desirable, at times it is necessary for isolated projects to follow their own route and rhythm.

Participants asked for clarification of the kind of help that is most needed and what is the best way of offering it. The discussion highlighted the need for caution. I made a plea for our not rushing in with impulsive acts that would run out of steam quickly and to avoid "flight into help or other acting-out attempts." Instead, we should "contain the tension that the deprivation creates," move prudently, and most importantly to work with our hosts in avoiding colonialist scenarios. As a priority Agrachev suggested the establishment of a proper system of training, including personal analysis.

A participant mentioned the model of the American Peace Corps which he found most impressive. According to this, analysts could make themselves available to spend two years or so working in these countries. This might be possible for analysts either at the beginning or at the end of their careers. These analysts would be able to leave their own countries more easily than the majority of analysts, who would find it difficult to abandon their practices and active participation in societal matters. This model has advantages in terms of cost, commitment and effectiveness. There are many analysts in the West who are natives of Eastern Europe and who could return for a time to assist groups in their countries of origin.

A second model was suggested: that some of the bigger, more affluent groups, especially the North American ones, would sponsor East European colleagues, to come for a minimum of two to three years for an intensive personal analytic experience along with seminars and other educational and training events. Both alternatives include the crucial element, personal analysis. The second model, however, would enable our colleagues to have their analysis with a senior training analyst so that they could return home and become senior trainers. (The danger was mentioned that therapists, after completing training in the West, might decide not to return to their countries.)

The discussion then focused on understanding the various traps that had been mentioned. Thomas Kirsch noted the personal sacrifice on the part of the visiting analysts. A great deal of time and energy is spent in organizing a visit, in addition to making the visit, when the analyst is away from his/her practice. All this has financial implications. What paybacks should we expect or do we expect?

Then he mentioned the issue of "conversion." The analysts going there are committed Jungians; do we expect our hosts to convert to our way of thinking? "Do I expect that their group should sign on the dotted line and become adherents of Jung; and then, what kind of adherents of Jung? What do you then do with your Neuro-linguistic training, what do you do with that part of you that likes object relations, classical psychoanalysis, and so on?" Further, he mentioned the more shadowy dynamics involving the visitors' expectations of gratitude, with the discomfort, helplessness and envy in the hosts. These dynamics should not be confused with the actual response which we have experienced so far: Our hosts have been extremely appreciative and generous to the visitors.

I mentioned three additional difficulties. The first is a visitor's traveling alone, making it difficult to contain the feelings that are evoked.

The second concerns the visitor's experience encountering a particularly creative and innovative application or understanding of a Jungian idea. Because our Eastern European colleagues have developed in isolation from the mainstream, occasionally we encounter amazing gems. For example, a psychologist in Belgrade has been using a Jungian framework for his research in neonatal psychology. When I showed my admiration, he was apologetic for not being familiar with the "proper" Jungian theories and was genuinely embarrassed by my interest. I emphasized to the forum that we should not forget the way that we are perceived there, as if we had magic powers and solutions to all problems. It is important that our contact with them help to restore their dignity.

The third difficulty concerns my personal response in my contact with colleagues from Russia and Eastern Europe: being faced with a powerful combination of wealth on one hand and material deprivation on the other. My response was a mixture of deep admiration and respect for their amazing resilience, for all the suffering they have endured – almost a feeling of shame for the wealth that we have in the West – with despair for substantial changes in their material situation in the near future. Overall it was a most moving and invigorating experience.

Agrachev said he was impressed by the degree of our understanding and our frankness in expressing it. He confessed that he, too, was concerned about these issues and that he had no solutions. Nevertheless, he felt that our talking about them in an open and trusting way was the best guarantee against falling into such traps.

The discussion then turned to the feasibility and advisability of connecting with other Western groups or institutions in assisting Eastern Europe. Some such institutions have had more experience than the Jungians in Eastern Europe. A major difficulty in such connection is the fact that most of these groups have not addressed what is perhaps our main problem, that of providing individual analysis as the backbone of training programs.

Samuels pointed out the problems of power dynamics and accommodation of theoretical differences, suggesting that we not waste time with joint efforts because of unfortunate experiences in the past based on these very problems. However, regardless of what "the consumers in these countries do with our product, we ourselves have to sell our thing." He also hoped that they would "blend it with other peoples' products," but that was up to them.

Despite the fact that no decisions were reached and perhaps no new elements emerged, most participants felt that this was a most important meeting both in emotional impact and historical significance.

Clinical Issues

Mirabile Dictu

Sidney Handel
Boston Massachusetts, USA
New England Society of Jungian
Analysts

"So it is a kind of magic," he comments: "you talk, and blow away his ailments." Quite true. It would be magic if it worked rather quicker;... magic that is so slow loses its miraculous character.

Sigmund Freud

In 1808, Jacob Grimm introduced the story of the Golem to Europe. In his version the Jews of Poland, after prayers and fasts, would construct a human figure – the Golem – from clay. When the name of God was pronounced the figure came to life and served its creators. It lacked speech and had a tendency to grow beyond control in size and destructive behavior.

The theme of an artificial man had a long history in Jewish thought. But its new audience was captivated by its underlying archetype, which expresses the mysterious conjunction of spirit and matter. This union is one of Jung's principal examples of an activation of the transcendent function.

The most startling expression of the transcendent function is a synchronicity, defined as the acausal meaningful coincidence of two events, one of which is experienced internally to the psyche and the other externally. It rests upon an archetypal foundation.

Jung attributed a central role to the transcendent function. It follows that the phenomena of synchronicity are of special significance for the individuation process. This is especially appropriate for a psychology whose roots go back to that set of negative synchronicities, or "transcendent dysfunctions," known as conversion neuroses.

Neumann (1979) remarked, "If the premise of synchronicity... can be validated this would mean... phenomena which have... been described in theological terms as 'miracles' are in principle contained in the structure of our world" (p. 254). According to the Oxford English Dictionary, "A miracle is a marvelous event (occurring within human experience) which cannot have been brought about through any human power or other natural agency and must therefore be ascribed to the Deity or some other Supernatural being. Often an act e.g. of healing transcending natural law."

This translates psychologically as follows: "Marvelous" refers to a strong subjective response of consciousness with an imputation of significant meaning. "Human experience and power" includes that contained in the conscious and the personal unconscious. It does not include the collective unconscious which contains "the Deity" corresponding to the Self, and "supernatural beings" analogous to the archetypes. "Natural" clearly implies adherence to natural law: the laws of space, time and causality.

Thus, the psychological rendering of the word "miracle" is: an event of strong subjective impact which transcends the bounds of space and time and has an archetypal basis. That is, a miracle is a synchronicity.

Rabbi Judah Loew ben Bezalel (c. 1525-1609) was known as the Maharal – an acronym of the Hebrew words meaning "Our teacher, the Rabbi Loew." He enjoys a kind of pseudo-frame as the supposed creator of the Golem of Prague, a Bohemian variant of the Jewish "artificial man." Since the theoretician often becomes identified with the practitioner it is not surprising that the apparent "miracle" of the Golem was attributed to a man who devoted so much of his energy to a study of the theory of the miraculous.

The creation of a Golem was first attributed to the Maharal only 150 years after his death, when the legend was transferred to him from another, unrelated sixteenth-century rabbi. The Maharal based his work on the Book of Exodus, which is both the story of Israel's redemption from Egypt and the most miraculous and/or magical book of the Bible.

Belief in miracle represents no theological challenge to the idea of a God still actively intervening in history. But, presumably, human beings are granted a certain autonomy to live their lives in conformity with nature, including its laws of causality. Some attempt must be made, from a religious perspective, to explain unpredictable contraventions of that nature. Otherwise the reality of will comes into question as does the point of human consciousness.

A similar problem is inherent in Jung's psychology. Given the theoretical distribution of intrapsychic forces and energies, why doesn't the Self simply intervene when the health or welfare of consciousness is at risk? Why, with an all-powerful Self, should there be any neurosis?

Presumably, humanity was able to evolve only in a relatively predictable universe of cause and effect. Similarly, ego-consciousness emerged within the context of a psychological world more or less amenable to will and prediction.

But for the Maharal there are two worlds. There is the "lower" one which is known to perception and measurement. Here natural law applies without restriction. There is, however, another realm. The Maharal calls it the "Nivdal" world, from the Hebrew word meaning separate, apart or abstract. It is a domain distinct from corporal reality, transcending matter. Completely abstract, it is the space of supernal powers. And it is the source of miracles.

Being completely other, the Nivdal realm is unknowable in any ordinary manner. Its properties can only be inferred from their intrusions into that perceptible world or approached through pure – speculative – intellect.

Describing the differences between "our" world and the Nivdal one, the Maharal observes that natural reactions and occurrences require time. But an abstract reaction – a reaction in the Nivdal world – does not.

Similarly, while the ordinary world is subject to boundaries and limits, the Nivdal world has no such constraints. In the abstract sphere there are no restrictions of space.

The Nivdal world corresponds to Jung's concept of the collective unconscious, which also cannot be represented in itself. It too is generally known only from its intrusions into consciousness through images, symptoms or symbols. However, it can be approached also through pure intellect as in, for example, Jung's theories.

Jung observed that, from the perspective of the collective unconscious, "space and time, and hence, causality, are factors that can be eliminated, with the result that acausal phenomena, otherwise called miracles, appear possible" (CW8, par. 995). Since for Jung the synchronistic event rests upon an archetypal foundation and the archetypes constitute the contents of the collective unconscious it follows that, just as the Nivdal world is the source of miracles, the collective unconscious is the source of synchronicities.

The Maharal follows traditional Jewish belief that for a miracle to occur, it is necessary for a prophet to be present. A miracle implies that a point of contact is made between the ordinary and the Nivdal worlds and the prophet is the agent of that contact.

So too for Jung: The synchronistic event consists of the simultaneous occurrence of two states, one which is normal and causally explicable, another which cannot be derived from the first. The point of contact is the archetypal image in the form of dream, premonition or symptom. And just as the prophet always brings a sense of the numinous, so must the archetypal image appear with a strong affect.

While the prophet mediates a link between two worlds, this can happen only where there is a possibility for that bridge to be formed. For the Maharal this means that miracles occur only where there is a predisposition for them; for example, in the temple courtyard.

Parallel to this notion is Jung's idea that, when there is a synchronicity, an *abaissement du niveau mental* (lowering of consciousness) is necessary so that the unconscious is touched. This happens where there is a permeability of consciousness. For this reason, a psyche bombarded with synchronistic experiences is highly vulnerable. A life experienced too synchronistically verges on the psychotic.

While all miracles take place where there is a predisposition, those whose existence is essential for the human drama happen only when there is an absolute need for them. The prototypical example is the entrapment of the people of Israel at the Red Sea. For Israel, which needed a miracle, there was one. For the Egyptians, who did not, there was none.

Jung noted that, when the psychological situation is at an impasse, synchronicity is most likely to occur. It is at such moments that archetypes appear with the greatest regularity.

The archetype is manifested through an image. This may be accompanied by a synchronistic event which is caused not by the image but by the underlying, irrepresentable archetype itself. So too for the Maharal. The need and the prophet must be present but only God performs the miracle.

At a psychological impasse an archetype is constellated in the collective unconscious. It appears affectively to consciousness in the form of dream or other image. If it finds an *abaissement du niveau mental* it may effect a meaningful bridge between two otherwise separate realms. These may be mental and physical, here and there or now and then. The bridge is experienced as a synchronicity.

So too when there is an historical crisis and God's people are stuck, Divine energies are mobilized. Through the agency of a prophet God may contravene the laws of nature with deeds beyond the constraints of time and space. The Divine and mortal realms come together at a place inherently sanctified or made so through prayer. This coming together is experienced as a miracle.

This analogy between the religious and psychological systems is natural since the notion underlying both miracle and synchronicity is itself archetypal. More illuminating, however, is the difference between the two systems.

Jung is explicit that the term synchronicity is purely descriptive. It does not explain anything. It is not a theory.

Because Jung held back from providing synchronicity with an explanatory power it has remained without one. No such limitation is to be found in the Maharal's theology. His metaphysical beliefs make his ideas a real theory of miracle.

Essential to the Judaic vision of history is the notion that God has an ongoing, interactive relationship with Creation. God intervenes in the historical process through the miracle. The minor miracles, those only incidentally good, serve as reminders of God's power, encouraging acceptance of the divine commandments. The "essential" miracles reshape the course of history. The overriding concern and purpose of the miracle is eschatological.

Implicit here is another difference between Jung and the Maharal. For the latter the miracle is always and unequivocally for the good. The unitary God has no shadow and divine intervention is always for the benefit of Creation. This is far from the case for Jung. Empirically, psychology has always had to deal with negative intrusions of the unconscious. Psychosomatic medicine also offers evidence that the workings of the collective unconscious are inconsistent, at best, with the welfare of the whole personality.

This understanding follows from the fact that there is a shadowy aspect to any archetype. Thus, while there is a tendency to describe the synchronistic experience as positive, the underlying archetype also carries a negative charge, which may even predominate.

This line of thought leads to a question which remains moot in Jung's writings. Is the Self but one of the archetypes? Or are there archetypes subordinated to, or contained within, a unitary Self? If the latter, then even the shadowy aspects of archetypal manifestations may serve the goal of individuation. But if the Self is simply first among equals, no such consolation may be taken. Then Jung's synchronicity would differ from the Maharal's miracle in that it is performed through an agency independent of the Self. Synchronicities might be, so to speak, the work of the Devil or the Devil's minions.

In this view individual synchronicities would be the work of individual archetypes, uncoordinated and perhaps even in conflict. This possibility hinges, of course, on whether Jung's psychology is regarded as "monotheistic" or "polytheistic." This question has been explored in depth – by Hillman (1971), for example – but remains unresolved.

While there might be much to gain by applying Jung's psychology to the Maharal's theology, the focus here is on several psychological aspects. First, there is a host of "trivial" synchronistic experiences. A typical example would be the dream of a long-lost friend followed the next day by a letter from that friend. Events of this sort, which would be termed simple coincidence were it not for the numinosity they carry, fit poorly with the belief that synchronicity occurs at a moment of psychic impasse. But they may be seen through the theory of the Maharal as affirmations of powers transcendent to the ego.

More important is a second analogy from the Maharal's theory. If the miracle is God's intervention in the historical process of humanity, synchronicity may be seen as a way in which the unconscious intercedes in ordinary life for the sake of individuation. This view is especially valid if the Self is the center and totality of a personality unitary even in its contradictions, and as long as Thanatos, especially as expressed in self-destructiveness, is honored with a role in the development of the personality.

But even were the Self just another archetype, synchronicity may be taken as the purposive advancement of the interests of a particular aspect of the unconscious. It might be dealt with then in terms of those interests and their relationship to other facets of the personality.

Of course, much of psychology involves not synchronicities but the making of Golems. For the ritual of analysis involves the equivalent of fasting and prayer. Various aspects of a problem (the *prima materia*) are collected and an underlying archetype is evoked by the ensuing dialogue of the work. Potentially destructive, for example, to relationships – society or Self – many complexes nevertheless serve the psyche, defensively and otherwise.

Although the Maharal, as far as is known, never himself attempted the creation of a Golem, he had no doubt as to the possibility of such an endeavor – ironically, because he considered such a work to be less than miraculous. He accepted the traditional view that the Golem lacked the power of speech, the faculty held in Jewish thought to be most essentially human. The Golem, being less than human, could be a natural product of human activity; the true miracle requires the transcendence of the natural.

For Jung the prerequisite psychological work is adaptation to reality. That is, first comes the task of harnessing or creating complexes. Then there can follow the *opus contra naturam* of individuation. It is this stage that requires the transcendent, sometimes manifested in synchronicity.

Jung's early thought was that the constellation of the transcendent function is an art which, once learned, enables the analysand to continue effective psychological work beyond the frame of analysis. But the art was to be developed within the context of the consulting room. So it is with the special case of the transcendent function represented by synchronicity. Although by no means restricted to the process of analysis, it is experienced, frequently, in that arena.

The notion of synchronicity has entered, or returned to, Western consciousness through Jung's consulting room.

References

Hillman, J. (1971). Psychology; monotheistic or polytheistic. *Spring*.
Neumann, E. (1979). *Creative Man*. Princeton, NJ: Princeton University Press.

Therapist Mediation of the Transcendent Function

Lionel Corbett
Santa Fe, New Mexico, USA
Chicago Society of Jungian Analysts

Movement from the unconscious into consciousness occurs in dreams or fantasies via the symbol: as transference elements within relationships, symptoms, slips of the tongue, jokes, creativity or directly as an experience of the numinosum. I propose a theory of the purpose of this movement – the working of the transcendent function – with special reference to the therapeutic situation.

Jung's Concept of The Transcendent Function

For Jung, coming to terms with the unconscious requires a bridge to consciousness, which is mediated by the transcendent function. The transcendent function describes the capacity of the psyche to change and grow toward individuation when consciousness and the unconscious join, revealing the essential person.

Jung regarded the transcendent function as a manifestation of the energy that springs from the tension of opposites. While the concept of the transcendent function itself has heuristic value, Jung's explanation of its origin does not withstand scrutiny and needs revision.

Many post-Jungian writers have questioned the notion that the psyche is necessarily structured in sets of opposites. This notion reflects a prominent feature of Jung's personal psychology but does not necessarily apply to everyone. Samuels (1985) pointed out that the perception of psychic functioning in terms of opposites ignores the concurrent mutual support, complementarity, incremental gradations of change and subtle transitions found within the psyche.

It is tempting to use Jung's concept of psychic energy to explain the movement of the unconscious into consciousness, for example as the result of a flow down a gradient from higher to lower intensity, or as movement from potential into kinetic energy. His concept is more psychological than Freud's biological speculations, but as Atwood (1989) points out, the concept of psychic energy projects into the psyche qualities of material objects and therefore does not deal with subjectivity. To use a reified term such as "energy" implies that we can force the psyche into a natural science model and violates Jung's own philosophical position. A different metaphor is needed to describe the movement of the unconscious into consciousness.

This movement is motivated by a need to join with whatever is missing from ourselves, in order to enhance the wholeness and cohesiveness of the personality. The missing quality is not necessarily an "opposite" one, even though Jung stressed that the alchemists represented the supreme act of union as a "chymical marriage" between masculine and feminine. What we need may be more of a certain quality which is the same as one that we already possess, such as masculinity or femininity. The transcendent function enables such movement toward wholeness to occur, either via symbol formation or by means of relationship with another person. Its function is to express the *telos* – goal – of the personality.

Personal and Mythic Manifestations of the Transcendent Function

The transcendent function is implicit in developmental theories which describe the growth of the baby out of an original blueprint and in psychoanalytic concepts such as the Zeigarnik phenomenon, which postulates an unexplained motivation (not based on the drives) for undeveloped structures to resume their development when conditions permit. Kohut (1977) used this idea as a rationale for the unfolding of the self's innate "blueprint" under correct conditions, leading to a selfobject transference. Wilfred Bion may have had something similar to the transcendent function in mind when he described the process by which raw sensory and emotional data – "beta" elements – are transformed into "alpha" elements that can be "digested."

The inexorable impulse for change familiar to all therapists marks the appearance of the transcendent function on the personal level. It is reflected also in myth, as the movement from chaos to cosmos; for example, as the situation prior to creation in which all is darkness and void until ordered by the word of God. Mythologies of the incarnation of the human into the divine, or of the emanation of the divine into the lower worlds, also express this sense of movement of an undifferentiated totality into limited form, corresponding to the idea of individuation.

Manifested as the creative process, we see this function in the vision of Kekulé – in which the solution to the problem of the structure of the benzene ring appeared as a uroboric snake image – or in the mind of Einstein working on the problem of relativity by imagining himself traveling on a ray of light. It also has its poetic representations; Dylan Thomas describes it as: "the force that through the green fuse drives the flower." Whence does this urge to completion arise, and how does it operate?

The Transcendent Function as the Movement From Implicate to Explicate Order

Bohm's (1980) concept of the "implicate" order refers to a level of undivided wholeness reminiscent of Jung's stress on the *unus mundus*. At this level of the totality, "everything is enfolded into everything else" (p. 177). This order unfolds into the "explicate" order, the usual mechanistic preoccupation of classical physics, in which things seem to be isolated and to occupy only their own discrete region of space and time. This explicate level of order constitutes the manifest world as we experience it. Unlike other analogies to the physical sciences, here we have not tried, mistakenly, to force-fit the psyche into a theory appropriate only to matter.

Bohm pointed out that consciousness must be brought into this universe of discourse. The unbroken, subtle background flow of the implicate order breaks up as we construct our conscious experience via memory and thought, which is so intense that we focus on what is static and fragmented, leading to the illusion that these fragments of consciousness are the basis of reality. We are not separate from what we observe.

Bohm referred to the totality of the movement of enfoldment and unfoldment as the "holomovement," a universal flux that includes mind and matter as different aspects of an unbroken movement. The transcendent function seems to be the carrier of the holomovement for the psyche.

The movement from the unconscious into consciousness means a movement from undifferentiation into plurality. As the implicate becomes the explicate order, an unbroken totality becomes the fragmented condition of everyday consciousness, which divides everything into parts. The purpose of the transcendent function seems to be to restore an original totality by producing symbols and relationships that tend to restore our sense of cohesiveness.

The origin of the fragmentation which the transcendent function seeks to heal lies in part in the way the brain works. Although the psyche is not a product of the brain, it works via the brain; its manifestations are affected by the properties of the brain, rather as a radio signal is dependent on the qualities of the receiver. Because the brain processes information such as language, memory and thought in a fragmented manner, the transcendent function compensates with a countertendency to form gestalts and symbols which restore wholeness. Hence our subjectivity oscillates between experiences of plurality and unity; for its completion, the incomplete (or explicate) personal self needs the experience of the (implicate) transpersonal Self.

The Transcendent Function in Relation to the Personal and Transpersonal Self

The movement into consciousness may be considered to represent a movement from the noumenal Self toward the phenomenal self. "Consciousness" involves linking elements of experience that have been separated, but which belong together. Isolated themes are then seen to belong to the same piece of music. This ordering process is calming even though initially the attempted superimposition of a new level of order onto the old may be terrifying. The need to organize experience seems to be one of our central motivational forces, so that material entering consciousness does not do so randomly, but fits into a subjectively meaningful context. It becomes organized via the archetypes on the basis of common themes and affective significance, into complexes. The archetypal basis of these schemata represents the extension of the order of the Self into the domain of the self; the archetypes are the psyche's morphogenetic principles. Equating archetype with spirit, the transcendent function mediates the function of spirit as an organizing principle which at the same time discriminates and unites.

The Transcendent Function
Manifested in the Selfobject Experience

Traditionally, the transcendent function was seen to manifest itself only as the psyche's symbol-making capacity. The search for wholeness was assumed to proceed more intrapsychically than interpersonally. Hence in the classical Jungian literature the relationship between analyst and analysand was seen as of secondary importance to the elucidation of symbolic material. But completion is also sought within relationships, and in such cases is mediated no less by the transcendent function than is the symbol. Kohut's (1984) selfobject psychology elucidates some of the processes by which we experience others as necessary for our own wholeness.

The term "selfobject" as used by Kohut – distinct from Fordham's (1976) use of the term – refers to another person who is experienced intrapsychically as necessary for the maintenance of the integrity and cohesiveness of the self. The selfobject needs of the child are: 1) the "mirror," for affirmation and affective attunement; 2) an idealizable figure as a source of values and soothing, and 3) the "twinship" sense of sameness, or the feeling that one belongs. These are archetypally determined elements of the Self which require human mediation. The degree of failure in the original selfobject milieu determines the degree of structural deficit in the vitality and wholeness of the self.

The analysand's selfobject needs are reactivated within the transference to the extent that they were not met in childhood; their emergence represents the constellation of the Self in the therapy, with all its potential for healing. The analyst is called upon to perform those functions which the analysand is unable to carry out for him/herself because they have never been internalized, but which are necessary for psychological survival. When the selfobject relationship is established, the patient feels alive and integrated. According to Kohut, cure is established by a gradual process in which the patient takes over these functions by a process of "transmuting internalization," in the course of which the interaction with the analyst is used to build personal self-structures.

Thus it takes both participants to experience one whole sense of self. I suggest that the transcendent function operates in therapy not only via the symbol but also via the movement into consciousness of early selfobject needs which, when they are met, will reestablish wholeness. I believe that Jung's (CW16) use of the Rosarium pictures to depict aspects of the transference actually illustrates the archetypal basis of what Kohut later described personalistically. These pictures express the idea of twoness which is at the same time felt as one-ness. The heads are not joined because cognitively the participants know that they are separate; the merger is at an unconscious level. The felt sense for the analysand is one of wholeness as long as the relationship with the analyst is intact.

The role of the analyst therefore is to mediate the demands of the Self as they unfold into selfobject needs, by allowing oneself to be used – in a symbolic sense – as a responsive and, when necessary, interpretive participant. Such unfolding represents the action of the transcendent function.

References

Atwood, G. (1989). Psychoanalytic phenomenology and the thinking of Martin Heidegger and Jean-Paul Sartre. In D. Detrick & S. Detrick (Eds). *Self Psychology: Comparisons and Contrasts.* Hillside, NJ: Analytic Press.

Bohm, D. (1980). *Wholeness and the Implicate Order.* London: Routledge & Kegan Paul.

Fordham, M. (1976). *The Self and Autism.* London: Heinemann.

Kohut, H. (1977). *The Restoration of the Self.* New York: International Universities Press.

Kohut, H. (1984). *How Does Analysis Cure?* Chicago: University of Chicago Press.

Samuels, A. (1985). *The Plural Psyche.* London: Routledge.

The Marionettes of the Self: The Transcendent Function at Work

Carlos Amadeu B. Byington
San Paulo, Brazil
Brazilian Society for Analytical
Psychology

After a century of dynamic psychotherapy many analysts recognize the limitations of exclusive verbal interpretation. Those glorious moments when the analyst gives the interpretation that produces insight followed by cure may be recognized today more as a wish-fulfillment left over from magic shamanism blended with nineteenth century rationalism than as psychological reality. In this respect, Jung was a pioneer. His discovery of active imagination and his introduction of drawing, painting, and sculpture – in his analytic practice and in his own process – pointed beyond mere verbalization toward expressive techniques to elaborate, understand and integrate symbols from dreams and fantasies.

The capacity of exclusive rational interpretation to cause psychic transformation seems to have reached its limit. Modern psychotherapeutic techniques seem to be directed increasingly toward the experience of symbols: body techniques to express emotion, techniques based on imagination, plastic techniques, oracular and divinatory practices and techniques producing altered states of consciousness.

Like all change, however, this one is suffering currently from exaggerated emphasis on the new and, reactively, on the old. Expressive techniques are mushrooming as alternative methods of therapy, each new technique announced as the latest marvel for cure, self-knowledge and well-being. Such an attitude tends to omit the four great acquisitions of twentieth-century psychology: 1) the transference (extended to include the whole analyst-analysand relationship); 2) the individuation process (extended to include the entire symbolic development of the personality together with ego formation and transformation); 3) the conscious-unconscious polarity and 4) the inter-relationship between defensive (compulsively fixed symbols) and creative (symbols developing freely) structures. When expressive techniques are employed without due consideration of these four dimensions, their practice is likely to become dangerous, irresponsible and unproductive. "Science without consciousness ruins the soul" wrote Montaigne (1533-1592) as far back as the Renaissance.

The present growth of such quackish and ignorant use of expressive techniques is enhanced by analysts and analytic training institutions that cling to the traditional verbal method of interpretation and declare some or all expressive techniques not to be analytic. Due to such exaggeratedly orthodox behavior they prevent candidates from learning these techniques in training seminars and training analysis. Such a castrating senex attitude has delayed the technical development of institutionalized analytic psychotherapy and has stimulated patients to look for new techniques among professionals who have not had analytic training.

Expressive Techniques in the Brazilian Society

Having returned to Brazil in 1966 after training at the Zurich Institute, I had the opportunity to train in group, family and couple therapy with Freudian and Kleinian analysts from Argentina. One of them, Fidel Moccio, coordinated workshops on expressive techniques such as painting, drawing, psychodrama and imagination integrated into the analytic method.

In 1977, when our group was admitted into the IAAP as the Brazilian Society for Analytical Psychology, I included expressive techniques in our training program to be employed not only in therapy but also pedagogically. This innovation created a problem with other analysts coming from Zurich later on, some of whom did not consider expressive techniques such as psychodrama and group work to be compatible with Jungian analysis. Thus, the present Congress brought relief and joy when I assisted Ellynor and Helmut Barz's presentation on their introduction of psychodrama for groups of candidates training in the Jung Institute in Zurich.

Expressive Techniques versus Rational Interpretation

Psychological situations often must be worked through intensely for their meaning to be grasped. This process of "working through" is necessary to understand complicated life situations, with their defenses and resistances. Such instances, which include all neurotic and psychotic, as well as normal archetypal symbolism, need painstaking symbolic elaboration to unravel their meaning. (I prefer the term "symbolic elaboration" rather than "working through." The latter has been used exclusively in psychoanalysis to denominate therapeutic work with pathological defenses. Symbolic elaboration includes expressive techniques and amplification in the work with all symbolic expression, including defenses.)

Rational interpretation may create an illusion of understanding that neglects the archetypal roots of symbols. In order to please the analyst, the analysand may accept interpreted meaning which is far from the life process.

The transference relationship is productive in the process of symbolic elaboration not only because it allows neurotic contents of the analysand's unconscious to be projected onto the analyst and worked through. More importantly, the ritual of analysis within which the transference occurs is in itself an expressive technique to build the analytic vessel which can take place the elaboration of what I call the "Therapeutic Self" (1985). The archetypal therapeutic transference is a soul-making ritual, fostering symbolic elaboration.

The Power of Expressive Techniques

Expressive techniques have an enormous power to enhance symbolic elaboration because they intensify the psychic energy of symbols. Three centuries of rationalism and materialism have inflated Western consciousness and accustomed it to lifeless words. Part of the soul withdrew from so much arrogance. Expressive techniques animate the soul to come back to life and diminish the identification of the analyst with the transcendent function by engaging the analysand actively and creatively in the process of symbolic elaboration.

Many analysts criticize expressive techniques as a directive method, as an intrusion by the analyst into the spontaneity and neutrality necessary for analysis. In my experience, quite the contrary happens. The adequate usage of expressive techniques turns the process of analysis into a creative participatory process between analyst and analysand not only on the therapeutic alliance of the ego level but also on the creative archetypal level of the Self.

I use many expressive techniques, including the couch, to elaborate symbols. Throughout the years I have come to recognize these techniques' enormous power to reveal the meaning of dreams, fantasies, conflicts and symptoms.

My recommendation, before using an expressive technique with an analysand, is to reflect on what you think is the meaning of the situation you are going to elaborate. Keep this to yourself and work through the symbol with the expressive technique. I am always surprised and enriched with the results.

Many analysts – including me – who have experienced the immense revealing power of expressive techniques, frequently do not use them, out of sheer laziness. When one employs expressive techniques, one has to get off the chair and move around (literally and figuratively). Parenthetically, a successful career of only sitting down may be crowned by physical ailments due to an unused body.

Expressive Techniques within the Transference

Expressive techniques are used spontaneously in play, fantasy, games and many instances of daily life. When used in therapy, they affect significantly the nature of the therapeutic relationship. Therefore, the first condition for their use is to realize that they are being employed within the field of transference. Any interpretation of the transference should be postponed until the exercise is carried out. Indeed, it is not necessary to interpret the transference but one must always pay attention to its dynamics. I usually participate actively in expressive techniques in some way. Hence, I find it productive after using expressive techniques to discuss what happened and how the analysand experienced my action and our relationship during the process.

Expressive Techniques and Personality Development

A further step in the use of expressive techniques is to place the symbols being elaborated within the scope of the development of the personality. How were these symbols dealt with in the past? Have they ever been worked through? Have they been experienced in neurotic, phobic or psychotic situations? How important are they and what role do they play in the person's life process? These requirements preclude week-end workshops using expressive techniques, unless the participants have been or are in analysis.

Expressive Techniques and the Conscious-Unconscious Polarity

The third requirement for the employment of expressive techniques is the permanent observation of the conscious-unconscious polarity in symbolic elaboration. In my understanding, life situations are always personal, cultural and archetypal. In so being, symbolic elaboration produces consciousness through archetypal activation which also reduces consciousness and produces unconsciousness. It is a never-ending process. The analyst must pay special attention to a high proportion of unconsciousness, which may diminish dangerously the analysand's capacity for adequate orientation in the life process.

Expressive and Defensive Structures

The fourth requirement in using expressive techniques is the polarity between creative structures and defensive structures in symbolic elaboration. Every psychic function may be constellated within the Self to function creatively and develop consciousness – or to function defensively, maintaining symbols compulsively, as they are expressed through what I call the "pathological shadow." The transference projections of analysand and analyst also may be creative or defensive.

Creatively endowed therapists may detect more easily functions that operate creatively and overlook their defensive presence, which blocks the process of symbolic elaboration. Conversely, analysts trained in the medical model, or poorly endowed with creativity, tend to overlook creative structures and to reduce symbolic elaboration to the working through of defensive structures. Each type tends – in its own way – not to handle adequately symbolic elaboration.

Overlooking defensive structures, dominantly creative therapists may aggravate pathological conditions, with danger of precipitating severe maladaptation and psychotic states. Reducing creative structures to defensive structures, dominantly pathologically-minded therapists may cripple the development of creative personalities.

Marionettes of the Self

This expressive technique uses puppets and toys similar to those of Kleinian ludotherapy and sandplay. The name of this technique originates in its creative effort to display these figures as the symbolic expression of the transforming Therapeutic Self. The marionettes are arranged by analyst and analysand in the middle of the consulting room, to express the dynamics of the Therapeutic Self, including the transference relationship.

Generally, the main human figures of the process such as parents, siblings, friends and relatives are represented by six-inch puppets. The disassembled marionettes remain ready for use and may be assembled readily in later sessions, changing their dramatic relationship as the analysis progresses.

Once the marionettes are assembled, priority symbols for elaboration become easily identified, including those dissociated and expressed through defense mechanisms. Further elaboration of these symbols may then be carried out through other expressive techniques such as drawing, painting, free association, psychodramatic expression, letter writing, active imagination, directed imagination, dancing and poetry. As symbolic elaboration develops, the marionettes are modified accordingly and other expressive techniques are chosen to continue the work.

This technique is useful for expressing, elaborating and clarifying any human situation. I have used it with good results in individual, couple and family therapy as well as in supervision and in teaching.

References

Byington, C. (1985). The Concept of the Therapeutic Self and the interaction of the defensive and creative transference in the transference quaternio. *Junguiana, 3,* 5-18.

Byington, C. (1986). The concept of the pathological shadow within a theory of symbolic psychopathology. In L. Zoja & R. Hinshaw (Eds.), *Symbolic and Clinical Approaches in Theory and Practice.* Zurich: Daimon.

The Interface of Developmental and Archetypal Images in Sandplay: The Ground of the Transcendent Function

Joel Ryce-Menuhin
London, England
Independent Group of Analytical
Psychologists

Jungian analysis has been on the leading edge of this century's psychotherapy in understanding how affect and image can be brought together in the construction of integrity.

John Beebe

Sandplay is categorized, sometimes, as an "Expressive Therapy." Although an analysand frees ego-control in sandplay, we restrict the possible clinical dimensions of its interpretation in using the term "expressive." I believe that a biological factor may influence the sandplay medium, interacting with the psychological factors.

The capacity for producing sandplays is built into human structure at fundamental levels; it may fit into what biologists call "super-normal sign stimuli." The term, "innate releasing mechanism" (IRM), designates the inherited structure in the nervous system that instigates behavioral response to sign stimuli. The ethologist Tinbergen (1951) wrote: "The innate releasing mechanism usually seems to correspond more or less with the properties of the environment, the object or situation at which the reaction is aimed... However, close study reveals the remarkable fact that it is sometimes possible to offer stimulus situations that are even more effective than the natural situation" (p. 223).

For example, when a male grayling butterfly pursues a female, the male shows a preference for females of darker hue. If a female is stained to a darker color than anything known in nature, as Tinbergen did experimentally, a male will prefer this butterfly to the darkest female of the species. This inclination to reach after and beyond nature is comparable to the transcendent function as it brings forward the unconscious, unrealized yearnings of human beings. Sandplay in its ritual play deals with super-normal sign stimuli, as Joseph Campbell (1991) indicated:

> Obviously the human female with her talent for play, recognized many millenniums ago the power of the super-normal sign stimulus; cosmetics for the heightening of the lines of her eyes have been found among the earliest remains of the Neolithic Age. And from there to an appreciation of the force of ritualization, art, masks, gladiatorial vestments, kingly robes, and every other humanly conceived and realized improvement on nature, is but a step – or a series of steps. (p. 43)

My sandplay room contains two sandboxes; one filled with dry sand, one with wet. There are about 1000 objects on shelves around the room. From these miniature figures, an analysand can build up a three-dimensional structure, allowing expression to both the rational and irrational parts of the personality. Sandplay of disturbed analysands is a reaching for something beyond both nature and circumstance. I am not equating it to an improvement on nature itself, as the ethologists have done in their biological experiments. I am suggesting, however, that the range and depth of sandplays indicate that the extremes of collective and personal unconscious may be present for psyche and soma, in terms of trauma, anxiety, pathology and vulnerability.

Analytical Psychologists are in danger of losing their interpretive skill in analyzing, reductively and synthetically, what psyche perceives in image. When the art of dream interpretation and of projective waking image-building is now of so little moment to many Jungian analysts, we are in danger of operating as some kind of inflated counselors – not analysts – in which self-reference is the omnipotent and pathetically non-Jungian mode of looking at the analysand's images. The narcissism of these crypto-Freudians in their ego-bound counter-transferences blocks the natural effect of the transcendent function.

A case illustrating my remarks – complete with photographs of sandtrays – can be found in an earlier publication (Ryce-

Menuhin, 1992, pp. 77-90). Sandplay heals where stress and development are most pointed. Its non-verbal power enabled an originally focused but shy young woman to experience, in the presence of a sustaining male analyst, the essence of entering womanhood. Sandplay excludes embarrassment, apology or dissembling. Its images to those initiated to its synthetic interpretation help nature itself to explore itself.

My sandplay interpretations are "adultomorphic," deliberately, because it inspires and stretches the imagination of those schooled only to rationality, discipline and materialism. Its free but firm grounding to transitory anxieties, gives it a holding power enabling nature better to take its course.

Unlike reductive methods which trace everything back to primitive instincts, the interpretation of Jungian sandplay by the synthetic method develops the material by differentiating it. This entails an introversion of libido, sacrificing a former attitude in favor of a new one, when image penetration reveals what this new attitude can be. The transition to a new attitude is the work of the transcendent function.

Sandplay, in its creativity, neither knows nor possesses symbolic meanings absolutely. Symbolic interpretation raises possibilities that may strengthen the analysand's ego, lifting its differentiation further from unconsciousness. The ego then may integrate the interpretation and reunite with Self.

Where psyche's projection is a living experience in sandplay, the idea does not petrify but receives visible three-dimensional expression by the sandplayers. This produces a new potential. After experiencing sandplays that may return to collective material or regress to the psychic conditions of prehistory, the retrograde process is reversed and renewed by here-and-now consciousness of relative meanings for the Self of the analysand. This impressive experience transforms the psyche's ongoing dynamic state.

Where a submission to instinct occurs, resistance to its dynamic chaos is compensated by a need for form and order. Sandplay enables a fast and flexible shift within the spectrum of the chaos/order dimension. The symbol points toward and partially enables release from the bondage to trapped energies. The images of childhood fantasies and the later projection of the child archetype in its conscious images strive for fulfillment and integration in the adult. Sandplay fantasy often foreshadows events in psyche.

Jung remarked more than once that a redeeming symbol comes from the place where no one expects it. Lack of prior assumptions is the most important attitude when building a sandtray. Symbolic play is a middle way in which opposites can flow together in a new movement. Functions that were inert come to life; the repressed and undervalued elements come into sandplay through the least valued function of conscious life. A restriction of the total potential of the sandplayer is what is stimulated and unblocked in sandplay. The psyche flows again away from the lure of a maternal abyss, a drowning in the oceanic depths of the Great Mother.

One of therapy's most powerful tools, sandplay stands out for its inspiration toward, and alignment with, archetypal and developmental personal projections, at a level which is outstanding among the projective therapies. A healing therapy of diagnostic and psychotherapeutic excellence, sandplay is indeed only at the dawn of its great potential to Analytical Psychology. Jung (CW8) has written: "Often the hands know how to solve a riddle with which the intellect has wrestled in vain" (par. 180).

We each have one face in *soma* and one in *psyche*. The face's left profile is the developmental aspect and the right profile is the archetypal aspect. Many physiognomists see this structure in each of our faces. Do some Jungians (e.g., the "London School") any longer recognize this structure in their splitting of the archetypal/developmental nature of the "face" of our work, with the interpretation of image and its affect?

Dora Kalff (1980) has pointed out that the course of psychic development in its interface, containing both the profile of the archetypal and the profile of the developmental, might be compared with flowing water. Hexagram 29 (K'an / The Abysmal Water) of the *I Ching* says:

It flows on and on, merely filling at the place it traverses; it does not shy away from any dangerous place, nor from any sudden plunge; nothing can make it lose its own essence. It remains true to itself in all circumstances. Thus, truthfulness in difficult situations will bring about the penetration of a situation within one's heart. And once a situation is mastered from within the heart, the success of our exterior actions will come about all by itself. (Wilhelm, 1951, p. 115)

References

Campbell, J. (1959/1991). *The Masks of God: Primitive Mythology.* London: Arkana.

Kalff, D. (1980). *Sandplay.* Boston: Sigo.

Ryce-Menuhin, J. (1992). *Jungian Sandplay: The Wonderful Therapy.* London/New York: Routledge.

Tinbergen, N. (1951). *The Study of Instinct.* Oxford: Oxford University Press.

Wilhelm, R., Ed. (1951). *I Ching or Book of Changes.* London: Routledge.

Animation of the Transcendent Function in Couples and Groups

Peter Schellenbaum
Zurich, Switzerland
Swiss Society For Analytical
Psychology

The spontaneous activity from the Self – as Jung defined the transcendent function – never occurs in an isolated individual personality. From the moment of conception the individual crosses boundary after boundary in an exchange with a larger and larger world. This exchange characteristically belongs to the Self. Therefore, the spiritual conflict that dissolves in the connecting "third" is to be seen not only intrapsychically but also between/among two or more personalities – couples and groups. I call the connecting third in interpersonal relationships the "third body." In order to understand this body we turn first to the concept of "resonance," then venture a critique of classical psychoanalysis and further draw the connection between the transcendent function and the self-healing of the individual in a couple's relationship or in a group.

Every self-transcendence of an individual is based on a resonance in a surrounding field, on oscillation in the interspace, on interaction. The individual never changes alone, but the field in which one lives changes, including all others that live in this field. The interaction may become increasingly beastly in sharper and sharper polarizations. Or it can cause a move toward harmony, thanks to a feeling awareness that includes the different polarities. The "magnetic field" in which we move is the source of our being at every moment. That which motivates us to transcend is not ourselves as individuals but our participation in a social field.

The concept of resonance comes from physics. It denotes the tendency to harmonization of rhythms. This phenomenon is universally valid: When oscillators in the same field pulsate at approximately the same rhythm they tend to "click into place" so that they come to swing in exact synchronization. In human interactions we detect adaptations of rhythm everywhere, such as the synchronization of the heartbeats of psychotherapist and client.

With people who get along well a harmonizing of gestures, voices and glances can occur. The word *Gestalt* denotes not only an individual personality; in being together with others we form a common gestalt that moves and changes as a dynamic unity and that is just as physical as an individual "third body."

The meaning of this body for individuation and healing cannot be valued highly enough. All psychophysical processes, such as illness or recovery, are processes of the third body. In a couple one partner may fall ill, representative of both, or the symptom of the one corresponds to a symptom of the other. Not only in the psychic but also in the somatic realm couples, families and groups form healing or illness-causing systems. The passage to a healing social system originates in the transcendent function.

We all are always symbiotic. The decisive question is whether we are aware of our symbiosis, whether we are able to feel and understand that which connects or separates in a larger whole, whether we withdraw from this larger whole by retreat or crumble by a loss of autonomy in fateful herding.

The loss of social harmony is simultaneously a loss of individual harmony. Harmony is not the absence of conflicts but self-organization of a social system through the connecting awareness of all concerned.

The relationship between analyst and analysand is a special kind of pair relationship. If I now express criticism of transference and countertransference in classical psychoanalysis, it is to show how in this model of a relationship the transcendent function is prevented. The power game that is inherent in psychoanalysis limits the possibility for resonance of the analyst as well as the possibility, for both analyst and analysand, of a connecting third body. As an example I choose a work of Kernberg (1985). He stated that it is a matter of "confronting all attempts of the patient that aim at dominating, controlling, and devaluating him omnipotently." It looks as if "[the patient] wants to achieve by it the analyst's feeling frustrated and a failure" (p. 293). In the narcissistic personality the old experience is revived: confronting distances one from the emotion, opposes it. The experience is contained also in the word countertransference.

That which Kernberg described takes place but is only the foreground of the unconscious interaction of the analysand with the analyst. As long as the interpretation moves in this foreground the analyst is trapped in the same imaginative system as the analysand. The analyst is conveying the feeling of frustration and of failure; the analysand now also has the feeling of frustration and failure in the relationship.

Even deeper than the unconscious intention of the analysand to devaluate the analyst and to impart the feeling of failure and self-doubt, to refuse anything helpful – out of jealousy – and to take only magical sustenance from the analyst (all these motives are listed by Kernberg), are feelings of the powerlessness of the small child who is not held, not mirrored, not enticed into growth. For the analyst and the analysand the resonance exists in the same powerlessness. The analyst whose powerlessness is not conscious dodges into the psychonanalytic power-game that in fact is a powerless power-game.

The deepest dimension in the analytic interaction is not a "counter," but a "with." In translating the language of the "counter" – the polarization in the foreground – into the language of the "with," of resonance and syntonic relationship, the analyst becomes aware of the powerlessness evoked within him or her. Only by starting from the zero-point of the jointly-sensed powerlessness can both find their way into constructive feelings and imagination. These are properties of the now-waking third body: spontaneous creations originating from the transcendent function.

In connection with the "interpretation of resonance" it becomes possible, and unavoidable, to put forward also the "interpretation of conflict," which has been the only one in psycho-analysis. It is important for the analysand to understand deep feelings, which he or she signals through the defense against anxiety. In the comprehensive connection of the real and felt "with," the secondary interpretation of the "counter" releases much less resistance or none at all. In this way most polarizations and power-games can be avoided. (So-called power-games are in fact powerlessness-games.) The analysand learns to form relationships outside therapy, with a connected awareness and a participating resonance. And the therapeutic relationship becomes a practice of the connected awareness of the third body and thus an activation of the transcendent function in a social organism.

In an example from couples therapy in a group, it becomes clear how the transcendent function awakens and sets in motion a shared process of change. A woman and a man, married for fifteen years, sit facing each other. The woman says that she is afraid. After a pause in which the two maintain eye contact – as they do throughout the exchange – the man remarks that he feels indifference. This situation reflects the polarization of feelings that has long existed. Their third body is now a suffering, torn organism that can express its truth only in contrariness; a common oscillation cannot be felt. It is futile to ask what was there first: the woman's fear with which she impedes her momentum of life or the man's indifference with which he protects himself from feelings. If one partner could break through the illness-causing system, it would cease to exist. In a Janus-faced third body one face reveals the fear of giving way to the momentum of life while the other reveals indifference as an effect of "stowed away" feelings. Between the two is an area of contact against which two backs are planted. They mean to push themselves free; in reality they hook themselves into each other because each wants to use the other as a launching platform for his/her vitality and emancipation. This is a pointless undertaking and an obvious opposition by which many of couples hinder their growth.

The atmosphere between the two is poisoned; no healing is in sight. In a second exchange the woman expresses rage, the man inattention and defense. Through a perseverance in a corresponding eye contact and through the exclusive attention to expression of their own feelings – the two rules of this partner-game – an intensification of the polarization takes place. This additional step into polarization is familiar to both. The fear of the woman finds a preliminary venting in the rage about lack of momentum in her life; the indifference of the man translates into a defense that hinders him from concentrating on the exchange that is currently taking place. So far little is new.

The pauses between the communications are long, the eye contact intense. In the eyes of the woman there are hot tears of rage; in those of the man ice-cold defense. For a long time nothing appears to happen. Both presumably have left the argument at this point many times: a fatal interruption in the formation of the third body, always in facing the same hurdle. But this time the argument continues – after I point out that it is important to continue. Now something decisive happens. By the continuing, uninterrupted awareness of feeling in the third body and the exclusive attention to their own feelings the two fall into an emotional vacuum. They both realize that they cannot continue like this; they are going nowhere. This decisive turn is not stated directly by either one. The all-filling nothingness – a new manifestation of the third body – does not permit one to name it. There is a long silence. In the group all are suddenly alert. In each member the same thing takes place as in the two partners.

Thus, at the emotional zero-point, the transcendent function starts moving – not only in these two, but in all the participants. Nobody realizes what has changed. But the mood is totally different: flowing like an invisible, inaudible, "unfeelable" stream. Indirectly the change – involuntary, radical renunciation of conceptions and pretences, of attitudes of victimization and manipulations – can be read from the interaction that followed. The woman says: "I feel exhaustion and relaxation." The man says: "Suddenly I am attentive and have a good feeling of interrelation." Each has let go of the pressure on self and partner. Now, at least within this ritual, there is no pressure, no expectation, no demand; both partners are simply there. They have found themselves in the same nothingness. The synchronized oscillation has engaged, in them and in the other group participants: revealed in the synchronized breathing, in the slow back and forth movements of their bodies and in the eye contact that has become mobile. Here the third body – the experience of the transcendent function – has taken place. Each expresses "I have trust." They have freed themselves toward the self-confidence of the third body, toward the trust in a connected growth. For both it is a matter of strengthening the feeling awareness in the joint third body, to enlarge the view from the individual half-measure – toward the wholeness of the couple, the laws of common growth and co-transcendence, and the solution of problems within this connected awareness.

The transcendent experience happens not only through a merely reasonable endeavor toward a solution of our points of controversy. Once in a while we need to look away from all reflections and words in order to meet directly, without control, in our own feelings, until the turn to that which is connecting occurs, even if this should mean separation.

An old alchemical text describes the symbolism of the third body. It can be read as an expression of the transcendent function within an individual as well as in a couple. Coming from the Simonian gnosis, it mentions the male and female primal principles in the world, that is, the polarity that in Christianity largely degenerated into polarization.

The "incomprehensible air" in the "interspace" is an image for the activation of energy through polar connection. The incomprehensible air is related as well to that of the "ether" that portrays the energy of life. The third body is an activation of energy through connection. The "between," of which philosopher Martin Buber speaks, is a space: a place of meeting between the poles, in a couple and in a group. Concerning the couple it means the "free space" without pressure, demands, expectations and self-interruption. In the "between" there is then room to breathe. Thus the "air" is the principle of creation: It has "neither beginning nor end."

The "air" – energy – that is created through coupling condenses into the third body which is no mere thought, but a bodily-spiritual reality, a comprehensive and centering power. This numinous central figure is an androgynous strength. The androgynous polarity is the human archetype of all polarity and its power of creation. As a result of sexual union creation happens, in the conception of a child. The androgynous central figure is independent of all that comes and goes in the history of the world, a primal principle of all being. Therefore it carries and nurtures us, is a source of security and spiritual nourishment in the couple and in all organic connections.

The transcendent function in the relationships of couples and in groups is animated and stimulated by the connected awareness that is related to entire systems. Hence, what is perceived on the outside is also experienced on the inside. The difference between the transcendent function in the individual personality and the transcendent function in a social system falls away. The connected awareness lets that which is on the inside looks outside and that which is on the outside, inside. Thus, individual therapy and couple- or group-therapy do not form an opposition, but two perspectives in the same "unus mundus."

Translated from German by
Yvonne Cherne

Reference

Kernberg (1985). *Borderline Disturbances and Pathological Narcissism*. Northwale, N.J.: Aronson.

Out of the Mouths of Babes: The Transcendent Function and the Development of Language

Elizabeth Urban
London, England
The Society of Analytical Psychology

The quest for the "mother tongue" is both my quest and that of a language-deprived, 10-year-old deaf girl. Both require an investigation into the developmental origins of language.

The Transcendent Function, the Self, and the Primary Self

Many years after he wrote "The Transcendent Function" (CW8), Jung recalled it as being among the first attempts at a synthetic view of psychic processes. This function is an essential aspect of Michael Fordham's postulate of a primary self, the psychosomatic integrate that contains the potential of the organism. From before birth the primary self has the functions of both integrating (Jung's "synthetic view") and dividing up (Fordham's "deintegration"). Development occurs through the dynamic between deintegration and reintegration. These processes constitute the concept of development that I shall use to describe the origins of language.

Clinical Material

The deaf girl, "Virginia," stole various things, such as money from home and small items of classroom equipment from school. Consequently, I saw her weekly at primary school, over her last four terms: from Easter of one year until July of the next. I shall examine what Virginia was trying to steal or, rather, to retrieve.

Although the cause of her profound perceptive (nerve) deafness was unknown, Virginia was presumed to have been deaf from birth. She had started to learn lipreading at age two, but, about the time I started to see her, sign language replaced oral communication in the curriculum. At that time, the impoverishment of her language was obvious.

In our painfully unpropitious first session, I understood virtually nothing of Virginia's communications. The feelings of being misunderstood and rejected which this evoked then became acted out, and she refused to see me the following two sessions. My supervisor, Dorothy Davidson, taught me how to rely on projective identifications – the thoughts and emotions that Virginia aroused in me – to understand Virginia's feelings. When I could see that my feelings of rejection had their source in Virginia, I had a way of understanding her.

To my surprise, she came willingly to the fourth session, and rejected me *in pretend*. This was the beginning of a regular pattern of play, in which she would march into the room adjoining mine and slam the door behind her. I would then pretend to beg her to let me play with her. Eventually she would let me in, and then order me about in her role of bossy teacher or cruel doctor.

The endings of the sessions were characteristically disruptive, because she wanted to take her toys away with her. Later I understood that her behavior was related to communicating. For instance, at the end of the fifth session, she insisted on taking the entire box of toys with her, yet brought them back to the subsequent session. This made what might have been stealing – or confiscation – into an exchange; she takes something from me and then gives something back. Hence the toys were a means of exchange, which because a fundamental link between us.

By the end of the term, there was a marked improvement in her confidence and ability to communicate, both in sessions and outside. To the best of anyone's knowledge, she had not stolen from home or school since the first time she saw me. However, when I took Virginia's toys home with me over the summer vacation, I noticed a strange toy. It was a tiny, soft cushion, probably part of furniture for a doll's house, that only Virginia could have put there. Something had been added to our means of exchange; she had contributed, albeit surreptitiously, something of her own to what passed between us.

The following autumn, a new relationship of mutuality developed and reached a climax in our last session before the Easter break, just a year after we started meeting. At the beginning of the session, she found some disused speech therapy equipment in my room. Using it and the procedure with which she was familiar, she pretended to give me a hearing test. She made vocalizations behind me and, pretending to be deaf, I raised my hand when I "heard." She reversed our places, and I gave her the "test," whereupon she indicated that she had heard me. We repeated the "test," and she repeated that she could hear. I asked her what word she heard me say, and she answered correctly, "Virginia." When I asked about the second word, she wrongly answered, "Elizabeth."

At the subsequent session four weeks later she pulled out the hearing test equipment, darkened the room and administered the test. She then insisted that I go with her into the hall, where we each copied a song chosen from several that were posted on the wall. When we returned to the darkened therapy room:

> She places me in the corner in front of the lamp and turns it on. She wants me to sing the song I chose, which I do with the spotlight on me, while she holds the music and, after a fashion, directs by signing the words. When we finish my song, she switches our positions so that she stands in the spotlight. She tells me to sign the words of her song, and we perform the song together – my inarticulate signing accompanying her nearly indiscernible words and flat yet enthusiastic tones. When we finish, she turns and stands opposite to where she stood to sing, applauds, and has me do the same. There is enthusiastic appreciation in the applause – and a curtain call.

The feelings that were aroused in me by Virginia during these two sessions helped me to understand what was happening. I felt an intense humbleness at the privilege of being "heard" by this deaf child, and an exquisitely painful tenderness at being allowed close to what felt at the time like her "primal wound." These feelings of idealized specialness and closeness were opposite to the rejection and worthlessness I had experienced at the beginning.

To summarize: When I started seeing her, Virginia equated being deaf with being unable to communicate and being rejected. After the first term, there was evidence in the tiny cushion that the foundations of communication had been established between us, accompanied by an improvement in her communication skills. During the autumn this development continued and gained momentum. It can be described as the unfolding (deintegration) of a complex fantasy of idealized good communication, in which there is a close and special togetherness with another, without the pain of not understanding or of being misunderstood.

In Virginia's fantasy, ideal communication occurred only if one could hear and, by implication, speak. Thus, she could "really" communicate only while in projective identification with an idealized hearing (and speaking) object. From what I felt at the time, she was in this state of mind in the two sessions involving the hearing test equipment. I think that she responded as she did because she knew from previous testing what to expect and not because she could actually hear. Thus, when she said she could hear, she meant that she was projectively identified with me as a hearing person and *felt* that she could hear. She also *felt* that she could speak/sing, while in projective identification with an idealized speaking (singing) object. In achieving this state of mind, Virginia had been able to acquire "honestly," that is, by hard work, what previously she had attempted to get only by stealing.

I have described so far Virginia's quest as one for the experience of being in communication with another. At this point a new question arises: If Virginia was deaf from birth and without a visual language until she was ten, how did she know what she was missing? Or, put differently, was Virginia stealing something that she did not have or retrieving something she once had but had lost? To address this question I turn to infant observation.

The following notes are of early exchanges between "Toby" and his mother. In the first observation Toby was 2-1/2 months old, by which time he had established a good relationship to the breast.

He sucked heartily at the left breast for several minutes, making throaty noises and moving his cheeks rhythmically. After several minutes his mother sat him up to wind [burp] him. She looked at him intently and talked to him, occasionally breaking into a broad grin.

Toby resumed vigorous sucking, then pulled away from the breast and looked at his mother's face. He began to suck again, but more slowly, then stopped, and she asked if he had finished. She pulled him toward her right nipple. Although he took the nipple into his mouth, she told me that he wasn't sucking. She turned him around. He looked at me and smiled. I noticed that he played with his tongue, moving it within his mouth.

She spoke to him affectionately; the questions she asked were spoken as if he might really answer. He began what she called his "conversation." He made a series of noises which had the rhythmic inflection of someone speaking. His mother looked down at him, smiled, and talked back to him, asking him to "Say that again?" While he was "talking," his face changed expression; he knit his eyebrows together with an intent expression, smiled, and looked around with raised eyebrows, as if expecting something.

This mutually satisfying feed includes not only taking in milk, but also touching, "talking to," and looking at one another. Toby lingers at the breast after sucking and holds the nipple in his mouth and, when he is taken from the breast, the nipple is replaced by his tongue. Thus, for Toby a good feed of various components is located in his mouth, first as a nipple in his mouth, then as his tongue in his mouth, and later as vocalizations in his mouth.

Influenced by Fordham's concept of deintegration and reintegration I view what is happening around Toby's mouth as an early step in development. I hope to show how the nipple-in-the-mouth of a good feed is a protophenomenon which deintegrates into the later phenomenon of a word-in-the-mouth.

In an observation when Toby was six months, 3-1/2 weeks old, he was in the kitchen playing with various objects, and I noted that his main preoccupation had shifted from people to things. Later his mother left temporarily. When Toby protested I held him on my lap, which quieted him.

He leaned forward and dug his fingers into a hole in the chair covering. I noticed that his mouth was pulled in, forming the letter B. I turned him around to face me. He leaned forward and reached out for my sweater and breasts. A couple of times he turned his head against my shoulder and breast, as if expecting to suck. I talked to him, and he relaxed. Feeling that my voice was soothing to him, I began to sing a lullabye. He watched my fingers rub his tummy, and then gazed into space, seeming to concentrate on listening to my voice. He relaxed and pulled his right arm around so that he could suck on his fingers. He looked at my face and at my mouth, reached for my mouth and touched it as I sang, still sucking on the fingers of his other hand.

As in the first observation, there is an experience at the breast – reaching for it – followed by an exchange with another person. However, there are developments. His interest has shifted from people (especially his mother) to things, which he can manipulate through developing fine motor control. Increased control also applies to his tongue and lips; his infant cooing, made up of primarily vowel sounds, develops to include consonants – the "B" mouth shape. Parallel to this is an increased awareness of inside/outside; fingers are used to explore this dimension, for example, the fingers into the rip in the chair covering and into his mouth and mine. Toby reaches for the "thing" in my mouth with one hand while simultaneously sucking on the fingers of his other hand. One can hypothesize that there is a link between the fingers-in-the-mouth (which derive from the nipple-in-the-mouth of the good feed) and the song/word-in-the-mouth.

The subsequent visit supports this hypothesis. Once again, the mother had left temporarily. When Toby started to cry, I picked him up, talked and then sang to him. He started to "talk" and reached for my mouth. He then made sucking movements.

In this observation, my song/word-in-the-mouth is linked, by Toby's reach, to his vocalizations-in-the-mouth and his sucked tongue-in-the-mouth. Thus, what became the song/word-in-the-mouth can be traced backward, via vocalizations, fingers, then tongue, to its source in the nipple-in-the-mouth of a good feed. All these thing-in-the-mouth experiences are inextricably bound up with emotionally colored exchanges with another person. This describes the mother tongue to which I referred in my introduction.

I believe that it was this "mother tongue" that Virginia was trying to steal or, more accurately, to retrieve. Before this conclusion can be accepted there is a point to add. To do this, I compare the part of the first observation of Toby's post-feed "conversation" to that of a baby girl the same age as Toby, 2-1/2 months.

> Amy looked at me and smiled, waved her arms and legs, and made 'eh' noises and raspy syllables in the back of her mouth. I could talk to her when she finished her vocalization, so that we had a "conversation." There was a series of waves and smiles, reaching a crescendo with her sounds. She "talked" in the crest of the wave; I talked in its fall.

The exchanges between Toby and his mother and between Amy and me are virtually identical; each infant is in relation to an adult via alternating vocalizations. It does not matter whether words are being used or understood. What does matter is that there is a meaningful exchange. The only significant difference between Toby and Amy is that Toby is hearing, and Amy is deaf.

Summary

I believe Virginia's quest was for the thing-in-the-mouth that is also a meaningful relationship, an experience which deafness does not preclude. By making a relationship with me in which the fundamentals of communication could be re-established and developed, Virginia was able to retrieve an experience of the thing-in-the-mouth that is also a relationship of shared meaning.

Psychotherapy Research: Implications For Analytical Psychology

Seth Isaiah Rubin
Sausalito, California, USA
Society of Jungian Analysts of
Northern California

Psychotherapy has taught us that in the final reckoning it is not knowledge, not technical skill, that has a curative effect, but the personality of the doctor.

C.G. Jung

Psychotherapy research has provided important findings about the process and outcome of psychotherapy ever since Carl Rogers – the founder of client-centered or non-directive therapy – began such research 30 years ago. Rogers and his colleagues were the first to demonstrate the clinical efficacy of empathy, a finding that has been replicated in different studies and in different centers. Thus, this finding has proven to be remarkably robust. Indeed, Hans Strupp (1989), a leading psychotherapy researcher of over 30 years standing and a psychoanalytic psychotherapist with a Sullivanian bent, has stated emphatically that "there is good evidence to show that no therapist comment, particularly interpretations, should be experienced by the patient as criticism, disapproval, or in other respects diminish the patients' already precarious self-esteem.... The emphasis should be on empathic understanding, which will also enhance the patient's collaboration with the therapist" (p. 722).

Until very recently, the effect of interpretation on therapeutic outcome had not been validated empirically. Lester Luborsky and his colleagues (1988) at the University of Pennsylvania have provided such validation with the publication of their 30 years worth of psychotherapy research. They have demonstrated that an accurate interpretation as defined by their Core Conflictual

Relationship Theme (CCRT) method is correlated significantly with outcome of psychotherapy. This highly important finding awaits replication.

While humanistic and psychodynamic forms of psychotherapy have demonstrated a willingness to make use of the methods and findings of psychotherapy research, Analytical Psychology has not. There is not a single psychotherapy outcome research study of Jungian analysis! Moreover, there is almost a total ignorance of the findings of psychotherapy research. Why is this? Jung claimed to be an empiricist. He was not above – or beneath – using statistical and experimental methods to suit his purposes. In the beginning of his career he used these methods to develop the Association Experiment. At the end, he brought them to bear on his attempts, in collaboration with Rhine and his associates at Duke, to prove the existence of extra-sensory perception.

I believe that, were he alive today, Jung would be open to the findings of psychotherapy research and willing to use its methods in studying and improving the practice of analysis. After all, this sort of research did not come into its own until well after his death. Whether he would be open to it or not, I believe that it is crucial for Analytical Psychology to become involved with psychotherapy research as consumers and producers, so that our field remains receptive to important sources of scientific knowledge and retains its reputation as a valid member in the community of scientifically respectable methods of psychotherapy. I, for one, do not want to see Analytical Psychology relegated by law or reputation to the status of rebirthing or other faddish techniques, with the manifold consequences such a redefinition would entail. Do you? Would Jung?

My purpose here is to explore two separate but related issues: 1) Some of the important ways in which psychotherapy research findings have supported Jung's clinical and analytic observations, for which Jung and Analytical Psychology get little, if any, credit; and 2) The explicit dangers the field of Analytical Psychology confronts in continuing to ignore the multidisciplinary enterprise of psychotherapy research. To give you an idea of our isolation from the psychotherapy research community, let me introduce you to the society for Psychotherapy Research: an international, multidisciplinary, scientific organization with over 1000 members from more than 26 countries. Some of the better known members include: Horst Kaechele, Aaron Beck, Albert Ellis, Jerome Frank, Mardi Horowitz, Otto and Paulina Kernbert, Lester Luborsky, Martin Orne, Hans Strupp and Mryna Weissman. There are but two Jungian members: Florian Langegger, Director of the Klinik Am Zurichberg, and I. Food for thought!

Psychotherapy Research Confirmations

Psychotherapy research brings to bear the methods of applied behavioral science on the study of the processes and outcomes of psychotherapy, of which Jungian Analysis is one form. These methods include the experiment or clinical trial, the comparative study, and the survey. Special emphasis is placed on collecting quantifiable data in order to insure that the data are amenable to sophisticated forms of statistical analysis. This has created a serious problem in the past, because so much that is meaningful to the nature and practice of psychotherapy cannot be quantified. However, newer forms of statistical analysis are now available for handling variables of a qualitative nature. My intent here is not to elucidate these important developments in behavioral science research methods and statistical data analysis, but to make the point that things have changed radically since Jung first directed his criticisms at the discipline of experimental psychology. Relevant and meaningful areas of investigation, such as the process and outcome of psychotherapy, are now subject to more rigorous research. They complement, but do not replace, direct clinical observation and case history-making.

It is rather uncanny just how many of Jung's observations and judgments about psychotherapy have been supported many years later by means of psychotherapy research. For example, Jung stated emphatically:

The question of psychological therapy is exceedingly complex. We know for certain that just any method or any theory, seriously believed, conscientiously applied and supported by a humanly congenial understanding, can have a most remarkable therapeutic effect. Therapeutic efficacy is by no means the prerogative of any particular system; what counts is the character and the attitude of therapist. (CW18, par. 1071)

Compare this statement with the assessments of Jerome D. Frank and his daughter Julia (1991), prominent psychotherapy research investigators:

These, then, were some of the way stations I visited in more than fifty years of studying and practicing psychotherapy. In the course of my journey, I have reached the following conclusions. The shared morale-enhancing properties of all forms of psychotherapy contribute importantly to their favorable outcomes. The interaction between particular therapists and patients, determined by the personal qualifies of both, contributes more to outcome than does therapeutic technique. Two probable exceptions to this general rule seem to be emerging. The first is that sufficiently prolonged exposure to an anxiety-provoking stimulus may relieve the anxiety linked to the stimulus. The second is that abreaction of an original trauma in a therapeutic context may be essential to alleviating posttraumatic stress disorders, a category whose ultimate borders are still unknown. These conclusions imply that in most cases, therapists should feel free to use whatever techniques are most congenial, and that therapists should not hesitate to adapt their techniques to accord with the personality, values, and expectations of particular patients. (pp. 300-301)

Also important are the personality of the analysand and the interaction of the analyst and analysand. In general, psychotherapy seems most helpful to people who have some capacity and willingness to enter into close relationships with others. Jung put great stress on the dialectical nature of the analytic process and the analyst's responsibility of being open to it, but much less on the characteristics of the analysand *per se*:

In psychotherapy, even if the doctor is entirely detached from the emotional contents of the patient, the very fact that the patient has emotions has an effect upon him. And it is a great mistake if the doctor thinks he can lift himself out of it. He cannot hope to do more than become conscious of the fact that he is affected. If he does not see that, he is too aloof and then he talks beside the point. It is even his duty to accept the emotions of the patient and to mirror them. That is the reason why I reject the idea of putting the patient upon a sofa and sitting behind him. I put my patients in front of me and I talk to them as one natural human being to another, and I expose myself completely and react with no restriction. (CW18, par. 319)

The frequency of analytic sessions is important. In Zurich, I was trained to conduct analysis at a frequency of one or two sessions per week. I understand that, while Jung might meet with analysands more frequently in the beginning stages of the analysis – during the reductive work – typically he would work with analysands at the lesser frequency. During my clinical training at the University of Pennsylvania, I heard Martin Orne compare Freud and Jung on just this issue. Orne pointed out that, based on the findings of psychotherapy research, Freud made the mistake of believing that a high frequency of therapy sessions was necessary to facilitate real personality change, whereas the critical variable was the length of time the analyst and analysand were connected therapeutically. (Two to three years was the minimum, according to Orne.) Orlinsky and Howard (1986) have essentially validated Orne's pronouncements, even though they were not able to pin down the exact optimal frequency of therapy sessions.

Orne believes, and I stand with him on this issue, that follow-up of the patient or analysand ought to be inherent to the process of psychotherapy or analysis. Under ordinary circumstances, at the beginning of analysis, analysands should be instructed, along with the other issues the analyst discusses – such as fee, frequency of visits, and any ground rules – that the analyst, as a part of the analytic process, will make contact with the analysand (or the other way around), after the analysis is terminated. This contract would occur at six months, one year, two years, and five years in order to find out how the analysand is feeling, thinking and doing. The follow-up can be structured or unstructured, tailored to the personalities of the analyst and analysand. The follow-up serves two purposes: 1) It maintains contact between analyst and analysand, thereby deepening the analytical gains; and 2) It provides the analyst invaluable information about the effects of his/her approach from which the analyst can learn and improve.

This follow-up is known as formative evaluation. Its counterpart, summative evaluation, serves the purpose of informing policy decisions with real consequences – such as funding or insurance coverage – on the basis of "pass" or "fail." My primary interest is in formative evaluation.

I do not mean to imply that there is only one way of doing things, or a narrow set of ways. To the contrary. I stand with Jung when he writes:

> Theory is important in the first place for science. In practice you can apply as many theories as there are individuals. If you are honest you will preach your individual gospel, even if you don't know it. If you are right, it will be good enough. If you are wrong, even the best theory will be equally wrong. Nothing is worse than the right means in the hands of the wrong man. Never forget that the analysis of a patient analyzes yourself, as you are just as much in it as he is. (CW18, par. 1072.)

I see the purpose of follow-up as providing each individual analyst with the means to enhance the effectiveness of his/her "individual gospel." Whatever works, in whatever form, often can work better.

Explicit Dangers

The handwriting is on the wall: Jungian analysis, as well as other forms of psychotherapy, will need to submit to outcome evaluation (formative at least; summative, I fear) in order to maintain its viability. In Germany, for example, Jungian analysis is excluded by law from the "scientifically respectable" category of psychotherapy, and lumped with faddish techniques for lack of any psychotherapy outcome research. This development portends ominous consequences; for example, what will happen to insurance coverage, health insurance for the analysand and malpractice insurance for the analyst?

We are not alone; we share this dubious predicament with surgeons, of all people.

> Surgeons are, understandably, among the most revered practitioners of medicine. It is the surgeon who tries to correct disease by his own hand. That hand is surprisingly free: surgery has never been subjected to the same rigorous evaluation as pharmaceuticals. A new operation does not have to be tested first on animals. Unless it has been explicitly identified by a surgeon as experimental, it can be performed without any sort of peer review; and there is no need for follow-up studies to review the new technique. (*The Economist*, 1991, p. 84.)

Unlike surgeons, Jungian analysts are not "the most revered practitioners of medicine." Most Jungian analysts have never even been trained to practice medicine. And Jungian analysts restrict their practice to the psyche rather than the body. But even so, as an instance of the paradoxical relationship between the opposites, there is a striking parallel between surgery and psychotherapy as far as evaluating effectiveness.

> There are drawbacks to random trials for surgery, which does not exactly lend itself to such investigation. Drugs have known ingredients and their effectiveness is largely unrelated to a doctor's skill. Although a doctor's diagnosis and recommendations about dosage play a part in the outcome, the result of prescribing a drug is mostly predictable, particularly if the recommendations of usage approved for the drug are adhered to. But surgical skills vary greatly. In the hands of one surgeon, an operation can be an outstanding success; in the hands of another, it can be a disaster. (*The Economist*, 1991, p. 85)

If in the paragraph above we were to substitute "psychotherapist" or "Jungian analyst" for "surgeon," no meaning would be lost. Surgery, because of the radical consequences it produces, is headed for clinical trials in one form or another. Must that fate befall Jungian analysis?

I do not believe so. If we are to be wise like the serpent, we will engage in voluntary formative evaluation such that we maintain our individual approaches and enhance our individual effectiveness. If we are to be harmless like the dove, we will assume a position from which we can answer our critics effectively without abandoning our identity as Jungian analysts. The choice is ours.

References

Frank, J.D., & Frank, J.B. (1991). *Persuasion and Healing: A Comparative Study of Psychotherapy*. Baltimore: Johns Hopkins University Press.

Luborsky; L., Crits-Christoph, P.; Mintz, J., & Auerbach, A. (1988). *Who Will Benefit from Psychotherapy? Predicting Therapeutic Outcomes*. New York: Basic Books.

Science Editor (1989). Guiding the knife. *The Economist*, May 4th, 83-85.

Strupp, H. (1989). Psychotherapy: Can the practitioner learn from the researcher? *American Psychologist, 44*, 717-724.

Play and the Transcendent Function in Child-Analysis

Verena Rossetti-Gsell
Rancate, Tessin, Switzerland
Swiss Society for Analytical
Psychology

It is my conviction that play is the original expression of the transcendent function in the infantile psyche. According to Jung this function is activated when one-sidedness of conscious behavior or attitude encounters resistance by unconscious instinctive needs. A convergence of opposite tendencies unites unconscious and conscious contents, making possible the passage to a new attitude regarding inner and outer circumstances, thereby overcoming stagnancy and freeing individual growth. In the developmental period, new orientation is required continuously by the changing of inner and outer needs.

Jung's paper on the transcendent function (CW8), written in 1916, when he was 41, was a result of a most intensive confrontation – already four years long – with his own unconscious fantasies and images. In his memoirs (MDR) he described these years, when he followed his inner pictures, as the most important time in his life. He also said that all his subsequent activity consisted in elaborating this material from the unconscious.

His interest was focused mainly on his own experience with the unconscious. Childplay was not a focus of his studies, but play was of basic importance in his life. He described some of his experiences – occurring between the ages of seven and nine – with passionate constructions of towers and their destruction by earthquakes; endless battles and entertaining a personal, eternal, holy fire.

It is not difficult to recognize the compensating and therapeutic meaning of this play. We can see it in relation to Jung's lack of security in the relationship with his mother, his nightmares, his attacks of breathlessness and the *"unbreathable"* atmosphere (MDR, p. 19) in his family.

At the age of 37, completely disoriented after the break with Freud, Jung began his confrontation with the unconscious. He started remembering the nine-year-old boy and playing again: looking for stones and building houses, a castle, a village, a church, an altar. Creative play, working with stones and drawing would remain his rites of entry to his thoughts and his scientific work.

Let us ask ourselves now where play occurs. The location of play in child-analysis can be seen in a threefold intersection: between consciousness and the unconscious, between inner and outer reality, between the child's and the therapist's psyches.

Jung defined the transcendent function as the function that brings together conscious and unconscious contents. Therefore play which is experienced at the threshold between consciousness and the unconscious, can be an arena for the transcendent function.

With regard to the child's developing capacity to distinguish an outer and an inner reality, we can follow Winnicott (1971). In his extraordinary observations and reflections on the development of the transitional space, we see that play occurs at the intersection between inner and outer reality, between psychological and material reality.

We ascertain also, with Winnicott, that creative play occurs in an interpersonal space; it needs reliable relational surroundings. The absence of these surroundings generates anxiety and play becomes defensive, obsessive or even impossible. The first "lonely playing" is possible in the mother's presence. Different needs are expressed in playing with mother, play with father, with siblings, with friends. In child-analysis, play occurs in the intersection of the child's and the therapist's psyche.

Now we ask ourselves about the dynamics of play. An example is a little boy's play in his initial therapy hours.

"Michael" is 4-1/2 years old; he has a brother of 2-1/2 years. Michael's symptoms consist in relational difficulties with other children in the kindergarten. He isolates himself, has tantrums at home, is aggressive toward smaller children and is clumsy with his hands.

During our first meeting, with his mother present, I invite him to play in the sand-tray. At first he puts the fire-engine in the tray, "to put out the fire." Then he builds a village: houses, a church, a cemetery. He digs a river and puts a bridge over it. The house near the river falls into the water. He takes a big crocodile and goes up to the mother to bite her and than comes to bite me. Quite excited he repeats the same attack with a big snake. The mother tries, verbally, to stop the aggression. My toleration helps her to share the game. Now Michael chooses "good" animals. A truck brings gasoline to the town but soon the house falls into the river again. This time it is saved by a tuna fish.

At the second meeting Michael is alone with me. His sand-play has the same beginning. The river now divides the village into an old and a new part. He prefers the old one. There is a kindergarten but no school. My supposition is confirmed that he is afraid, that things are too difficult there. Today, Michael only looks at the wild beasts; he does not touch them. However he activates the gasoline truck again.

At our third meeting the construction of the village, digging the river and the arrival of the gasoline truck are repeated. The house near the river again trembles and falls in to the river. While I worry about this accident he orders me to call for help. The tuna fish comes and saves the house. The scene is repeated but the house – together with mother, father and child – continues to fall into the river. The house is swallowed by a big shark, the parents by the crocodile. The beasts laugh "ha-ha-ha!" The child cries "Mama! Papa!" They are regurgitated and saved.

During the fourth session sand-play begins again in the same way. When the child falls into the water I have to cry and scream. Upon my interpretation regarding his possible wishes to see such a thing happen to his brother, he answers "yes" in an absent-minded way. Thus, it is important that the play continues. Now crocodile, shark and snake are called "the monsters." They devour the child and the parents three times. Michael is very excited and shows great pleasure in identifying with the beasts. They eat "yum!" and laugh "ha-ha-ha!" He imitates a thunderstorm, making noises of thunder and spitting. I am participating with his feelings and containing them at the same time.

When the thunderstorm is finished, Michael changes register: He declares himself a woodcutter and asks for a saw. With a saw from the toolboard he saws the monsters into pieces and frees the swallowed-up persons. A new, terrible thunderstorm throws the houses around and finally deep into the earth. The woodcutter returns. Finding a field he decides to plow it. Plowing and cutting the earth with his saw he touches something. Michael exclaims: "Something hard! What can this be?" He digs out all the houses, showing wonder and surprise at every finding. During the next hour, playing out this scene, the woodcutter Michael cuts the field geometrically in all four directions, asking me if he has forgotten any. He reconstructs the village with his discoveries. Michael continues to develop this game in six more sessions. As transference evolves it is the analyst who is eaten up.

I will indicate the dynamic of the transcendent function in this play. Jung observed that the initial procedure of the transcendent function is directed toward finding emotionally-charged contents. He found that the most convenient way to make visible these contents is by activating spontaneous fantasies.

In Michael's spontaneous play such unconscious contents are expressed from the beginning of our encounters. His first focus is on the fire engine. To me this means that there are emotions burning dangerously somewhere. The boy's spontaneous fantasy makes the dangerous unconscious emotions visible by means of dramatic play-scenes. In the trembling and sinking house the abandonment anxiety is expressed. With the crocodile's attack on the mother and me, oral aggressivity and devouring rage is transformed into images and transferred to the analyst. We can see how emotional unconscious contents are put in contact with the conscious infantile capacity to act and how confrontation between ego and unconscious is initiated. Michael's play with good animals makes evident that, in addition to the negative feelings there are good ones too; his activating the gasoline truck

shows that in the infantile unconscious energy for further movement is available.

The timing of the confrontation is determined by the infantile
ego. After the first "coming out," the play during the second
meeting expresses the fear of new orientation. The ego prefers
the old part of the village and no school. Negative feelings are
now repressed, the beasts only looked at. More energy (gasoline)
is needed for the confrontation with dangerous emotions.

In the third hour the therapeutic relationship seems to be
reliable enough. Having shown empathy, I must lend my voice to
the fear, the anxiety of losing the house, the protective motherly
container. This emotion being shared and contained, the frightening, aggressive, devouring rage now can be expressed and dra-
matized. The affective value being fully invested, confrontation
can evolve.

Following Jung's description of the transcendent function, the
confrontation is guided by two principles: 1) creative representation, making the formal aspect clear and guided by the esthetic
tendency and 2) understanding, making the content clear and
guided by the intellectual tendency.

During the fourth hour creative representation of the unconscious affective contents is differentiated and the boy's emotional state comes to an apex in the excitement of making thunder-
storms, laughing and spitting. His ego, sustained by the analyst's
seeing and attempting interpretation dares now to interact with
the overwhelming affects. We can observe in Michael's psyche a
masculine ego figure being activated. The woodcutter figure
seems to me a forerunner of the fighting hero. In Neumann's
(1980) terms, the ego is actually at a magic-phallic level. This
infantile ego tries to save the parental images and to bring under
control the frightening destructive emotions. The ego-agent has
to differentiate in all directions, respecting the psyche's need for
totality. He has to save and recompose the village, to reconstruct
a functional, civilized context for evolution and growth.

We see, in this example, that the way of representing the
unconscious fantasy depends on the child's personality but is
influenced, evidently, by the character of the analyst, by the

choice of play material and through pleasure in creative play. The quality of intellectual understanding, guiding the interaction, is in close relationship with the maturity of the infantile ego. It is sustained by the analyst's effort to make sense, to understand and to interpret, and by patience, by a capacity to respect the timing of the infantile ego. The short play sequence I have described is evidently just the beginning of a dialogue, of a process which will need time to evolve.

After this attempt to show how the transcendent function is activated in infantile psyche, we may ask ourselves what conditions are needed to make creative play possible. I consider three conditions fundamental:

1. Creative play needs space, time and freedom to use them.
2. Play needs a receptive and containing relationship.
3. Play needs a minimally self-confident ego.

The first condition is not guaranteed when physical and psychological surroundings force the child to too early an adaptation. A child having activated an "emergency ego" in Neumann's terms or a "false self" in Winnicott's terms is limited in play, is not free. Excessive limits by behavioral norms leave little space and time for play.

The second condition, a receptive and containing relationship, is not guaranteed if the parents and relatives are unable to receive projections of archetypal contents or expressions of instinctual needs and to contain the emotions connected to them. For instance, it may be impossible for a mother to tolerate the negative mother projection and the aggressivity connected to it during the separation period at the beginning of the second year. Or for a father to confront rivalry and competition. The cultural context may limit the parents' capacity to accept expressions of instinctive drives; they may not accept infantile sexuality nor contain the excitement connected to it. Parents' capacity to tolerate play and to play themselves is limited by their own complexes.

The third condition, the need for a minimally self-confident ego, is not guaranteed if the infantile ego is not sustained by the adult ego in a way that corresponds to the child's level of ego-growth.

When a child requires psychotherapy, these conditions have not been guaranteed sufficiently by the natural surroundings. The therapist's job is to assure them, in order to activate or reactivate the transcendent function, thus to make play possible.

In child-analysis the first condition is met by the setting in space and time, the second by what Jung called the symbolic attitude of the analyst and by the involvement in the dynamics of transference and counter-transference, the third by the analyst's ego – sustaining the infantile ego in its confrontation with the unconscious contents.

References

Winnicott, D.W. (1971). *Vom Spiel zur Kreativität*. Stuttgart: Klett-Cotta.

Neumann, E. (1980). *Das Kind*. Fellbach, Germany: Bonz.

From the Three Suns to the Three Bridges: The Transcendent Function and Therapy with Children

Jean-Pierre Falaise
Grenoble, France
French Society of Analytical
Psychology

How does doing therapy with children help us to understand the transcendent function? And what does this function bring to the child's development and psychological treatment? These are two sides of the same question: consciousness and integration.

Two key times in the therapy of a five-year-old, Simon, are illustrative. Each is centered on an archetypal image: the sun for the first and the bridge for the second.

I intend to consider how the transference has been able to insure a relationship for this boy, whose parents have been prisoners of an intense negative mother complex and were divorced when he was two years old. The violent conflicts between the parents after Simon was born revealed their depressive core.

The therapy started at the mother's request, since she was confused and worried by her own reactions as well as by Simon's symptoms: eczema, unsteadiness, sadness, fits of anger and stubborn refusal to sleep at his father's home. The father contained his depression in solid defenses which amplified Simon's conflicts and insecurity: Who tells the truth? Whom should I trust? This man did not respond to my requests to meet him.

Let us look at the facts over a nine-month period, beginning at 4-1/2 years of age. The first seven sessions were similar: In a ritual way Simon, huddled between his mother and me, puts all the animals on the divan and without a word animates several of them in scenes of fighting. Dinosaurs, lions, tigers and horned animals are particularly active; the others are witnesses or victims. My role was to express the perceptions, ideas and emotions of a bear cub that, with its parents, watches the events.

We might consider these games as a way of cautiously discovering his impulses. There was also the reactivation of traces of traumatic violence and the internal tension between the levels of psychic organization. One should notice the importance of the phallic impulses, too: active aggressivity, manhood, impulse for knowledge and spiritual values opposed to chthonic values. Images, then, of a differentiating masculine mixed with defensive positions.

And while Simon is completely invested in the primitive motor pleasure of handling things and making noises, like a baby, I – as the alter-ego bear cub – play the more developed part of his ego: put the events into words, operate the transition from thing-presentations to word-presentations, bridge the gap between the sensory and the psychic universe. I have to identify, name, comment and find words, to give shape to the things and events in a relationship. Using the relationship and the language, I must transform the sensations into emotions. It is in the relationship between us that the archetypal images, are animated. They will give shape and meaning to the impulsive pressures and organize the imaginal life.

It is no surprise, then, that the image of the sun appeared after Simon reclaimed his impulsive vitality. The sun god has in all times been the main archetypal image of consciousness and of human development. The sun brings warmth and light, emotion and knowledge, the feeling that one is an acting subject.

Three more points will help in understanding the integrating power of the image. First, just before the sun's surge another image appeared in the animals' game: a human baby laid on a stag's antlers. We could see a promise of development, risen from mother earth and borne toward the sky in the protection of the stag's horns. When the corporal self and the relational self are well established they constitute a positive maternal complex which supports the differentiating masculine, the meeting with the father and the integrating ego. The separating masculine principle organizes the different stages in the ego's evolution to "solar ego": self-awareness.

Second point: the urge toward the unknown. During the game, an animal dares to cross the gap between the divan and the sand-tray, on the opposite side of the room. It is a clever fox cub, bearing the projection of the trickster. In addition the creature will be the origin of the death and of the recovery of the parents. Simon ventures, then, into the air and for the first time in the exploration of space to the sand-tray, stopping on the way by his mother's armchair. He reaches a more confined space, better suited to play where the esthetic dimension of the transcendent function can be activated: putting into a dramatic shape what, on the divan, is mere chaos; giving shape to the internal conflict in "another stage of intricacy." This trickster is going to invite the other animals to follow him in what he calls "the other world" or "the other land." The other's world as well as the dead's world, and spiritual universe opposed to the universe of primary attachment.

Third point: during this same setting Simon gets, in the game, an opportunity to speak about his father, as I ask him about an elephant that tramples down everything in its path. I ask whether the elephant is really evil or is just playing tricks. Simon replies at once, in the game and out of it: "My dad, he's always kidding." I learn then that the father's mother uses the same word to criticize her son. There is a grave conflict between this man and his mother because she always refused, while he was a child, to tell him who was his father.

One can understand the significance of this moment, when the energy of the unconscious organizers and the emotions of individual history are combined in the transference. "In order to gain possession of the energy that is in the wrong place, [one] must make the emotional state the basis or starting-point of the procedure.... The whole procedure is a kind of enrichment and clarification of... the affect.... This work by itself can have a favourable and vitalizing influence" (CW8, par. 167).

When it is time to leave, Simon suddenly shows desire to draw with the colored pencils. It is the first time that he wishes to use the graphic mode – a sudden step forward in the integration of his inner world. It is time to part but I feel that he is in an intense emotion that drives him to realize something, in both senses of the word. He draws very quickly three suns: a medium one, a small one and a big one, on three different sheets.

The medium one is located on top right. Its broad smile and rays send a flood of light on Simon's first name, written on the bottom edge of the sheet, as on firm ground. It is the first graphic expression of the feeling of identity. He cuts the small sun out with the scissors to "stick it on his heart," as he says. I help him to hang this celestial lamp to his breast, to warm up his intimate universe. Then he cuts out the large one as well and takes it home. Later, I learn that he stuck it to the car's window. Maybe to say loudly, in the social space, in front of everyone, that he does feel alive.

The medium sun will stay on my table, as a trust. It means that here, in this activating relation, lies at the moment his vital axis, the ego-Self axis. With these suns, we shall say: night and day, earth and sky, large and small, inside and outside, private and social, hiding and showing, lies (joking) and truth, suffering and satisfaction, evil and good. The differentiating light of consciousness is putting tension between the opposites which, in the unconscious, are not separate.

We have seen, with the animals' fights, that consciousness is at first sensorial: sensations that take on meaning in the relationship and are, then, emotions. We can say now that this consciousness (we could use the word "conscience") is moral. In the following months the sessions will picture plentifully, in the sand-tray, the conflicts with the environment, always linked to the archetypal themes until they come close to consciousness and require the active intervention of the interpretation.

It is now six months later (Session 19). During this time some elements have appeared that have allowed me to provoke the separation from the mother. Simon is now alone with me in the sessions. The game starts with seeking a bin to hide a small animal in it. Then this bin becomes a little yellow bridge under which Simon buries a pangolin in the sand. It is like a tunnel – maybe an image of wounded narcissism that tries to protect itself, for the pangolin is an animal with a carapace and a nasal appendix to swallow ants. And Simon notes that "there are red ants that eat men" (whether "men" or "human beings" is unclear), thus confirming the two symbolic sides of the ant: food and destruction, as the two sides of the mother complex.

This little bridge located in a corner of the tray gives Simon the idea of putting another – medium – bridge between the first one and the center of the tray where three dinosaurs plus a foal form a sort of four-pointed star. An image of centering that had appeared several times in former sessions, provides counterpoint and compensation for the restoring aspect of the ego-Self axis. This medium bridge seems, then, to link the archaic libido with the narcissism.

Then comes a third bridge which soars from the little yellow bridge over the edge of the tray. It covers, with a succession of little arches, the space between the tray and the divan. On this established link the pangolin can set forth to fetch the black panther that, this time, has stayed on the divan.

As if answering the trickster's innovative impulse, today the pangolin and the bridges confirm that a dynamic intrapsychic link has been constituted. Simon, better connected to himself, can quit the heroic position of defensive phallic erection. He is able to cope with the negative experiences and the active aggressivity of the developments now appearing inside him. And his behavior is improving.

Just after the session with the suns, he had a pharyngitis; after that his eczema and his unsteadiness diminished. Following the bridges, his father at last answered my invitations to meet him. Simon was very proud to build the bridges again before his father, who was happily surprised. On this day I had an opportunity to give an important interpretation of the differences between sexes and generations, because of a slip of the tongue Simon made: to make a child, a mother and a father are needed, and a father is also needed to grow up.

The next session confirmed the integration that dawned in the bridges and was supported by the interpretation. As soon as he came into the room, looking grave with eyes in a slight daze, he told me: "I told my teacher: My mum and dad, they're divorced."

It was the first time he used the word "divorce." I thought then that if, inside him, the parents were "divorced," the pictures were now two differentiated, integrated inner realities.

Integration: ability to hold together the differences. Suns and bridges. Differences and relations. But we shall go further in analyzing Simon's speech. We can hear:

"I told my teacher": social space, the sun on the car's window; "persona" side of the ego, large bridge that crosses the border toward the outside and, at the same time, confirms the unification of the maternal picture beyond the cleavage. Isn't the paternal function supporting these moves?

"My mum and dad": I have two parents and now two differentiated images: guarantee for my identity and my sexual identity via the integration of the differences between sexes and generations.

"They are divorced": intimate space of my secrets and my wound. Place where the archaic relationship and the feelings are connected.

The latin etymology of the transcendent function, trans-ascendence, clearly indicates the passage from one state to another; differentiating and linking. The bridges show that in Simon's unconscious some links are now established, which support the process of integration. The educative environment and the link with the parents' psyches must now support and strengthen what has been made. But the therapy must go on, although the mother is in therapy and the father started one nine months after we met.

The psychic activation caused by the transference relationship has been able to heal by stimulating the unconscious organizers' energy and, at the same time, traces of the individual history.

Translated from French
by Florentin Blanc-Paris

Forum: Psychology and Art

Leonardo's Mother Revisited

Christian Gaillard
Paris, France
French Society of Analytical
Psychology

I invite you to a stroll into the history of art, to cast a fresh look at the work of Leonardo. "The Virgin, Jesus and St. Anne" (Fig. 1) is the starting point of my reflection, and will remain at its core. In order to get in touch with its meaning, I suggest an exercise: sitting together in front of the painting, under its gaze, in silence borne as long as possible.

This silence is necessary for us to keep at a distance and discard the first words that come: the title of the painting, the names of the characters on the canvas. These words confine the painting within the area of what is already known.

We are interested here in something different: allowing the slow emergence of impressions, of sensations which surge from very deep levels, hardly perceptible at first, unutterable still. The point is to let oneself be impressed, by sensations and emotions.

It is not easy, nor an everyday experience. Perhaps the young artists in my class at the National Academy of Art in Paris achieved it more easily than do students of psychology. Art students learn to remain open to inchoate forms fumbling for expression. Let us listen to what they were able to grasp.

Two ways of perceiving the painting gradually emerged. I found myself belonging to the group that was moved by the picture's very human dimension: something nearly trivial, from everyday life. True, when we ramble in Italy, from Ravenna to Siena, or when we follow the same course within the Siena Art Gallery, going over the rooms set in chronological succession, we come to experience again the gradual bringing together which Italian art is working out, from the fifth to the sixteenth century. Soon we can recognize ourselves in it. Golden backgrounds break into landscapes and perspective is invented. Holy figures put on flesh. And bodies are quickened.

In this painting, no more golden backgrounds. But rocks, a real tree and the real earth under the feet. No more halos; they vanished. We have left the empyrean of the Christian myth enshrined within a church.

More bewildering, not only have we left the metaphysical heavens of religion but we are still moving lower down. We are drawn downward by the weight of the infant's body, at the bottom of the picture, on the right, and by the gesture of the mother, of the mothers, to whom he is connected – essentially through the exchange of looks – with the lamb he is playing with, a flesh and blood lamb, an animal he is mistreating.

I know a child, about the age of this one, a very precocious girl, who is permeated by strange inklings. One day she assaulted her baby brother with some brutality. She was scolded: "What has he done to you?" We heard her say, in a voice from else-where: "He pushed me into the world." Which was, of course, quite to the point – and gnostic enough.

Well, this child here is not really "pushed into the world." He is on his way to it, forwarded by his mother's gesture of accompaniment and by the dynamics of the picture. Hence the gravity of the scene. A physical gravity, felt through the senses.

The center of gravity is being shifted down to the earth where we rest. And our feelings are loaded by sensations, by the weight and impetus of the bodies themselves. In this way I first perceived this painting, with a group of my students.

But then, another group made me perceive it quite differently. During a longer lapse of time they managed to refrain from too quick words which reduce the unexpected and enigmatic event to what was seen and known already, in order to make room for a more inclusive and at first dumb apprehension of the work and its impact.

They obeyed the rules that I had suggested better than I did myself. They let themselves be affected by the painting in a very different way. Actually they made me aware of the eerie and ominous presence in this work.

Figure 1

Figure 2

Figure 3

Figure 4

Three feet emerge from the living pyramid which underlies the composition. To what body, what element can we connect the left arm, folded across the line which divides the picture in the middle, once we have seen two heads springing, so it seems, from a single bust?

I do not know if we are all able to practice this kind of gaze which, disconnected from ordinary modes of perception, allows itself to scan what is offered without reuniting the parts into a familiar whole. Ehrenzweig (1974) – one of the fathers of the most recent psychology of art – makes use, in this context, of the word *scanning* – a gaze which first remains unconscious, thus allowing the development of more primary modes of perception and association.

Commitment to this essentially unconscious gaze boils down to the practice of "*poised attention.*" This type of attention is not a hazy mood but is based on sensations. It is both a sensory and visionary perception: in accepting and practicing a welcoming of impressions aroused, conjured up by the enigmatic texture of what is given to see.

Indeed, this is one of the basic conditions of our clinical work, especially of interpretation. Interpretation should always emerge from distant origins and proceed from our "evenly suspended and poised attention," basically regressive.

Thus, in the analysis of art, interpretation takes its form as did the work itself. There lies the challenge: emulating and cooperating with the creative impulse of the artist, in the moment he or she molds the substance of the work.

Thus, we are puzzled by the disquieting presence of this fanciful, inhuman or infrahuman body, by this patchwork of overlapping bodies building up an uncouth and dreadful polypus, gradually looming under the smiles. Yet, I keep in mind my own first impression of an all-too-human scene.

What then? Are we confronted with a non-human presence rising from nowhere, or with a familiar scene so obviously human that we feel both reassured and inclined to dreaming? How can we find our way through two opposite impressions?

We must step back. We must look at this masterpiece from a greater distance, in order to scrutinize the painter's attempts and his rough sketches, in this area where his work is fumbling for shape.

Here is the "London Cartoon" (Fig. 2), presently exhibited at the National Gallery in London. It is a charcoal sketch for a work which was never realized. What strikes us first is the faces – these so human faces that look at one another, respond to one another and are doubly reflected. We never tire of experiencing inwardly the movement of this double feminine face which leads to the two children, themselves fascinated by each other, and conversely from the children to the feminine faces. There is no end to it.

Freud (SE11) admirably perceived this movement and this bond. There lies the impact and success of his essay on Leonardo. Freud understood also the homoeroticism Leonardo reveled in and within which he remained secluded. He showed how the homoeroticism of a boy proceeds from the love his mother bore him when a child, how the memory of this love remains inscribed in his body and how it will be found again in his homosexual attachments as well as in his fascination for the enigma of woman.

When, in 1910, Jung received Freud's essay on Leonardo, he immediately wrote: "[Your] Leonardo is wonderful.... It is the first essay of yours with whose inner development I felt perfectly in tune from the start" (Let-I, p. 21).

Of course we share Jung's first enthusiasm. But today? To what extent can Freud help us in our present relation with Leonardo's work, after the split between Freud and Jung and the new development in the psychology of the unconscious?

Today we can consider this work with a different outlook, more tolerant and more anxious. If you gaze at this drawing beyond the faces, if your glance moves from this plane to what stands beyond explicit, blatant and immediately identified figures, if you commit yourself to the vacant, "scanning" look, you may feel, as I do, that this sketch is more impressive and far more disquieting than the Louvre painting.

Here, the interweaving of bodies into a single composite presence is more evident. Not only are feet, arms and heads connected to the same inhuman or infrahuman body but, at the core of the work, legs are also interwoven so intricately that one becomes unable to say which is whose.

From whose weird and disconcerting body does this child emerge, in the center of the drawing? To whom belong these two parted knees under him? What is this appendage looming in the aperture of these two knees?

Was Freud really able to see this work according to this perspective? I do not think so. For his theory was sealed by his view of the recollection from childhood. He thought he could explain everything by memories from the artist's childhood, by the too close kisses the husbandless mother gave to her child Leonardo. And through the pseudo-memory, in which Leonardo himself believed, was the image of a vulture which would have alighted upon the child's cot, introducing its tail into the child's mouth. Freud's disciples discerned it, overtly, in the Louvre painting.

Here it is (Fig. 3) with its tail in the child's mouth. It is especially impressive because, according to a widespread tradition, the vulture was capable of begetting a brood without the intervention of the male, and since Freud relied on it to make us understand a vast section of Egyptian mythology, particularly the elements relating the mighty goddess Mut to the vulture.

The image was so impressive that Jung let himself be impressed. He wrote in the same letter of June 10, 1910: "The transition to mythology grows out of this essay from inner necessity" (Let-I, p. 21), and he even added that he had seen a vulture in the painting, though with a slight difference: For him, the beak of the vulture was inserted into the mother's pubis.

What then is true about this extravagant bird story? With or without a real bird around the cot, and inscribed on the canvas, what remains true is the mother-attachment at the core of all Leonardo's work, an attachment which left very little room for the father.

We can find evidence for this in the painting of one of Leonardo's disciples, Bernardino Luini (Fig. 4, "The Holy Family with John the Baptist and St. Anne"). This excellent man – short of being an excellent painter – attempted to find a place for Joseph. But we cannot say it was a success; we keep wondering if the poor chap is about to slip out of the frame!

What remains equally true about this vulture story is that the mother's body is endowed with overpowering presence: an all-pervading threat, like that of a bird of prey.

This threat may account for the well-known mistake of Freud in identifying a vulture; in reality the bird the artist spoke about was a kite. Why did Freud make such a mistake?

We can understand it, once we realize that if a vulture is a dreadful bird, a kite is still worse. In French a "kite mother" is a bad mother; she ill-treats her brood, starving them, evidently out of jealousy. Thus to see a vulture in the painting was less disquieting than to see a kite.

Finally, in this visionary but not fully worked out perception which Freud, and Jung after him, could have of Leonardo's work, the following remains true: For a boy, it can be terribly hard to relate to his mother and initially, on a physical plane, with his mother's body. Starting from there, growing up into a man is by no means a matter of course. In Leonardo's work – different from Michelangelo's – we can see neither a man nor a father.

Here is "John the Baptist" (Fig. 5) and here is his "Bacchus" (Fig. 6). They are strangely akin, like cousins or brothers, so close that we could mistake the one for the other, although one comes from the Bible and shouts in the desert, while the other is the Greek god of drunkenness and women. Leonardo, I think, resorted to splendid insolence when he gave a similar treatment to his Bacchus and to John the Baptist, thus challenging both his audience and the ecclesiastical hierarchy with such a mingling of characters and genders. But does not this imply, also, a denial of differentiation and individuation?

Freud, we must acknowledge, contributed enormously to the progress of our awareness. In spite of his headstrong adhesion to the pseudo-memory from Leonardo's childhood, in spite of his

Figure 5   *Figure 6*

sham vulture in which he did not dare to see a representation of the Terrible Mother in the form of a kite mother and, more radically, though he was unable to consider the bird as a real symbol – the best expression for a while, but for a while only – of what he had begun to explore through the painter's psycho-biography, he was a great help in our understanding of the drama experienced by the man Leonardo.

But if we read Freud again with profit, it is according to the new perspective opened by Jung, as early as 1910, and especially after his "Symbols of Transformation" (CW5), in the perspective of our practice and theory of symbols. Freud helped us along. But he stopped midway and now walks behind us. Or we can say that we met him on our way.

For we deliberately started, not from the psychology of the man Leonardo, but from his work. We committed ourselves to a relation with the work largely different from Freud's and we developed quite another perception of the relationship between child and mother in this work. We placed ourselves before the created work and started from a perception of a very human and familiar scene and history, but we also relied on our perception of a very inhuman theme and tragedy.

We must now take one step forward. A very recent discovery is a drawing by Leonardo which had remained concealed for a long time in the collection of Queen Elizabeth II of England (Fig. 7). This drawing was exhibited in New York only in 1991.

According to historians of art, this is not John the Baptist. Nor is it a Bacchus. It is an Angel, even an Angel of the Annunciation. The historian who exhibited this drawing in New York gave it its title: "The Angel in the Flesh."

We are confronted again with the provocative and even wonderfully alluring presence of the figure called John the Baptist. The face becomes nearly plain and even frankly ugly. In addition, the sexual ambiguity of the character is made still more blatant by the obvious outline of the unveiled breast. But the greatest wonder lies in the powerful erection which the pseudo-John the Baptist, a would-be Angel, allows us to perceive under his garment. Here provocation reaches a climax, supported by

Figure 7   *Figure 8*

the information that the model for this drawing was Leonardo's closest and most faithful companion, the one who followed him everywhere to his very last day.

Here is a blasphemous and almost pornographic challenge. It may be a material proof of the psychobiographical interpretation Freud gave in his essay on Leonardo. And a Freudian analyst (André Green, 1992) will tell you that, in its open bisexuality, this drawing discloses the fantasy of narcissistic enjoyment and denial of the threat of castration; Leonardo was clinging to both since his infancy. I believe, however, that if Freud understood the man Leonardo and some of his minor works well enough, he misunderstood the masterpieces and what was at stake there.

Even concerning such an apparently Freudian drawing, what could Freud have said of the almost unbearable contradiction between the erect penis and the gesture pointing upward or into a space behind the scene? Between these two opposite poles, is there a room for an angel? And above all, is there an opportunity for becoming a man? A creative man?

Freud was not so far from this question by his psychobiographical approach. But my hypothesis is that Leonardo's art, in its time, was able to forward the matter far beyond the measure which Leonardo could solve in his own life. Any work of art, as a symbolic achievement, stands much ahead of the artist's life, much ahead of the relationship he enjoys with his own body and with the body of his mother.

The gesture of the "Angel in the Flesh" is repeated in the Bacchus (Fig. 6), in the John the Baptist (Fig. 5) and in the London Cartoon (Fig. 2). What then does the finger signal? Is it the absent father? Is it the father's Law? I do not think so, for the same contradictory movement is present at the core of the Louvre masterpiece (Fig. 1), far more accomplished.

The contradiction is expressed here by the dynamics of the picture and the tension between the diaphanous, ethereal, surreal background of the painting – out of which the first head emerges, dominating the whole. At the other end of the scene the child, no longer caught – as in the London Cartoon – in a doubly mirrored relationship with his closest image, but at grips with a real, recalcitrant lamb.

In the bipolar opposition which conveys to the painting its dynamics, its contradiction, and – should I say – its meaning, the composition gives us to see out of what intricacies, out of what disquieting interweaving of bodies the child stands out. Meanwhile we begin to perceive how the woman who remains most humanly close to the child is moving free, but hardly so, from the massive, polymorphous and hardly recognizable presence which still contains her.

The complex body of this work, a masterpiece from the sixteenth century, might take us to another region than the artist's childhood and the various episodes of his adult life. It might take us elsewhere than to the body of his mother Catarina or his stepmother, Dona Albiera, elsewhere than to this perfectly virgin mother in which the church of those times, and the very title of the painting, would induce us to believe.

But then, *what reality* is being staged here? What deeply human, but also terrible inhuman conflict are we given to see? Freud is of no help to us because his sensibility as well as his theory could not allow him to see the formal and structural mold of the painting and to perceive what unconscious pattern is being worked out here.

Here it is, Masaccio's "St. Anne, The Virgin and Jesus" (Fig. 8). We have left psychobiography; we have come to another time-space disclosed both by the genealogy of shapes – unexpectedly composed, as never before, in Leonardo's masterpiece – and by the so-called surreal background of it.

Figure 9

This work was painted about 1420, Gozzoli's (Fig. 9) in 1925.
(Leonardo's painting in the Louvre is dated 1510 or 1515.) There
appears, nearly a century before Leonardo, the analogy and the
structural homology of these works, resting on their pyramidal
and trinitarian composition. Weird trinities. They are female
ones, whereas the Trinity which henceforth ruled the Christian
world was all male.

There is, of course, much to be said concerning the historical
and cultural conditions which, at the outburst of the Renaissance,
induced the Trinity of dogma to give way to these female trinities, which spread into Italy and Germanic countries until the
beginning of the Reformation. Here are some specimens: Veit
Stoss' "Heilige Anna Selbdritt" and Andrea Sansovino's "Santa
Anna Metterza" (Fig. 10).

Figure 10

The style of these popular works and the presences embodied
here are blatantly archaic when compared with Leonardo's. In
referring to archaic antecedents after seeing Leonardo's work,
the point is to make us aware of the difference in scale between

figures represented here. In D. Mauch's work (Fig. 11), for example, the figure called St. Anne is out of proportion; it exists in an extra-human dimension in its relation with the one called Mary, and with the child.

Such a presence, which can be called extraordinary, even gives the names to these trinities: They are called *Metterze*, from the Italian *terza*, which means "the third one." And the prefix *met*, with its Latin origin, stressed it: *Metterze* (Maiolani-Gérard, 1991) It is as though this person who bears the mother and the child introduced herself under this name, saying "Here am I, the third one, the Mother, who has upheld, contained and, for a long while, included the human mother – little Mary – and the child."

But what is brought about by Leonardo's work? In this work (Fig. 1), the Mother is always eminently present. From her all things proceed, and her head is always situated in another dimension. But she has drawn closer to our world. And above all now the human mother, whose skin and gesture are so human to our senses, evades her and, by slow degrees, gets loose from her.

Figure 11   *Figure 12*

Then the child, this one a real boy, a creature totally different from the Holy Ghost of male Trinities, this flesh and blood child, who really has ceased to be Jesus Christ, can set foot very near to us, and play. He is playing with a lamb, and this lamb may well be the greatest invention in this painting. This naturalistic lamb, domesticated and rebellious, is the fourth figure of this Trinity. We had been expecting him so long, and he has come at last. We are indebted to Leonardo for his presence.

Here, of course, at first sight he stands as a reminder of Christ's fore-ordained sacrifice and death. But he is also a reminder of the animal condition of infancy. The child must grow out of it. His mother pulls him out of it, as much as she accompanies him.

Finally he is a true symbol, a very ancient and quite new one, created by the painting. New, because now no longer confined within the Christian faith. He stands aloof; he lives his own life. And he watches us; he demands understanding.

You can see now that this work does not tell only the story of a child abandoned by his notable father at Vinci. Its origin is far more remote. Here is being worked out a task, which for ages has engrossed us, unconsciously at first. This work emerges from the depths of our collective story.

Let us take a step back. Back to Eleusis (Fig. 12). This relief dates back to the fourth century before Christ. Who could say that we are here presented with Catarina, Dona Albiera and the son of a Vinci notary? Or even with Ann, Mary and Jesus? Here the story is said to be about Demeter, the Great Mother, and Kore, her daughter – who will become Persephone – and the boy Tryptolemos, who will teach the Greeks agriculture.

At Eleusis, in the fourth century before Christ, this was already an old story; the Mysteries were celebrated for nearly 2000 years. In the main, these rituals have remained unknown to us. But we know that the crucial, secret and intimate experience of the initiate consisted in familiarity with the story of Demeter and of Kore-Persephone, the story of their separation. Meanwhile the initiate grew more and more familiar with his or her own death.

Demeter, in her distracted quest of her lost daughter carried away by Pluto, was reenacted in song and mime. Her bereavement was lived anew – such bereavement as strikes the soil with sterility and makes corn die.

Kore also was frequented. Kore whose statues are ageless, and first so sexually undifferentiated that she often might as well be seen as a *Kouros* (a boy) and like Artemis, with so much of a virgin about her that she could mistake herself for a flower, as Narcissus did.

But through her dramatic separation from her mother, through her encounter with Pluto in the underworld, Kore learns about sharing and about life cycles. She becomes a mediator between Demeter's ever-revolving universe and the netherworld. Then can the boy Tryptolemos be confronted with Demeter, and in his turn teach humans the laws of agriculture.

Here is Demeter's smile (Fig. 12, left). Through this smile, I am coming back to Leonardo (Fig. 1). Better than in Eleusis, better than in the still medieval times of the Metterze, better even than what Leonardo himself might have said and thought, and Freud was able to teach, this work tries to recapture the dim knowledge of myths and religions, to bring it nearer to us and make us recognize it with the help of what our lives have already taught us.

With such a painting, this ancient knowledge descends at last from mythical heavens, to make us aware of the familiar but dramatic and enigmatic experience of our attachment to our mother's body, to her face, her look, her skin, her taste. Never before this painting had we so closely perceived the place occupied by the mother figure in our attachments and our parting, as well as her mediating function. She has proved so durably, so closely, so strangely, commingled with the world she originates in, we can dream of her, fear her, reluctant to detach ourselves from her in order to alight at last, and walk toward our own destiny.

Translated from French
by Simone Rosenberg

References

Ehrenzweig, A. (1974). *L'ordre Caché de l'Art*. Paris: Gallimard.

Green, A. (1992). *Révélations de l'Inachèvement*. Paris: Flammarion.

Maidlani-Gérard, J.P. (1991). Le "Souvenir d'enfance" de Léonard, son impact sur le travail de Freud. *Psychanalyse a l'Université, 11*.

Figures:

1. Leonardo da Vinci, *The Virgin, Jesus and St. Anne*. Le Louvre, Paris.
2. Leonardo da Vinci, *The Virgin, Jesus, St. Anne and John the Baptist*. National Gallery, London.
3. The Freudian Vulture.
4. Bernardino Luini, *The Holy Family with John the Baptist and St. Anne*. Ambrosiana, Milano.
5. Leonardo da Vinci, *John the Baptist*. Le Louvre, Paris.
6. Leonardo da Vinci, *Bacchus*. Le Louvre, Paris.
7. Leonardo da Vinci, *The Angel in the Flesh*. private collection.
8. Masaccio, *St. Anne, the Virgin and Jesus*. Uffici, Firenze.
9. Gozzoli, *St. Anne, the Virgin and Jesus*. Museo Civico, Pisa.
10. *left:* Veit Stoss, *Heilige Anna Selbdritt*. Skt Anne Kirche, Vienna.
right: Sansovino, *Santa Anna Metterza*. Chiesa San Agostino, Roma.
11. D. Mauch, *Ste Anne trinitaire*. Musée Grobet-Labadié, Marseille.
12. Relief from Eleusis. National Archeological Museum, Athens.

Anselm Kiefer: The Psychology of after the Catastrophe

Rafael López-Pedraza
Caracas, Venezuela
IAAP Individual Member

In the early 1960s, at the Zurich Institute, discussions on German mythology, the phenomenon of National Socialism and the Second World War were part of the teaching of Jungian psychology. These discussions were based on Jung's *Essays on Contemporary Events* (now in CW10), in which a great psychologist brought a psychiatric approach to the tragedy of the Second World War. The study of these essays is essential to the learning of Jungian psychology; their reflection of historical events teaches about the shadow in its most collective and darkest manifestation, precluding any possibility of idealized projections.

I believe that we can learn psychology from art and that the work of the German painter, Anselm Kiefer, supports Jung's psychological view of the collapse of Western culture's central religious and spiritual supports. For this reason I have taken Jung's title "After the Catastrophe" to subtitle my exposition on Kiefer's work.

Anselm Kiefer was born in 1945, the year World War II ended. He seems to be representative of a generation of Germans who are under the tremendous pressure of coming to terms with an almost impossibly difficult and terrible history.

Kiefer has demonstrated that he has a strong enough psyche to activate in himself the German past – its mythology and history – from its primitive beginnings to Hitler and National Socialism. One of the "tools" Kiefer's psyche uses to mobilize his imaginative creativity is regression. Through it he reaches a symmetry with the psychology he wants to approach. This approach is exemplified in the series of photographs, "Occupations," where he can be seen ironically giving the Nazi salute in a variety of absurd locations.

His effort is a painful and risky game, possible only within a hermetic boundary. Kiefer has said that he does not identify himself with Hitler but he has to re-enact, psychically, what Hitler did, in order to understand his madness. For this purpose Kiefer borrows the technique of the actor and so is contained by the archetype of theater. The figure in these photos can be viewed as an actor rehearsing, or acting, in a play and thus achieving an acquaintance with evil.

I will start with "Operation Sea Lion I" (Pl. 14)[1] because it gives us immediate access to Kiefer's psychology, to his intention and his personal, ironic point of view. Operation Sea Lion was the code name for the German plan to invade Britain. The German High Command practiced the operation in a bathtub. With a macabre dramatism and an ironic humor, Kiefer paints, in reddish browns, grays and black, an image of the German generals, with the passive ranks of ordinary soldiers massed behind them, playing with little toy boats in a bathtub. Above are three empty chairs, probably signifying an absent or meaningless Trinity. The generals play their omnipotent game, revealing their madness and stupidity. With this image, Kiefer depicts humanity's infinite capacity for playing stupid games when possessed by power and destruction.

Kiefer's ability to depict stupidity qualifies him as a great psychologist. Modern psychology has failed to bring into discussion sheer stupidity as a relevant aspect of human nature, or to reflect on its own stupidity.

Kiefer's irony and sarcasm as regards human stupidity gives him the psychological distance for reflecting the mammoth cultural shadow which is the main theme of his paintings. Nazism has been seen as the paradigm for evil. Now, with the help of Kiefer, we may add that it can be seen as the paradigm of stupidity as well. To view it as such brings about psychological movement; a door is opened into the exploration of the shadow –

1. All paintings mentioned, except "Parsifal," appear in Rosenthal (1987).

one that helps us to detect when our own stupidity makes us fall into an identification with the dementia we call evil.

Jung, in his essay "Wotan" (CW10), described the German god as "the god of storm and frenzy, the unleasher of passions and the lust of battle" (par. 375) and as "a fundamental attribute of the German psyche" (par. 389). He also wrote: "As an autonomous psychic factor, Wotan produces effects in the collective life of a people and thereby reveals his own nature. For Wotan has a peculiar biology of his own, quite apart from the nature of man" (par. 391).

Jung identified the volatile danger inherent in such a mythology: a mythology that leads to sudden states of possession. According to Jung, Wotanic German mythology gives a picture of a powerful irrationality that conflicts strongly with historical reality. The complex in its repetitive manifestations suggests an extreme autonomy and a form of suffering that seems to be at the core of the German people's fate. Could it be that this Wotanic biological factor gives to the German people their ethnic character?

The massive painting "Parsifal" (Fig. 2) is one of Kiefer's reflections on a German mythological motif. An old friend and colleague wrote to me after seeing this powerful work in the Zurich Art Museum. His vivid and emotional "reading of an image" conveys more than any intellectual commentary of the art critics:

Then I found this socking great Kiefer!! Its size alone is moving. What it means I have no idea. An enormous claustrophobic wooden room with no windows; empty, threatening and uncanny. Two monstrous constructions of wooden beams in the room and reminiscent of gallows. A bucket of blood in the middle. Amfortas is down below in spirit and unredeemed. Parsifal is up in the air in spirit. The myth doesn't seem to work, and the myth not working is a claustrophobic building with pompous constructions – empty!

Kiefer offers a reflection of the horror of the myth's not working. And we are faced suddenly with an unknown stratum in human nature. The work transmits an emotion which has no

precedent in art. We are taken to outlandish spaces, interiors and
exteriors, enclosed claustrophobic places, devastated landscapes,
eerie forests and burnt-out buildings, containing all the memories
of German myth and history. Could we say that Kiefer's works
express a horrifying realm of human nature? Are they an expression of that peculiar Wotanic biology observed by Jung?

There is another painting, "Ways of Worldly Wisdom," in
which Kiefer portrays the most historically representative faces
and names of the German academy: its poets, writers and thinkers. The academic heads loom out of a ghostly petrified forest. In
the lower left is the head of a dead German soldier, an image that
reflects the inflation and unreality embedded in the German
tradition of knowledge. Kiefer's intention seems to be to connect
to Germany's historical roots and perhaps, through the scenario
of the eerie forest, to connect to the strange biology we have been
questioning.

German philosophy had, with its arrogance, dominated Western thought; but after the World War II it became suspect. This
was not because it stirred and justified the German attitude and
behavior but because its ultimate product was the disastrous
horror of the War. Obviously there was something wrong with
the German establishment, its academy and philosophy. Kiefer
himself seems to be a well-grounded man, with a down-to-earth
vision which here moves us to reflect on the representatives of
the German academy as being possessed by the same demonic
forces that impelled Germany into the catastrophe.

As well as mythological and historical themes, Kiefer has
rendered his reflections concerning the failure of Western culture's religious values and virtues in such striking and thought-
provoking paintings as "Father, Son, Holy Ghost" (Pl. 9) and
"Faith, Hope, Love" (Pl. 29). He seems to imply that perhaps the
only protection for the psyche and the only resource humanity
has for facing reality today is with art and psychic creativity.

Portraying the German psyche at its deepest and most biological level, Kiefer paints mostly from the part of the archetype that
touches on instinct and the world of nature: "the infra-red" end of
the archetype, as Jung dubbed it. I want to use it here metaphori-

cally because it allows me to refer to a part of human nature that always remains obscure. For me, the adventure of Jungian psychology lies in this realm.

Kiefer's explorations are contained in a sound knowledge of the history of painting and the possibilities offered by this century's discoveries in the plastic arts which, to him, lend themselves as the proper net in which to catch his creative process. Kiefer's paintings hint at the conflicts underlying the expressionist distortions, the strange forces that nourish this tradition. More than this, he gives an unexpected turn to historical painting.

Kiefer brings a very personal approach to Judaism which is neither moralistic nor guilt-producing. He has evidently asked himself some searching questions about the history of the Germans vis-a-vis the Jews. His 1984 trip to Israel seemed to be a pilgrimage in search of answers to such questioning. He seems to have found some answers in the way he has approached certain Jewish themes in a long series of paintings. Concerning the painting "The Red Sea" (Pl. 69) Mark Rosenthal, curator of the exhibition of Kiefer's paintings in the USA, writes:

> Kiefer brings the Exodus tale into a German context in *The Red Sea*. The connection is forged by the carryover of the National Socialist bathtub from the "Operation Sea Lion" series. The tub full of red liquid links two biblical events, the first plague in Exodus, when Aaron turned water to blood with his rod, and Moses's parting and closing of the sea.... A glass plate like the one that held the chairs of the Trinity aloft appears above the earth holding a white "pillar of cloud." (1987, p. 127)

"The Red Sea" is a powerful conception. As Rosenthal says, Kiefer makes an unmistakable connection between a Biblical Exodus motif and the Nazis' Operation Sea Lion. He portrays the Red Sea motif in a similar way to his portrayal of the German generals playing in the bathtub. Kiefer's imagination is able to relate the German generals' fantasy of crossing the English Channel with the Biblical fantasy of Moses crossing the Red Sea. He seems to treat the Jewish legends in a rather similar way to his treatment of German mythology and the Christian tradition, as reflecting a similar stupidity.

Is he suggesting that the Jewish complexes are also fated, like the mythological and religious complexes of the German people and Western culture? That the Jewish psyche is repetitively struggling with complexes that no longer nourish the Jewish soul? I find that Kiefer, who himself is suffering from a mammoth historical failure, is at least questioning and trying to reflect the old Jewish complexes in relation to their present historical reality.

Kiefer's conception in "Jerusalem" (Pl. 19) turns upside down our collective traditional imagination concerning the Holy City. The painting is an expressionist abstraction, elaborated with acrylic, emulsion, gold leaf, lead and two steel bars. The latter are particularly striking. And it is the abstraction of the painting that stirs my imagination and allows me to bring my own image of Jerusalem.

One of the most important occasions at the 1983 IAAP Congress in Jerusalem was a morning devoted to representatives of three monotheistic religions – a Jewish scholar, a Catholic priest, and a Muslim imam – talking about the meaning of Jerusalem for each religion. A beatific spirit of tolerance floated in the crowd that morning. There was not the faintest allusion to the shadow and hatred that the three religions, living together in a city, constellate. The atmosphere of that meeting was far from a basic premise of Jungian psychology: to learn from the shadow. The myth of religious tolerance had thrown a smoke-screen over the bloody history of the religious shadow.

The three religious conceptions of Jerusalem, psychologically speaking, are inflated in the face of the history of the city. The image alone, a place where three monotheistic religions cohabit, where the psyche has to deal constantly with three exclusive religious systems, is an infernal image. Does not religion show its most psychologically paralyzing aspect in the inevitable, never-ending friction among the three religions? We owe it to Jung's genius that religion was brought into the study of psychology. It is within this Jungian legacy and according to the psychological times in which we are living, the times after the catastrophe, that we can give attention to the relation between psychology and religion and bring some differentiation to what sometimes seems to be one and the same. This may help us to adopt a less hypocritical attitude and become more aware of the shadow constellated by the historical religions.

In the self-portrait "Broken Flowers and Grass" (Pl. 44) Kiefer shows an important aspect of his personal psychology. He is lying on a bed, eyes closed, dressed in a black tunic. The entire forefront of the painting is strewn with painted flowers and grass. He looks as if he might be dead. The image has that hermetic freakish touch of rehearsing one's own death. But, psychologically speaking, he is transmitting an image of his depression.

The flowers give the opportunity to say something about flowers in relation to feeling and depression. For these are flowers that could bloom only in the subterranean realm of Persephone. Kiefer's feeling, artistic creativity and depression are bound together indissolubly in his personality and individuation.

"Broken Flowers" moves the discussion on depression and psychic creativity to a new level. The great bulk of Kiefer's work gives the impression that all his reflections about humanity's historical tragedy come through a particular level of depression and are only to be expressed through art. At any rate, it is a demonstration of an artist who has the necessary psychic force to hold his depression and accept its importance to his nature and creative process. Furthermore, we have to take into account not only Kiefer's deep depression but also his unimpressive physique; he tackles enormous canvasses which, in addition to their creative conception, require a tremendous physical stamina.

Kiefer has many and varied ways of expressing the depressive level of his personality. In "Emanation" (Pl. 77) he moves almost into abstraction. Other depressions are expressed in fragments. "Emanation" is a heavy load of lead blotting out the sky, evidently an expression of depression. On the other hand, Kiefer gives the impression that the lead is not inert but, falling; paradoxically, lead is an expression of psychic movement. Those interested in symbolism could have a symbolic reading of a seminal mercurial lead uniting a cloudy sky and a dark earth. For me, however, the painting has the imaginative reading of a strange abstraction to express depression. I would go so far as to see "Emanation" as having healing properties in the same way as a dream.

One is amazed at Kiefer's creativity at the level of depression; here he gives us his greatest lesson. His work points to a path in psychology that moves my psyche tremendously, a path of exploration where I feel my passion for psychology is properly nourished.

Reference

Rosenthal, M. (1987). *Anselm Kiefer*. Catalogue, The Art Institute of Chicago and the Philadelphia Museum of Art.

Minotauromaquia

James Wyly
Chicago, Illinois, USA
Chicago Society of Jungian Analysts

The etching shown in Figure 1 and known as "Minotauro-maquia" (1935; Bloch 288) could be considered the climax of Pablo Picasso's long series of works devoted to the Minotaur, which occupied him throughout the 1930s. The Minotaur is, of course, the mythic bull with a man's body which King Minos of Crete kept in the labyrinth until Theseus slew it. When Picasso took up the Minotaur it seemed to represent the raging, raping male-animal instincts of the human psyche; thus he drew and painted it up to the time of this work. But after this etching the Minotaur begins to develop another kind of appearance and eventually becomes a rather amiable character. We can compare a 1933 Minotaur (Fig. 2. Picasso's Vollard Suite No. 87), en-gaged in one of his favorite pursuits, with a 1938 one (Fig. 3; Duncan, 1974, p. 153).

The Minotaur never again achieves that level of ferocity after the etching of 1935. It is thus a climactic work; if we are to understand the Minotaur's transformation we could do worse than to examine "Minotauromaquia" closely in an effort to deter-mine what is happening in it.

We see a confrontation between the Minotaur and a young girl holding a candle and some flowers. Evidently the girl wants to illuminate what is between them: an unconscious or dead female bullfighter on her eviscerated horse.

The Minotaur is traveling, for he carries a backpack and he seems to have come from the sea, behind him. With his right hand be blocks the light, as though he does not want to look at what is before him.

Surprisingly, the young girl does not flee, but remains static and fearless. Not only does she want the Minotaur to see, she seems to offer him flowers. Is this a gesture of welcome?

Meanwhile the bullfighter lies unconscious with her breast exposed. Her last conscious gesture was evidently to turn her sword, which is still in her hand, from the beast she was planning to kill.

So both the Minotaur and the bullfighter have behaved uncharacteristically: She refused to kill him and he refused to see, though the bull operates in the bullring by sight. His sight is what makes him dangerous; the matador's skill at manipulating his vision can determine which of them survives the encounter. The Minotaur's gesture is therefore suicidal, while the matador's parallel self-sacrifice will keep him alive; the girl with the flowers seems to welcome this event! Why should this be? Both the female matador and the Minotaur have histories in Picasso's earlier work which will clarify this.

When the Minotaur became an important symbol in Picasso's work in the early 1930s he used it to represent a masculine force that repeatedly attacks the anima-figure whose presence is necessary both for human relatedness and creative work. The eleven "Minotaur Plates" of the Vollard Suite (Nos. 83-93, executed in May and June of 1933), show the Minotaur in action. In Plate 83 (not shown) the Minotaur is having a glass of wine with a young woman. In the next three Plates the party becomes a drunken orgy as more figures appear. The Minotaur passes out and in Plate 87 (Fig. 2) he rapes the young woman – or he dreams of raping her, for the rape is mysteriously transformed into the Minotaur's death in an arena, at the hands of a young hero, before a crowd of onlookers. Picasso's imagery clearly implies the slaying of the Minotaur by Theseus (Fig. 4, Plate 89). But later, at a party celebrating the Minotaur's death, the young hero tries on a Minotaur costume (Fig. 5, Plate 92), and this gesture revitalizes the Minotaur force, for in Plate 93 (not shown), the raping continues.

Figure 1

Figure 2

Figure 3

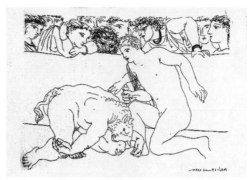

Figure 4

Figure 5

Figure 6

Figure 7

Figure 9

Figure 8

Picasso placed the four "Blind Minotaur" plates immediately after this in the Vollard Suite, though they were executed more than a year later. In all four, we see the blind Minotaur groping for a relationship with a young girl who is reminiscent of the one in "Minotauromaquia" (Fig. 6, Plate 94). Again, vision is the issue, and now we can perceive that he can have a non-violent relationship with the feminine when he cannot see what he is doing. Of course we are also reminded of the blind Oedipus, led to Colonus by his daughter, Antigone. And as in "Minotauro-maquia," the Minotaur has come ashore from a sea voyage. Part of the mystery is clearer now; the Minotaur's blindness is, like Oedipus's, self-imposed. Like Oedipus, he cannot bear the sight of his connection with the feminine who, the analogy to Iocasta reminds us, is both his mother and his consort. Oedipus could not stand to see that he was married to his mother. When the Mino-taur sees a woman she reminds him of this connection. He cannot stand it and must subdue her. Furthermore, even the young hero who kills the Minotaur becomes a Minotaur when his violent victory over the original Minotaur is celebrated!

Now let us turn to the female matador, the woman with the blade. Surprisingly, we also find her in the first of the four "Blind Minotaur" plates (Fig. 6). There is a painting on the wall of the building the Minotaur is approaching, and close examination shows it to be hung upside-down and crossed out. This double message of denial tells us that it shows what is not to happen; and if we enlarge it and turn it right side up (Fig. 7), we see some-thing chilling: A crazed-looking woman is stabbing a man in a bathtub, while the light of the sun streams in through the open window.

This is a scene which Picasso had executed twice before, on Christmas Day 1931 and on July 21, 1934. It is the famous assassination of the French revolutionary propagandist, Jean-Paul Marat, who was stabbed in his bath in 1793 by the young and deluded Girondin agent, Charlotte Corday. Picasso was fa-miliar with Jacques-Louis David's 1793 painting of the same event; the astonishing fact that Picasso executed the 1931 "Woman with Stiletto," when he was exactly the age of Marat when he was killed, suggests something about Picasso's psychological involvement with his subject matter. In the Corday figure it is easy to see the vengeful feminine retaliating for her rape, and we are reminded of a remark Picasso is supposed to have made to Françoise Gilot: "A Minotaur keeps his women lavishly but he reigns by terror, and they're glad to see him killed" (Gilot and Lake, 1964, p. 50).

Women with stilettos, women with butcher knives. They are not so far removed from women with swords. This thought leads us to an important theme both in Spanish mythology and in Picasso's earlier work: the female matador. Just as Charlotte Corday thought she was eliminating a counter-revolutionary and destructive force when she murdered Marat, Picasso's female matadors seem to try to eliminate the most archaic and counter-revolutionary aspect of masculinity, the Minotaur. This leads us to more women who murdered counter-revolutionary men in their bathtubs; both Agamemnon and Minos died in the same circumstances as did Marat. Clytemnestra murdered Agamemnon in the bath she offered him when he returned from Troy with Cassandra, interrupting her new relationship with Aegisthus, and the daughters of King Cocalus of Sicily murdered Minos himself when he came to their island to take away that revolutionary and creative man, Daedalus.

So we see everywhere the ancient theme of the raped or betrayed woman who reassembles her life and then refuses to submit to the return of her abuser, and in "Minotauromaquia" we expect her to defend herself once again. But that painting was crossed out and hung upside-down. That solution had been tried before, and in the long run it changed nothing. So now, instead, the female matador bares her breast and turns her sword around while a young woman meets the Minotaur with light and flowers. A different solution is necessary, and "Minotauromaquia" shows us what it is.

The feminine figures have given up revenge and instead force the Minotaur to look at them. Here is a different outcome for Oedipus' and Iocasta's disastrous self-discovery. If she refuses to kill him and he does not blind himself to who she is, they will have to submit to the influence of each other's ongoing presence. The feminine cannot oppose the Minotaur's potential for violence and the Minotaur cannot blind himself to its effects. In the end, neither the Minotaur nor Oedipus can wiggle out of the fact that he is married to his mother; and the mother must confront her son-husband as he is, and not attempt to deny his nature as did Pasiphae when the original Minotaur was confined to the underground labyrinth. Here Picasso is in agreement with recent feminist psychology, which is reexamining the classic assumption that individuation requires the severance of the mother-tie. I think the Minotaurs Picasso made after "Minotauromaquia" show us something about the effects of this revision.

In Picasso's work subsequent to "Minotauromaquia," the Minotaur is never again unambiguously terrible, and is often beautiful. Plate 27 of the *Vollard Suite* was made in June of 1936 (Fig. 8). Again the Minotaur is approaching a woman, but he is totally changed in appearance, and his sensitive gestures remind us more of the love affair of Eros and Psyche than of the Minotaur-rapes we have become accustomed to seeing.

And after "Minotauromaquia" the Minotaur does other things than pursue women. In the Minotaur works of 1936-38 Picasso was free to depict him in the underworld, undergoing various kinds of transformations, engaged in different activities, and even transformed into a woman (Fig. 9, Bloch 289). Figure 3 shows the Minotaur's final form in Picasso's work. After this, for all practical purposes Picasso made no more Minotaurs.

Picasso said, "We are not merely the executors of our work; we *live* our work" (Ashton, 1972, p. 43). It is as though Picasso's Minotaurs prepared him for the shattering world events that were then approaching. In 1936 the political Minotaur came alive again with the outbreak of the Spanish Civil War. As Picasso's own Minotaurs went through the evolution we have seen that Picasso's world sank into ever more violent chaos. The war was a clear sign to Picasso, as it was to many others, that Fascism was bringing a holocaust that would consume all of Europe. Events climaxed in early 1939, when Hitler's entry into Prague, the fall of Spain to Franco and the death of Picasso's mother all occurred within two and a half months of one another.

These events correspond with the end of Picasso's intense concentration upon Minotaur imagery. Psychologically, the Minotaur had done its work, and Picasso was now prepared to wait out the war with some sense that the catastrophe was not final, and that other solutions were possible to the age-old conflict that lay behind it. If Picasso's Minotaur and his ladies could develop a nondestructive relationship, then perhaps the violent oppositions in the world could as well. The trick is evidently for them to remain fully aware of each other and change under each other's influence.

It is encouraging to understand the Minotaur adventures of Picasso as the psyche's response to the times through which Picasso was living. The works give us a graphic account of the psyche's mythmaking function as it responded to appalling political events of the 1930s. As events in our own time bring out the archaic Minotaur in our own civilization, perhaps we can see in the art a little of what we are called upon to do if we are to live through them. It is not that we are to assume mindlessly a set sequence in time, from raging Minotaur to a happy-ever-after resolution. But we can see that awareness of what is going on and a willingness to encounter it head-on can result in a breakdown of the original opposition, a regression of libido to the transforming depths of the unconscious and an emergence of a new awareness, form or attitude that transcends the original difficulty.

To search for solutions to oppositions in this kind of process instead of our usual idea of destroying the "enemy" without changing our own position would seem to be the psychological attitude to which "Minotauromaquia" has led us.

References

Ashton, D. (1972). *Picasso on Art*. New York: Viking.

Bloch, G. (1968). *Pablo Picasso. Catalogue de l'œuvre gravé et lithographié. Tome 1: 1904-1967*. Bern: Kornfeld and Klipstein.

Duncan, D. (1974). *Goodbye, Picasso*. New York: Grosset & Dunlap.

Gilot, F. & Lake, C. (1964). *Life with Picasso*. New York: McGraw-Hill.

Forum: Ethics in Analysis

Murray Stein
Wilmette, Illinois, USA
Chicago Society of Jungian Analysts

As an association of Jungian analysts, IAAP is concerned about the quality of care delivered by its members. A major derivative of the quality-of-care issue is an imperative to collective reflection on ethical concerns as these apply in our profession. Putting aside questions of research, publishing and teaching, the issues remaining are (1) the necessary ethical conditions of an analytic situation that is to assure quality care and service and (2) the needed ethical qualities of the analyst who is providing that care and service. It is incumbent upon Analytical Psychology to reflect collectively and continually upon the principles and rules that are taught and maintained regarding the therapeutic setting and upon the ethical qualities of the persons practicing Jungian analysis. Thus, there are two tasks: to develop principles and rules of ethical conduct in analysis and to foster deeper understanding of the psyches of the persons practicing analysis, who are called upon to deliver psychotherapeutic care in an ethical manner.

With respect to the first task, it must be recognized that we as members of IAAP share this concern for ethics and this need for ethical reflection with members of many other professional therapy organizations. To generate and refine ethical principles and rules of behavior for Jungian analysts is not essentially different from doing this in any of the helping professions. Perhaps we can bring greater sensitivity to such phenomena as transference reactions than some other professions might. On the second point, however, we do have something more special to contribute: In reflecting on the very human nature of the persons who are expected to follow the rules and to live by the principles that the moral philosophers among us have evolved, we can offer insights that are perhaps more encompassing and complete than general ethicists can offer. We have something to contribute about the understanding of human nature and the psyche as these bear upon questions of ethical behavior by analysts.

For example, if we agree with Jung's fundamental insight that the psyche is essentially paradoxical, it follows that when we increase the intensity of light we also deepen the shadow. We can polarize the psyche by emphasizing too much the standards of perfection that our rational, morally principled minds can generate. When we do this, we create a split and lay the groundwork for unconscious acting out. We know that it is extremely important how we carry out the rules of moral and ethical behavior, and how we apply them to ourselves and to others. It is critical to have sound rules and principles but the harder task is to become successful in carrying them out in a satisfactory way.

An Analytical Psychologists we should not be overly surprised when even famous moral philosophers and theologians, or gifted and sensitive artists, stumble and fall into the precise morass they can transcend with such grace in their conscious works. This is the paradox of human nature. And it is no more surprising in prominent figures of culture than it is in the members of our own IAAP Societies and Institutes. Moral consciousness is no guarantor of ethical behavior, and at times the very intensification of such consciousness will constellate the opposite in behavior. To compensate for the Apollonic brilliance of a perfect moral and ethical stance there is an irresistible pull to Dionysian chaos and dismemberment, driven perhaps by the death-and-rebirth archetype and by the individuation drive itself.

This panel on ethics was included in the Congress program at the request of the Executive Committee. This request came in response to a recommendation from the Council of American Societies of Jungian Analysts (CASJA) – suggested by the San Francisco Institute – to include a statement about ethics in the Constitution of IAAP. The Executive Committee decided to initiate a discussion about ethics that would add to the literature in the field and would also carry the level of reflection beyond a statement of rules. To that end, I invited five analysts – three European, two American – to contribute statements to this discussion of ethics and analysis.

Peter Rutter
San Francisco, California, USA
Society of Jungian Analysts of
Northern California

Let us remember: What hurts the victim most is not the cruelty of the oppressor, but the silence of the bystander.

Elie Wiesel

Petra Affeld-Niemeyer's paper elsewhere in this volume is a significant transformational event. It links this forum with the psychological development of consciousness in the world around us.

In helping us to understand and feel the petrifying and soul-murdering effects that incestuous invasions cause, Affeld-Niemeyer offers to us as Jungians and to our society an extremely important way to reverse the scapegoating of victims of power abuse – political, economic, ideological or intimate.

Affeld-Niemeyer has chosen a quintessentially Jungian way to undercut the denial of the reality of incestuous abuse that has been the shadow-heritage of the history of psychoanalysis. Her way has been to deliver us the reality of the psyche, by giving us several clinical moments where archetype, symbol, dream and once-unhealable wound all come together in the transference, in the *mysterium coniunctionis*, to create a truly new opportunity to transcend the seeming impossibility of healing the person's wound. When stone comes to life in a dream, when the reality of such a symbolic healing moment lives between analyst and analysand, we are brought back to the core of Jungian analysis. In this experience we regain hope for our analysands and for ourselves. Furthermore, we create a hopeful model of renewal through facing the reality of the psychic trauma that the destructive shadow inflicts. This transcendent model of bridging seemingly irreconcilable splits is one which the society around us also desperately needs.

But even as we contemplate this transcendent healing possibility that we invite our patients to experience, we must attend constantly to the shadow of this very process, to the deadening stone that Affeld-Niemeyer speaks of, to the life experiences of our analysands that have deadened them and to the shadow of the healing relationship itself, including the possibility that we as analysts at times contribute to the deadening of, the silencing of, our analysands.

This, to me, is why we are in this work. We have an ethical task. But because we are a clinical organization, our ethical standards must derive from the core of our work, from our understanding of the reality of the psyche as it manifests between analyst and analysand. Affeld-Niemeyer, by demonstrating so palpably the vulnerability of the patient's psychic core, reminds us that there is an inescapable clinical mandate for establishing ethical standards regarding the maintaining of boundaries. Every person in analysis is engaged at a level of core vulnerability.

It is not too great a leap, then, to assert that every therapist at every moment with every patient has a duty to protect the core vulnerability of the patient that, in the unconscious, may be engaged with the therapist, whether or not there is any conscious evidence for this level of vulnerability. As we psychotherapists allow ourselves to see incestuous abuse as real, we are allowing our patients to tell us about the reality they have endured, and are discovering that patients are now presenting to us innumerable experiences and varieties of the incest wound. Whether we understand the concept of incest as literal/physical, psychological, symbolic, or a dynamic with a family system or the culture, we see that incest deadens. We assuredly know enough about the transference and the presence of unseen, pre-verbal unconscious elements, to make it clear that it is the responsibility of the therapist to hold in trust most of all the vulnerable core of the patient, whether or not any direct evidence of a visible incest would ever manifest itself.

The clinical reality of the transference makes boundary crossing not only unethical but a question of competence. Therapists who involve themselves in dual relationships with patients –

whether those relationships are personal, sexual or financial – are exploiting the vulnerable core of patients and, in the light of what we know about transference, are making a quantum departure from the competent standard of practice. The healing arts require the highest possible standard of humanity and professionalism. We must accept that those practitioners who do not hold to these standards are, consciously or unconsciously, asking us to relieve them of their privilege to practice their profession, so that they can return to the task of confronting their own wounds, of trying to make themselves whole in more ordinary ways, without being burdened by their demonstrated failure at the extraordinary task of shadow containment for others that the healing arts require.

Two tasks in clinical ethics confront the IAAP, as well as all organizations representing helping professionals whose practice is based on the trust of those who are served. First, such organizations, including the IAAP and each of its member Jungian societies, should establish ethical codes that are also understood to be standards of clinical practice. Such ethical standards are not, as is sometimes alleged, incursions on individual autonomy, but are chosen consciously by each individual who wishes to link his or her professional identity to the collective professional identity (e.g., "Jungian analyst") that the organization establishes in the mind of the public. We must keep in mind also that such a professional identity carries with it, in the experience of the beholder, not only social power but also archetypal power.

Second, each organization needs to have the wisdom to devise clear procedures for hearing ethical complaints and communicate to the public that it values receiving such complaints. Procedures must recognize and reflect the legal and due process rights of all parties to an ethics complaint. Beyond this, an organization must also have the courage, when a violation of a standard of practice has been found that might endanger others, to inform the profession and the public of the name of the practitioner and the nature of the violation. In this way we break our collaboration with the secret-keeping of the incest pact and ensure that we will not be the silent bystanders to whom Elie Wiesel refers.

Every clinical organization needs clear, yet dialectically evolving, ethical standards and procedures not only as a focus for the clinical/ethical consciousness of its own members, but also for the world outside us. We have, at the very least, an obligation to protect the public. Beyond that, I firmly believe, we as Jungians can claim a central role in bringing the transcendent function, and all the hope and healing it represents, to the outside world as well – to the cultural consciousness of our world – through our demonstrated ability to live into, and articulate, the quintessentially human values that we meet in the deepest realms of the psyche.

I conclude with a quotation from Jung:

> The shadow, as we know, usually presents a fundamental contrast to the conscious personality.... Confrontation with the shadow produces at first a dead balance, a standstill that hampers moral decisions and makes convictions ineffective or even impossible.... Stripping off of the veils of illusion is felt as distressing and even painful. In practical treatment this phase demands much patience and tact, for the unmasking of reality is as a rule not only difficult but very often dangerous.... Self-knowledge is not an isolated process; it is possible only if the reality of the world around us is recognized at the same time. Nobody can know himself and differentiate himself from his neighbor if he has a distorted picture of him, just as no one can understand his neighbor if he had no relationship to him. The one conditions the other and the two processes go hand in hand. (CW14, pars. 707, 708, 739)

Denyse Zémor
Paris, France
French Society of Analytical
Psychology

The traditional sources of ethics, religion and philosophy – which are collective myths – are absent from our contemporary world or seem to have lost their credibility; they no longer stand as a moral reference for individual responsibility. Is it possible that, in practice, morals have moved toward ethics?

The English word "ethics" summons up in French three ideas: The first is *la morale*, the science of good and evil. The second is *l'éthique*, ethics, which becomes morals when applied to individuals in values and conduct. The third is *la déontologie*, the code of ethics governing a certain profession.

We notice that: 1) A code of ethics is on the side of the rule, while ethics are linked with values. 2) A code of ethics is legally compulsory, while ethics are somewhat optional. 3) A code of ethics is an agreement, a collective compromise concerning a practice, while ethics are individual, connected with one's identity which is under continual questioning and of continual concern. 4) A code of ethics concerns the laying down of rules from outside, whereas ethics concerns conscience, with the intuitive idea of what we think is good and cannot be codified.

Ethics represents a value judgment on one's action as analyst, yet this action itself involves judgment. If I interpret a dream in a specific way, it implies an evaluation. In addition, a part of my action remains hidden for me, in the transference and countertransference. Is not the analyst both judge and participant at the same time?

Jung was interested in the subject of ethics throughout his life. He showed the coexistence of good and evil and the relative aspect of each, while recognizing the omnipresence of moral judgment.

For Jung, neurosis originates in moral conflict. Ethics – deciding between good and bad – is a creative act which is both intra- and inter-subjective: including a subjective experience as well as a moral one. Thus, ethics carries out morals creatively within the analytic relationship. This moral law is only an archaic superego, but corresponds to an archetypal model. Morals are the conscious aim of the ego, the inner voice of the individual.

Throughout the psychological process, the main point lies in acknowledgment of the shadow, followed by its integration. Accepting one's shadow is difficult for one's morality, because consciousness must take the unconscious into account.

And now the question of ethics in France. For French Jungian analysts, fostered as we are in college and university with Freudian culture which provides us with safe and useful limits, problems of the code of ethics are not in the foreground. Ethics and codes of ethics are closely linked; both are necessary. In our work as analysts, ethics deeply enlighten our code of ethics.

The training of the analyst, with its different stages, includes ethics. Indeed, the estimation of countertransference is a value judgment. Understanding of ethics is part of supervision – individually and in groups. This work parallels the deepening of the personal analysis which, for the analyst-in-training, is the very test of personal ethics.

The ethics code includes the mastery of sexual impulses, the abstinence rule and interdiction of sexual acting-out, thus protecting the symbolizing process of the analysand. Ethics, however, concerns not only the code but also the analyst's personal attitude and countertransference.

This code concerns also the control of the omnipotence drives of the analyst, maintaining the secrecy of the analysis and the countertransference. Without control of this drive the analyst risks maintaining the analysand in infancy by being inflated as the one who knows, identifying with the Great Mother or Father.

What are the foci of ethics in analysis? The first focus concerns relationship to the other: This relationship is being lived through eros, just as the link with the unconscious and the union of opposites are being experienced in the relation between man and woman.

The second focus is individuation; a process of becoming a psychologically un-divided person. It is essential, as a Jungian, to know that the growth of personality starts from the unconscious.

Needless to say, the ethical position must be an individual one, but it should not be connected only with the subject's desire. It must take the collective into account, although sometimes going against it.

In the Freudian view, the ethical dimension develops from the subject's desire and the resulting conflicts. Jung differed from Freud, insisting that repressed drives should not be destroyed. Rather, they must be developed further by dealing with the shadow. For Jung the very nature of the unconscious is creative; it is not enough to make the unconscious become conscious. It is also necessary to connect with consciousness the dynamic contents emerging from the unconscious. Thus, Jung provided us with an ethical scope that is larger, more open and more differentiated than the Freudian.

Yet this gratifying endeavor appears to be full of traps, especially Jung's saying that the ego should be deprived of its central position in favor of the Self. This sacrifice is induced while acknowledging the Shadow, the losses and the mournings that an individual experiences. At the same time, Jung showed the dangers of identifying with the Self: an ego inflated at the cost of the Self.

A sacrifice of the Self to omnipotence results in hindrances to life and liberty. The ego is the answer to the conflicting unconscious movements; it is responsible for the ethical commitment and for the choices of the individual among the various archetypal constellations.

The ethical position takes the totality of the subject – the conscious-unconscious relationship – into account. This relationship consists in a structure which offers the possibility of being entirely oneself. The Jungian point of view thus appears to be narcissistically gratifying.

Jung made a distinction between ethics and morality. The purpose is not for humans to be good, but to become autonomous. He specified that each ethical law may change into its opposite, if one drives it to its limit.

Difficult to hold is the idea that one should stay between the opposites without suppressing them. One conditions the other, but one is not the other; a conflict arises when the contents of the Shadow claim to be joined to the conscious contents.

Jung insisted that when there is a conflict the opposites are activated; an opportunity arises to compare the ignored and rejected part of the individual with the illusion of that which one thinks one knows. If this experience is carried out on the affective level – and not only on the intellectual one – a third, paradoxical possibility is born. Union of opposites is the aim of the individuation process: the conscious achievement of the Self, which is the stake of Jungian analysis. It is also the means used by the conscious to fulfill this aim: "The unconscious only works in a satisfactory way if the conscious fulfills its task to the end" (CW8, par. 568).

The question of psychic incest – in Jungian terms "psychic infection" – is at cross-purposes with the union of opposites. There is no doubt of the seriousness of the wound to a person whose analyst transgresses the interdiction against sexual acting-out. This transgression is an attack on the analysand's psychic space and nullifies the symbolizing process.

Coming from France, I am surprised at hearing and reading in the media of the United States and Canada so much about sexual abuse. Of course, abuse happens in France but it is rarely spoken about. In our French Society, the SFPA, a special committee deals with transgressions of the abstinence rule.

But what about psychic incest? Jung spoke of the importance of the concept of incest and incestuous desire. However, his idea was that of endogamous libido which arises in the unconscious and is fruitful for the human psyche.

This endopsychic libido is active in the analytic relationship and sets up the transference. In the individuation process one must get out of the incestuous family intimacy. The containment of this incestuous libido is the very basis of our analytic work, along with the separation process.

The question then arises: How is it possible to give some limits to this incestuous drive without drying it up? How can we avoid falling into shared unconsciousness and at the same time remain connected to the unconscious dynamisms which are being reanimated by the incestuous relationship? We may watch our own errors when, while being influenced by our counter-transference, we allow ourselves just one little sentence of suggestion or personal association, taking a position similar to "participation mystique."

The difficult point is to be able to maintain ourselves during the sessions at a certain distance, self-contained as far as the relationship is concerned. The risk of common unconsciousness is also a danger, not holding the other in his or her differentness.

It appears that both theoretical ethics and clinical ethics have to do with practice. I could put it in this way: "I don't have to see where my analysand and I are alike, but where we differ." That is what he or she needs from me: to become a person who is different from others, and different from me.

Jung said that becoming conscious gives meaning to our whole existence and, at the same time, that the unconscious dynamisms define the human condition. The difficulty of ethics in Jungian analysis lies in this living contradiction, that the unconscious seems to yearn toward the light of consciousness while feeling reluctant to reach it.

Aldo Carotenuto
Rome, Italy
(Resigned from IAAP, 1993)

Sexual behavior has been the pointless cause of scandal and an obstacle to a clear vision of, and a calm approach to, the dynamics of the analytic relationship. I shall attempt, therefore, to explore this sacred ground, which has always been the object of psychoanalytic investigation. Recent research data (Bouhoutsos, 1985) reveal that 65 percent of therapists claim to have treated patients with a history of sexual involvement with previous therapists. Only a very small percentage of those cases were reported to authorities. The first step, therefore, for a real comprehension of the question of sexual involvement between therapist and patient is in the direction of increased awareness. Only thus will the therapist succeed in avoiding the trap of dangerous "selective inattention": establishing a priori what sentiments, what desires are legitimate. Only by considering the facts as they come to our attention, and not what they should be in order to confirm an abstract rule, can the therapist avoid condemning or concealing a colleague's actions. At the same time the therapist will be able to assume calmly and autonomously the weighty ethical responsibility which the analytic relationship implies.

"Whatsoever house I enter, there will I go for the benefit of the sick, refraining from all wrong-doing or corruption and especially from the act of seduction, of male or female." That part of the Oath of Hippocrates illustrates most strikingly how, from the very beginning, the requirement of moral integrity on the part of the physician was considered a vital element in the constitution of the science and art of treating illness. Thus, physical intimacy between physician and patient, that relationship of confidence and trust, can be approached correctly only if the patient becomes for the physician a value – an end rather than a means.

If we shift from the treatment of the body to the treatment of the "soul," matters become even more complicated. The therapist is no longer aided in maintaining emotional distance from the object of investigation by the fact of dealing with organs but is dealing with a universe of emotions, desires, fears – which confer a subjective and individual quality to each organism. Paradoxically, the fact that the psychotherapist's renouncing physical contact makes possible the therapeutic relationship which, developing unilaterally on the imaginal plane, involves desire and corporeity as impossible objects. And it is precisely that impossibility which renders them even more powerfully fascinating.

Thanks to this imaginal vision of the relationship, the particular basis of which is the presence of the analyst's individuality, the analysand is induced to form a unique relationship with the analyst. Thus, the analysand makes the analyst the receiver of projections and the container of the analysand's interior world. The analyst thus becomes the container of those parts of the analysand's psyche which are not fully developed, aspects the person would like to disown or, in any case, those aspects which have not yet been integrated.

One point, which is fundamental if we are to understand the important role the psychotherapist's integrity plays, is that the field of forces generated by the client/therapist encounter cannot avoid being affected by an asymmetry between the partners, one of whom asks desperately, without knowing what is being asked; the other prepared to give and demonstrating knowledge of what is being asked. Let us examine briefly a few of those aspects of the analytic relationship which make essential the professional rigor and total awareness of the analyst.

The analytic relationship represents, first, an exemplary space in which the individual learns to transform need into desire: the passage from a purely natural condition to self-awareness. The indispensable condition for this process is substituting interpretation, on a symbolic level, for acting out.

Second, on the affective plane, the analytic relationship must function as a corrective emotional experience in which the pathogenic relational models which the analysand previously felt driven to repeat in interpersonal relationships are not confirmed.

The analyst's intervention must be cautious; it must break the circle of repetition-compulsion while preventing putting into action any compulsion, in particular the sexual drive, since that passage to action would be equivalent to rendering impossible the process of growth. In addition – always in the context of the preservation of the dynamics that must exist if the therapy is to be successful – it would be wise to keep in mind Freud's words: "I shall take it as a fundamental principle that the patient's need and longing should be allowed to persist in her, in order that they may serve as forces impelling her to do work and make changes, and that we must beware of appeasing those forces by means of surrogates" (SE17, p. 165). Ferenczi also warned against the risks involved in satisfying the patient's libidinal needs, either during or outside the treatment.

Let us move now to the rules related to the inevitable "inequality" of the therapist-patient relationship. As in any other relationship between two individuals, one of whom unconditionally submits to the other, this inequality will cause the patient to regress and to over-estimate the therapist. The vulnerable position is due not so much to the fact of exposing the patient's most intimate nature as to the fact that the help the person searches for is so particular and so profound. It is precisely this condition that permits the patient to project onto the therapist what Jung called the "savior archetype," severing the capacity for self-treatment from a "wounded" image and attributing that capacity entirely to the therapist.

The therapist may possess minimally, or not at all, the attributed powers, which are bound intimately to the past experience and psychology of the patient. Thus, it is clear that any intimacy with the patient will produce a very different impact than it would in another type of relationship. We could compare the impact to that of incest or rape; both those "relationships" also involve one person who is at least perceived as being much stronger and another who is extremely vulnerable.

This "handing oneself over" is a psychological condition actively solicited, particularly during the early phases of therapy, by the analysis of the patient's resistance and the overcoming of defenses, in order to make "analysis" possible. What triggers the condition of unconditional trust, to which the patient is induced to regress, is the certainty of not being betrayed by the therapist. It is precisely because the patient's vulnerability has been induced deliberately by the therapist, that taking advantage of it would be absolutely unethical.

It becomes clear that the therapist who fails to contain the dynamics of the transference/countertransference is guilty of betrayal, because of the asymmetry of the relationship and because the decision to go into therapy is made by the "healthy" part of the patient which has permitted, perhaps for the first time, a gesture of faith in another and consequently in himself or herself. Depriving the patient of the possibility of experiencing a relationship without ulterior motives can cause psychological devastation.

We cannot ignore, therefore, the depth and intensity of the dynamics in the analytic relationship which are capable of activating the analyst's unconscious. One illustration of this possibility is the difficulty a therapist sometimes experiences in containing the extraordinary seductiveness of some hysterical patients. The intensity with which hysterical analysands experience their transference love, and the fact that they often are unable to distinguish it from manifestations of real love, can cause emotional problems for the analyst. Another example is the contagious quality of analysands with structural disorders of the ego. The presence of a pregenital disorder in the analysand can require the introduction of variations in the relational technique. As these analysands often perceive anonymity and neutrality as an attitude of rejection or even hostility, the analyst must relate to them with a "loving presence." A result may be a deep mobilization of the unconscious of the analyst, who may fail to distinguish between the analysand's and the analyst's needs.

Thus, there is a wide variety of collusion that can be traced to the various forms of the therapist's "madness." In certain cases we can observe a reversal of roles: The therapist becomes the center of the relationship, perhaps even the sole real content of the sessions. The patient's psychological subjection is particularly dangerous in provoking in the therapist fantasies of omnipotence and false healing. Sexual satisfaction can be one of the manifestations through which that treatment is expressed. The patient is likely to respond dutifully to the unconscious needs of the therapist, acting in accordance to a combination of needs, which are bound to the asymmetrical character of the therapeutic relationship. One of the patient's needs is to please the therapist, combined with the desperate need to do anything to feel better – the basis of entering therapy. The therapist who fraudulently offers sexual intimacy in place of valid treatment, or who exploits the patient's desires, deliberately confusing what is erotic with what is not or treating a positive transference as if it were not the result of the therapeutic relationship, will find the way unbarred.

A factor common to all such cases would appear to be an unresolved narcissistic need which results in using the patient as an extension of the therapist; the sexual experience cannot be considered then as anything more than a personal experience in a relationship which is not personal in the usual sense of the term. Thus we must set aside false beliefs which are only pretexts: that the ethical question should be raised only if sexual involvement occurred before the end of the therapy, and that sexual involvement is acceptable if it takes place outside the session.

Statistical surveys have studied therapists who were sexually involved with their patients. Approximately 95 percent of these therapists are men. Sixty percent of them justified their sexual involvement as a consequence of their patients' identification with the father figure. Sixty percent recognized their dominant role in the relationship. Fifty-five percent were frightened by the intimacy. Ninety-five percent experienced fear and a sense of guilt for what had occurred. Only 40 percent requested counsel or help from a friend or colleague. Finally, 45 percent rationalized their behavior by their patients' need for intimacy. The ingenuousness of these statements is overwhelming.

The fact, as Pontalis (1990) pointed out, is that the analyst is not a magic notebook, in which observations are simply set down and preserved, but a highly sensitive film. If the analyst's own

analysis missed certain aspects, if his or her work is not constantly verified through comparisons with colleagues, it is possible
that gradually and imperceptibly such an analyst could unwittingly become "enslaved." On the other hand, Freud's categori-
cal judgment was that the destructive consequences of sexual
involvement with a patient had an undesired and unpredictable
effect: a widespread and uncontrolled suspicion on the part of
analysts of any form of sentiment toward the analysand. The
result of an excess of zeal, in some cases, was an opposite
distortion: the analyst's phobic attitude toward internal affects.

Observing the rule of abstinence cannot be considered a foregone conclusion. Wherever an encounter with the unconscious is
constellated, eliminating danger becomes impossible; we can
only attempt to control it. Here the professional capacity of the
analyst comes into play: acquiring a profound knowledge of
oneself and the unconscious complexes which could compromise one's work, and mastery in the use of counter-transference
as a means to acquire knowledge of the patient. The trick is to
remain a neutral analyst without becoming a neutral being, adjusting to each specific case, taking an empathic attitude without
sliding into a fusion of affects.

Jung associated the theme of sex in analysis with the archetype of *coniunctio* – the psychic union of opposites, the goal of
individual and collective psychic development. He considered
the correct interpretation and control of erotism in analysis the
turning point between regression to a prehuman condition and its
opposite: freedom, in the form of self-knowledge. The reappear-
ance of the Oedipus complex constellation during analysis is a
specific example of the more general problem of incest, which is
archetypal. Consequently, the Freudian reduction of it to a sexual
need represents a deviation from the true nature of the problem.
Jung exhorted the analyst not to stop at a literal comprehension
of incestuous desire; thus, we should be even less willing to stop
short of activating such desire in the analytic relationship. It
presents an important aspect in freeing the patient to evolve. The
immediacy of desire, however, must be brought into the symbolic realm. "The empirical truth never frees a man from his bond-

age to the senses; it only shows him that he was always so and cannot be otherwise. The symbolical truth, on the other hand, which puts water in place of the mother and spirit or fire in place of the father, frees the libido from the channel of the incest tendency, offers it a new gradient, and canalizes it into a spiritual form" (CW5, par. 335).

Thus the actualization of the incestuous tendency binds rather than liberates; this becomes clear in the instance of acting out during analysis. Sex in analysis is incest because it is not a free act of sex between equals, but occurs between the analyst – who has become idealized, superhuman – and the child self of the patient. Should sexual desire then be repressed in analysis? No; many patients come into analysis as a result of the poisonous consequences of excessive repression. Instead, the phantasm of desire must be transformed, always keeping in mind that the archetype of *coniunctio* is at the same time the model of transfer-ence and the goal of analysis. Thus, we could say that the image of the analytic couple is present from the first encounter and its internal consolidation the horizon toward which the path leads.

Translated from Italian

References

Bouhoutsos, J. (1985). Therapist-client sexual involvement: A chal-
    lenge for mental health professionals and educators. *American
    Journal of Orthopsychiatry*, *55*, 177-82.
Pontalis, J. (1990). *La Force d'Attraction*. Paris: Éditions du Seuil.

Paul Brutsche
Zurich, Switzerland
Swiss Society for Analytical
Psychology

When we speak about ethics we feel immediately concerned. Ethics touches us in an inner area; we don't want explanations given by others. Ethics belongs to the realm of personal values, close to the Self. And being close to the Self means: being religiously involved, with the undeniable danger of becoming dogmatic and judgmental, even fanatic.

When some American students at the Zurich Institute heard that I would take part in a panel discussion on ethics in analysis, they immediately connected the topic to sexual abuse and warned me that this question might become very hot. It was with some resistance that I agreed to concentrate on this specific topic because "ethics in analysis" includes much more interesting areas than situations of sexual abuse which, of course, concern colleagues but not ourselves. By speaking about such abuse we easily fall into a kind of animus-possessed moral discourse, whereas in our normal analytic experience we meet ethical questions that are connected with our own attitudes.

The perennial ethical questions arise from problems of divorce, abortion, suicide or subtle forms of unrelatedness to the other and to ourselves. For example, adopting the attitude of the one who has an answer, even when we have no answer, can be unethical just as is sexual acting-out. I do not want to minimize the problem of sexual abuse with all its traumatizing consequences, but ethics should not be absorbed by this question alone. I can not decide whose behavior was more immoral: Jung's having had – probably – an affair with Sabina Spielrein and his desperate struggle and later effort for sincerity, or Freud's sovereign position of undisturbed correctness with its underlying tendency toward authoritarian dogmatism.

How can it happen that an analytic relationship turns into a sexual relationship? Among the many reasons, four seem most relevant to me.

1. The analyst has a split-off power-shadow which becomes overwhelming and causes misuse of the analytic relationship. In our Institute we were confronted recently with such a case: a candidate whose training we had to stop because he had an affair with a drug-addicted client. This candidate was problematic long before this happened; he was too kind and too much identified with an analytic helper-persona. Having put aside self-esteem, self-affirmation and healthy aggression he became a classical victim of the compensatory shadow which had degenerated into a cynical psychopathic impulse. Although such cases are not frequent the literature on the subject refers mostly to such pathology; where conscious or unconscious power seems to be the main issue.

2. Perhaps sexual acting-out can be understood as another form of compensation too: for a wrong ego-power attitude, a false security as an experienced analyst, an experience of an ethical deficit, a human weakness, professional failure which compensates one's ideal self-image and one's professional status. Such acts of sexual abuse seem mainly to be committed by experienced analysts with established professional reputations. Interpreting this surprising phenomenon "finalistically" we could think that the psyche itself provokes such professional failures in order to shake a therapeutic attitude that has become possessive and too much involved in technique, strategy and knowledge.

This compensation of a rigid and self-sufficient attitude does not always take the form of a sexual acting-out. It can be experienced also through a complicated, unsolvable or even tragic transference problem. Such an experience can function as a reminder of the enigmatic quality of psychic reality that never can be controlled by the therapist's ego. The unfortunate turn of events in Jung's work with Sabina Spielrein can be understood as such a critical initiation into the unpredictable autonomy of psychic reality which cured the psychiatrist in him from its naivete and blindness.

3. Jung wrote somewhere that the more analysts try to be distant the more we activate sexual fantasies in our analysands. This is very true. On the one hand it is essential that we are aware of boundaries in our analytic relationships: boundaries which allow natural feelings of sympathy and closeness to evolve into a soul-generating experience grounded in a mysterious human encounter. (Such boundaries summarize what ethics in analysis is all about.) On the other hand, if boundaries serve only our own defensive need to keep control over the spontaneous process, they become destructive. If we keep emotions, feelings, body energy and body language completely out of our work, that is, if we change libido and energetic experience into a one-sided consciousness, we inevitably constellate the suppressed power of sexuality.

4. Sexual abuse occurs seemingly when an analyst is unfamiliar in personal life with the numinous quality of a soul relationship: that a relationship between a man and a woman can go far beyond attraction and social partnership and become a vessel for soul-sharing and a creative discovery of the polarity of feminine and masculine consciousness. The analyst who has never experienced the transcendent function within and through relationship inevitably will be overwhelmed sooner or later by this archetypal, numinous fascination. Such an analyst then runs the risk of missing the differentiation between the archetypal reality and the concrete situation, and of being overrun by the evidence of the sacred, constellated between the analyst and analysand.

Beverley Zabriskie
New York, NY, USA
New York Association of Jungian
Analysts

In following the collective psyche's archetypal imagery, the Jungian analyst is led to the symbols and symbolic systems which in previous times and distant places attempted to plumb the human psyche. The Jungian analyst is thus aligned not only with other current practitioners of psychotherapy, depth psychology and psychoanalysis, but also with the scholars and seekers, mythmakers and adepts who preceded modern theorists of human behavior.

An ever-present tension thereby exists in the work and self-image of Jungian analysis and the Jungian analyst. Moving between unknown mystery and known data, straddling the boundary between the unconscious and consciousness, emphasizing individuation rather than adaptation, Jungian practice is poised on a creative edge, open to the transcendent as it speaks through the psyche.

Within the world of psychoanalysis, the liminal placement of the Jungian tradition has been intensified by the personal bitterness between Jung and Freud. Freud's view of Jung as an apostate and traitor, the defensiveness within Jung's despair at Freud's disapproval and Jung's refusal to be bound by Freud's demand of allegiance to his authority and his theory, thrust Jung into exile from the very tradition which most closely shared his belief in the existence of psychic reality outside the ego. Jung's analytical psychology has been in the shadow cast by this conflict between the founders, which kept Jungians apart from the psychoanalytic tradition. Indeed, some Jungians have come to identify more with shamans and priests, prophets and psychics than with other analysts, perhaps thereby circumventing or defending against an ego wound inflicted by the denial of peer recognition and professional legitimacy. While sustained by the matrix of the unconscious, while related to many traditions, Jungian analysis and analysts have not been contained by any one discipline.

More than any other, then, the archetype of the orphan has shaped the collective Jungian psyche. The freedom to be oneself is the birthright of the psychological orphan: allowing for originality and the initiative of one without accepted origins, not initiated into any tribe. In its positive aspect psychological orphanhood creates psychic soil for the inspired and individual stance, unbound by collective convention. As Jung wrote: "Everyone who becomes conscious of even a fraction of his unconscious gets outside his own time and social stratum into a kind of solitude" (CW14, par. 258). But in its negative form, exclusion breeds a defensive belief in one's own specialness, the birthright claimed is entitlement, so often companion to nursed injury, by which one believes oneself granted right and privilege beyond the given to make up for the never received or too soon lost. If not understood and soothed, inflation and corrosive envy breed contempt and spawn disdain for more settled – and more restricted – mortals and their mores. The uncontained may claim not to be accountable and the orphan becomes the renegade, answerable only to needs, drives and appetites.

This entitlement is an especially treacherous underside in those who claim to help and guide. In analytic practice, the psychologically orphaned may disdain professional tenets of practice and ethics. A particularly Jungian distortion is the analyst's mandate to recognize and mediate the collective unconscious, taking the posture that the individual Self is beyond the limitations of ego, has archetypal dimensions and so is not bound by ethical codes designed to protect both analyst and analysand from exploitative human failing. Individuation is then confounded with a narcissism that confuses creative engagement with libidinal license, so that the impulses and drives of the analyst's id are disguised in breast-beating self-absorption, self-serving theories or the *force majeur*, archetypal prerogative. All boundaries are rejected as the inflicting of Freudian patriarchal superego.

It is true that once an exploring ego has experienced the living reality of the unconscious, of the archetype and of that non-ego psychic center, the Self, the individual needs relevant meaning – not just rules and regulations – for choices and behaviors. For a Jungian analyst, as for Jung himself, a transcendent perspective is essential in achieving an ethical stance which emerges from a consciousness-based conscience.

In his temperamental and professional orphanhood, Jung found a psychological home in the orphan tradition of alchemy:

> Alchemy has performed for me the great and invaluable service of providing material in which my experience could find sufficient room, and thereby made it possible for me to describe the individuation process at least in its essential aspects. (CW14, par. 792)

Alchemy's wholeness included the dark side excluded by the ideal of perfection in the Protestant Christianity with which Jung was familiar. Alchemy accepted mess and chaos different from Jung's ordered Swiss surround. Jung's reflections on himself from and through alchemy provided his deepest going analysis of his best and worst self, far more confirming and central than his short-lived mutual work with Freud. It was truly as if he needed to go back to the seventeenth century and its alchemy to cure his dissociation and alienation.

Jung found the Orphan to be a central image in alchemy, the beginning and end of the work, the burdensome stone of internalized rejection at the beginning, the jewel-like solitaire of claimed individuality at the end:

> Like the apprentice, the modern man begins with the unseemly prima materia which presents itself in unexpected form, a contemptible fantasy which, like the stone the builders rejected is flung into the street and is so cheap that people do not even look at it. He will observe it from day to day or until the fish's eyes or sparks shine in the dark solution, for the eyes of the fish are always open and therefore must always see, and so are a symbol of perpetual attention. The light that gradually dawns on him consists in his understanding that his fantasy is a real psychic process which is happening to him personally. Although he is also an acting and suffering figure in the drama of the psyche. (CW14, pars. 752-53)

Jung was drawn particularly to the eroticized imagery of the alchemical conjunction between the masculine and the feminine, perhaps because it addressed a shadowy aspect of his professional life, his sometime difficulty in the handling of erotic transference and countertransference.

If here, in this discussion of ethics and its codes, its observance and violations, we turn with Jung toward alchemy, we find there the transcendent scintillae or "eyes" from which to reflect on and stay present to ourselves and our work as "acting and suffering figures in the drama."

As therapists, we hold ourselves accountable in a client-centered professional, contractual space. As analysts, we attempt to understand the dynamics which have formed the individual who comes and entrusts, so that we may abstain from tampering with what is sound and intact, while facing what has been spoiled by neglect or abuse, corrupted by human bitterness. As Jungian analysts, we desist from intruding on an individual's connection with the enhancing and restorative energies of the archetypal psyche. We attempt to hold ourselves accountable to the workings of psyche itself, with the humility which allows us to suffer our smallness. It is demanding and difficult work, and the alchemists never forget its inherent dangers:

> For them the dark side of the world and of life had not been conquered. In their eyes, the fire point, the divine centre in man, was something dangerous, a powerful poison which required very careful handling if it was to be changed into the panacea. The process of individuation likewise has it own specific dangers: "There is nothing in nature that does not contain as much evil as good." (CW14, par. 49)

In the language of our work, there is constant unconsciousness with consciousness, shadow with ego, potential for malpractice within the practice.

In both the insights and the ravings of alchemy, Jung found the understanding necessary to guard against the inflation and entitlement which may make the analyst a carrier of "poison." Particularly compelling to Jung was the alchemists' notion of the fateful alternatives in life as between bitterness and wisdom, carried by the symbolism of salt, and connoting on the one hand the stinging and biting corrosiveness of bitterness and on the other the preserving savor of wisdom. It is salt in the wound to admit to the limitations of our professional consciousness not only in regard to the collective unconscious – which as Jungians we have always acknowledged – but also the personal unconscious. Can we admit that while we have pridefully eschewed being merely reductive in the Freudian sense, we have often been reduced to acting out repetition compulsions, recasting personal shadows over clients' souls and lives?

It is not chance that our keener focus on ethics and its abuses coincides with a time of rapprochement between Jungian and other psychoanalytic traditions which have attended to the early unfoldings of the human personality and bring greater understanding of the intense and delicate pre-oedipal needs of our wounded clients and selves. It is also a moment in both our culture and in our profession when a stronger and surer feminine voice is raised and heard, speaking from feminine values. These, I believe, inform our growing sensitivity regarding ethical practice and conduct.

The salt of alchemy was associated with the embodied nature of the feminine, which brings us into worldly embodiment, into context, into reality, of life lived between the salty tears of birth and death. It is the feminine capacity for discrimination which does not abstract or deny, but attends to the reality of context. It is the contextual sensibility of the feminine which discriminates what belongs within and what violates the temenos, the vessel, the cauldron of analysis; which knows it as the space for the young and raw, weary and wounded, vulnerable and thus manipulatable, injured and so manipulative. It is Psyche's sensibility, as she sought to see and find Eros, to know her context, to carry out her sorting tasks. It is not at all the patriarchal superego fondness for commandments and prohibitions, although it would be naive to imagine that the superego cannot wrest Psyche's lamp and turn it into a torch to inflame rather than illuminate.

We may insist that the eros which occurs in therapy and in analysis must be through the opus, the work. If it is not therapy or analysis that is occurring, but a violation of its boundaries, there is no therapeutic eros, but rather its mockery, power and collusion masked in Eros' disguise. If events within the analytic relationship abscond with and block vital energy, it is terrible therapy and cheap imitation of life. From the feminine perspective, we may attend and relate to the form and content, frame and fabric of analysis, its rituals and its language. In the service of psyche, it is crucial that we keep our troth with discriminating language, and not confound power with sex, sex with eros, eros with cupidity, contact with intimacy, connection with intimidation, relatedness with seduction, discharge of desire with the care of concern. Then we will not confuse transference and counter-transference with either a love relationship or with the power axis of domination and submission, seduction and compliance.

Although there are many forms of analytic failure and exploitation, perhaps because human relations and thus the ethics that inform them are a prime feminine concern, the most highly charged ethical issue now current in our profession is sexual abuse – which by and large takes place between a male analyst and female analysand. Let us – especially women – state clearly that the current concern about sexual abuse arises not from some arrested, unsophisticated, puritanical attitude toward sex, but a feeling discrimination between a mutual peer relationship embracing sexuality, and the misuse of transferential leverage in violations of need and trust.

We might expect that as members of a professional body with growing awareness of the power of the transference and who avow respect for individuation, we would hold ourselves and our colleagues accountable for gross violations of the boundaries of our clients' selves. Perhaps, while Jung himself stressed the constancy of the dark side, in our need to be special children of the special father, there has been a prevailing tendency not only to lighten Jung's shadow, but also to accommodate to those who invoke this shadow as the parent and giver of personal license masquerading as professional technique. Perhaps because the penetration of narcissism has been traditionally weak in Jungian training analysis, the rapaciousness of the analyst who envies and wants for himself whatever he is not, including femaleness, has not been sufficiently confronted or contained.

It is striking that in issues of malpractice, and most especially of sexual violation, our community which espouses individuation and consciousness has functioned in the most common collective fashion, with the denial typical of a dysfunctional family which either does not see or does not say truthfully what is seen, which cannot admit that its own violate those in their care. Our associations and our institutes mis-function as silent tribes which allow a ghastly psychologized permutation of the old *droit de seigneur*, enabling a colleague to be a self-appointed initiator who takes the pick of the crop.

Here again, we must call on the feminine, and on female analysts, to hold ourselves accountable, not to conform like collusive mothers who entrap the children while insulating the violator in infantile entitlement. Let us not forget that we are responsible first to the clients who come for understanding and release from the repetitious, the neurotic and the destructive. And let us not imagine that it is compassionate friendship and colleagueship not to confront but rather abandon those with whom we practice, to a monstrous appetite or addiction which devours professional identity and responsibility. We can recognize the pathos, but what does it serve to leave a colleague awash in pathology?

Let our precepts and principles be filled with yin, described in a Chinese text as a mother tiger stalking the jungle in the protection of her cub. Let our ethics have a yang, sometimes calling to task, but more deeply calling us to becoming and being a stable, attentive, reflective, embodied presence: neither sadistically intrusive or withdrawn, neither killingly helpful nor murderously indifferent. Let our codes have savor, permeated with bitterness from past violations now transformed into wise discrimination. Let our ethics codes be codes of practice – salty texts of wisdom and humility – based on consciousness of the limits of human nature, the force of personal complexes, the shadow of the profession, and the unwieldy enormity and power of the psyche.

Forum: Supervision in Training

Supervision and the Interactive Field

Mario Jacoby
Zollikon/Zurich, Switzerland
Swiss Society for Analytical
Psychology

Supervision is considered by all schools of depth psychology to be an integral part of the training of candidates who want to practice the art of analysis. Candidates are required to reveal their analytic procedure and their experience with analysands to a designated supervising analyst. What a candidate may learn from such an encounter depends a great deal on the supervisor's attitude and ideas as to what analysis is all about. In the classical Jungian tradition one shared Jung's skepticism about any kind of technique. It is not what the analyst says that is important, but what he or she lives and emanates as a personality. The main emphasis is placed, therefore, on the personality of the analyst and his or her maturation in the individuation process.

There is something else about which Jung was adamant: Analysts must learn, to the best of their ability, to understand the language of the unconscious. For this reason it is required that they study symbolism in wide areas of our history and culture and that they focus their ability to use a symbolic approach on the unconscious material of the analysand. Foremost importance in training was given, therefore, to the personal analysis of the candidate and to the study of amplification. Supervision was regarded as being necessary but less important. The task of a supervisor most often consisted in adding interpretations of the dreams of the candidate's analysands and perhaps adding some advice on how to relate these ideas to their conscious situations. The question of how often to see the supervisor was left to the candidate's own judgment.

Today the process of training is regulated in part, by the quantity of supervisory ("control") sessions. "The more hours the better." There still is discussion as to whether this great number of supervision hours furthers the quality of training. Some colleagues argue that candidates may rely on their supervisors too long or that candidates may come just to get the required number of hours. One hears the opinion that candidates should come to supervision only when they feel stuck in the process.

I am in favor of an increased number of sessions. Yet, in order to change quantity into quality, it is necessary to reflect on how to use these hours productively. For all those schools which require an analytic technique, a detailed discussion of the different moves and interactions is needed. But also in the schools of Analytical Psychology, which allow much freedom and individual openness, encounters with a good supervisor serve an essential purpose.

This is especially so since, for many analysts, there has been a shift in emphasis. The focus on the so called "contents" of the unconscious has been enlarged to include also a more sensitive awareness of the unconscious dynamics as they express themselves in the here and now of the "therapeutic space" or of "the interactive field." I do not think that there is an "either-or": focus on dream content or transference/counter-transference, symbolic or clinical approach. It is well known that the effectiveness of dream interpretation depends as much on the person who interprets as on the content of the interpretation. On the other hand, interpreting everything in terms of the transference may not do justice to certain contents coming up from the unconscious. Although Jung was the first to discover the mutual influence in the analytic encounter (the relationship founded on mutual unconsciousness) this whole area remained quite neglected and undifferentiated for a long time, with the exceptions of some training centers such as the "London School."

As soon as the subtleties of the interactive field between analysand and analyst-candidate are included in the supervision session, matters become much more complex. The focus will be put on questions such as: How perceptive are the trainees in terms of the non-verbal communication of the analysand, his or her body language, voice inflections, undertones? And, how differentiated is the awareness of candidates regarding what analysands are evoking in them? How do they react to love, aggression, devaluation, ambivalence? Do they take those affects too personally and retaliate in an unconscious and subtle way? Or are they unaware, repressing their feeling reactions? And once they are open to what happens within them, can they differentiate their own unconscious projections from their perceptions of what may come from the analysand's unconscious? That is, is there the capacity to discriminate between what Michael Fordham called "illusory" versus "syntonic" counter-transference?

Those distinctions are difficult to make. The most difficult task is to differentiate the ability to stay in touch with oneself while "standing back" and trying to see oneself through the analysand's eyes. Can candidates understand those subtle issues when the supervisor tries to point them out? And once they have become sensitively aware, can they develop enough therapeutic flair and instinct to follow through with their insight, perhaps to verbalize parts of it for the benefit of the analysand in an effective way? Can they integrate enough knowledge of the symbolic approach and of whatever theories they cherish to be able to use them according to the necessities of the individual situation? These are all important questions to be dealt with in the course of supervision.

So far I have focused on the ability of candidates to be perceptive enough regarding their place and their differing roles in the dynamics of the interactive field. In my experience as a supervisor I find that some candidates seem very unaware in this respect. They also seem confused or resistant when confronted with questions of that nature. As a consequence, I may feel frustrated about their lack of any "feel" for the art of analysis. I may doubt their giftedness for this profession and also doubt that they will ever be able to learn it. I may begin also to question myself about my ability to evoke their potential. Sometimes I may notice that they are in the grip of a complex during a supervision session; disturbances in the mutuality of our dialogue may arise. Yet with other candidates, the sessions may bring a lively give and take, a mutual inspiration for new insights.

As important as it is to keep analysis and supervision separate, the rule cannot be inflexible because an interactive field between candidate and supervisor is constellated. The supervisor must take into account that nearly everything that candidates share with him or her may be influenced by what is going on in the interactive field between them.

How then can the supervisor grasp what really is taking place in the sessions of candidates with their analysands? Usually the supervisor has to rely on the candidate's account. I obviously listen to what candidates are telling me. At the same time I try to become aware of how I am affected by their presence and personality, which partly reveals itself by voice intonation, facial expression and body-language, as well their vitality, harshness, softness, warmth or lack of emotion. Sometimes there are facets of a candidate's way of being with me that puzzle me; the analysand he or she talks about may hardly appear before my "inner-eye." The candidate stays in the foreground of my attention. But the analysand, too, may come alive for me in his or her particular individuality. For fleeting moments, in fantasy I may get into the shoes of a described analysand and even get a glimpse of how he or she may feel in the presence of the analyst-candidate. This is all very well as long I take into account that I may project the feelings I experience while sitting with the candidate. But it may be also that in this way I perceive something essential to their interactions.

It is not easy for candidates to transplant, so to speak, the analysand/analyst field to the interactive field with the supervisor. Some do it more successfully than others. Telling me the dreams of the analysand and, more or less, the contents of the sessions is relatively easy. It is more difficult to get a grasp of what is going on in relation to the subtleties of emotional interchange or of what influence certain personality characteristics of the candidate may have on the interactions with the analysand. The candidate may be quite unaware of those implications.

I often try to verbalize the issue according to the way I myself feel affected by the presence of the candidate. I may express, as I did in one case, my feeling of being invaded by the candidate's temperament and the space he needs. I thus asked him in what way his invasive vitality may affect his clients and whether he has made any observations in this respect. He remarked that it was a matter of course to be much more passive with clients than with me. I had doubts as to what degree he could restrain himself, but the two clients he supervised with me were doing quite well. It may be that they could incorporate some of his surplus energy.

I tend to express to candidates the way I feel in their presence. Thus I try to sensitize their awareness as to how their personality features and their manner may shape the interaction with analysands. Such expression is an important part of supervision and yet it can be counterproductive as it may touch sore spots which are so vulnerable that they cause a depressive insecurity and may even harm the treatment. Furthermore, some candidates may be too defensive or may not have the antennae to "hear" what I say.

An essential aim of analysis is to further consciousness and understanding of self and world. How does a candidate learn to acquire a more differentiated understanding of psychological interconnections and an ability to convey these to the analysand? Is this possible without theoretical concepts and methods – not to mention techniques – of how to implement these? I think it is an illusion to conceive of oneself as working without theories, concepts or methods; our minds cannot function without them. On the contrary, we have to study many different theoretical ideas in order to be more or less conscious of which ones to apply. Only by being aware can we handle such ideas flexibly and individually enough to get a sense of those models which suit our way of proceeding. Thus, I feel that discussion of theories and methods, in addition to eventual recommendations for further reading are part and parcel of supervision.

Analysts have, by necessity, their own ideas about analysis. I remember seeing a woman for supervision, quite a strong personality, who seemed to know what she wanted. She handled the issues of her analysands in a very directive way, gave much advice and took a great deal of initiative. She felt sure that this was the right way to act and she could always tell me of some progress her analysands had made. I was terribly frustrated about her insensitivity in analytic matters, but what could I say in view of her clients' progress? Many roads lead to Rome. Some patients may need a more directive approach; it does not matter to me whether we call this analysis or not. What was so frustrating in this case was my impression that this woman was too well defended against her unconscious power issues; there was no flexibility, not even a receptor for what I wanted to convey to her.

Another candidate was just the opposite. She tried her best by reflecting on her procedures in terms of Jung, Kohut, Winnicott and others. Yet it seemed all too theoretical and was not related to the spontaneity of her "true" feelings. I suspect that she did this partly to fulfil what she fantasized as my expectations. But it became obvious that she tended to be absorbed by theories in the situation with analysands as well. This had to do with lack of trust in her own subjective reactions, identifying instead with the teachings of authority figures.

I sometimes wonder whether we are asking too much of our candidates. Such processes of finding oneself, of trusting one's subjective reactions and being critical at the same time, of getting personally involved yet remaining simultaneously a figure of the patient's fantasy – all this takes time and experience. Yet I am often amazed to what extent some gifted candidates can use the slightest hints from supervision to develop their own ways of proceeding. They develop their flair for symbolic understanding in addition to their skill in verbalizing and their feeling for the right timing and even the right tone for certain interventions. Of course there may be phases when they tend to identify with the person of the supervisor and introject his or her way of proceeding. It is advisable, therefore, for trainees to work with more than one supervisor.

Analysis is essentially an art and therefore difficult to teach. As supervisors we are often limited to lending support toward the differentiation of natural talent. And last but not least I feel that supervisors, by being part of the learning process of the trainee, may also learn something. Supervising gives us the opportunity to reflect with another person on the subtleties of our work. There is also a healthy narcissistic gratification if one can share one's ideas. I must confess also that candidates may handle certain difficult situations in an astonishingly effective way, often better than I probably could have done. Thinking of the truth of Jung's statement that the analyst is also in analysis, I feel it appropriate to say that as a supervisor, by doing one's job, one may experience a good bit of supervision.

Styles of Supervision

Judith Hubback
London, England
Society of Analytical Psychology

I do not like the term "Control Analyst," and I think I would not, even if I were a member of a Society where it was considered correct. It confuses the boundaries between analyst and supervisor. There are objections to the term supervisor, but lesser ones. "Control Analyst" can convey a picture of the senior analyst looking over the candidate's shoulder in a possibly persecutory way, but I think it has more the quality of a helper than that of a controller.

It is difficult to be sure what is going on in an analysis that the candidate describes. Some candidates give a much clearer and more convincing account of the process of the development of the patient's ability to symbolize and of the transference projections and of the countertransference ones, than other candidates do. The transferences to the supervisor and to the candidate/supervisor relationship are usually significantly at work. Probably all analysts would agree that we find it difficult to relate to some of our candidates; others we find very congenial. Thus, transference and countertransference between supervisor and candidate are factors to be monitored.

A Symposium was published in the April 1982 *Journal of Analytical Psychology* (Dreifuss et al., 1982), with the title "How do I assess progress in supervision?" Alfred Plaut had submitted a brief communication on that subject; I as Editor asked additional contributors to respond to the question, without seeing the others' papers: Gustav Dreifuss, Michael Fordham, Joseph Henderson, Elie Humbert, Mario Jacoby, Ann Ulanov and Hans-Joachim Wilke.

The Spectrum of Styles

The spectrum of styles runs from the permissive to the didactic. From conversations with colleagues and professional meetings on the subject, it seems that each supervisor differs from any other. The same applies to candidates. In addition there are the cultural variations within IAAP.

On the permissive end of the spectrum of styles, the supervisor comments little and intervenes even less. That may be suitable for very gifted candidates, but they can be anxious as well as gifted. I have heard such people complain that they wanted more guidance, or encouragement, or suggestion of other approaches than the one they were using. The supervisor may be well advised to think it best for the candidate to find his or her own pace and to feel for the pace at which the patient can go. My experience in the main is that such a candidate can benefit from the more experienced supervisor's style, that of a senior colleague relating to a junior colleague, who may well have something valuable to offer but who is not insisting on being right.

In the didactic approach and style, it is important for the supervisor to convey that he or she has something to offer the candidate who is willing to accept the junior role and to combine that with a healthy amount of humility. Humility is necessary because, at least in the early days of working together, the supervisor possibly does not know the candidate well, and only gets to know the analysand through the reporting of the candidate. Both of them may have been influenced by the report of the assessor – the person who conducted the assessment interview. The transference projections into that interview may turn out to be very different from those that emerge in the supervision. In the early stages, then, there are probably four psyches that must be taken into account: the assessor's, the candidate's, the analysand's and the supervisor's.

It is necessary, also, to remember that the candidate almost certainly is still very much under the influence of his or her own analyst's style and personality as well as the models of the psyche and the technique that that analyst uses. The candidate's analysis and its boundaries must be respected by the supervisor.

Something that can lead to friction with the candidate is the asking of questions. I think there is very little room for questions in analysis; that is, the analyst asking questions of the analysand. I find questions to be directive and not therapeutic. For example, it is more analytical to comment on the fact that the patient seems to be holding back on something, and to suggest that there is some difficulty in the way. That draws the patient's attention to a block, or a defense, or a more serious resistance, much better than can be done by putting a question. A question aims more for content than for the interaction between the two people concerned. But I think it is in order, and good quality supervision, to ask the candidate to explain why he or she said such and such, which seems to have gone nowhere, and would there have been some other factor to pursue, or some other response? That approach leads, usually, to a colleague-type discussion, as a result of which one or the other will be convinced of the value of going into detail.

Also within supervision I suggest papers that the candidate could benefit from studying. They should include papers which do not conform closely to the supervisor's views.

In sum: In considering style in supervision, I think the key words are enabling and facilitating. As supervisors we do not, I hope, split off our main characteristics as analysts in general and the particular analyst that each of us is. Enabling the candidate to become an analyst includes a certain amount of empowering and strengthening the candidate to improve his or her abilities. Facilitating includes helping the candidate to find the work gradually a bit easier through the decrease in anxiety which usually goes with improved understanding of the art, the craft and the method of analysis. Those developments happen only and not automatically as a result of a set, or required, number of supervisory sessions.

Reference

Dreifuss, G.; Fordham, M.; Henderson, J.; Humbert, E.; Jacoby, M.; Plant, A.; Ulanov, A.; Wilke, H-J. (1982). Symposium: How do I assess progress in supervision? *Journal of Analytical Psychology*, 27-2, 105-130.

From Training Candidate to Supervising Analyst

Paul Kugler
Buffalo, New York, USA
Inter-Regional Society of Jungian
Analysts

For many years I have been interested in supervision, not simply as a technique, but as an essential component in the life of a training institute. Here I am focusing on the psychological context of becoming a supervising analyst. Generally it is assumed that a graduate in Analytical Psychology needs to wait a certain number of years before engaging candidates as a supervisor. To understand better the role of this transitional period in the development of the identity of the analyst, I shall explore some of the psychological and social dynamics encountered during the transition from training candidate to supervising analyst. We have analyzed in great detail the development of our analysands' identities, their intra-psychic and inter-psychic conflicts, past and present, as well as their personal and cultural contexts. Traditionally we have assumed that the analysis of the other half of the therapeutic dyad takes place during the analyst's training analysis. And to a certain extent this is true. But only to a limited extent. A significant amount of the identity of the new analyst develops only after receiving the diploma in Analytical Psychology and often takes place outside the context of personal analysis.

The transition from training candidate to supervising analyst is a complicated psychological process. The recently graduated analyst carries a burden of expectations which he or she may not be equipped to fulfill immediately. There is a certain pressure to maintain a presence, a persona of maturity, stability, authority and confidence that may not coincide with psychic reality. There are also unconscious institutional dynamics relating to issues of training that confront the new analyst. And rarely are these dynamics in the development of the analyst's identity made conscious or spoken about directly at the level of the training institute.

The Stages of Professional Development

Essentially there are four phases in the professional life of an analyst. The first is the period of candidacy during which the person receives formal education in a training institute. During this period we acquire experience in personal analysis, attend didactic seminars, participate in case conferences and are supervised. Then, at some institutes, there is the writing of clinical cases, a thesis and an examination process.

The second phase extends through the five or so years immediately following the completion of the diploma. During this period of professional development the analyst is often referred to as a recent graduate or junior analyst. The new graduate sometimes receives reduced rates on conference fees or professional dues and is at times restricted from participation in certain aspects of training. This phase involves becoming integrated into the professional community, adopting the analyst's persona, and developing a personal style of analysis.

The third phase begins roughly five years after graduation. Analysts at this middle stage are referred to variously as supervising analysts, training analysts, and senior analysts. This phase involves for some analysts active participation in the training of candidates. For those who choose to pursue this aspect of professional development, many new facets of individuation emerge. There is increased attention to the existential concerns associated with the everyday running of a training institute. The idea of training is less idealized and more realistically approached as the senior analyst confronts the painful realities associated with the problems of training. During this phase we develop our clinical capacity to supervise and conduct case seminars. We focus our attention on training analysis, analytic technique and the process of conceptualizing the clinical case and conveying this capacity to candidates in didactic seminars, as well as in the process of chairing clinical cases and thesis committees.

There is a fourth and final phase in the analyst's professional life. This phase involves retirement from training activities and clinical practice. Analysts in this phase might be characterized as elders of the analytic community. Our profession is one in which retirement from analytic practice is almost unheard of except in cases of health problems or the development of a different vocation. Simply retiring from private practice at age 65 or 70 is the exception, not the rule.

My focus here is primarily on the second phase, the period immediately following the completion of formal analytic training through the assumption of the responsibilities of a supervising analyst. This transitional period can be emotionally turbulent as the new graduate works to build up an analytic practice, undergoes acculturation into the professional community, transforms the perspective on analytic training from candidate to analyst and begins to develop the necessary analytic, didactic and clinical skills to function as a supervising analyst. Perhaps by becoming more conscious of some of the intra-psychic and inter-psychic tensions encountered during this transitional period we may provide for a more integrated experience in the process of becoming a supervising analyst.

The Transition from Training Candidate to Analyst

The first issue is the effect that receiving the diploma has on the analysands of the new analyst. When I was a director of admissions I observed that every year or so there would be two or three applicants to the training program who were in analysis with a recently graduated analyst. Often these applicants were ill prepared psychologically and their applications for training were unsuccessful. When they were asked during admissions interviews why they had decided to apply for training, often there was an uncomfortable moment when they replied that their analyst had encouraged them to pursue training or had interpreted a particular dream as a calling to become a Jungian analyst. The question I always asked myself at this moment was whether it was the applicant's desire to become an analyst that motivated the application or was it their analyst's desire?

While the new graduate has objectively received the Diploma and is an official member of the professional community, on the subjective level assumption of the analyst persona may take many years. The new analyst may project aspects of still partially-unconscious professional identity onto analysands, especially those who have activated an idealized countertransference. The constellation of this process may result in the new analyst's looking actively for "analyst material" in analysands. This results in a confusion between the recent graduate's desire to integrate psychologically the analyst's persona and the analysand's personal identity.

Dis-Identification from the Student Image

Another dynamic that appears during this transitional period is the movement toward dis-identification with the "student image." The new analyst has spent many years with an identity firmly intertwined with this image. This identification does not end immediately upon graduation. The new analyst's relationship to the archetypal syzygy of student-teacher may take various forms. After graduation the analyst may remain identified with the student pole. When this happens the new analyst tends to become over-identified with candidates still in training and to assume the role of "candidate advocate." The new analyst repeatedly locates him or herself between the candidates and training committees when conflict arises.

The recent graduate has spent many years with unconscious aspects of identity intertwined with various portions of the training program. Prior to graduation the candidate's relation to supervisors, teachers, personal analysts and other students is infused with unconscious contents ranging from shadow material to Self projections. This infusion allows for a powerful and rich psychic experience during training. Personal analysis and supervision provide a container to differentiate and integrate this psychic material. Upon graduation the new analyst, like the young adult leaving home, must either introject these psychic contents or find new places to house them in other inter-personal relationships.

Separation from the training program, while providing relief from having to meet outer requirements, presents a new set of issues. Suddenly the new analyst is on his or her own and often is confronted with a disquieting anxiety about competence and analytic ability. To compensate for self-doubt and insecurity about professional capabilities, the beginning analyst may look for security and certainty in a particular mentor or school of thought. Either or both may function as an idealized Self-object for the developing analyst, providing a sense of security, cohesion and direction. The community of analysts connected by a common ideology or mentor replaces the student "family" lost upon graduation. Eventually a healthy degree of disappointment may surface as the Self projection is withdrawn and the school of thought or mentor is viewed more realistically.

Another reaction to the student-teacher syzygy may be for the recent graduate to disidentify with the student pole and over-identify with the teacher. In this case, the graduate has a strong desire to teach, do supervision and assume immediately all the training responsibilities that, until only recently, have been carried out by his or her training analysts and supervisors. The movement out of the student image and into the assumption of the analyst persona is often accompanied by a re-activation of unresolved adolescent conflicts. New analysts may find themselves acting out old family patterns. This is sometimes experienced in exaggerated needs to idealize or repudiate "parental" figures in the profession in order to individuate and achieve an analytic identity.

Boundaries and Training

As the new graduate works to establish a psychological relationship to a training institute many dynamics will be encountered. There are the usual institutional transferences, the struggle between the so-called clinical and symbolic perspectives, the question of standards for admission into training institutes and professional societies and the potential for generational conflicts between the older, more established analysts and the recent graduates needing to find their own individual voices and authority.

During this period immediately following graduation, many complicated boundary issues also are encountered. For example, how "friendly" might the new analyst be with students who only a short time ago were colleagues? When the new analyst speaks to candidates their comments are now colored with the "analyst image," its power and authority. This is not such a problem when the analyst graduates from a foreign institute and returns home, but it is a problem where the recent graduate continues to be involved with the institute where he or she trained. When the new analyst begins to sit on admission and evaluation committees, teach and give exams, other boundary issues arise. For example, should new analysts teach candidates known during their student period? From what discussions should recent graduates absent themselves in training meetings? Should they participate in evaluations of candidates who were in training with them? These concerns are complicated and need to be balanced carefully between the value of the training experience for the new analyst and the need to respect the boundaries of candidates.

Assimilation of the Analyst's Persona

Often during this period of dis-identification with the student image and the assimilation of the analyst's persona, the recent graduate may experience emotional fluctuations between feelings of inflation and those of insecurity and inadequacy. When inflated there is a strong desire to teach or to form a new institute and an overconfidence in analytic capacity – a feeling of knowing more than past teachers and supervisors. The new analyst may have the feeling that the institute's entrance requirements for training are not high enough, the clinical experience of applicants not extensive enough or the requirements for the completion of the diploma not strict enough. There is a tension between the outer requirements to be an analyst as defined by the institute and the newly developing inner identity of the analyst. Until the inner professional identity is established and the person feels comfortable with individuality and uniqueness, the analyst may feel threatened by outer regulations used to define "Jungian analyst." During this phase the analyst's persona is still unstable and vulnerable and may look for confirmation through an outer reification of its image in institute requirements.

On the other hand, when deflated feelings surface, the new analyst may question the choice of vocation and capacity to practice as an analyst, and may fear being discovered for all he or she does not know about the theory and practice of analysis. Dreams may appear in which the analyst has failed the final exams or forgotten to complete all the requirements for the diploma. Integration of the analyst's persona involves meeting not only the outer institutional requirements but also the requirements of the psyche itself. These inner requirements are often more difficult to meet than those objectively spelled out in The institute's guide to training. As we struggle to discover and fulfill our own psychic requirements to be analysts it becomes more and more apparent that these requirements are not necessarily the same as those formalized at the institute level. No longer are the judges located on the Admission Committee or the Evaluations Committee or the Examinations Committee. Now they are inner figures, aiding in the process of personal admissions, re-evaluation and self-examination. When these figures are left in projected form, we may try to institutionalize them, creating the outer institute and its requirements in our own image.

If we are able to differentiate our inner requirements from the outer institutional ones, we will be better able to lobby hard in professional discussions for our unique point of view, while also being able to accept modification or rejection of our proposals without feeling narcissistically wounded. More psychological differentiation of inner requirements from outer ones may lead to less institutional splitting and more tolerance of differences and individuality in analytic training.

Summary

There is a period of time immediately following the completion of the diploma through the assumption of the responsibilities of a supervising analyst in which the analyst's professional identity is being integrated. During this period of acculturation into the analytic community we may experience more inflation, deflation, rigidity, zeal, vulnerability, and inferiority than during other periods of our professional life. Awareness of the possibility of these intra-psychic and inter-psychic tensions may allow for a more conscious and less turbulent passage through the phase of professional development immediately following graduation and leading up to the assumption of the role of supervising analyst.

Selection and Training of Supervisors

Marga Speicher
New York, NY, USA
New York Association For Analytical
Psychology

Our work as supervisors is based on the work we do as analysts but it requires capacities and skills that are different from those we use as analysts. The papers in this forum are intended to focus on the features unique to supervisory work.

A survey was conducted in 1991 and 1992, seeking to discover what Jungian training programs actually do in three areas: (1) what type of supervision is required and recommended; (2) what is required or recommended preparation for supervisors; (3) what support and ongoing educational opportunities are provided, required, recommended for supervisors. Replies were received from 18 of the 21 training programs.

The questions about preparation of supervisors were addressed by nearly all the programs which have been in existence for some time and have 30 or more candidates. Clearly this is an area of concern whenever a program grows to such a size. Responses fell into two groups:

(1) A few programs take the position that continuing training beyond receiving the diploma is solely the responsibility of each analyst; training programs have neither responsibility nor authority to set standards and criteria for training that relates to functioning as supervisor or training analyst. Some of these programs indicate, however, that the fruits of self-directed continuing training become evident; it becomes obvious who can function as supervisors and control analysts. The designation "supervisor" seems to develop in an informal manner that contains evaluative components. The model seems to be one similar to that of determining that an artist is an artist or that a scholar is a scholar. An

important point, as I understand it, is the intentional absence of institutional criteria.

(2) Programs that have discussed issues relating to designating supervisors repeatedly state that it is difficult to establish external criteria by which to assess the qualities needed to be a supervisor. Most programs require that an analyst have a set number of years of experience as an analyst after completion of training before functioning as a supervisor. The range is from five years through eight years; most require five years. Number of years of experience is not a sufficient criterion *per se* but such a span of time provides for a period of transition following completion of training during which the analyst can consolidate identity as analyst and full member of the professional community.

Many programs named qualities that are needed and desirable in a supervisor and stated that they look for demonstration of these qualities although they do not indicate the nature of such demonstration:

- Personal and professional maturity.
- Ability to pursue analytic work in depth.
- Ability for analytical reflection.
- Capacity to tolerate the uncertainties inherent in the analytical process, to reduce the tendency to compensate by pseudo-certainty.
- Capacity to reflect on and work with the interpersonal dynamics between analysand and candidate and between candidate and supervisor.
- Capacity for integration of theory and analytical practice as well as the ability to articulate that integration. Such capacity can be demonstrated in the form of papers or public lectures. Some programs require such demonstration.
- Experience as teacher; demonstrated ability to teach.
- Participation in a series of workshops or lectures dealing with issues specific to supervision.

One program has developed a series of lectures on supervision in which analysts are expected to participate before beginning to supervise. Other programs report that they are considering establishing workshop-type programs and/or that they hold periodic workshop-type meetings where active supervisors can review issues of common concern.

For most societies number of years' experience is the only formal criterion for designation of supervisors. They consider this criterion worthwhile but insufficient. In some societies small committees of senior analysts or the entire board or training committee have the responsibility and authority to designate supervisors. The responses to the questionnaire did not give us detailed information about how those societies fulfill this responsibility. A future project could explore that matter. In general, respondents to the questionnaire stressed that training programs have to guard against the formation of rigid structures with ever-increasing requirements; they must remain flexible and able to respond to training needs as they become apparent.

One society president referred to the process of becoming an analyst and to the process of becoming a supervisor as processes of initiation. Therefore, in her view, in the process of selection to become either an analyst or a supervisor, democratic principles do not apply. To me, however, democratic principles do not conflict with images and dynamics of the process of initiation. Democratic principles speak against autocracy, dictatorship, oligarchy – forms of government that we do not want to see in our institutes, in selection of candidates and in selection of supervisors. The democratic tradition calls for a process of selection for those who are qualified according to openly-stated criteria and rejection of those who are not qualified. Processes of democratic fairness do not conflict with and do not contradict the process of initiation.

Indeed, the process of initiation may serve as the archetypal image and process that directs selection and development of analysts as well as selection and development of supervisors. That archetypal image typically contains (a) qualities that the applicant must possess; (b) tasks, steps, phases through which she or he must proceed; and (c) a designating moment when the applicant as well as those around her or him know that the process has been completed.

In regard to training analysts, our training programs have named (a) the qualities a candidate must possess; (b) the tasks, steps, and phases through which a candidate must progress to become an analyst; and (c) the moment she or he attains the designation "analyst." Current supervisors have begun to explore that process as it relates to potential supervisors: to name the corresponding qualities, tasks, steps, phases involved in the process of becoming a supervisor. Our candidates deserve having the process of designating their supervisors and teachers to be taken as seriously as we take the process in which we select, teach, and designate candidates to be analysts.

Index of Authors

Abimbola, W. 321, 325
Abramovitch, Henry Hanoch 250
Adler, Alfred 76, 238
Agnel, Aimé 101, 116, 118-121
Amati, S. 40f, 52
Angst, J. 62, 74
Ashton, D. 482, 484
Athanasius 299, 301
Atwood, G. 396, 401
Auerbach, A. 435
Bach, S. 281, 290
Baldwin, J. 361, 363f, 367
Bank, S. 76ff
Barz, Helmut 173, 190ff
Bascom, W. 317, 325
Beebe, John 116, 193, 409
Berliner, B. 213, 229
Bias, J. 100, 313, 355
Bion, W.R. 26, 30, 248f, 396
Bleger, J. 39ff, 52
Bloch, G. 475, 482, 484
Bohm, D. 397f, 401
Bouhoutsos, J. 498, 504
Bovensiepen, Gustav 242
Brome, V. 295, 301
Brutsche, Paul 381, 505
Bührmann, M.V. 343, 350
Buitenen, J. Van 250, 256
Bullough, Vern L. 205, 211
Byington, Carlos Amadeu B. 402, 408
Campbell, J. 410, 413
Carotenuto, Aldo 498
Carpy, D.V. 170, 172
Cassian, J. 299, 301
Cassirer, E. 89, 93
Chu Hsi 305, 309
Confucius, 302-309
Conte, G. 85, 93
Coomaraswamy, A. 96, 98, 100
Corbett, Lionel 395

Darwin, C. 68, 74
de Troyes, C. 104, 107, 115
Dehing, Jef 15, 31, 33, 36
Di Lorenzo, S. 80, 93
Doniger, W. 156, 165
Dreifuss, G. 524, 527
Dumont, L. 297, 301
Duncan, D. 475, 484
Dunham, B. 70, 74
Eco, U. 85, 93
Eenwyk, John R. Van 273, 275, 280
Ehrenzweig, A. 454, 466
Ernst, C. 62, 74
Exupéry, Antoine de Saint 168
Falaise, Jean-Pierre 443
Fechner, G. 117, 122
Fierz, H.K. 281, 290
Fleming, M 204, 211
Fordham, M. 136, 138, 142, 246f, 249, 401, 519, 524, 527
Frank, J.D. & J.B. 209, 430f, 435
Franz, M.-L. von 195, 208, 211, 283
Franzini, E. 91, 93
Freedberg, L. 63, 74
Freeman, W. 278, 280
Gadamer, H.G. 99f
Gaillard, Christian 451
Garber, M. 204, 211
Gardner, R. 331, 333
Giegerich, W. 119, 122
Gillette, D. 198, 211, 234, 239ff
Gilot, F. 481, 484
Gleason, J. 319, 325
Green, A. 90, 149, 287, 328, 397, 460, 466
Hall, C. 251, 256, 342, 423
Halligan, F. 241
Handel, Sidney 387
Hegel, G.W.F. 123ff, 128-132, 134f, 140, 142, 146ff, 150, 257

Heidegger, Martin 95, 98, 401
Henderson, J. 37, 524, 527
Hillman, J. 87f, 93, 354, 360, 393f
Hitler, A. 64f, 69, 74, 218, 467f
Horney, K. 213, 229
Horowitz, J. 272, 430
Hubback, Judith 126, 142, 148, 150, 381, 524
Hulley, C. 327-333
Humbert, E. 524, 527
Jackson, Andrew 60, 86, 362
Jacoby, Mario 517, 524, 527
Jaffé, A. 281, 283, 290
Johnson, Margaret P. 63, 343
Kahn, M. 76ff
Kalff, D. 412f
Kast, V. 157, 165, 371
Kernberg, O. 265, 272, 416, 420
Khan, M. 214, 229
Kiepenheuer, Kaspar 281, 290
Klein, M. 54, 137f, 142, 221, 229
Kohut, H. 214, 229, 396, 399ff, 522
Kojeve, A. 146, 150
Kott, J. 262, 264
Kugler, Paul 528
Kujawski, Pedro 315
Lacan, Jacques 20, 123, 152, 165
Lake, C. 202, 288, 332f, 481, 484
Layard, J. 235, 241
Ledermann, Rushi 265f, 272
Lifton, R. 41, 52
Loi, F. 81f, 87, 93
Loomis, Mary 334f, 342
Luborsky 428, 430, 435
Lynd, H. 68, 74
Malcom X 367
Mandelbrot, Benoit 276f
Mann, Thomas 296
Mattoon, M. 11, 14, 356, 360
Maupoil, B. 316ff, 325
McAlindon, T. 263f
McGuire, W. 117, 122
Meador, Betty De Shong 53, 194

Meier, C.A. 281, 290
Meltzer, D. 132, 142
Menaker, E. 213, 229
Mertens, W. 169, 172
Miller, A. 64, 74, 142
Mintz, J., 435
Moore, Robert L. 27, 30, 198, 211, 233f, 239ff
Moravia, A. 80, 82, 84, 93
Morgenthaler, F. 167, 172
Morin, E. 92f
Nagy, Marilyn 293
Nemerov, H. 165
Neumann, E. 83, 93, 387, 394, 442
Nietzsche, F. 117, 122
Nordby, G. 251, 256
Ogden, T. 54ff, 58, 152, 154, 157, 165
Papadopoulos, Renos 368, 371
Pareyson, L. 85, 91, 93
Pemberton, J. 315, 322, 324f
Petchkovsky, Leon 326
Piontelli, A. 246, 249
Pitt, William 61
Plant, A. 50, 338, 527
Pollock, J. 86, 93
Pontalis, J. 502, 504
Pool, R. 275, 279f
Powell, S. 27, 30
Racker, H. 139f, 142
Reale, Basilio 79, 93f
Rhi, Bou-Young 302
Ricoeur, P. 106, 115, 273, 280
Roloff, Lee 195
Rosati, Maria Pia 94
Rosenberg, B. 62, 74, 465
Rosenthal, M. 468, 471, 474
Rubin, Seth Isaiah 428
Ruck, C. 204, 211
Rutter, Peter 489
Salman, Sherry 143
Salzmann, M. 115

Samuels, Andrew 353f, 356, 360, 370f, 374f, 378, 384, 395, 401
Sandner, Donald F. 31
Savitz, C. 153, 165
Schafer, R. 162, 165
Schellenbaum, Peter 414
Segal, H. 138, 142
Shea, J. 241
Solomon, Hester McFarland 123, 143, 148
Spare, G. 27, 30
Speicher, Marga 536
Stein, Murray 13, 484, 487
Stepelevich, L. 124, 129, 142
Stewart, Louis H. 59, 74, 76f, 259
Strahan, Elizabeth 189
Strupp, H. 160, 165, 428, 430, 435
Sun Bear 338f, 342
Takeuchi, Makoto 310
Taylor, E. 117, 122
Tinbergen, N. 409, 413
Trevi, M. 84ff, 93
Ulanov, Ann Belford 193, 212, 524, 527

Urban, Elizabeth 347ff, 362, 421
Valéry, P. 91, 93
Ventura, M. 343, 354, 360
Verger, P. 315, 324f
Vico, G.B. 88, 93
Wabun 338, 342
Walcott, William O. 361
Walsh, R. 32, 37
Wilhelm, R., Ed. 413
Wilke, H-J. 524, 527
Willeford, William 257
Winnicott, D.W. 21f, 26, 29-33, 35, 37, 84, 93, 137, 142, 153, 157, 214, 229, 375, 437, 442, 522
Wirtz, U. 40, 52
Wisdom, J.O. 35, 57, 95, 113, 229, 306, 322, 470, 491, 511f, 514
Wöhrle, Andreas 166
Wolff, T. 117f, 234, 236f, 241, 295
Wright, R. 362ff, 367
Wyly, James 475
Zabriskie, Beverley 75, 508
Zimmerman, F. 172
Zémor, Denyse 493

Subject Index

Aaron 69, 430, 471
abaissement 105, 390f
abandonment 42, 81, 86, 89, 112, 168, 176, 208, 219, 240, 270, 365, 382, 435, 439, 514
Aboriginal Culture 326, 330f
~ Myth 326
abortion 505
Abraxas 34f, 295
abreaction 244, 431
abuse 49, 53f, 57, 331, 489f, 496, 505ff, 511ff
abyss 96, 153, 412
active imagination 20, 33, 59, 65, 80, 87, 113, 145, 147, 189-192, 222, 245, 294, 402, 408
~ participation 33, 175, 382, 529
Adam 371
addiction 184, 514
Adler 76, 238
adolescent 41, 83, 253, 299, 532
adult baby 205-210
Africa 71, 316, 325, 343f, 364
aggression 49, 137, 162, 213f, 219, 221-224, 228f, 238f, 356, 358, 370, 438f, 441, 444, 447, 506, 519
Aids 110
albedo 323
alchemy 13, 22, 77, 101, 114, 126, 138f, 143, 148f, 209, 226, 315, 322f, 396, 419, 510ff
alcohol 158, 270, 378
alienation 69, 97, 112, 157, 205, 229, 510
ambiguity 39ff, 50f, 53, 55f, 140, 262, 281, 459
ambiguity nucleus 40f
ambition 363f
American Presidency 60
amplification 182, 191, 246, 255, 404, 517

amplify 195, 443
analytic attitude 26
~ container 190
~ couple 504
~ experience 192, 382, 505
~ identity 532
~ practice 92, 402, 509, 530
~ process 15, 19, 79, 94, 194, 251, 276, 323, 431f
~ reflection 167
~ relationship 139, 145, 167, 494, 496, 498f, 501, 503, 506f, 513
~ setting 168, 199
analytical psychologists 302, 310, 315, 368, 409f, 488
ancestor 64, 76, 318, 330
Ancestor Spirit 344-349
androgyny 201
angel 45, 63, 186, 226, 459f, 466
anger 45, 68, 99, 191, 243, 251, 254, 304, 361ff, 443
anguish 90, 259
anima 75, 106, 119, 138, 174, 180f, 185, 227, 229, 239, 245f, 255, 476
anima/animus 251
animus 75, 138, 204, 239, 331, 505
annihilation 56, 214, 243, 316
anthropology 156
anxiety 27, 43, 98, 108, 142, 145, 159, 184, 190, 192, 204, 210f, 213, 244, 251, 297, 301, 410f, 417, 431, 437, 439f, 526, 532
Aphrodite 194, 202, 205, 210
Apollo 77, 183, 192f
Apollonian 183f, 191, 193, 270
Aquino 61
archaic relationship 448
~ symbol 246
archetypal affects 67
~ aspect 307, 412
~ basis 388, 399f

~ coniunctio 140
~ constellation 184, 305, 370, 495
~ content 113, 441
~ dimension 509
~ drama 54
~ dynamics 194
~ experience 250, 266f
~ father 108
~ figure 75
~ forces 202
~ image 39, 42f, 71, 138, 167, 189, 390, 409, 443f, 508, 538
~ level 405
~ model 124, 494
~ nature 17
~ pattern 130, 249, 251f
~ psychology 143
~ realm 77
~ roots 67, 404
~ structure 84, 245
~ symbol 43
~ unconscious 54
archetype of conformity 251
~ the self 132, 135, 305, 343
archetypes 14, 17, 112, 151, 166, 202, 207f, 212, 236, 241f, 245, 249, 280, 313f, 388, 390ff, 399
Ares 205
Aristotelian 95
art 57, 82, 84-87, 91, 94-100, 120f, 190f, 193, 201, 219, 325, 328, 330f, 380, 394, 410, 448, 451, 454, 459f, 467, 469ff, 473f, 483f, 491, 498, 517, 519, 522, 526
Artemis 77, 465
artistic creation 82, 94, 98f
~ expression 88
Asia 217f
assimilation 96, 113, 146, 198, 365f, 533
associations 11, 110, 117, 195, 290, 373, 514
astronaut 312

Athena 222, 225, 227ff
attitudes 64, 113, 127, 182, 306, 331, 376, 418, 505
Augustine 97, 99, 298
aunt 75, 201
authority 71f, 106, 198, 206, 213, 295, 340, 498, 508, 522, 528, 533, 536, 538
autism 54ff, 249, 401
autocracy 538
baby 26, 48, 70, 88, 137, 202, 205-210, 226ff, 267f, 271, 396, 427, 444, 452
bad mother 457
Barbie Doll 201f
bath 480f
battle 119, 134, 317, 363, 366, 436, 469
beard 315, 374
beast 438, 440, 476
beauty 57, 90, 95-98, 120, 194, 326
bed 43f, 48ff, 89, 197, 227f, 283, 316, 473
Beebe, John 116, 193, 409
bell 84, 288
belly 46
Bethlehem 288
betrayal 49, 51, 263, 501
Bhagavat Gita 250
bi 68
Bible 95f, 233, 251, 298, 364, 372, 388, 457
bicycle 84
bipolarity 128, 132, 138, 236, 240f, 461
bird 90, 101, 164, 324, 456ff
birth 19, 48, 60, 62, 68, 70, 74, 76f, 95, 100, 125, 127, 138, 182, 195, 202, 212, 216, 220, 245ff, 253, 274, 290, 304, 324, 330, 338, 341, 421f, 424, 512
bitterness 508, 511f, 514
black moses 349

~ Power 365
blind 32, 38, 107, 480ff
blindness 35, 480, 507
blood 57, 104f, 119, 131, 154, 369,
    452, 464, 469, 471
boat 286, 468
boundaries 60, 168, 189f, 196, 340f,
    353, 362, 389, 490, 507, 509, 513,
    524, 526, 532f
Brazil 315, 402f
breakdown 21, 26, 103, 137, 253,
    483
breast 137, 221, 227, 244, 271, 424ff,
    446, 459, 476, 481, 509
brutality 65, 452
Buddha 330
Buddhism 163, 296f, 306
Bulgaria 378
bull 475f
bullfighting 475f
butterfly 171f, 409
Cabala 95
Canaan School 348
cancer 217, 338f, 364
Carnival 252
castration 213, 403, 460
Castro 61, 71
catastrophe 113, 118, 147, 467, 470,
    472, 483
catharsis 88, 95, 222
Catholic 472
channel 125, 195, 218, 471, 504
chaos 79, 102f, 114, 127, 161, 163,
    252, 258, 275f, 278ff, 316-319,
    324, 343, 378, 397, 411, 445, 482,
    488, 510
childhood 29, 31ff, 38, 40, 45, 47ff,
    54, 62, 76, 138, 157, 160, 179,
    204, 208, 217, 268, 334, 336f, 400,
    412, 456f, 461
childish 110
China 71, 306, 514
Chosen People 95

Christ 217, 271, 288, 297f, 464
Christ Child 226
Christianity 22, 100, 119f, 130, 280,
    297ff, 344, 419, 451f, 462, 464,
    471, 510
Christmas 159, 480
Chronos 71
Church 343f, 347ff
cigarette 244, 374
civilization 33, 353, 364, 483
clinging 460
clinic 158, 281
clinical application 236
~ case 108, 529f
~ example 29
~ experience 84, 533
~ issues 384
~ material 357, 421
~ observation 266, 430
~ practice 358, 491, 530
~ reality 490
~ research 237
~ work 141, 354, 380, 454
Clinton, Bill 72f
cohesiveness of the self 399
cold 47, 105, 177f, 181, 418
Cold War 59
coldness 56, 316
collective consciousness 147
~ cultural masquerade 252
~ Unconscious 24
color 54, 86, 88, 90f, 159, 317ff, 328,
    333, 362, 365, 409
colored bird 90
compensate 43, 208, 318, 398, 411,
    488, 506, 532, 537
compensation 105f, 108f, 112f, 146,
    447, 506
compensatory 101, 109, 145, 279,
    294, 301, 506
competition 272, 357, 441
compulsion 193, 207, 212ff, 220,
    228, 243, 310, 500, 512

confession 99

confidence 42, 99f, 226, 303, 355, 419, 422, 498, 528

confidentiality 184

Confucianism 307

coniunctio 132f, 138-141, 149, 503f

conscience 81, 145ff, 446, 493, 510

conscious experience 43, 398

~ understanding 120, 140

conservative 117, 151, 376

constellation 144, 184, 305, 323, 328, 370, 394, 400, 495, 503, 531

constitution 66, 72, 488, 498

corpus 245f

corruption 498

countertransference 139f, 167, 170ff, 181, 185, 225, 266, 415f, 493f, 497, 511, 513, 524, 531

countertransferential somatic response 199

couple 137f, 140, 234, 239, 332, 359, 403, 408, 414f, 417, 419f, 425, 504

Coyote 36, 336

creation 29, 34, 67, 72, 81f, 84, 94, 96, 98f, 138, 261, 322, 388, 392f, 397, 416, 419f

creative impulse 82, 454

creativity 22, 80, 83, 85, 97, 110, 143, 147, 149, 243, 265, 320, 395, 407, 411, 467, 470, 473f

Creator 64, 95

Creatura 121

crocodile 438

cross 61, 110, 153, 201, 211, 213f, 237, 297, 343, 445, 496

crucified christ 271

crucifixion 213

cult 193, 233, 331

cultural malaise 208

Czechoslovakia 370, 379

daemon 83

dark sky 287

daughter 39, 43-51, 61, 70f, 73, 75, 158, 217, 221, 226f, 285, 289f, 313f, 431, 464f, 480f

death 27, 34f, 41f, 45f, 50f, 108, 128, 134, 165, 203, 205, 210, 216, 221f, 225, 238, 251, 263, 283, 297f, 302f, 318, 324, 363, 388, 429, 445, 464, 473, 476, 483, 488, 512

death instinct 137, 213

deconstruction 200, 202, 204, 233, 238, 358

Decree Of Heaven 302, 306

defeat 198, 213

defenses 55, 108, 148, 208, 266ff, 404, 443, 501

deification 240, 370

Deimus 205

deintegration 116, 132, 136, 148, 425

deintegration/reintegration 138, 148, 247

deintegrative 267

deity 388

Demeter 464f

denial 16, 31, 38, 41, 55, 268, 457, 460, 480, 489, 508, 514

dependence 15, 161, 266, 276

dependency 38, 118, 238, 339

depression 73, 159, 173, 176, 180f, 244, 253, 282, 331, 443, 473f

depressive position 54, 137

destiny 71, 95, 107, 200, 302f, 308, 311, 313f, 320, 324, 326, 356, 465

destruction 22, 29, 41, 132, 200, 202, 243f, 318f, 323f, 436, 447, 468

destructive action 316

devil 34, 81, 98, 148, 299f, 392

dialectical space 154ff, 163

Diamond Body 233-237, 240

diaphanous 460

dictatorship 59f, 67, 71, 538

dinosaur 443, 447

Dionysos 184, 191, 193, 270, 488

Dionysus 183, 188, 192f
disappointment 267, 532
disgust 47, 68, 110
disorientation 112, 145
dissociation 21f, 27, 29, 67, 101, 214, 321, 330f, 510
divination 318ff, 322f, 325
divine child 135
~ eros 98
divorce 193, 448, 505
dog 217
doll 202
dolls 201
Dostoevsky 98
dream analysis 13
dreaming 20, 29, 223, 381, 454
Dreifuss, Gustav 524, 527
drunkenness 65, 457
dualism 294
Dulles, John Foster 63
dying 226, 283
eagle 42, 171
earth 90, 221, 258, 270, 296, 317, 320, 330, 332, 335, 338f, 342, 347, 439, 444, 446, 452, 470f, 473
earthquake 436
Eastern Culture 310, 313
~ Europe 59, 71, 368ff, 372, 378-383
eccentric 359, 364
Eden 372
ego consciousness 198
~ development 312f
~ formation 403
~ function 113
Egypt 70, 297, 299, 388, 391, 456
Eisenhower, Dwight 63, 73
Eleusis 464ff
Ellis, H. 430
emotional body 257
~ experience 20, 26, 51, 186, 247f, 499
~ impact 384

~ problems 501
emperor 303
enactment 206f
encouragement 525
Eros 82, 98, 193f, 205, 482, 512f
ese 320f
esoteric 183, 191, 238
Eve 371
evil 34f, 46, 60, 63f, 66ff, 89, 95, 114, 119, 148, 265f, 268, 294, 297, 327, 329-332, 349, 364, 366, 445f, 468f, 493, 511
exile 250f, 508
experience of extreme destruction 41
experimental psychology 430
extraversion 106, 113, 334, 353
extraverted 76, 182, 193
extremes 313, 410
Exupéry, Antoine de St. 168
fairies 220, 222f
fairy 45, 50, 220, 258
fairy tale 45f, 110
family life 62
~ therapy 75, 408
fantasy 43, 45, 53f, 56, 88, 114, 125, 130, 137f, 154, 173f, 176f, 179, 212, 214, 219f, 226, 255, 274, 336, 357ff, 378, 406, 412, 424, 439f, 460, 471, 510, 520, 522
Fastnacht 252
fate 32, 118, 255, 321f, 356, 434, 469
father archetype 313
~ figure 502
~ image 236
fathers 116, 454
fear 35, 41-44, 47, 50, 66, 68, 89, 91, 99, 108, 110, 153, 159, 168, 182, 188, 193, 205, 210, 217, 221, 243f, 253, 337ff, 363, 365, 417f, 433, 440, 465, 499, 502, 534
feeling of loss 94
femaleness 201, 514

feminine power 228
~ Psyche 236
~ self 236
femininity 221, 396
Fetus 249
fire 46, 241, 288, 331, 366f, 436, 438f, 504, 511
Fisher King 104, 107
fixation 205, 207
flower 225-228, 287, 397, 465, 473, 475f, 481
forced identification 53
forest 45, 50, 85, 90f, 470
fractal 276-279
freedom 67, 70ff, 96, 254, 297, 301, 307, 317, 376, 441, 503, 509, 518
French 14, 72, 101, 115, 297, 443, 448, 451, 457, 465, 480, 493f, 496
French Revolution 71f
Freudian 21, 102f, 109, 114, 119, 148, 163, 204, 212, 233, 235, 237, 240, 371f, 403, 460, 466, 494f, 503, 509, 512
Freudian analyst 109, 460
~ school 145
Freudians 410
friendship 20, 65, 514
Gaia 221
Gandhi, Mohandas K. 61, 63f, 71
Garibaldi 61
gender 62, 77, 85, 200, 202, 254, 353, 375ff, 457
Genesis 242, 251
Genetic 25
genius 79, 91, 183, 193, 272, 472
ghost 65, 84, 164, 283f, 290, 364, 464, 470
Giacometti 112, 115, 120
gnosis 22, 26, 148, 198, 419
Gnostics 36, 126
god 34f, 44, 46f, 71, 81, 92, 95f, 108, 111, 120, 130, 148, 155f, 164, 183, 188, 203, 215, 217, 223, 225f, 228,
295, 297-300, 307, 315, 317f, 320, 323, 325, 330, 349, 371, 387f, 391f, 397, 413, 444, 457, 469
god of divination 322
Goethe, J.W. von 98, 296, 324
gold 111f, 472
good mother 109, 254
Gorbachev, Mikhail 62, 368
Gore, Al 73, 212
Gorgon 222
grandfather 57
grandmother 201, 347
gratification 138, 523
great mother 14, 194, 412, 464, 494
Greek Tradition 99
grief 41, 68, 300
group psychotherapy 373f
guilt 45, 68, 99, 114, 161, 221, 290, 336, 340, 370, 471, 502
hallucinations 43f, 47
Hamlet 327, 364
Hansel And Gretel 45f
harmony 86, 92, 95f, 170, 205, 210, 263, 305, 307, 310, 414f
hate 27, 64, 116, 258, 265ff, 298
heart 46, 114, 148, 203, 225, 283, 299, 302, 306, 341, 361f, 366, 369, 413, 446
Heaven 302-308
Hegel, G.W.F. 123ff, 128-132, 134f, 140, 142, 146ff, 150, 257
Heidegger, Martin 95, 98, 401
hell 98f
helplessness 48, 244, 382
hermaphrodite 226
Hermes 92, 149
hero 64, 71, 74, 250ff, 297, 300, 310, 440, 476, 480
hidden god 215
hierarchy 62, 296
higher power 33f
Hindu 96
Hiroshima 120

Hitler 64f, 69, 74, 218, 467f
Ho Chi Minh 61
holidays 159
Holocaust 32, 120
holy 35, 94, 288, 344f, 364, 436, 452, 457, 464, 466, 470, 472
Holy Spirit 130, 344-348
Homecoming 250, 255
homosexuality 199, 455
Hopkins, A. 435
hospital 197, 224, 226f, 344, 374
hotel 372
husband 43, 49, 57, 154, 158f, 270, 315, 345, 482
hypnotist 372
I Ching 281, 322, 412f
IAAP 11f, 368-371, 375, 378, 380f, 403, 467, 472, 487f, 491, 498, 525
id 103, 125, 200, 294, 509
idealization 110, 161f, 170, 224
idealized self 532
~ transference 169f
idealizing transference 160-163
identity as a sacrifice 42
~ on the level of instincts 41
ideology 240, 372, 532
imago 47, 97
immortality 95
impotence 266, 370
imprint 105
inadequacy 94, 213, 533
Inanna 194
Inborn Potential 25
incest 38f, 41-45, 48, 51, 53, 109, 133, 192, 219f, 489ff, 496f, 500, 503f
incubation 77
independence 39, 57, 377
India 297f, 301
Indian 250f, 301
individuality 13, 499, 510, 520, 534
individuation 18, 20, 65, 67, 107, 124, 135, 168, 236, 238-241, 252f,
278, 302, 305, 307, 309f, 336, 360, 392-395, 397, 415, 457, 473, 482, 488, 495, 508f, 511, 513f, 529
individuation process 17, 66, 107, 130, 135, 150, 239f, 250, 252, 265, 310, 334, 387, 403, 496, 510, 517
infancy 19, 243, 266ff, 460, 464, 494
infant 26, 55, 57, 68, 108, 110, 128, 130ff, 137f, 207, 242ff, 246-249, 285, 331, 424, 426f
infantile ego 440ff
~ relationships 248
~ root 272
~ sexuality 51, 441
inflation 29, 240, 252, 470, 509, 511, 533, 535
initiation 37, 214, 506, 538
injury 33, 104, 212, 509
innocence 105, 341
insecure 49
instinct 38, 41f, 66, 84, 124, 137, 209, 215, 268, 411, 413, 470, 475, 519
instinctual impulses 266
integration 100, 107, 113f, 122, 124, 126f, 135, 138, 147, 149, 168, 220, 237, 249, 252, 311, 313, 323, 365, 378, 412, 443, 445, 447f, 494, 534, 537
intercourse 138
introjection 139
introversion 66, 77, 106, 110, 113, 219, 334, 353, 411
intuition 18, 22, 97, 101, 107, 110f, 113f, 117, 151, 175, 184, 234f, 237, 239, 334
intuitive concept 31
~ perception 50
Isis 77
isolation 214, 354, 372, 383, 430
Israel 95, 224, 250, 253, 344, 361, 364, 391, 471
Israelites 69, 364

Italy 376
Japanese 112, 310
jealousy 68, 220, 416, 457
Jerusalem 144, 250, 472
Jesus 297, 364, 451, 461, 464, 466
Jewish 64f, 70, 218, 361, 387f, 390, 394, 471f
Joan Of Arc 61, 63, 70f
Job 115
Johnson, Lyndon 63
Judaism 471
Jungian analysis 75, 158, 163, 192, 233, 240, 272, 404, 409, 429f, 433f, 487, 489, 496f, 508f
  ~ analysts 11, 31f, 53, 59, 109, 116, 151, 187, 189, 233, 240, 257, 273, 293, 326, 334, 343, 361, 373, 387, 395, 410, 428, 434f, 475, 487ff, 494, 508, 511, 528
  ~ approach 379
  ~ attitude 305, 308
  ~ psychology 11, 119, 204, 211, 233, 256, 293, 328, 368, 373, 467, 471f
kairos 198
Kant, Immanuel 94, 123, 282
Kennedy, John F. 60
king 70, 104, 107, 211, 239, 241, 315-319, 362, 475, 481
King Arthur 105
  ~ Lear 327
  ~ within 198, 211, 241
kingdom 147, 250, 252, 255, 297, 317
kiss 258
Kleinian 54, 130, 132, 192, 403, 407
Kleinian Theory 137
Kore 464f
Krishna 255
labyrinth 234, 475, 482
lamb 452, 461, 464
laziness 405
leadership 59ff, 63, 69

Leonardo Da Vinci 79, 466
lesbian 46, 205, 254
libido 98, 132ff, 180, 241, 411, 447, 483, 496f, 504, 507
Lilith 220, 222
liminality 508
Lincoln 61
Little Prince 168
Logos 82, 89
Lord 64, 323
loss 16, 40, 47, 94, 104, 106, 111, 293, 415
lover 234, 236, 238f, 241, 254, 257f, 260ff
Macmillan, Harold 61
mad 21, 32, 62
magician 234, 236, 238-241, 364
magnetic field 414
Mahabharata 250, 252, 255f
maleness 199, 201
Mandala 310
manipulations 86, 252, 418
marriage 65, 138, 184, 194, 202, 218, 270, 297, 364, 396
martyr 298
Martyrdom 298
Marx, Karl 123
masculine role 223
  ~ values 105
masculinity 221, 223, 396, 481
Masochism 213, 229
masochistic 219, 223, 228
masturbation 213
materia 207, 393, 510
maternal imago 47
  ~ reverie 26f
maturation 238, 307f, 517
meaninglessness 28, 36
mechanistic 275, 397
medication 57
medicine man 338
menstrual 57
Mercurius 258, 324

Mercury 114
Messiaen, Olivier 101, 120
metaphor 88, 126, 139, 157, 169, 273, 275, 279, 357, 396
Michelangelo 364
Midsummer Night'S Dream 257
Minerva 147
minotaur 257, 475f, 480-483
miracle 225, 288, 387-394
mistrust 365
money 217, 362, 375, 421
monster 47, 268, 285, 288, 330f, 438f
moon 224, 282, 309, 312, 327, 329, 331f, 338f
Moses 63, 69ff, 349, 364, 471
mother archetype 202, 221, 313
  ~ earth 444
  ~ figure 221, 465
mothering 55, 255
mourning 495
Muse 81
mythology 22, 33f, 42, 71, 87, 89, 91, 104, 182, 192f, 204f, 234f, 239, 283, 301, 315f, 319, 322, 326-331, 333-339, 341, 397, 413, 452, 456, 467, 469-472, 481
myths 155f, 194, 204, 319, 322, 326, 332f, 465, 493
narcissistic 76, 169, 243, 265-268, 271f, 296, 410, 446f, 460, 509, 513
narcissistic gratification 523
  ~ need 502
  ~ personality 272, 416
  ~ wound 210
National Socialism 467
Nazi 218, 468, 471
Nazism 468
needy 336
negative experience 447
  ~ mother 441, 443
  ~ transference 162
Negro 363

neurosis 83, 108, 173, 204, 214, 266, 314, 387, 389, 494
neurotic 27, 103, 109, 114, 214, 404, 406, 514
nigredo 322
nipple 213, 221, 227, 425f
Nixon, Richard 63
numinous 136, 148, 226, 241, 358, 390, 420, 507
Oedipus 42, 213, 219, 331f, 480ff, 503, 512
omnipotence 86, 170, 265, 370, 494f, 502
omnipotent 168ff, 354, 410, 468
ori 320f
Other, the 13, 15, 17, 38, 40, 61, 65, 104, 108f, 111, 124, 128f, 131f, 154, 175, 229, 252, 337f, 348, 374, 473, 537
Otherness 147, 154
Otto, R. 430
owl 147
Palestine 224
panic 45, 47, 50, 205, 210, 244, 253
Paracelsus 114, 324
paradise 285
paranoid 54f, 130f, 191, 253
parent 44, 53, 62, 64f, 76f, 108, 110, 137f, 195f, 213f, 216ff, 220, 245, 268, 285, 288ff, 296-300, 326, 356, 408, 438, 441, 443, 445, 448, 513
Parsifal 104f, 107, 119, 121, 468f
partnership 507
patriarchal 377, 509, 512
penetration 411, 413, 513
penis 57, 204, 213, 460
Persephone 464, 473
persona 118, 225, 250-255, 307, 334f, 448, 506, 528f, 531-534
personal analysis 373, 381f, 494, 517, 528f, 531
  ~ psychic element 85

Phaedrus 95

phallus 48, 198, 213f, 221, 262, 331, 440, 444, 447

Pharaoh 70, 364

philosophy 100, 123, 128f, 131f, 142, 147, 150, 166, 294, 470, 493

Phobos 205

Picasso, Pablo 86, 475, 480-484

planet 151, 168, 278, 314

Plato 95, 97, 99, 123

Plaut, F. 524

Pleroma 34

Plotinus 96

plurality 398

poetry 81ff, 87ff, 95, 98, 205, 304, 306, 309, 408

polarity 403, 406f, 419f, 507

Political Leadership 59f

politics 61, 63, 69, 301, 353ff, 358ff, 367, 375ff

possession 103, 175, 353, 445, 469

posttraumatic stress disorder 431

predictability 357

pregenital 501

pregnancy 117, 246, 286

prehistory 411

prejudice 305

pride 46, 365

priests 320, 372, 508

primary ambiguity 39

primordial unconscious identity 39

prison 43, 286

prisoners 443

projection 27, 40, 63, 65, 82, 106f, 139f, 162, 185, 194, 211, 225, 239, 247, 296, 407, 411f, 441, 445, 467, 499, 519, 524f, 531f

projective identification 26, 40, 139, 161, 193, 422, 424

prophecy 158

Protestant 115, 217, 510

psychiatric association 373

~ diagnosis 21

psychiatry 281, 290

psychic conditions 411

~ creativity 470, 473

~ development 25, 412, 503

~ differentiation 40

~ Energy 273

~ factor 469

~ function 407

~ material 251, 532

~ pain 94, 100, 214

~ process 510

~ reality 22, 25f, 142, 506ff, 528

~ structure 155, 208, 241, 311f

~ totality 135

~ transformation 402

psychodrama 173, 176, 179, 181, 184-190, 192, 194, 403f

psychological change 133, 141

~ development 66, 83, 251, 354f, 358, 489

~ experience 127

~ growth 274, 278

~ identity 40

~ implications 369

~ reality 402

~ relationship 532

psychosis 21, 31f, 57, 103, 113, 252, 266

psychosomatic 242f, 247, 249, 281, 284, 392, 421

psychotic 21f, 26, 32, 113, 169, 268, 272, 390, 404, 406f

psychotic image 158

puberty 217

punishment 38, 44, 213f, 219ff

Purim 252

queen 236, 239, 257f, 315ff, 459

rabbi 388

rape 42, 260, 476, 481, 500

rapist 110

rapport 243

Reality Functions 38

rebellion 370

rebirth 238, 488
reconciliation 18, 34, 262, 319
reconstruction 39, 53, 56, 141, 200, 204
redemption 35, 99, 365f, 388
regression 38f, 41, 51, 54f, 205, 209f, 287, 378, 467, 483, 503
reification 23f, 534
reintegration 132, 136, 149, 247f, 421, 425
rejection 68, 369, 422, 424, 501, 510, 534, 538
religion 100, 181, 193, 212, 217, 226, 262, 295, 298, 301, 313, 315, 318, 452, 465, 472f, 493
religious system 318, 472
Renaissance 262, 368, 403, 462
repression 20f, 38, 67, 103, 295, 297, 320, 504
resistances 114, 404
restructuring 169
rite d'entrée 80
ritual 33, 80, 349, 393, 404, 410, 418, 443
rituals 194, 214, 219, 221, 223, 272, 344, 348f, 464, 513
Roman Empire 297ff
Romanticism 85
Rome 86, 94, 498, 522
Ross Perot 73
Rousseau 296
rubedo 323
Russia 63, 74, 368-372, 375, 381, 383
Russian 327, 368, 371f, 375f, 380f
sacred 239, 364, 498, 507
sacrifice 19, 42, 48-51, 118f, 215, 223, 225, 298, 310, 323f, 382, 464, 476, 495
sadism 29, 223, 271
sadness 95, 443
saint 35, 71, 168, 205, 298, 325
sake 297, 393
salvation 297f, 300, 366

sand 171, 191, 285f, 288, 310, 410, 438, 445f
Sandplay 13, 409-413
scapegoating 489
schizoid 54f, 130f
schizophrenia 21, 31f
schizophrenic 32
school 50, 84, 97, 143, 145, 158, 189, 199, 201, 213, 234, 285, 288, 327, 348, 363, 373, 380, 412, 421f, 438, 440, 517f, 532
sculpture 244, 402
sea 63, 311, 344, 391, 468, 471, 475, 480
security 28, 43, 110, 166, 226, 295, 420, 436, 506, 532
Self Psychology 214, 401
sensate experiences 55
sensory contiguity 56
separation 39, 42, 82, 103, 109, 111, 113, 119, 246, 254, 268, 288, 294, 299, 310, 419, 441, 446, 464f, 497, 532
Seven Sermons To The Dead 13, 20, 33, 103, 121, 126, 144, 148, 295
sexual abuse 496, 505ff, 513
~ assault 42
~ fantasies 507
~ trauma 38
sexuality 33, 41, 51, 217, 226, 238, 241, 299, 307, 356, 358, 441, 507, 513
shadow 32, 66, 75, 102, 104, 114, 117ff, 121f, 147ff, 186, 190f, 193, 215, 236, 239ff, 251, 266ff, 307, 330, 334, 392, 407f, 467f, 472f, 488-492, 494ff, 506, 508, 511-514, 531
Shakespeare, William 264, 364
shaman 32, 241, 508
shamanism 37, 402

shame 46, 68, 74, 114, 161, 336, 340, 383
shark 438
Shembe 349
sin 221
socialism 467
Socratic 130
somatization 43
son 60f, 63f, 71, 73, 75, 103, 130, 158, 194, 198f, 218, 221, 313f, 316, 324, 330f, 445, 464, 470, 482
Sophia 220, 223f, 227f
sorcery 107
soror mystica 77
soul 35, 40f, 51, 65, 79, 95, 98ff, 131, 149, 184, 191, 199, 204ff, 210f, 215, 224f, 241, 245, 248, 262, 281, 284, 288, 290, 300, 315, 349, 361, 365f, 379, 403ff, 472, 498, 507, 512
South Africa 71, 343f
spell 54, 105, 257, 271, 328
Spinoza 123, 130
stable of bethlehem 288
star 35, 42, 44, 70, 151, 317, 447
Star Maiden Circle 334-339, 341
state of ambiguity 40, 51
stepmother 461
stress 191, 397, 411, 431
stress disorder 431
subjective level 531
suicide 42, 48f, 243, 270, 378, 505
sun 31, 34, 61, 105, 164, 168, 283, 288, 317ff, 327, 335, 338f, 342, 443f, 446ff, 480
superego 125, 494, 509, 512
supernatural 388
surrender 49
sword 196ff, 476, 481
symbiosis 415
symbol formation 16f, 19, 133, 396
symbolic events 187
~ image 273

~ level 185, 499
~ understanding 11, 522
Symbolism 85
Symposium 95, 99, 524, 527
synchronicity 282, 284, 387f, 390-394
synchronization 415
synthesis 61, 73, 84f, 88, 96, 124, 126-129, 132, 135ff, 146-149, 156, 215, 257
Taoism 306
Tarzan 286
teleological process 147
Terrible Mother 160, 458
thanatos 220, 393
the i 132, 281, 306, 322, 412
~ republic 97, 317
~ Symposium 95, 99
therapeutic analysis 172
~ process 167, 285
~ relationship 155, 157, 161f, 169, 171f, 285, 406, 417, 440, 499, 502
~ work 404
Theseus 257, 262f, 475f
tolerance 472, 534
training analysis 403, 513, 528f
~ analyst 373, 382, 529, 532, 536, 539
~ programs 190, 384, 536, 538f
transcendent 12, 16, 23, 94, 107, 112, 120f, 127, 151, 195, 198, 204, 210, 212, 215f, 226, 257, 274, 282, 285, 290, 305f, 387, 393f, 419, 489f, 508, 510f
transcendental self 152
transference countertransference 25, 138f, 172, 190, 501
~ relationship 265, 404, 407, 448
transferences 77, 245, 372, 410, 524, 532
transformative potential 83
transitional object 214
transsexual 195, 199ff, 204, 210f

transsexuality 199f, 204
transvestite 200, 220, 250
trauma 38, 53-57, 246, 340, 356, 410, 431, 489
trickster 251, 253, 258, 315, 322, 325, 336, 445
trinity 462, 464, 468, 471
trust 57, 104, 110, 157, 161f, 267, 303, 341, 361, 419, 443, 446, 490f, 498, 501, 513, 522
Twisted Hair Teaching 335
typology 88, 235, 334f, 341, 379
uncanny 120, 324, 430, 469
uncle 75
unconscious attitudes 127
~ compensation 106, 108f
~ content 18, 77, 126, 144f, 148, 153, 183f, 323, 437, 439, 442, 531
~ dynamism 497
~ elements 16, 135, 490
~ fantasy 53f, 56, 130, 138, 440
~ projection 162, 519
unconsciousness 152, 162, 200, 207, 406f, 411, 497, 511, 518
underworld 194, 465, 482
union 18f, 35, 61, 96, 126, 138f, 145, 149, 153, 175, 183, 187, 194, 306, 321, 327, 377, 387, 396, 420, 494, 496, 503
unisex 201
United States 11, 60, 101, 192f, 345, 361, 375f, 496
Universal Love 146
~ psychic element 85
universality 152
unknowable archetype 152
uroboric 397
Utopian Society 64
vegetable kingdom 147
verbalization 402

vicious circle 286
Vinaya 296
Vinci, Leonardo da 79, 364, 464, 466
Vollard Suite 475f, 480, 482
vulnerability 121, 410, 490, 501, 535
war 59, 64, 66, 72, 101f, 120f, 123, 134, 216, 218, 244, 255, 294, 316, 372f, 467, 470, 482f
warrior 234, 236-239, 241, 250
Washington, George 60
water 31, 164, 197, 306, 330, 347f, 353, 412, 438, 471, 504
weakness 103, 250, 506
West 315, 317f, 325, 369, 374, 380, 382f
Western Culture 299, 310, 313, 332, 472
wholeness 112, 124, 128, 130, 135, 147f, 215, 228, 238f, 241, 253, 265, 281, 396-401, 419, 510
wilderness 12f, 69
wisdom 35, 57, 95, 113, 229, 306, 322, 470, 491, 511f, 514
witch 45f, 50
Wolff, Toni 117f, 234, 236f, 241, 295
wood 258, 262, 283, 288
word of god 95, 397
~ War I 120f
World War I 64, 102, 216
World War II 66, 120, 244, 372, 467, 470
Wotan 469
wound 32, 193, 210, 423, 448, 489ff, 496, 508, 512
Yahweh 63, 69f, 331
Yoruba God 315
Zeus 42, 71, 99
Zulu 343ff, 348

JERUSALEM 1983

Symbolic and Clinical Approaches
in Theory and Practice
edited by Luigi Zoja and Robert Hinshaw
375 pages, hardbound, illustrations

This handsome volume, drawn from the Ninth International Congress of Analytical Psychology in Jerusalem, contains contributions from 25 prominent Jungian analysts from around the world. Among the authors are Alfred Ziegler and Adolph Guggenbühl-Craig from Zurich, Rafael López-Pedraza from Caracas, and Aldo Carotenuto from Rome. The essays reflect on the meaning and significance of contemporary analytical work.

BERLIN 1986

The Archetype of Shadow in a Split World
edited by Mary Ann Mattoon
456 pgs., paper and hardbound,
numerous pictures and diagrams

The Tenth International Congress of Analytical Psychology was held in West Berlin September 2-9, 1986. Its theme, **The Archetype of Shadow in a Split World,** was the focus of 25 major papers, with prepared responses to 14 of them. Congress participants were several hundred Jungian analysts.

PARIS 1989

Personal and Archetypal Dynamics
in the Analytical Relationship
edited by Mary Ann Mattoon
530 paper and hardbound,
numerous pictures and diagrams

The 11th International Congress for Analytical Psychology was held in Paris from August 28 through September 2, 1989. It is no surprise that the theme of "Personal and Archetypal Dynamics in the Analytical Relationship" succeeded in drawing widely varying and controversial responses.

Susan Bach
LIFE PAINTS ITS OWN SPAN
On the Significance of Spontaneous
Paintings
by Severely Ill Children
with over 200 color illustrations
Part I (Text): 208 pgs., part II
(Pictures): 56 pgs., 240 x 200 mm
ISBN 3-85630-516-5

SUSAN BACH

LIFE PAINTS ITS OWN SPAN

ON THE SIGNIFICANCE
OF SPONTANEOUS PICTURES BY
SEVERELY ILL CHILDREN

DAIMON

Life Paints its own Span with over
200 color reproductions is a comprehensive exposition of Susan
Bach's original approach to the physical and psychospiritual
evaluation of spontaneous paintings and drawings by severely ill
patients. At the same time, this work is a moving record of Susan
Bach's own journey of discovery.

Rivkah Schärf-Kluger

The Archetypal significance of
GILGAMESH
A Modern Ancient Hero

DAIMON

R. Schärf-Kluger
THE GILGAMESH EPIC
A Psychological Study of
a Modern Ancient Hero
Edited by H. Yehezkel Kluger
Foreword by C.A. Meier
240 pages, paper, illustrations
ISBN 3-85630-523-8

The long-awaited life-long opus of Jung's
brilliant disciple, Rivkah Kluger, this book
consists of a detailed psychological
commentary on the ancient Sumero-Babylonian epic myth of
Gilgamesh. The great beauty and depth of the Gilgamesh epic, one
of the world's most ancient myths, render it a unique instrument
for learning about the human soul. Rivkah Kluger ably applies it to
illustrate the significance of myths for an understanding of the
development of consciousness and of religion: we are shown how
an ancient myth is highly relevant to the state of our world today.

Heinrich Karl Fierz
JUNGIAN PSYCHIATRY
Foreword by C.T. Frey-Wehrlin
Preface by Joseph Wheelwright
illustrations and index
430 pages; paper
ISBN 3-85630-521-1

This newly translated book is the life work of the well-known psychiatrist and co-founder of the renowned Jungian "Klinik am Zürichberg" in Switzerland. From the contents: Meaning in Madness / The Attitude of the Doctor in Psychotherapy / Psychological-Psychiatric Diagnosis and Therapy / Psychotherapy in the Treatment of Depression.

Verena Kast
SISYPHUS
The old Stone, a new Way
A Jungian Approach to Midlife Crisis
ca. 130 pages, paper,
ISBN 3-85630-527-0

Verena Kast refers to Sisyphus as the "myth of the forty-year-olds," who often experience their lot in life to be a Sisyphus task. Are our human efforts all in vain, or is there some meaning to be found? In the end it is a struggle with death itself.

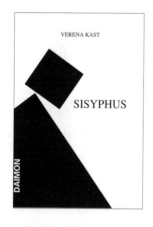

Verena Kast deals with a problem that also fascinated Nietzsche and Freud. ... This book is packed with down-to-earth experience, clinical anecdotes, wit and insight.

Murray Stein

ENGLISH PUBLICATIONS BY **DAIMON**

Susan Bach – *Life Paints its Own Span*
E.A. Bennet – *Meetings with Jung*
George Czuczka – *Imprints of the Future*
Heinrich Karl Fierz – *Jungian Psychiatry*
von Franz / Frey-Rohn / Jaffé – *What is Death?*
Liliane Frey-Rohn – *Friedrich Nietzsche*
Yael Haft – *Hands: Archetypal Chirology*
Siegmund Hurwitz – *Lilith, the first Eve*
Aniela Jaffé   – *The Myth of Meaning*
                 – *Was C.G. Jung a Mystic?*
                 – *From the Life und Work of C.G. Jung*
                 – *Death Dreams and Ghosts*
Verena Kast   – *A Time to Mourn*
                 – *Sisyphus*
James Kirsch   – *The Reluctant Prophet*
Rivkah Schärf Kluger   – *The Gilgamesh Epic*
Rafael López-Pedraza   – *Hermes and his Children*
                 – *Cultural Anxiety*
Alan McGlashan – *The Savage and Beautiful Country*
Gitta Mallasz (Transcription) – *Talking with Angels*
C.A. Meier   – *Healing Dream and Ritual*
                 – *A Testament to the Wilderness*
Laurens van der Post – *A «Festschrift»*
R.M. Rilke – *Duino Elegies*

Jungian Congress Papers:
Jerusalem 1983 – *Symbolic and Clinical Approaches*
Berlin 1986 – *Archetype of Shadow in a Split World*
Paris 1989 – *Dynamics in Relationship*

Available from your bookstore or from our distributors:

In the United States:

Atrium Publishers Group
P.O. Box 108
Lower Lake, CA 95457

Chiron Publications
400 Linden Avenue
Wilmette, IL 60091
Tel. (708) 256-7551
Fax: (708) 256-2202

In Great Britain:

Airlift Book Company
26-28 Eden Grove
London N7 8EF, England
Tel. (607) 5792 and 5798
Fax (607) 6714

Worldwide:

Daimon Verlag
Hauptstrasse 85
CH-8840 Einsiedeln Switzerland
Tel. (41)(55) 532266
Fax (41)(55) 532231

Write for our complete catalog!